The Seminoles

The Civilization of the American Indian Series

Osceola, best known of the Seminole war leaders.

The Seminoles

Edwin C. McReynolds

NORMAN AND LONDON
UNIVERSITY OF OKLAHOMA PRESS

By Edwin C. McReynolds

Oklahoma: A History of the Sooner State (NORMAN, 1954)

The Seminoles (NORMAN, 1957, 1972)

Oklahoma: The Story of Its Past and Present (with Alice Marriott and Estelle Faulconer) (NORMAN, 1961, 1967, 1971)

Missouri: A History of the Crossroads State (NORMAN, 1962)

Historical Atlas of Oklahoma (with John W. Morris) (NORMAN, 1965)

Library of Congress Catalog Card Number: 57-11198

ISBN: 0-8061-1255-7

To Johnny and Danny
who liked Indian history

Preface

ALTHOUGH THE TRIBE has always been small in number, and through most of its history relatively backward in acquaintance with the arts and sciences of white men, the Seminoles are a great people. They deserve a separate and special place in the records of American Indians, for it is impossible to grasp fully the contributions of native Americans to the broad current of national culture without considering the record of the Seminole tribe. Furthermore, the total effect of United States Indian policies cannot be judged without careful scrutiny of this fragment. Adversity may produce in a people characteristics that are readily discernible, and certainly the qualities of present day Seminoles—full blood and mixed blood—and the Negroes who have long been associated with the tribe can be studied effectively only in the light of history. The virtues of the Seminoles are, to a great extent, the product of hardship, war, and their struggle for existence. Physical courage ranks high among them, loyalty is expected of all, and modesty is a persistent trait of Seminole women. No people have fought with more determination to retain their native soil, nor sacrificed so much to uphold the justice of their claims. Removal of the tribe from Florida to the Canadian Valley was the bitterest and most costly of all the Indian removals.

Before they mingled with Europeans, their blood in a large

degree was that of the Muskogee, or Creek tribe. Both Seminoles and Creeks belong to the Muskhogean language group, as do the Choctaws and Chickasaws. The residence of the Seminoles apart in Spanish Florida, however, and the gradual development of interests that were not only distinct, but in some cases positively hostile to those of the Creek Indians, render separate treatment of the two tribes a necessity. In recent years the best of the writers on the Creek tribe have not regarded the two as a unit; and the determination of the Seminoles to establish a separate tribal government was so strong that it defeated the plan of the United States Indian Office to unite them with their relatives in a single organization.

Relations of the Seminole tribe with the United States were similar in many respects to the relations of other tribes removed from eastern states to the territory of Louisiana. At the time of removal, the Seminoles as a people understood less than the other Civilized Tribes about the mysterious purposes and methods of white men. John Ross of the Cherokees was a man acquainted with the processes of Georgia politics, and he knew also important facts concerned with the business of buying and selling cotton and other chattels, and highly significant principles involved in the value of farm land, such as the effect of population growth upon the demand for real estate. Coacoochee of the Seminoles, who lived in the same period with Ross, was familiar with the process of losing hostile white soldiers in the swamps, and the effect of a night attack upon a sleeping enemy camp. John Ross possessed qualities that would have made him a great military leader if his tribe had been engaged in war, and very possibly Coacoochee had personal traits that would have made him useful in the conduct of business. Both men were able diplomats and popular leaders who commanded the respect of their people—but in widely different fashions.

Starting late in its struggle for adjustment to the laws and customs of white people, the little Seminole tribe has not produced so many eminent men and women in politics, law, medicine, or education as the number credited to the Cherokee, Choctaw, Chickasaw, or Creek tribes. Perhaps no group of three thousand persons of any race or color has done so. Certainly it was not to be expected that the Seminoles, who often played a minor part, because of their small population, even in common concerns of the Indian nations, should equal the larger Oklahoma tribes in the election of senators, governors, and state justices during the first half of the present century.

Seminoles have shown the same aptitude for politics and law, however, as their Indian neighbors; and have produced their share of capable persons in many fields of human endeavor. Osceola, Coacoochee, and Billy Bowlegs as war chiefs during the struggle of the tribe to hold its beloved homeland; Fuch-a-lusti-hadjo as an Indian statesman of the removal; John Bemo as a missionary to his own people; John Jumper as a chief and religious leader after the American Civil War; John Chupco as an incorruptible executive during the troubled period of reconstruction; and John F. Brown as the greatest exponent of modern adjustment—are but a few of the talented Seminoles who have left in the heritage of their labors a contribution to American life.

The author of this volume is indebted to a long list of friends and colleagues for aid in its production. Librarians and archivists have been particularly cordial and helpful in making sources available. Arthur M. McAnally, Stanley McElderry, Opal Carr, Helen E. Williamson, Don N. Rickey, Orris E. Carter, and Sandra D. Stewart of the University of Oklahoma; Mrs. Rella Looney, Mrs. Myrtle Jeanne Cook, Mrs. Louise Cook, and Secretary Elmer Fraker of the Oklahoma Historical Society; Miss Muriel Wright, editor of the *Chronicles of Oklahoma;* Director Ralph Hudson and Mrs. Geraldine Smith of the Oklahoma State Library; and Justice N. B. Johnson of the Oklahoma Supreme Court, have all given generous help in assembling documents and locating vital manuscripts, pictures, and maps. Miss Dorothy Dodd of the Florida State Library gave hospitable and valuable aid in the use of rare books and other materials; and Mark F. Boyd of Tallahassee, who has a vast knowledge of Florida, its Indians, and the sources for Seminole research, gave the author the benefit of highly useful suggestions. Harold Hufford, Oliver Wendell Holmes, and Frank A. Caflisch of the National Archives;

and Percy Powell of the Manuscript Division, Library of Congress, lived up to the high standard of service that researchers have learned to expect in these great national depositories.

The writer is grateful for aid given by the Faculty Research Foundation of the University of Oklahoma, and for the reduction of teaching load that made it possible to complete this study during the present semester. Miss Angie Debo, formerly of the Oklahoma State University at Stillwater, has been particularly helpful in the loan of valuable materials and in friendly suggestions. Professors Gilbert C. Fite, Duane H. D. Roller, Edward Everett Dale, Donald J. Berthrong, and Roy Gittinger, have all given assistance on special problems. Professor Kenneth W. Porter of the University of Illinois gave highly useful suggestions in regard to the Florida wars, the Indian and Negro persons concerned with removal, and especially the career of Coacoochee. Professor Charles C. Bush and the late Professor Morris L. Wardell were kind enough to read entire chapters of the manuscript, and their critical suggestions were of real value.

Finally, the author is deeply appreciative of the assistance given by his wife, Ruth, in collecting materials and in criticizing and typing the manuscript.

EDWIN C. MCREYNOLDS

Norman, Oklahoma

Contents

Illustrations

The Seminoles

CHAPTER 1

Seminole Beginnings

"The word Seminole means runaway or broken off."

WILEY THOMPSON

"**I** NEVER BEFORE WAS AFRAID at the sight of an Indian," wrote William Bartram, describing his first meeting with a Seminole. The young English colonial botanist was making a field trip, in the spring of 1773, from Philadelphia to Florida, a new British province by the terms of the Treaty of Paris, and home of the Seminole Indians. Bartram had traveled by boat to Charleston, South Carolina, and was making his way southward across Georgia towards the St. Marys River.

The Seminole crossed his path at a considerable distance in advance, and the young scientist, observing that the native horseman was armed with a rifle, tried to avoid discovery by keeping large trees between them; but the Indian spurred his horse forward at a gallop. "At this time I must own that my spirits were much agitated," Bartram admitted, in the journal of his travels. "I saw at once that being unarmed, I was in his power; and having now but a few moments to prepare, I resigned myself to the will of the Almighty. . . . My mind then became tranquil, and I resolved to meet the dreaded foe with resolution and cheerful confidence."

The Seminole stopped a few yards in front of the traveler and silently regarded him, "his countenance angry and fierce." He shifted his rifle from shoulder to shoulder, showing clearly by his manner that he was on the point of committing murder.

3

"I advanced towards him, and with an air of confidence offered him my hand, hailing him brother; at this he hastily jerked back his arm, with a look of malice, rage, and disdain, seeming every way discontented; when again looking at me more attentively, he instantly spurred up to me and with dignity in his look and action, gave me his hand."[1]

Later, the trader at the crossing of the St. Marys said to Bartram: "My friend, consider yourself a fortunate man; that fellow is one of the greatest villains on earth." The evening before, white officers had taken the Indian's gun away from him and broken it. He received a severe beating; but afterwards escaped, carried off a new rifle, and vowed to kill the first white man he saw.

The incident is a summary of countless relations between Europeans and the red natives of North America through a period of four hundred years. Misunderstanding, suspicion, and sometimes fear and hatred there were, on both sides. There were some evidences, too, of good will and a desire for harmony.

European settlement of Florida, like that of other portions of the Atlantic coast, began slowly. Spain required three-quarters of a century to establish a firm foothold in the peninsula. The romantic appeal of this land was powerful from the start: persistent stories of the Fountain of Youth, traditions of a water passage to the western ocean, rumors of vast stores of rich jewels and precious metals; and with these more or less unsubstantial products of native imagination and European eagerness to be deceived, the obvious attractions of a friendly land. There were acres of blooming flowers spread before awed visitors in the colorful designs of nature, dense growths of shrubbery and forest with an endless variety of green foliage and cool shadows, and the mystery of hidden waters and remote havens of fertile soil.

Many Europeans who came to Florida in the sixteenth century were men who fitted well into the romantic background of an enchanted land. Pánfilo de Narváez, a red-haired, one-eyed man with a tall, powerful frame, who landed on the shore of Santa Rosa Island in October, 1528, with a remnant of his ill-fated band, was a person to stimulate the attention of all who

[1] William Bartram, *The Travels of William Bartram*, 44, 45.

4

are intrigued by the inner conflict of personality traits. He was a bold and enterprising man, capable of greatness in the wide sweep of his imagination and the courage with which he took a calculated risk; but doomed to failure by his slovenliness, and a strange lack of resolution in the presence of disaster. Perhaps Hernando Cortes gave a fair estimate of the man, when Narváez failed to carry out an assignment in Mexico. The assignment was to arrest Cortes and bring him back a prisoner; but when the military expedition became simply a relief party for the conqueror of Mexico, Narváez said, "Esteem it great good fortune that you have taken me captive." Cortes answered, "It is the least of the things I have done in Mexico."[2]

Juan Ponce de León, seeker of the fabled Fountain of Youth, who died of a wound inflicted by an Indian's arrow in Florida; Hernando de Soto, who left a remarkable narrative of discovery, adventure, and tragedy, in his contacts with the natives of Florida and the adjacent lands; Tristan de Luna, Pedro Menéndez de Avilés, Sir Francis Drake, and a long list of contemporary soldiers of fortune, were all men around whom legends easily grew.

The native population found in Florida by the first European visitors was of three different linguistic stocks: Timuquan, Calusan, and Muskhogean. The Timuquan Indians lived in the valley of the St. Johns and westward across the Suwannee; the Calusan tribes occupied territory south of the Mosquito Inlet; and the Muskhogeans were along the west coast, from Apalachee Bay to the Apalachicola River.[3]

The French and Spanish observers who have left descriptions of the Timuquan Indians in their primitive state are in general agreement concerning their physical characteristics. The men were tall and strong, the women were possessed of unusual grace and comeliness. The hunters were armed with yew-wood bows so sturdily fashioned that they could be bent only by a powerful man. With feathered arrows, and arrowheads made of flint or fishbone, perhaps tipped with a viper's tooth, the weapon was

[2] Richard L. Campbell, *Historical Sketches of Colonial Florida*, 10, 11.
[3] Verne E. Chatelain, *The Defenses of Spanish Florida, 1565-1763*, 5-8, 11, 12.

5

deadly up to two hundred yards. The Timuquans killed alligators by ramming sharpened poles down their throats. The physical prowess of the women was almost equal to that of the men; Spanish invaders were astonished to see these native women cross a wide stream by swimming, at the same time holding aloft an infant in one hand.

The earliest European visitors regarded the Mayucas and Ays of southern Florida as particularly ferocious in their warfare. Some of the colonial writers referred to them as cannibals. The Tegesta tribe and the Tocabagos in the region south of Lake Okeechobee were ruled over by an able chief whom the Spaniards called Carlos.[4]

Bishop Calderón who died in 1676, left a vivid record of his life in Florida, with valuable information concerning the Indians of his period.[5] There were 13,152 Christianized Indians in the four provinces—Timuqua, Apalachee, Apalachicola, and Guale. These natives were commonly naked, or clothed only in the skin of an animal from the waist down. Some of the women dressed themselves in a tunic made of Spanish moss, which covered them from head to feet. According to his account, the good bishop prevailed upon 4,081 of the ladies, less modestly garbed, to wear tunics like the others.

Their principal foods were beans, pumpkins, game, fish, and a "porridge which they made of corn with ashes." Certainly there is a close similarity between the food patterns of this seventeenth century culture and that of the eighteenth and nineteenth century Indians in the same region. The Timuquans and their neighbors drank water and also a hot beverage called *cazina,* a bitter draught made from a weed that grew along the coast. This drink was non-intoxicating.

Their houses, made of straw on wooden frames, had no windows, but each was provided with a door about three feet high and half as wide. Inside the house, in bad weather, they slept on a *barbacoa,* a bed consisting of a timber frame and cover-

4 *Ibid.,* 11, 12.
5 Gabriel Díaz Vara Calderón, "17th Century Letter," *Smithsonian Miscellaneous Collections,* Vol. XCV, No. 16, 12.

ings of bear skin. Through a large part of the year, they slept out of doors on the ground. The *garita* was their storage place for corn and small grain, and other foods.

It was the custom of these seventeenth century Indians in Florida to burn the grass and weeds from their fields in the fall, as their hunters circled the burning area to slaughter deer, wild ducks, and rabbits. They also gathered in large parties when they hunted for bears, cougars, and the forest bison. Game killed by these organized hunting groups was turned over to the town chief, who divided it among the families according to their needs. The chief himself was privileged to keep the hides in his own possession. The chief's fields were cultivated by the common labor of his people.

Near the middle of each village there was a large, round structure used for the meetings of the council and for general assemblies of the people. The largest of these buildings would accommodate about 3,000 persons; and, like the dwellings, they were built with a wooden framework covered by cleverly fitted grass, with an opening in the top to allow smoke to escape. Intended primarily for the public purposes mentioned above, the buildings could be converted into sleeping quarters for visitors, if the need arose. Visiting in large parties was a common practice among these natives.

The Florida Indians showed little interest in gold or silver as ornaments, or for other purposes. The Spanish goods which caught the attention of native traders were knives, scissors, axes, hatchets, hoes, glass beads, bronze rattles, coarse cloth, and a variety of garments.[6]

Spain explored some parts of the Florida coast and attempted a map of the peninsula as early as 1502; but sixty-three years passed before Pedro Menéndez de Avilés established the first permanent settlement at St. Augustine. In the meantime, French claimants had appeared—first a Huguenot party under the leadership of Jean Ribaut, and soon afterward another Huguenot group led by René de Laudonnière. Menéndez murdered Huguenot settlers, "not as Frenchmen, but as Lutherans;" and a few

[6] *Ibid.* 13.

7

years later a French leader, Dominique de Gourges, allied with the powerful Indian chief, Saturiba, fell upon Fort San Mateo, took prisoners and massacred them, "not as Spaniards, but as traitors, robbers, and murderers." The native population must have been deeply impressed by the severity of civilized warfare.

The Florida Indians were sometimes in revolt against Spanish rule during the seventeenth century. The Apalachee tribe, who gathered products of the forest, hunted for game, fished in the streams of middle Florida, and cultivated their crops of corn, beans, and melons, were asking the Spanish invaders as early as 1607 "for missionaries to come to their area and baptize them."[7] But Apalachee uprisings in 1638 and 1647 were followed by a general Indian revolt in 1656, in which the Muskhogean tribes joined with the Timuquans, against the insatiable demands of Spanish officials and churchmen for laborers on new fortifications and for the products of Indian agriculture.

Only in the decade, 1690 to 1700, did the Spanish authorities attempt to expand on a large scale their settlements to regions west of the Atlantic seaboard. Pensacola was founded in 1696, to challenge French control of the Gulf coast.

The planting of British colonies south of Virginia brought to the Florida frontier a conflict which was to continue for more than one hundred years. Virginia settlers established themselves at Albemarle on the Chowan River in 1653. A charter was issued to the eight proprietors of Carolina in 1663, and a few years later the settlement of Charleston began. The British settlers of South Carolina incited the Indians of Spanish Guale to raid white plantations about 1680, and the missions of the region had to be moved to the St. Marys River. Lord Cardross established a Scottish settlement at Port Royal, off the coast of South Carolina, in 1683, and soon this British leader prevailed upon the Yamassee Indians to attack the Spanish settlement on Santa Catalina. In 1686 a Spanish party destroyed Port Royal. Clashes occurred between the Apalachees, led by Antonio Matheos and supported

---

[7] Mark F. Boyd, Hale G. Smith, and John W. Griffin, *Here Once They Stood*, 107.

by Spanish troops, and the British-dominated Apalachicolas, a branch of the Lower Creeks.[8]

By 1685 there were 2,500 settlers in the Carolina province, including the French and English religious dissenters.[9] After 1682, France was making her bid for control of the Mississippi Valley and the coast of West Florida, both of which were important factors in the wider contest for dominance of North America, and in the world-wide struggle among European nations for expansion of territory. Indian tribes adjacent to the provinces of the warring powers—England, France, and Spain— were hopelessly confused as to their best policy for survival. It must be admitted, too, that the ablest statesmen of the European nations were not altogether clear in regard to the ultimate results of their own alliances and their long, exhausting conflicts.

In 1701 the War of the Spanish Succession found France and Spain in alliance against the British and their allies. In 1702 a military party from South Carolina captured St. Augustine, but lacked the power to garrison and hold it; so they burned the town before withdrawing. In 1703 and 1704 a party of fifty British soldiers, with some thirteen hundred Creek allies, led by James Moore of South Carolina, fell upon the Apalachee towns, burned the missions, killed many of the Christian Indians, and carried off captives whom they enslaved. The commander of the Spanish garrison and about 200 Apalachee warriors were among the dead. The prisoners who were carried back to Carolina numbered about 1,400, most of whom, in the course of time, were absorbed by the Creek tribe.[10] Two years later a Spanish and French force attacked Charleston, but were driven off. The English retaliated by sending armed parties into Middle Florida in 1708 and 1722.

Before 1740 the British had planted Georgia between the Carolinas and Spanish Florida, and in that year Governor James Oglethorpe, supported by a naval force, attempted the conquest

[8] *Ibid.*, 8.
[9] H. E. Bolton and T. M. Marshall, *The Colonization of North America*, 207, 208.
[10] Frederick Webb Hodge, *Handbook of American Indians North of Mexico*, I, 67, 68.

of St. Augustine. The invasion was a failure, and the Georgians were forced to beat off a counterattack upon Savannah. Oglethorpe again led an expedition against Florida in 1745, but Spain still held St. Augustine when hostilities were suspended by the terms of the treaty, signed at Aix-la-Chapelle in 1748.

A final struggle for control of the North American Continent was shaping up, even while the diplomats were negotiating peace terms. The colonists of France and those of England were shooting each other, along with Indian allies, on the Pennsylvania frontier and elsewhere before the end of the year 1754. The French and Indian War, American colonists called the struggle; in Europe it was known as the Seven Years' War, and its results were of deep significance, in widely separated parts of the globe. In North America, France was eliminated as a contender for territory, with only a dream of French empire in the West remaining for the restless imagination of Napoleon Bonaparte in the next generation. Great Britain, her title to the Hudson Bay area confirmed, received unchallenged possession of Canada and all the land east of the Mississippi River, excepting only the Island of New Orleans on the left bank below Lake Pontchartrain. The Treaty of Paris in 1763 thus placed Florida and the Seminole Indians in British hands.

The new owners divided Florida into two parts, with the Chattahoochee and Apalachicola rivers separating the East from the West province. East Florida included the peninsula, with its northern limit the St. Marys River and a line extending westward from its source to the mouth of the Flint River; West Florida, the territory west of the lower Chattahoochee and the Apalachicola, to the Mississippi River. The northern limit of West Florida was placed at the 31st parallel, but in 1767 the British ministry moved it up to 32 degrees and 28 minutes, north latitude. West Florida was separated from the Spanish-occupied Island of New Orleans by Lakes Borgne, Maurepas, and Pontchartrain.

The exact relationship between the Indians of Spanish Florida in the seventeenth century, and the people who came to be called Seminoles about the time of British occupation, 1763–83, cannot be known. When the records of colonial wars state that Creek invaders practically exterminated the natives of the peninsula, the picture emerges vaguely. Certain it is that the Seminole Indians of William Bartram's account, at the outset of the American Revolution, were a mixed people. There were elements of Muskhogean stock—Apalachicolas and Apalachees—whose language was related to that of the Creek invaders. There were Timuquan remnants, and undoubtedly there were descendants of the wild Mayucas and Ays of the east coast, and of the Tegesta tribe in the southern peninsula.

Even the invaders contained diverse peoples of separate Indian linguistic stock. The Hitchiti who lived on the Flint River below the mouth of Kinchafoonee Creek, spoke a language that was clearly Muskhogean, yet so different from that of the Creeks as to raise many questions concerning the background of the two tribes. The Hitchiti were "absorbed" by the Creeks, becoming an "integral" part of the Creek people.[11] The process was comparable, though not precisely parallel, with that by which Slavic elements of the Balkan Peninsula, speaking a language related to that of the ancient Hellenes, have become an "integral" part of the United States people. In either case, examination of all the ethnological factors involved in the ancestry of the mixed people would be an extremely difficult task. Furthermore, it would be an exercise of doubtful value, because of incomplete data. The Yamassee Indians, crushed as an independent tribe by their wars with the Creeks, spoke a dialect of the Hitchiti language, as did many other tribes of the Southeastern area: Chiaha, Oconee, Sawokli, Apalachicola, and Mikasuki.[12] In Bartram's time, about half of the Florida Seminoles spoke Creek and the other half, Hitchiti; but in later years, the speech of the Seminole Indians became more closely related to that of the Creek tribe. The Mikasuki were the Seminoles living in the area about Miccosukee Lake, in present day Leon County, Florida. Their speech and their place-names indicate kinship with the people of the Sawokli towns, on the lower Chattahoochee River, near the borders of Georgia, Alabama, and Florida.

[11] *Ibid.*, I, 61, 68, 551, 860, 861; II, 481, 500, 501.
[12] *Ibid.*, I, 551.

Fifty years after the end of the American Revolution, an intelligent Indian agent in Florida explained to a friend the meaning of the term, Seminole, and gave an official view of all the Florida Indians. "The word Seminole means runaway or broken off," Wiley Thompson wrote; "Hence . . . applicable to all the Indians in the Territory of Florida as all of them ran away . . . from the Creek . . . Nation. The treaties made with the Seminole Indians embrace all the Indians in the Territory except some Bands on the Apalachicola River who were provided for in a seperate [sic] Article in the Camp Moultrie Treaty."[13]

The early history of the Seminoles is closely associated with that of the Creek tribe. The United States made separate treaties with the Florida Indians long before the Creek tribal government recognized the separation. A brief glance at the Creek Confederacy from the time of its organization late in the seventeenth century until the Florida Indians had seceded, approximately one hundred years later, will clarify some phases of Seminole beginnings.

The original Creek Confederacy, organized in Georgia and Alabama, perhaps with the ultimate design of forming an extensive Indian union against European invaders, contained thirty-seven towns.[14] The immediate purpose of Chief Old Brim, in 1716 was to strengthen his people for their war against the Cherokees and to provide a durable foundation for his "balance of power" policy. Old Brim understood the need of France, England, and Spain, in their long contest for territorial possessions, to have the friendship of Indian tribes in strategic locations; and he expected to find advantages for the Creeks in the diplomatic bids of the great powers for Indian support.[15]

Most of the peoples combined in the Creek Confederacy were Muskhogean, but a few bands of unrelated Indians, such as the

13 Wiley Thompson to Judge Augustus Steele, March 31, 1835, National Archives, O. I. A. Letters Received, Seminole, 1835.

14 It is probable that an earlier confederacy existed in the area, at the time of De Soto. John R. Swanton, *Early History of the Creek Indians and their Neighbors,* 257; Charles H. Coe, *Red Patriots,* 5, 6; Angie Debo, *The Road to Disappearance,* 3, 4, 40, 50.

15 R. S. Cotterill, *The Southern Indians,* 20ff.

Yuchi, had been incorporated.[16] Tribes conquered by the Creeks were generally added to the union, and by this process the Alabamis, Hitchitees, Koasatas, Natchez, and Tuskegees became identified with the Creeks. A band of Shawnees, related to the Algonquian tribes north of the Ohio River, found their way into the Creek Confederacy.

During the two decades of British ownership, steps were taken to make the province of Florida an economic asset to the Empire. Governor Andrew Turnbull imported 1,500 Minorcans to cultivate indigo at New Smyrna on the east coast. A program of road-building was undertaken, and in three years the government spent $580,000 in East and West Florida. As a result of the prosperity incident to government expenditures, most Europeans in Florida were loyal to Great Britain during the American Revolution. A military party from Florida co-operated with a British force from New York in an attack upon Savannah, Georgia, in 1778. In the following year, after Spain's declaration of war against Great Britain, Don Bernardo de Gálvez, Spanish governor at New Orleans, began the seizure of British posts in West Florida. He captured Pensacola in 1781.

The period of vigorous British colonial activity was not long enough to affect deeply the conditions of Indian life; and for thirty-six years following the British provincial experiment, Florida was in the hands of its native population, excepting the slight authority maintained by Spain from its trading centers and missions, such as Pensacola, St. Marks, and St. Augustine.

Seminole Indians lived by hunting and fishing, together with a considerable activity in farming and stock-raising. Many parts of Florida were overrun with wild animals in numbers astonishing to Europeans. William Bartram relates an incident in which he and a fellow hunter were stalking, simultaneously, a herd of deer and a flock of wild turkeys in the vicinity of Lake George. At the same time a huge wild cat was stealthily approaching the turkeys; and as Bartram was about to level upon the cat, his companion fired at a deer and missed it. Lynx, turkeys, and deer

[16] Muriel Wright, *A Guide to the Indian Tribes of Oklahoma*, 29ff., 128ff., 157, 264.

all escaped harm. "Thus we foiled each other," the botanist rue-
fully summarized the adventure. On another occasion, Bartram
fished in the Little St. Juan with a single companion in a boat.
His fishing partner was expert in taking trout, and as they drifted
two miles downstream, the catch was large enough to supply
their two households. "Some of the fish were so large and strong
in their element, as to shake his arms stoutly, and drag us with
the canoe over the floods before we got them in," wrote the
young scientist. Evidently they were catching trout of the larger
variety.[17]

During the British period an attempt was made to replace
military control with civil government in Florida, and encouragement was given to immigration and trade, which resulted in
a host of new problems in the relations of the Europeans with
Indians. Frequently the difficulty could be resolved into a single
question—How can the white population be prevented from
selling intoxicants to the natives, and thus exploiting and de-
bauching them for the sake of profits? Sometimes the problem
took an entirely different form, such as—How can the white
trader protect his scalp, or how can the remote settler keep possession of his livestock and save the lives of his wife and children? Inevitably, the relations of the two peoples became more
complicated when there was intermarriage.

An employee of the Spaulding Trading Company on St. Johns
River was married to a young Seminole woman. Unacquainted
with the processes of accumulating property, but delighted by
the trinkets, fabrics, and other goods handled by the strange
creature who had become her husband, the lady was inclined
to give away his possessions to her amiable and equally delighted
relatives—a countless horde of brothers, sisters, aunts, uncles,
and cousins. Desperate because she was reducing him to poverty,
the trader alternately begged her to desist, and threatened to
shoot her; but, as Bartram tells the story, had not "the resolution
even to leave her."[18] The Seminoles did not approve of her conduct; but in spite of Indian support for the trader, and a tribal

17 Bartram, *Travels*, 109, 194.
18 *Ibid.*, 110, 111.

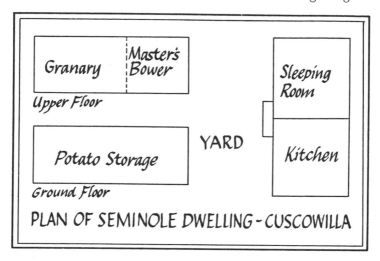

Granary	Master's Bower		Sleeping Room
Upper Floor			
Potato Storage		YARD	Kitchen
Ground Floor			

PLAN OF SEMINOLE DWELLING - CUSCOWILLA

law which forbade a second marriage for the wife, the unhappy young husband's only consolation was found in "deep draughts of brandy."

Cuscowilla was the tribal capital of the Alachua Indians who moved into Florida from the Oconee River of Georgia about 1710. These transplanted Lower Creeks, mingled with the conquered peoples of earlier times, continued customs of the Muskogees, and became an active element of the Seminole tribe.[19] Cuscowilla contained some thirty dwellings, each consisting of two houses standing twenty yards apart. One unit was about thirty feet long, twelve feet wide, and twelve feet high. It was divided into two rooms, one of which was used for cooking, the other for sleeping. The second unit had a similar length and width, but it was higher, with two stories. A considerable part of both floors was used for storage, usually with potatoes on the lower level, grain and other foods on the upper. An elevated, shaded, open platform, which could be reached by means of a portable ladder, stood at the end of this two-story building, adjacent to the front door of the other unit. This pleasant, airy space, supported only by pillars, was reserved for the head of

[19] Hodge, *Handbook*, I, 34.

the family. Here he received visitors, and here he found comfort during the hot summer weather.

Each of these buildings was constructed on a frame, with heavy pillars fixed in the ground at the corners, lighter posts along the sides, and cross pieces of timber to strengthen the walls. The square yard around the houses was invariably swept clean, and the streets of Cuscowilla and other Seminole towns were neatly kept, free from all sources of contamination.

William Bartram described the chief of the Alachuas at Cuscowilla in 1773 as a "tall, well made man, very affable and cheerful, about sixty years of age, his eyes lively and full of fire, his countenance manly and placid, yet ferocious, . . . his nose aquiline, his dress extremely simple, but his head trimmed and ornamented in the true Creek mode." His Yamassee slaves, captured in war, served him with signs of abject fear and in general behaved in a mild, tame fashion. "The free Indians, on the contrary, were bold, active, and clamorous." Slaves were permitted to intermarry with free Indians and the children of these mixed marriages were free.

Each family at Cuscowilla supplied itself with vegetables from a small individual garden in which corn, beans, tobacco, and melons were raised. The common plantation, situated at a distance of two miles from the town, on fertile ground enclosed by a fence to keep out domestic animals and the wild animals of the forest, was farmed by the whole village. Each family had its own part of the land, clearly marked off at the time of planting. Cultivation was a common enterprise, but each family gathered its own crop for storage in its private granary. Standing near the center of the plantation was a building used for common storage, however, and to its public food supply each family contributed grain and potatoes. Visitors and indigent members of the tribe were supplied from this public granary. Each year when the grain in the fields was beginning to ripen, children of the tribe were stationed in the planted area at intervals, to scare away crows, blackbirds, and jackdaws by constant "whooping and halooing."[20]

[20] Bartram, *Travels*, 164–70; James Adair, *History of the American Indians*,

William Augustus Bowles, self-styled principal chief
of the Creeks and the Seminoles.

From a painting by Thomas Hardy
Photograph courtesy Dr. Mark Boyd

"I, Micanopy . . . do hereby fully acknowledge and confirm
every Article of the same [Articles of Capitulation]."—March
6, 1837.

From McKenney and Hall,
Indian Tribes of North America

The Florida Indians along the Little Juan fashioned canoes from cypress trees, large enough to carry twenty or even thirty warriors. In these large boats they traveled along the coast and sometimes to the Bahamas and Cuba. Coffee, liquors, sugar, and tobacco were among the articles imported; and for these things the Indians bartered deerskins, furs, dried fish, beeswax, honey, and bear's oil. Apparently the Spaniards valued this commerce highly and treated the visitors from Florida with marked consideration, entertaining them lavishly and serving their most highly prized beverages. Spanish fishermen visited St. Marks and many widely separated places on the Florida coast, exchanging their fish for pelts and furs.[21]

Most of the Lower Creeks and Seminoles who sprang from that branch of the Muskogee tribe, were influenced primarily by Spanish elements of European culture. A Christian Indian of the Alachuas was likely to wear a little silver crucifix fastened to a small chain or to the wampum collar about his neck. The Spanish Catholic missions left many evidences of their training, which were altered but slightly by the brief period of British rule.

The Florida Indians produced an abundance of food in their fields and from the forests, streams, and lakes. To visitors such as William Bartram and James Adair, they probably served their best. Certainly the travelers were impressed by Muskhogean hospitality and lavish in their praise of the Indian cooks. Bartram mentioned with enthusiasm the venison, hominy, milk, and corn cakes that were served to him, and recalled the feast that was prepared as a farewell gesture for him by the "white king of Talahasochte." Bear's ribs, venison, varieties of fish, roasted turkeys, hot corn cakes, and "a very agreeable cooling sort of jelly which they call *conte* . . . prepared from the root of the China briar," were placed before the guest. The jelly was made by chopping the roots into small segments, pounding them to a pulp, and mixing with water. Later this mixture was strained and the sediment was dried in the open air. The resulting fine powder

---

406ff.; Swanton, *Early History of the Creek Indians and their Neighbors;* Debo, *The Road to Disappearance,* 20.
[21] Bartram, *Travels,* 194.

was mixed with warm water, sweetened with honey, and served cool. The jelly could also be stirred into corn meal, and cooked in bear's oil in the form of hot cakes.

Meeting an Indian family on the road back from a hunt, Bartram observed that the man, his wife, and the children were all mounted on good horses and that their pack animals were laden with game, hides, and honey. The Indian gave to the botanist a fawnskin full of honey, and Bartram had presents for the hunter and his family: metal fishhooks, sewing needles, and other useful little articles.[22]

There were occasions when some of the Seminoles, both men and women, engaged in drunken revels that were quite demoralizing. The feasting, dancing, and "sacrifices to Venus" might continue for several days and nights—usually until the supply of intoxicants was exhausted. Indians suffering from the effects of their debauchery were likely to become desperate for more liquor. According to contemporary accounts, the Seminole squaw frequently turned this situation to her own advantage. During the dance it was customary for a warrior, possessed of a full bottle of rum, to offer a drink from the bottle to any damsel with whom he danced or engaged in conversation. "But the modest fair, veiling her face in her mantle, refuses at the beginning of the frolick; but he presses and at last insists.

"She being furnished with an empty bottle, concealed in her mantle, at last consents, and taking a good, long draught, blushes, drops her pretty face on her bosom, and artfully discharges the rum into her bottle, and by repeating this artifice soon fills it: this she privately conveys to her secret store, and then returns to the jovial game, and so on during the festival; and when the comic farce is over, the wench retails this precious cordial to them at her own price."

The Long Warrior, commanding a Seminole war party en route to West Florida to campaign against the Choctaws, took no part in his men's revelry, but was unable to veto their excesses. The agent for Spaulding and Company on the lower St. Johns, Mr. McLatche, had to consider the problem of credit

[22] Bartram, *Travels*, 164, 203, 206.

for Long John and his warriors. The Seminole's proposition was to fit out his men with clothing, food, and other supplies, with payment promised when the party should return from the Choctaw country. The Long Warrior expected to bring back furs, pelts, and other valuables.

Mr. McLatche hesitated, and finally told the Indian that he had no authority to grant so much credit for so long a time. The Long Warrior was deeply offended. "Do you presume to refuse me credit?" he asked. "Certainly you know who I am, and what power I have: but perhaps you do not know, that if the matter required, and I please, I could command and cause the terrible thunder, now rolling in the skies up above, to descend upon your head in fiery shafts, and lay you prostrate at my feet, and consume your stores, turning them instantly into dust and ashes."[23]

Mr. McLatche was not intimidated, but was willing to meet the Long Warrior half way. "Show me what you can do with the thunder on that Live Oak yonder by the road," he suggested. Then, when the great chief declined to use the tree as a target for his thunderbolt, the trader offered to extend credit for the band's absolute needs, such as shirts and blankets: one half to be paid at once, the balance upon their return from Mississippi. On that basis the deal was closed.

The Seminoles called William Bartram *Puc-Puggy*, meaning "flower-hunter." In their camp near the trading post on the St. Johns, a large rattlesnake caused a near panic by coming among their shelters and gliding into the place where the food was stored. The Seminoles hestitated to injure a rattlesnake, because of their belief in the power of "manes," the kindred or spirit, of a dead snake. Three of the young men came to *Puc-Puggy*, however, and begged him to free them from the presence of the great snake, since it was the pleasure of the botanist "to collect all their animals and other natural productions of their land." They declared he was welcome to the snake.

He went with them, killed the snake with a pine knot, cut off

[23] It is possible that William Bartram, who reported the incident, edited the comments of the Long Warrior; for they are somewhat more ornate than the language commonly employed by a Seminole chieftain. It is likely that the Long Warrior talked to Mr. McLatche through an interpreter.

its head, and took out its fangs for his collection. The Indians were impressed by his bold action; but presently three young warriors returned to him with an interpreter, and said they would have to scratch him, taking out some of his blood to make him "less heroic." When two of them flourished their scratching instruments, Bartram resisted; whereupon the third warrior took his part, pushing off his companions, and declaring that the botanist was a brave warrior and his friend. The two who had seemed bent upon scratching him immediately dropped their fierce scowls, "whooped in chorus," shouted with laughter and said the visitor was a sincere friend of the Seminoles, a worthy and brave warrior, and that no one thereafter should attempt to injure him. Evidently they had been enacting a farce for the appeasement of the more superstitious Indians.[24]

The Seminole Indians, in common with other tribes of the Muskhogean stock, were inclined to be proud of their valor and hardihood, haughty in their dealings with strangers, particularly with Europeans advancing claims that contradicted Indian rights, and arrogant in their fierce determination to rule their own land or die in the attempt. No person who fought against them and became thoroughly acquainted with their qualities, from the time of the first Spanish invasions to the end of the Seminole wars, ever doubted their courage. Perhaps the inevitable tragedy surrounding their relations with European peoples added a touch of gallantry to their behavior as soldiers. Experienced army officers, long in conflict with the Seminoles, declared that their warriors never surrendered. The women and children of the tribe were caught in the midst of the struggle for existence, and often there was no distinguishable civilian population. The charge that the Seminoles condemned prisoners of war to death by burning is probably true; but there was precedent for that cruelty in the heartless attitude of De Soto, Narváez, Ponce de León, and many others who were less prominent among the conquering foreign armies.

To an English trader who begged a party of Seminoles to spare the son of a Spanish governor whom they held with two

24 Bartram, *Travels*, 214–20.

other youths under sentence of death, the Seminole spokesman answered: "You know that these people are our cruel enemies; they save no lives of red men who fall in their power; you say that the youth is the son of the Spanish Governor, and we believe you; he is our enemy; if we save one we must save all three; but we cannot do it. The red men require their blood to appease the spirits of their slain relatives; they have entrusted us with the guardianship of our laws and rights, we cannot betray them. However, a third is saved by lot: the Great Spirit allows us to put it to that decision; He is no respecter of persons." The lots were cast, but the Governor's son lost and was burned.

In spite of their severity in combat, the Seminoles were merciful to beaten enemies in the matter of sparing lives. It is true that they followed the common practice of their area in the enslavement of captured enemies. As noted previously, intermarriage of slave population was permitted and the children of intermarried slaves became free. Incorporation of conquered peoples was the accepted practice of both the Seminoles and their parent tribe, the Creeks.

The traveler, William Bartram, wrote that he never saw an Indian beating his wife, or even reproving her in anger. In that astute observer's opinion, "Muscogulges" ranked high in their domestic relations. "Just, honest, liberal, hospitable, temperate, and persevering," are among his descriptive words.[25]

[25] Bartram, *Travels*, 382–85.

CHAPTER 2

Return of the Seminoles
to Spanish Rule

"I, Tustenuggee Harjo, am ordered to bring you these sticks."

TUSTENUGGEE HARJO

B Y THE TERMS of the Treaty of Paris in 1783, the United States of America was recognized as an independent state, and the province of Florida, with its Seminole population, was returned to Spain. The newest power and the oldest in North America were thus brought into close contact as neighbors; and the native populations, on opposite sides of the international boundary, were blood relatives with complicated problems of tribal relationship already existing.

After the departure of the British officials and a considerable part of the English settlers, the Indians came into unrestricted control of a large area in the peninsula, together with the lower Suwannee and Apalachicola river valleys. The Spanish authorities in Florida exercised jurisdiction over St. Marks, Pensacola, and St. Augustine, maintaining military protection of a sort for trading posts operating under Spanish grants. The inhabitants of St. Augustine habitually remained within the protected area of the city. Some of the Minorcans, brought to New Smyrna by Dr. Andrew Turnbull in 1767, remained in Florida under Spanish rule, living at St. Augustine.

Bella Vista, Governor John Moultrie's country estate, and other valuable properties abandoned by British owners in East Florida, were destroyed by bands of Indians. Most English colonists who remained after Spain recovered Florida settled in the western province. William Panton of the trading firm, Panton, Leslie, and Company, had influence with the Spanish provincial government which he used for the benefit of English settlers who were interested in commerce or industry. A part of the British inhabitants of Florida, fearing the attitude of Spain in regard to religious conformity, removed to Georgia or South Carolina.[1]

The Indians ran their towns according to Seminole customs, largely the same as the customs of the Creeks, but separate from the Creek Confederacy. The Indians of Florida represented one of the difficult factors of diplomacy in the relations of Spain with the United States.

Many elements of friction appeared on the Georgia frontier and along the international boundary to the west during the two decades following Spanish recovery of Florida. Negro slaves, escaping from the hard labor of the Georgia or Carolina plantation, found refuge among the Seminoles in Spanish territory. The Spanish authorities were inclined to accept the fugitives as free citizens; and loss of slave property by the Georgia planters, the natural desire of the Negroes to win their freedom, and the friendly attitude of the Seminoles toward escaped slaves, all combined to create a diplomatic puzzle. Clash of interest between white settlers north of Florida and the native population south of the St. Marys did not arise suddenly. Indian slaves of the early Carolina provinces usually fled south in making a break for freedom; and their example was followed by plantation Negroes before the end of the seventeenth century. This situation was an important factor in the planting of Georgia in 1732; but slave labor was soon admitted to the new province, and the problem of fugitive slaves continued during and after the American Revolution.[2]

The situation of Spain on the southern and western borders of the United States was an invitation to her officers in America to carry on intrigues with the Indians of the region. Spain's traders and agents were well acquainted with the Indian leaders,

---

[1] Carolyn Mays Brevard, *A History of Florida*, I, 4.
[2] Joshua Giddings, *The Exiles of Florida*, 2, 3; Bolton and Marshall, *The Colonization of North America*, 316, 335, 336.

and Spanish diplomats studied the temper of American settlers in the Mississippi Valley. Holding both banks of the Mississippi River for several hundred miles above its mouth, Spain had in her hands a powerful weapon for advancing her interests in the West. Every community along the Ohio River and its tributaries was dependent upon the river outlet to world markets through New Orleans and the Gulf of Mexico. Spanish officials considered three means for promoting the interests of their country by exploiting the powerful position of Spain on the lower Mississippi: first, to assert rights guaranteed by the Treaty of Paris in control of river commerce, with domination of both banks up to the mouth of the Yazoo; second, to incite the Indians to warfare along the western frontier of American settlement; and third, to carry on intrigue with western Americans themselves, for the purpose of separating their communities from the government on the Atlantic Seaboard.[3] Among the persons of European descent enlisted in the Spanish cause were Dr. James O'Fallon of South Carolina, James Wilkinson, an officer of high rank in the United States Army, John Sevier of Tennessee, and James Robertson, who named his western settlement "District of Mero" for the Spanish governor of New Orleans.[4] Alexander McGillivray, whose activities will be touched upon later in the story of Seminole relations with the United States, was the son of a Scotch trader and a Creek-French mother. He was in the pay of Spain, but his loyalty was unwavering in the support of Creek tribal interests. Among all the careers of intrigue on the American frontier, none was more remarkable than that of McGillivray.

By 1789, the year in which George Washington took office as President of the United States, the Creek Confederacy had expanded to include sixty Upper Creek Towns on the Alabama River, and about forty Lower Creek Towns on the Flint and Chatahoochee rivers. Henry Knox, secretary of war, reported that most of the Creeks lived within the United States but added: "Some of the southern towns of the Creeks, or Seminoles, are

[3] A. C. McLaughlin, *The Confederation and the Constitution*, 93.
[4] John Spencer Bassett, *The Federalist System, 1789–1801*, 70ff.

within the territory of Spain, stretching toward the point of Florida."[5] The "gun-men," or warriors of the Creek Nation, numbered about 6,000 according to the Secretary's report.

White settlers, moving westward in small bands, had begun to occupy the upper valley of the Tennessee in 1770, by 1780 had made settlements at Boonesborough in Kentucky and Nashville on the Cumberland River, and by 1785 were pushing for recognition as the state of Franklin, in the eastern part of the region that became the state of Tennessee some eleven years later. The founders of the Watauga settlements, John Sevier and James Robertson, disappointed by the failure of statehood in that area, listened attentively to the offers of Spanish agents in the hope of finding a solution for the problem of commercial outlet.

The state of Georgia promoted settlement of the lands it claimed in the West, including most of present day Alabama and Mississippi. The Georgia legislature made grants to three companies in 1789: the Tennessee Company which established a short-lived settlement near Muscle Shoals on the Tennessee River; the Virginia Company which did not reach the stage of actual settlement; and the South Carolina Company which proposed to plant a colony in the region south of the Yazoo River, in dispute between the United States and Spain. Dr. James O'Fallon, at the head of this enterprise, conspired with General James Wilkinson to obtain aid from Spain in making the settlement, and carried on negotiations with the Spanish governor at New Orleans. President Washington warned western people to remain aloof from the scheme, and the state of Georgia annulled O'Fallon's charter.[6]

Of all the men who took an active part in the diplomatic intrigues of the western frontier, perhaps Alexander McGillivray was the ablest. He was the son of a leading citizen of provincial Georgia, who, as Secretary Henry Knox pointed out in his report to President Washington, "adhered to Great Britain in the late war," and as a result had his property confiscated by the state.

[5] *American State Papers: Indian Affairs*, I, 15.
[6] Bassett, *The Federalist System*, 72, 73.

Alexander McGillivray's mother was Sehoy (Two-kept-on-after-the-Enemy) Marchand, daughter of a French general and his fullblood Creek wife. Lachlan McGillivray, the Loyalist who lost his property for supporting Britain against the revolting American Colonies, left daughters whose descendants were among the first families of Alabama. His son, Alexander, became the foremost citizen of the Creek Confederacy, and one of the most astute diplomats of his time. The Creek Indians valued his leadership because he was well educated, he understood the ways of the white men thoroughly, and he was able to match wits with the best in private business or in the diplomacy of the Creek Nation. At Pensacola in 1784, he negotiated a treaty with the Spanish officials by which it was agreed that Spain should enjoy a monopoly of the Creek trade, and give protection to the "whole Creek-Seminole Nation."[7]

William Augustus Bowles was an adventurer whose activities sometimes brought disaster to the Creeks and Seminoles. Born in the British province of Maryland, Bowles entered the army when he was thirteen and became an ensign two years later while serving in Jamaica. At Pensacola, after the British set up their provincial government in West Florida, Bowles was charged with insubordination and reduced to the ranks. He deserted, threw away his uniform, and fled to the Creek country, where he was well received and accepted as a member of the tribe. He married the daughter of a Creek town chief.

A Spanish force, laying siege to Pensacola in 1781, gave Bowles a chance to recover the good will of British officials, lost by his desertion from the army. He lifted the siege with a Creek war party, and afterward was put on a basis of half pay in the British Army, apparently for service expected of him among the Creeks. His career took strange and diverse patterns: as an actor in a troupe which he contacted at New Providence in the British West Indies; as a painter of portraits; and finally as a trader in a post that was established on the Chattahoochee

---

[7] *American State Papers: Indian Affairs*, I, 15, 19, 73; Debo, *The Road to Disappearance*, 38–43; Brevard, *History of Florida*, I, 4ff.; Giddings, *The Exiles of Florida*, 10, 17.

to compete with Panton, Leslie and Company for the profitable trade of the Creeks.

He came to Florida for the first time in 1788, five years after Spain had regained title to her province. From that time until the end of his life, Bowles was engaged in the effort to oust Panton, Leslie and Company from their monopoly of Creek commerce and to expel Spain from her control of Florida. He was supported by John Murray, fourth Earl of Dunmore and former Governor of Virginia, and by John Miller, a wealthy merchant who was interested in the Indian trade. On at least two occasions, Bowles led raids of the Seminole Indians upon Panton, Leslie and Company's store at St. Marks, and on one of these forays he captured the Spanish fort, but was unable to garrison and hold it. He conducted a delegation of Seminoles, Creeks, and Cherokees to England in 1790 to obtain support for his trading activities.

Alexander McGillivray, regularly in the pay of the Spanish-chartered company of Panton and Leslie, and holding a modest investment in that firm, was a persistent opponent of Bowles. John Sevier and William Blount, citizens of Tennessee, were at one time fellow-conspirators of Bowles with deep-laid plans for driving Spain out of Florida and Louisiana. McGillivray died in 1793, but the United States agent for the Southern Indians, Benjamin Hawkins, remained to offset the influence of Bowles with the Creeks. It was the combined stratagem of President Washington's agent and the great diplomat of the Creek Indians, at the end of his career, that induced Governor Carondelet at New Orleans to order Bowles arrested. After imprisonment at Havana and Madrid, he was on his way to the Philippines in 1797, still a prisoner of the Spanish Government, when he made a spectacular escape and obtained British financial aid for another try at trade in Florida.

From his camp near the mouth of the Apalachicola River, Bowles led a party of Seminole Indian warriors in a great variety of raids. A merchant vessel, grounded on the Florida coast, was captured by this band who recovered six barrels of powder and a large supply of rum. With the military supplies thus obtained,

Bowles determined to attack St. Marks. The Seminole and Creek warriors were led by a Mikasuki chief named Kinhaizie, and the expedition was accompanied by Bowles himself. To the Indian chief the Spanish authorities proposed a parley; Kinhaizie agreed to accept their hospitality, see the entertainment prepared for him, and hear their proposals. Apparently, he was not thoroughly committed to support for the English adventurer and was seriously considering the Spanish offers of valuable presents for the Seminole warriors in exchange for the surrender of Bowles, when a breach of Indian etiquette caused a sudden change in his attitude. At the suggestion of the commandant's wife, Kinhaizie was asked to lay aside his bad-smelling pipe; he agreed, and stalked out of the meeting.

Almost immediately afterward, Bowles and Kinhaizie attacked with a force of 300 Seminoles, a small party of Creeks, and 10 white men. When the first assault was repulsed, Bowles settled down to a siege. Of three supply vessels sent to relieve the Spanish garrison, one got through, one was turned back, and one was captured by the Indians. After six weeks, the Spanish commandant surrendered, whereupon Bowles declared war upon Spain, assuring the Seminoles that he had orders from Great Britain.

The Spanish Governor, Vicente Juan Folch, acted promptly by sending a strong fleet to recapture St. Marks and posting a reward of $4,500 for the arrest of Bowles. Recognizing the overwhelming force of the Spanish expedition, Bowles withdrew, at the same time throwing open the doors of the warehouses to his Indian followers, to carry away such goods as suited their fancy.

The Seminoles were ready to make peace, and some of the head men agreed to surrender Bowles, who had taken refuge at Mikasuki, Kinhaizie's town. The chief was still resentful over the affront offered him in regard to his pipe, however, and refused to surrender the fugitive. On the contrary, he aided Bowles in escaping to the Creek country. The respite was brief, however, for the Creeks turned him over to Governor Folch who sent him to Cuba, and there he was imprisoned in Moro Castle.

As a prisoner, Bowles undertook a hunger strike during

which the Governor sent a message saying that he wished to have a conference. "I am sunk low indeed," Bowles answered; "but not so low as to receive a visit from the Governor General of Cuba." The prisoner died in 1805, survived by his Creek wife and several children. Among the descendants of this line was Chief Bowles, the friend of Sam Houston.[8]

In the conflict between Bowles and McGillivray, the United States had generally supported the latter, although Commissioner of Indian Affairs James Seagrove pointed out that the Creek diplomat was not giving his full support to the interests of President Washington's government. "A Spaniard, or an Englishman, is respectable all through the Creek Nation," Seagrove wrote to Secretary Henry Knox; "but it is very dangerous for any person, known to belong to the United States, to travel or be in that country."[9] McGillivray's having more than one master, the Commissioner thought, was responsible for the lack of respect accorded to United States citizens by the Creek tribe, and the scant prestige enjoyed by United States officials in the Indian country. All of George Washington's appointees, however, including Seagrove, were inclined to condemn Bowles and to deplore his persistent agitation among the Indians. His pretensions of great power and high position were offensive to plain men who faced dangers of the frontier casually and took pride in qualities of simple worth, such as courage and honesty. David Craig, reporting to the Commissioner of Indian Affairs, called attention to a picture of Bowles with two Indian chiefs, beneath which was written, "General Bowles, commander-in-chief of the Creek and Cherokee Nations."

To the assembled chiefs at Rock Landing on the Oconee, Seagrove explained that their land was in an uproar because of the efforts of bad white men—particularly "in consequence of the villainous imposition of a low adventurer, of the name of Bowles." The Commissioner exhausted his vocabulary of abuse—

[8] *American State Papers: Indian Affairs,* I, 184, 264, 296, 299, 300, 304; II, 792; Brevard, *History of Florida,* I, 16–23; *Dictionary of American Biography,* II, 519–20 (article by Arthur P. Whitaker, on William Augustus Bowles).
[9] Seagrove to Knox, May 24, 1792, *American State Papers: Indian Affairs,* I, 296.

Bowles was "too lazy to work for a living," he was regarded by the British Army as a bad man and "a coward," he was "obliged to fly his native country, or be hanged." Then he added, "Brothers, I could tell you much more about this bad man Bowles." But he refrained because Bowles was in the custody of Spanish officials and probably would make no more trouble.[10]

A new element was introduced into the diplomacy of the Southwestern frontier by Citizen Charles Genêt when he came to Charleston, South Carolina, in 1793 as the minister of Revolutionary France. Perhaps his primary purpose was to involve the United States in the war against Great Britain, but he also hoped to gain the support of the Mississippi Valley settlers in an attack upon Spanish Louisiana and Florida. The attitude of President Washington, stiffly neutral, brought Genêt's recall, even though the appeal of the unseasoned foreign agent to the people of America enlisted in his favor, among other frontiersmen, the great George Rogers Clark. Genêt's ignorance of diplomacy was an important factor in the defeat of his plans.

In November, 1794, Thomas Pinckney of South Carolina, United States minister to Great Britain, was instructed to take up his residence in Madrid, and to enter into negotiations for the settlement of two stubborn diplomatic problems: navigation of the Mississippi, and the northern boundary of Florida. Almost a year passed before Pinckney and Emmanuel Godoy, head of the Spanish ministry, were able to agree upon terms. The "Prince of Peace," as Godoy was called in Europe after his settlement with France, was inclined to meet American demands in a liberal spirit; furthermore, Godoy was disturbed by the possibility of growing friendship between England and her former American colonies, suggested by the conclusion of the Jay Treaty in England, during the time of Pinckney's residence in Madrid. The Treaty of San Lorenzo, signed by Pinckney and Godoy on October 27, 1795, placed the boundary of West Florida at the 31st parallel, and gave the people of the United States liberal use of the Mississippi with the right of deposit at New Orleans. Clearly, Godoy was determined to win the friend-

10 Seagrove, talk to Creek Chiefs, May 18, 1792, *ibid.*, I, 299.

ship of the United States as a safety measure against possible British aggression in the Mississippi Valley or Florida in alliance with the new American Republic.[11] Thomas Pinckney's diplomacy effectively settled the problem of western secession tendencies during the brief period of Spain's continuance in Louisiana Territory.

The death of Alexander McGillivray in 1793 had been a severe blow to the Seminoles and Creeks. For the Creeks of the Upper and Lower Towns, he had exercised an intelligent, restraining influence; for the Seminoles, he had been a leader for the principle of confederation, with enough imagination to understand the separate interests of a people physically divided from their kinsmen in the North. Violence along the border of Florida broke out after his death. Algonquians from the region north of the Ohio River came among the Creeks and urged them to join in a united Indian war against the westward surge of white settlers. The Lower Chiefs, especially, were influenced by the prospect of a war against the frontier whites, and numerous raiding parties were formed for the purpose of striking at the outposts of western settlement. John Galphin, a white adventurer who had strong influence with the Cowetas, led a party of thirty warriors in plundering the post at Traders Hill on the St. Marys, killing six of the defenders and carrying off Negro slaves, livestock, and goods from the store.

Upon the demand of Superintendent James Seagrove that the tribe take action against these raiders, the Tuckabatchee chief, Oche Harjo, ordered five of the hostiles executed, and arranged to surrender Galphin along with the property taken at Traders Hill. He sent notice of this action to Colerain by his young cousin, David Cornell. Unfortunately the messenger's party, including besides their leader a young Indian lad and two warriors, were met outside of Colerain by a band of Georgia militiamen who were bent upon revenge. Cornell and the Indian boy were killed, their two companions saving themselves by flight. Seagrove and Governor Edward Telfair of Georgia prom-

[11] *American State Papers: Foreign Affairs*, I, 252, 533–49; Brevard, *History of Florida*, I, 8; Bassett, *The Federalist System*, 82.

ised that the men responsible for these murders should be punished; but to the Creeks the event remained a striking evidence of the white man's treachery.[12]

Clearly, the disorders along the frontier in this period were not due entirely, or even principally, to a lawless tendency among the Southern Indians. While the Treaty of San Lorenzo was being negotiated in 1795, an outlaw named Benjamin Harrison and his accomplices murdered twenty Creek Indians on their own hunting ground. It was natural that the Creeks should strike back, and in the process of their revenge they killed innocent white citizens. Although the authorities of Georgia and the United States were agreed that Harrison should be prosecuted, Indian leaders were disappointed to learn that the white criminals were imprisoned to await trial for their enormous offense.[13]

To the council at Colerain, thirty miles above the mouth of St. Marys on the Georgia side, the Creeks sent about four hundred warriors and head men in May, 1796. Colonel Benjamin Hawkins of North Carolina, Andrew Pickens of South Carolina, and George Clymer of Pennsylvania represented the United States. Lieutenant Colonel Henry Gaither was sent with a federal military force to keep order; and the Indians, skeptical in regard to pledges of safe conduct, placed carefully hidden stores of food along a line of convenient retreat. The state of Georgia also sent a militia force to the conference; but the federal commissioners enforced rigidly the rule that no armed men unauthorized by the United States should land at Colerain.[14]

The Georgia commissioners presented a list of claims for property losses: 89 Negro slaves, 825 horses, 1159 cattle, 495 hogs, 115 houses burned. Total damage, as stated in this bill, amounted before the Treaty of New York to $70,000; and after that settlement, to $40,000. Regret was expressed for the depredations of Benjamin Harrison and other whites; but the Georgia

---

[12] Debo, The Road to Disappearance, 55ff., 72, 89.

[13] Ibid., 61–65.

[14] American State Papers: Indian Affairs, I, 472–87, 495–501, 551–60, 586–618; Niles' Register, Vol. LIII (1837), 66; Debo, The Road to Disappearance, 62–66; Cotterill, The Southern Indians, 113–17.

men thought the principal blame should rest with the Creeks for failure to carry out the treaties of Augusta, Galphinton, and Shoulderbone.

Angie Debo, in her history of the Creek Indians, catches the temper of the tribal leaders in her description of the meetings at Colerain. "Fushatchee Micco was spokesman. They conducted themselves with firmness and dignity, and their feeling of solidarity, their intelligent conception of issues, and their grave sense of responsibility were impressive indications that even after twenty years of war and disintegrating influences the great confederacy could gather its forces for a supreme effort of self-preservation.... When the Treaty of Galphinton was mentioned they asked who signed it; when the hogs were mentioned in the list of stolen property, they laughed."[15]

Later, in conversation with the Federal Commissioners, Creek leaders asked how the men from Georgia could tell whether their hogs had been stolen by Indians or killed by bears. "The Georgians have done us much evil," their spokesman said; "but we never blamed them for the hogs we lost."

The Indians at Colerain agreed upon ratification of the Treaty of New York, admitted United States traders under protection of federal troops, accepted the Apalachee fork of the Oconee River as their boundary, and ceded a tract of twenty-five square miles from Creek lands on the Oconee, as the site for a factory. Two blacksmiths with strikers were provided for the Creeks, and goods to the amount of $6,000 turned over to them. Edward Price, who came to Colerain as factor in 1796, moved the supply of goods from that place to the new site on the Oconee, Fort Wilkinson, in the spring of 1797.[16]

The Treaty of San Lorenzo provided that the United States and Spain should each appoint a commissioner and a surveyor to run the line of the international boundary. President Washington appointed Andrew Ellicott as commissioner and Thomas Freeman as surveyor. Spain appointed Major Stephen Minor

[15] Debo, *The Road to Disappearance*, 63, 64.
[16] Charles J. Kappler, *Indian Affairs: Laws and Treaties*, II, 46–50; Cotterill, *The Southern Indians*, 115, 116.

of Philadelphia to act as commissioner and surveyor. The commissioners were instructed to make the necessary arrangements as to equipment and helpers, to run the lines with as little offense to the Indians as possible, and to mark the boundary with mounds and cedar posts. In March, 1798, the work began at Natchez.

It was clear from the first of the conferences with the Creeks and Seminoles that the whole project was viewed with suspicion by the natives. Andrew Ellicot met with Benjamin Hawkins, United States agent for the Indian tribes south of the Ohio, and with the Spanish governor, Juan Folch, at Pensacola. Several hundred Indians came to the meeting, all expecting presents and giving Hawkins to understand that the Spanish Governor would have given them presents if the Americans had not been there. Hawkins was not ready to comply, and the resentment of the Indians was obvious. Governor Folch sent out messengers to the Seminole towns, to secure safe conduct for the commissioners, and Andrew Ellicott asked Benjamin Hawkins for fifty warriors as a more tangible form of protection; for it became evident that the agents of the United States, unattended by a military police force, were not safe in the land of the Seminoles.

At the first Seminole town the Indians took all of Ellicott's horses and threatened the lives of the entire party. Thus the request of the Commissioner for military protection assumed a reasonable aspect. Colonel Hawkins went so far as to demand of Chief Alexander Cornell (Oche Harjo) that the offending population of the town be punished; and after some weeks of waiting, received a "talk" from the Chief, conveyed by one of the head men.

"I, Tustenuggee Harjo, am ordered to bring you these sticks. . . . The Tallassee people who violated our law by insulting and plundering the commissioners of Spain and the United States have returned to this town. . . . Oche Harjo called a meeting of the chiefs to punish the guilty at once." The account of the punishment was gruesome and left no doubt of the earnest intention of the Indian leaders to keep order. In regard to the foremost of the trouble-makers, Tustenuggee said: "We pulled down and set fire to his house. We beat him with sticks until he was on the ground as a dead man. We cut off his ears and a part of his cheek. We killed all his fowls and hogs, and broke all the pots, pans, and furniture in his house." Two hundred and fifty warriors were then sent as an escort for the commissioners.

Commissioner Ellicott, however, had changed his general plan of procedure. He traveled down the Chattahoochee by boat, around the peninsula, and up the St. Marys to its headwaters. He determined to mark only the beginning of the boundary line on the St. Marys, and the end at the mouth of the Flint, leaving the line to be run later. Accordingly on February 26, 1800, he erected a mound to mark the eastern point of the boundary line. Although the agent, Benjamin Hawkins, complained that Ellicott was inexcusably slow, that he burdened his party with unnecessary luggage, and traveled long distances to avoid possible clashes with the Indians, it must be admitted that Seminole hostility, together with the normal difficulties of surveying a wilderness line, would account for the failure to complete the job at the end of two years. Perhaps Hawkins himself, although he was one of the ablest of the early Indian agents, had failed to handle the initial meeting with head men and warriors at Pensacola, in the tactful manner demanded by the occasion. Furthermore, an adequate military force was not provided until a part of the surveying party had become demoralized by the peril of their situation.[17]

Ellicott had other difficulties, not directly connected with dangers from Indian attack. Thomas Freeman was employed as a surveyor, probably through political influence. His attitude toward the work, and his relations with the Commissioner, is shown in a note that he wrote to Ellicott on June 30, 1798. "The chainbearers, I conceive, are under my direction," he informed the boss. The Commissioner found him insufferably arrogant, a detriment to the work of running the line; and finally suggested his removal.

[17] Brevard, *History of Florida*, I, 10–15; Debo, *The Road to Disappearance*, 66. Miss Debo says of Hawkins: "He was the ablest man that ever represented the United States among the Creeks."

The secretary of state, Timothy Pickering, answered Ellicott. "The conduct of the Surveyor, Mr. Freeman, . . . is wholly unwarrantable. Should he be recalled, it will be on your responsibility, for the information you gave concerning him. . . . He and all the hands employed, and the military escort, were intended to be and must be under your command."[18]

There was more than one view as to the actual danger involved in the task of surveying the line. Daniel Clark, a merchant with large holdings of property in the Indian trade, wrote to Ellicott: "It is said that Major Freeman in his journey through the Creek Nation narrowly escaped being murdered by the Indians, on suspicion of being employed . . . to run the line with Spain, through their country."

From his camp on the Chattahoochee, Ellicott wrote to Will Panton on August 16, 1799: "We have been much pestered by the Indians . . . and I fear they will continue to steal our horses." The Commissioner complained that the Indians had stolen, also, a silver spoon marked with an E on the handle, and asked that Panton stop the sale of the spoon, should it appear in Pensacola. David Gillespie sent to Ellicott the news that the Mikasuki warriors under their king, "a man of violent passions," had marched on July 4, 1799 to stop the surveyors. He added that the Indian leader had cooled off when he heard from Spain and the United States.

Stephen Minor, a member of Ellicott's party, was critical of his chief in much the same tone as that used by Agent Benjamin Hawkins. A letter from Minor to David Gillespie, given in part below, reveals his view of the situation in 1799, on the Spanish border.

"I am happy to learn by the Negroe Hector that you are on the point of returning safe to the Chatahouchey. The information is the more pleasing as the disposition of the neighboring tribes of Indians seemed to have changed. By this time you will have been informed of our precipitate departure from the mouth of the Flint; and of the motives of it; but probably report may

[18] Freeman to Ellicott, June 30, 1798; Pickering to Ellicott, Oct. 4, 1798, Andrew Ellicott Papers: Correspondence, II.

have magnified the danger of our situation, and have represented it as more disturbing than it really is. It is true it cannot be called agreeable: and I apprehend that we are surrounded by numbers of Indians who have embodied, some with a view of extorting presents from us, and others with a design of plundering us; but I suspect that by taking a route different from the one we have commenced, we shall completely balk them. These two last nights they have stolen upwards of twenty horses from us, but I flatter myself that they will all be returned to us upon the arrival of the 50 warriors sent for by Col. Hawkins, who has been with us since the 12th inst. on the approach of danger. Mr. Ellicott, listening to the whispers of his *familias spirit*, and keeping in view the principles of his Sect and the irreparable loss that society would suffer by his death, prudently embarked with his family, including Parks the parrot, Bit the squirrel &c. in Bernard's Schooner, and gently glided down the stream into the bosom of safety. When we next meet we will talk this matter over; some circumstances of which will offer you a little entertainment.

"Should Poston apply to you for horses and you have any to spare I shall thank you to let him have them. Permit me to suggest to you that it would be prudent for you to join us as soon as possible, that we all keep in a body and be able to repel, with more efficacy, any attempt of the Indians against us. . . ."[19]

[19] Clark to Ellicott, June 14, 1798; Minor to Ellicott, Sept. 22, 1799, Andrew Ellicott Papers: Correspondence, II.

CHAPTER 3

Seminoles and Border Diplomacy, 1801–12

"This bargain was as fair a purchase as ever was made from red men, since the treaty of William Penn."

JOHN FORBES

THE POLICIES of President Thomas Jefferson with respect to Indian tribes of the United States cannot be reduced to a simple formula and stated in a short sentence. His interest in the growth of agricultural production made him an ardent expansionist and a strong supporter for the westward movement of the population. On the other hand, his humane spirit was a guarantee of genuine sympathy for oppressed people, and the Indians were already feeling the heavy burden of exploitation heaped upon them by the mounting numbers of white residents in their homeland. Jefferson was eager for the development of Indian skill in agriculture, to reduce the acreage of fertile soil required for subsistence, and to make land available for citizens of the United States; but he was sensitive in regard to human rights, and keenly aware of past tendencies to ignore the principles of justice, when white settlers clashed with Indian interests.

With every passing year, the Indians became more reluctant to give up their lands for the use of western settlers.[1] Jefferson was not the man to use his authority as President to beat down the demands for fair treatment of the Indians; yet there is evidence that he was willing to permit them to drift into debt, and that he saw no injustice in using the pressure of their unaccustomed financial obligations to bargain with them for their lands.

[1] Edward Channing, *The Jeffersonian System*, 256–57.

Jefferson appointed experienced Indian agents for the tribes south of the Ohio River. To meet with the Creeks at Fort Wilkinson on the Oconee in May, 1802, Secretary of War Henry Dearborn sent Benjamin Hawkins, Andrew Pickens, and General James Wilkinson. The Upper Creeks were well represented at the meeting, but the Lower Creeks were at that time engaged in supporting William Augustus Bowles in his raid on St. Marks. The Tame King of Tallassee and the Little Prince of Broken Arrow had joined Bowles, the self-styled "Commander-in-Chief of the Creeks," with several hundred warriors, and the Lower Towns were practically unrepresented at Fort Wilkinson.

Efa Harjo spoke for the Indians, and General Wilkinson delivered the "talk" for President Jefferson. The technique employed by the United States commissioners was one which grew familiar in the years to come. James Wilkinson presented a long list of treaty violations by the Creeks and charged the Indians with many crimes. As indemnity, he proposed that the tribal leaders should cede a wide strip of Georgia land to the United States. He urged also their acceptance of an annuity and proposed two additional blacksmith shops on Creek land for a limited period.

Efa Harjo (Mad Dog) countered with a list of Indian grievances, at the top of which stood the murders of David Cornell and other Creek citizens. He complained that settlers in the Cumberland Valley were encroaching upon Creek hunting grounds by their farming activities, and that a new wave of settlers were invading the Alabama and Tombigbee areas. He showed a strong interest in the white man's iron farming implements and spoke in favor of additional blacksmiths for the Creeks. Some of the Indian leaders were interested in learning the white people's textile methods, and two chiefs proposed that skilled women should be sent to teach Creek matrons the art of spinning and weaving.

Opposition to further cessions of land was so apparent in Efa Harjo's talk and in the attitude of other Creek leaders, that the main purpose of the meeting seemed likely to fail; but the Indians were eager to get back to their fields, and as the confer-

39

ences dragged on into June their anxiety grew. The agent, Benjamin Hawkins, demanded better tribal control of the young warriors, and spoke in strong terms against the protection and support given to William Augustus Bowles by the Seminoles. Efa Harjo and his fellow chiefs yielded suddenly, agreeing to a cession of Tallassee land along the border of Florida, and about half of the land between the Oconee and Ocmulgee rivers that was desired by the United States Commissioners. The Creek chiefs also sent a message to the Seminoles, demanding that they give up their support of Bowles and their hostility to Spain. Withdrawal of Seminole assistance resulted in the immediate downfall of Bowles, and his final imprisonment by Spanish authority. In consideration of the land cessions, the United States agreed to a permanent annuity of $3,000 for the Creeks, a ten-year annuity of $1,000 for the tribal chiefs, $15,000 for debts and the damage claims of Georgia citizens, and two blacksmith shops.[2]

At the Treaty of Colerain in 1796, the Creek Confederation —with Lower Creeks who lived north of the Florida border and Seminoles south of that line practically unrepresented—had agreed to return fugitive Negro slaves to their owners in the United States. This was the issue which made separation of Spanish Seminoles from the Creek tribe of the United States a permanent division. During the eight years of Jefferson's presidency, the forces of separation were steadily at work. The United States was to gain possession of the Seminole country in the purchase of Florida a decade after Jefferson's second term ended; but the process of creating a separate tribe was complete, and all efforts of United States officials, extending over forty years of planning, legislation, and treaties providing unity, were destined to fail.

In 1804, John Forbes, junior partner in the firm of Panton, Leslie and Company, obtained a grant of land from the Seminole Indians, to cover losses resulting from the raids of Bowles and his followers. The agreement, drawn up at Cheeskatolfa on

[2] Kappler, *Indian Affairs: Laws and Treaties*, II, 58, 59; *American State Papers, Indian Affairs*, I, 668–80; Debo, *The Road to Disappearance*, 72–74; *Compilation of all the Treaties Between the United States and the Indian Tribes*, 100.

May 25 was signed (by means of the "x" mark), by Yohalla Emathla, Talaya Micco, Tustanagy, Hopoy Hapo, Panas Micco, William Perryman, and sixteen other chiefs of the Seminoles and Lower Creeks. In a letter to Secretary of War Henry Dearborn, dated September 5, 1806, John Forbes commented upon his land grant as follows:

"Finding the Upper and Lower Creeks unwilling to admit, as a part of my claims on them, the robberies committed by Bowles and his Seminoles, I treated for and obtained from the Seminoles, as an indemnification, a tract of land lying within the Spanish limits, for the cession of which, according to Indian laws, they were fully competent, by which means my general claims against the nation were reduced within $40,000. This bargain, I do assert, was as fair a purchase as ever was made from red men, since the treaty of William Penn, and has been formally ratified, in presence of the King of Spain's representative. . . ." The grant to Forbes, lying between the Apalachicola River and the Wakulla, on which the St. Marks store of Panton, Leslie and Company was situated, contained approximately 1,500,000 acres.[3]

The Jefferson administration followed John Forbes' example in obtaining Indian lands as a means of settling debts of the tribal members. A powerful anti-American sentiment, led by the aged Tame King of Tallassee, kept alive among the Creek Indians a determination to hold their remaining lands in order that they might live in their primitive fashion with common fields to cultivate, and wide areas reserved for game. The personal credit of Creek chiefs and warriors, however, a credit that was based upon their ability to pay and their record for payment, was the factor which proved most potent in wringing new land cessions from them. They gave up their property as a means of settling their debts. The pressure for payment of just obligations —and some of the claims did represent goods sold to the natives without fraud, except in the violence done to the fiduciary obli-

[3] *American State Papers: Indian Affairs*, I, 750, 751; *Public Lands*, IV, 86–96; Giddings, *The Exiles of Florida*, 22; Cotterill, *The Southern Indians*, 144, 145 n.16.

gation of the United States to protect the Indians—was a form of coercion which the Creeks and Seminoles, along with many other tribes, could not withstand.

In 1805 the Coweta chief, William McIntosh, visited Washington with five other Indian delegates, including the mixed-blood chief of Tuckabatchee, Oche Harjo. After talks with President Jefferson, the visiting statesmen signed a treaty on November 15, authorizing the United States to build a road from Fort Stoddert to the Ocmulgee River, and ceding the remaining Creek lands between the Ocmulgee and the Oconee. In addition to the settlement of tribal debts, the consideration included an annuity for eighteen years.[4]

Among the complex causes of war between the United States and Great Britain in 1812, the conditions in East and West Florida may be regarded as a powerful contributing factor. The Seminole Indians, offshoot of the Creek Confederacy in the United States, occupied Spanish territory but were never thoroughly under Spanish official control. Seminole hostility toward westward expansion by the people of the United States was strongly reflected in the attitude of the Creeks. The dominant tendency of American citizens to expand the national domain, to push the boundaries westward beyond the Mississippi Basin and southward to the Gulf of Mexico, was an active force during the Jefferson and Madison administrations. Jefferson's explorations of the Columbia River and the Río Grande, and the casual references of the "War Hawks" to the annexation of Canada, indicate the general trend of national thinking; but it was on the Spanish border east of the Mississippi that the desire for expansion became intimately bound up with the Indian problem. In the words of Kendrick C. Babcock, "The persistent desire of the United States to possess the Floridas, between 1801 and 1819, amounted almost to a disease, corrupting the moral sense of each succeeding administration."[5]

As Great Britain and the United States balanced precariously

---

[4] Cotterill, *The Southern Indians*, 145, 152–53; Kappler, *Indian Affairs: Laws and Treaties*, II, 85, 86; Debo, *The Road to Disappearance*, 57, 68, 75.

[5] Babcock, *The Rise of American Nationality*, 22.

on the brink of war in the early months of 1812, British agents worked diligently among the Indians who lived west and south of Georgia. The Creeks were especially unhappy over the recently opened road between the Chattahoochee River and Mims' Ferry on the Alabama. The road was filled, constantly, by a stream of immigrants; and the Creeks became worried over the prospect of being hemmed in between the restless population of Georgia on the east, and the new settlers of the Tombigbee on the west. The State of Georgia was the leader in hostile activities against the Creek and Seminole Indians, who had valuable land directly in the path of expansion by white settlers.

Spanish officials, employees of a weak and poverty-ridden government, looked with disfavor upon the advance of pioneers from Georgia to the Tombigbee. British agents found receptive listeners among the Spaniards, the Seminole Indians of the Spanish province, and the Creek Indians of Georgia and Alabama. The descendants of British colonists who had lived north of the St. Marys River were spreading out westward across the Flint and Chattahoochee, and these frontiersmen inherited a tradition of hostility toward the Seminole Indians. Spanish officers had used the Florida Indians in campaigns against colonial Georgia settlers; and after the United States became independent, rumors of Indian uprising always brought tremors of apprehension along the Southwestern frontier. Moreover, people who lived south of the Ohio River, including settlers of the Virginia, Carolina, and Georgia frontiers, linked together the policies of Indian removal to the West and expulsion of Spain from Florida. As Kentucky and Tennessee grew into statehood and the territories of Mississippi and Alabama filled with settlers, it was inevitable that frontier views should have weight in the national capital.[6]

The people who lived north of Florida were inclined to exaggerate depredations of the Seminole Indians, to minimize the theft and violence of their own citizens, and to blame Spain for lawlessness along the border. The village of St. Marys, situated

[6] Julius W. Pratt, *Expanionists of 1812*, 67.

on the north bank of the boundary river near its mouth, had become the fifth town of Georgia, with a population of 585 in the year 1811, and was the center of a flourishing trade with the Seminoles, who exchanged beef, pork, venison, pelts, and furs for guns, ammunition, shirts, cotton cloth, pots, and beaver traps. Colerain was upstream from St. Marys, also on the Georgia side of the river.

General George Mathews of Georgia became an active participant in Florida affairs in 1810, when William H. Crawford obtained for him an appointment as a commissioner to confer with the Spanish Governor at Pensacola. Specifically, Mathews was to discover the attitude of Governor Vicente Folch in regard to acceptance of a bribe for the delivery of West Florida to the United States.

General Mathews was Virginia born and a veteran of the American Revolution. Reared in the backwoods, he was almost illiterate, but possessed of keen intelligence, a passion for information, and a strong desire to serve in public affairs. His record in frontier warfare, with narrow escapes, dangerous wounds, and many daring exploits, gave him prestige in Georgia, where he removed in 1785 at the age of forty-six. Within a period of ten years, he had served as brigadier general of militia, governor, member of Congress, and governor for a second term. He was appointed territorial governor of Mississippi in 1798, but President John Adams withdrew his name from consideration by the Senate because he was suspected of being a party to the Blount conspiracy in West Florida, and of irregular conduct in Yazoo land speculation. As governor of Georgia, Mathews had signed the Yazoo Act. It was said that he started for Philadelphia to cane President Adams, but changed his mind when he heard that his son had received a federal appointment.[7]

During the winter following his visit to Governor Folch, Mathews and his colleague, John McKee, met again with the Spanish official at Mobile, but failed to obtain actual delivery of West Florida to the United States. Early in 1812, General

[7] *Dictionary of American Biography*, XII, 403–404 (article by Isaac J. Cox); Rembert W. Patrick, *Florida Fiasco*, 4–15.

Mathews planned an "uprising" in East Florida, which he hoped would have the appearance of a spontaneous revolt against Spain by the colonial population. John H. McIntosh led a band of Georgia volunteers across the St. Marys on March 12 and joined the party of Florida settlers who were declaring independence. The force with which Mathews threatened Spanish authority in Florida consisted of a small band of English residents, a handful of recruits from Georgia, and volunteers from the United States regular troops.[8]

The original plan of conquest had been to march directly from the crossing of the St. Marys upon St. Augustine; but the refusal of Commodore Hugh Campbell of the United States Navy to furnish gunboats for the support of such an enterprise, placed it beyond the resources of General Mathews. For that reason he changed his plan and moved against Fernandina on Amelia Island.

Justo López, Spanish commandant at Fernandina, sent messengers to General Mathews to ask what he proposed to do, and also sent Joseph de la Maza Arredondo to ascertain from Major Jacint Laval at Point Petre, the attitude of the United States government toward the invasion. Since Major Laval had refused the request of Mathews for the use of 140 regular soldiers as re-enforcements, and had ordered Mathews to leave Point Petre and never again to set foot upon the place, his reply might have been anticipated. General Mathews had reminded Laval that both of them were veterans of the American Revolution, and suggested that President Madison was eager to carry the "freedoms" of the American republic to Florida.

"Yes, General Mathews," answered Laval, "I fought for your American freedoms and my American ideals. But I did not leave my native land to die in battle so that avaricious men could grab land by debasing the ideals of Seventy-Six."[9]

To Arredondo, Major Laval gave a straight denial of participation by his government in the Mathews invasion. "The United States are neither principals or auxiliaries," he said; "and I am

---

[8] *Ibid.*, 83–85.
[9] *Ibid.*, 72–74.

not authorized to make any attack on East Florida." In conference with Mathews, however, Arredondo heard a different version of the situation. "I have instructions from my Government," the General said, "to receive East Florida or any part of it from the local authorities, or to take it by force to prevent its occupation by a foreign power."

"Do you . . . consider those rebels, who call themselves Patriots, the local authorities of East Florida?" asked Lopez's messenger.

"I do," answered General Mathews; "and . . . I have . . . information of a British plan to land two regiments of Negro troops in East Florida."

"Who gave you that information?"

"A man in whom I have every confidence."

Arredondo was not deceived. "This is an American invasion of East Florida," he declared. "Most of those in arms against us are Georgians, brought to our province by your promises of 500 acres of land. If you withdraw all guarantees of American support, we will drive these rebels pell-mell back into Georgia, within a week. If we should fail to do that, Colonel Lopez will deliver Amelia Island to you."[10]

Commodore Campbell kept open the question of his cooperation in the attack on Fernandina, until the hour of invasion. On the morning of March 17, 1812, five of his gunboats anchored within two hundred yards of the shore at Fernandina and prepared to bombard the Spanish batteries at an order from Campbell who was anchored within signal range in Cumberland Sound. At the last moment, the commander decided not to support the Patriots, and sent an order to his gunboat 62: "Under no circumstances will you fire upon the Fernandina battery."[11]

Colonel López was not aware of Campbell's indecision, however, and the townspeople were obviously shaken in their resolution to fight the invaders by the presence of gunboats. "We must surrender," Lopez said to the people who gathered at his house awaiting the attack; "resistance would be unavailing."

10 *Ibid.*, 90, 91, 92.
11 *Ibid.*, 96.

46

George John F. Clarke, an influential trader of Fernandina, volunteered to carry the white flag of surrender to the advancing patriots. Clarke was the son of an English colonist in Florida who had remained in that province after its recovery by Spain in 1783. Three years later, when he was twelve, George had been apprenticed to Panton, Leslie and Company, and when he reached mature years he became the common-law husband of Flora, a Negro slave whom he purchased from John Leslie. By Flora, Clarke had eight children; and after her death, four more children by another slave woman named Hannah. His trading enterprises had prospered on Amelia Island, and Clarke had been one of the citizens who advised resistance against the invasion by General Mathews.

Colonel López signed articles of surrender to General George Mathews, Lodowick Ashley, and John H. McIntosh, who signed as commissioner for the patriots. It was agreed that Amelia Island should be ceded to the United States within twenty-four hours. Mathews, Ashley, and McIntosh kept good order during the period of negotiation and afterward, which is evidence of control over hungry followers who had looked forward to plunder as a part of their compensation for the adventure.[12]

During the advance upon Amelia Island the Seminoles occupied a position of neutrality. King Payne, principal chief after the death of the Cowkeeper, took no part in the Spanish efforts to organize a defense and did not offer his services to McIntosh and Ashley against Spain. The old chief, Cowkeeper, had been a bitter enemy of the Spaniards; according to a tradition in Florida, he had vowed to kill one hundred of their men and when he was about to die, with only eighty-six of the hated invaders slain, he made his two sons agree to kill fourteen more. The younger son, Bowlegs, seemed ready to carry out the promise, for he proposed to join the invaders against Amelia Island, and was deeply offended when his offer was declined by John H. McIntosh.[13]

Fundamentally, the Seminole people had more to fear from

[12] *Ibid.,* 97.
[13] *Ibid.,* 104, 180.

the advance of American settlers than from Spanish control in Florida. Particularly the Negroes, who were associated with the Seminoles and often allied with them in war, had a strong interest in the conflict between the Americans and the province of Spanish Florida. Almost a century had elapsed since an entire colony of refugee slaves from the British settlements in the north had been received at St. Augustine and planted as free persons in García Real de Santa Teresa de Mose, a few miles distant from the capital. At intervals after 1730, more fugitives had joined these colonists or settled in other parts of Florida.

Some of the Seminole chiefs had bought slaves, usually paying for them in livestock. Ownership of slaves enhanced the prestige of an Indian leader and usually added but little to his material wealth. The custom of the Seminoles was to permit their slaves to live apart, in separate villages, paying a small tribute in the form of grain or livestock as a recognition of their servile status. The Negroes had more knowledge of soil-cultivation than their Indian masters and frequently the slaves, as well as the free Negroes, developed a very substantial prosperity in cleared fields, crops, and livestock. The Negroes dressed very much like the Seminoles, scantily when they were at work in their fields but with colorful splendor of adornment—turbans and shawls, smocks, moccasins and leggings, glittering metal ornaments—when they were bent upon the enjoyment of a festive occasion.

Many military actions, all of minor importance, were fought in Florida during the war with Great Britain from June, 1812, to January, 1815. Lieutenant Colonel Thomas A. Smith, commandant at Point Petre, failed to take St. Augustine in September, 1812, when Governor Sebastian Kindelan used Indian and Negro troops to cut off his supplies. Colonel Daniel Newnan, whose volunteer force had covered the retreat of Smith's army from St. Augustine, fought against an Alachuan party under King Payne and suffered greater losses than did the Indians. Newnan's situation, deep in the Indian country, became so desperate that the remnant of his force had to be rescued by a

Ye-how-lo-gee, "Cloud" (top left); Ee-mat-la, "King Phillip" (top right); Co-ee-ha-jo (below left); and La-shee, "Creek Billy" (below right).

From George Catlin's
North American Indians

Billy Bowlegs, who said in 1849, "Wild Cat is my great friend! Tell him not to come into our country until I send for him."

little party of dragoons, released with great reluctance for that purpose by Colonel Smith.

King Payne planned a union of all the Indians of Florida and a general uprising against the whites, particularly against Georgians; but in the conference that he called for the purpose of organization, his scheme was opposed by Wolf Warrior of the Mikasuki band and by most of the Seminole chiefs. He gave up the idea and sent a messenger to Benjamin Hawkins asking for peace. While his messengers, as a means of obtaining the desired amnesty, were offering to surrender all property including slaves captured from the citizens of Georgia, King Payne died; and his more active and belligerent brother, Bowlegs, became chief of the Alachuan and Alligator bands.

In the meantime, Governor David Mitchell of Georgia had for a brief period taken over the command left vacant by the removal of Mathews; and Mitchell, in turn, was replaced by Thomas Pinckney of South Carolina. The new commander, born in 1750 of a distinguished family, had served as a soldier during the American Revolution and in various civil offices afterward, including governorship of South Carolina, ministry to England, and another diplomatic post in which he negotiated the widely acclaimed Treaty of San Lorenzo with Spain. In 1796, Pinckney had been defeated for the office of vice president of the United States by Thomas Jefferson.

Tall and erect at the age of sixty-two, Thomas Pinckney had the self-assurance, courtesy, and dignity of the aristocratic planter. He had also the intellectual capacity of his family and was regarded by his contemporaries as a great man. His limited services as a military commander furnish little basis for an estimate of his stature in that occupation.[14]

General Pinckney was opposed to the ambiguous policy of the Madison administration in regard to Spanish Florida. He told Secretary James Monroe, frankly, that it was the obligation of the United States either to occupy East Florida with a force sufficient to hold it against British attack, or withdraw from all

----

[14] *Dictionary of American Biography*, XIV, 617–19; Patrick, *Florida Fiasco*, 182–83; 218–36; 254–59; 263–65; 266; 271, 273.

parts of the Spanish province; but in spite of his personal views on the matter, Pinckney was unable to comply with Benjamin Hawkins' request that he use his federal force to prevent invasion of Florida by Tennessee volunteers. Colonel John Williams invaded with the state troops early in 1813. Colonel Thomas A. Smith, Laval's successor as commandant at Point Petre, also marched into Florida with 220 men. Thomas Flournoy, adjutant general of the United States Army, had ordered Smith "to punish those Indians who had taken the warpath, burn all their property which could not be transported, execute without mercy Negroes captured under arms, and take all other Negroes as prisoners."[15]

The invading forces started with the intention of exterminating the Florida Indians; but they found in the path of their march, for the most part, abandoned towns and Indians who were not on the warpath. One such band, not connected with either the Alachuas or Alligators, was attacked by the Tennessee Volunteers who killed one old man and two squaws, and took seven prisoners. After fighting one indecisive engagement with the Alachuas, Colonel Smith resolved to make a complete withdrawal of his forces from Florida. The invaders had destroyed many Indian houses and other property, and were able to carry away about 300 horses and 400 cattle, but had not inflicted serious damage upon the Seminole armed forces.

While these events were taking place in Florida, the Creek agent, Benjamin Hawkins, was engaged chiefly in plans to civilize and reorganize the Indians who were under his care. To the Secretary of War, Hawkins sent reports that varied from extreme optimism to despair.

On February 3, 1812, he wrote: "Our Indians are, many of them, occupied in spinning, weaving, making new settlements, and improving those heretofore made. I believe nine-tenths of the Lower Creeks have left their old towns and have formed, or are forming settlements, on the creeks and rivers where the lands are good, and the range for stock good." Three months

[15] Quoted by Patrick, *Florida Fiasco*, 231, from the *Nashville Clarion and Tennessee Gazette*, July 13, 1813.

later Hawkins reported the murder of Thomas Meredith, an emigrant bound for Mississippi Territory, by the old Creek head man, Maumouth; and on May 11, 1812, gave in detail the results of a Lower Creek Council in which the chiefs announced that they would not "interfere in the wars of white people," and that they would "prepare the minds of their young people to be neighborly and friendly."[16]

[16] *American State Papers: Indian Affairs,* I, 809; Albert James Pickett, *History of Alabama and Incidentally of Georgia and Mississippi,* 515.

CHAPTER 4

Indian Alliance
Against the United States

*"It struck me forcibly that the general should take nearly eight
million acres from the friendly Upper Creeks."*

BENJAMIN HAWKINS

R APIDLY, THE CREEKS AND SEMINOLES aligned themselves on the British side of the war in America. The Shawnee, Tecumseh, was the most effective advocate of Indian unity,
and eventually of support for King George III's cause in North
America. Records concerning the parentage of the great Indian
leader are not in complete agreement. In Alabama, there is a
tradition that his Shawnee father, Pucksinwa, lived at Souvan-
ogee on the Tallapoosa River. Most of the authorities are inclined to the view that Tecumseh's mother also was Shawnee,
though there is evidence that at one time Pucksinwa was married to a Creek woman, and that she went north with him into
Ohio. In any event, Tecumseh and his twin brother, Tenskwatawa, were born near Oldtown, Ohio, about 1768, and were
among the Indians who retreated westward before the advancing tide of white settlement in the Northwest Territory. In 1808
the family lived near the mouth of Tippecanoe Creek on the
Wabash River. Pucksinwa had been killed in war with the whites.
Tenskwatawa had become renowned as a prophet among his
people, and Tecumseh had established a wide reputation as a
warrior and as a promoter of Indian unity.[1] He had fought

[1] *American State Papers: Indian Affairs*, I, 761, 763, 800; Debo, *The Road
to Disappearance*, 76–79; Babcock, *The Rise of American Nationality*, 34; Pickett,
History of Alabama, 510–15; *Dictionary of American Biography*, XVII, 358–60
(article by Katherine Elizabeth Crane, on Tecumseh).

against the white frontiersmen at Big Rock, Ohio; at the battle
on the Little Miami; and at Paint Rock, in 1793. He was with
the Indian party that attacked Fort Recovery in 1794, and he
fought at Maumee Rapids in the same year. He had visited with
the Cherokees and Creeks for two years when he was a young
man, and knew personally many of the leaders and warriors
south of the Ohio.

Early in 1812, Tecumseh held conferences with British offi-
cers at Detroit, and then traveled south with a party of mounted
Indians. He visited the Chickasaws and Choctaws, and went into
Florida where the Seminoles were approached on the subject
of intertribal harmony. Whether the visit to the Seminoles took
place early in Tecumseh's mission or later, as Professor R. S.
Cotterill suggests, it may be assumed that the influence of the
Shawnee was not needed to create resentment of the Florida
Indians against the United States.[2]

Returning to Autauga on the Alabama, Tecumseh won many
Creek followers; and at Coosawda, the Hickory Ground, and
Tuckabatchee, had similar success. His visit at the latter town
coincided with a conference called by Colonel Hawkins. Five
thousand Creeks and a considerable number of Cherokees and
other southern Indians, together with white traders, soldiers,
government workers, and several hundred Negroes, were assembled on the Tuckabatchee Square daily. The wily Tecumseh
would deliver no "talk" while Hawkins was present; but with
the Agent's departure, the apostle of Indian unity quickly found
an occasion to deliver his address.

In the meantime he paid close attention to Indian ceremonial
practices, and made an impressive entry at the daily meetings.
He and his thirty followers from the land north of the Ohio
marched into the square every morning, with faces painted black,
naked warriors except a loin cloth and waist band for dragging

---

[2] R. S. Cotterill calls attention to certain discrepancies in the contemporary
evidence regarding Tecumseh's visit to the South. The primary purpose of the
mission, in his view, was intertribal harmony, and not necessarily war against
the United States. The visit, he states, "had no connection with the War of 1812
except to precede it. Far from bringing about the Creek Civil War, Tecumseh's
mission actually delayed that event." Cotterill, *The Southern Indians*, 166–75.

a buffalo tail behind them, and a head dress of splendid eagle feathers. The Creek chiefs were met by the visitors with a friendly grasp of both arms and a ceremonial exchange of tobacco. All of the assembled Creeks reacted in cordial fashion except Captain Isaacs, Chief of Coosawda, who shook the buffalo-horns of his head dress at Tecumseh, refused tobacco, and declared that he, Isaacs, was as great a chief as the visitor.

It was Tecumseh's theory that North America belonged to all the Indians, and that no tribe had the right to cede a part of the land, since all were injured by the advance of white settlements. Destruction of game and all wild life, conflict of interest between Indians and Europeans, the gradual loss of freedom and independence by the red men, were results that followed inevitably upon the white man's occupation of territory. Thus, the condition of every native tribe was a common problem and the solution was to be found in unity. Tecumseh was a practical statesman, and understood fully the need of alliance with a powerful nation. He selected Great Britain as an ally and the United States as the object of attack, because the one was distant and competent, wealthy and well established, the other was close, restless, and the most immediate threat to the Indian way of life.[3]

Tecumseh told the eager Indian listeners at Tuckabatchee that the white men would ruin the forests with their clearings and ploughed ground, pollute the streams, and make it impossible for an Indian to live by means of his own weapons. Then the Europeans would enslave the native population. He believed that his people should fight with war club, bow, and scalping knife—not with the weapons of the invaders. The King of England, ready to engage in trade for the products of the North American forest, would help to expel the settlers who were pushing west across the Indian lands.

From British military officers, Tecumseh learned the date of an expected comet, and he used the information to impress the Creeks with his powers of magic. The arms of the great chief

[3] Pickett, *History of Alabama*, 512–13; *Dictionary of American Biography*, XVII, 358–60.

would appear, he told them, "stretched out across the heavens." A prophet of the Upper Town Creeks declared that the Great Spirit had sent Tecumseh among them; and most of the head men whose bands were visited by the party from the North gave their promise of support. Tustenuggee Thlocko (Big Warrior) refused to join in the movement because he was fearful of the power wielded by Colonel Benjamin Hawkins and his government; and as a result of his attitude, Big Warrior received a dire warning.

"In Detroit, I will stamp my foot and shake down every house in Tuckabatchee," Tecumseh told him. Tustenuggee made no answer, "but puffed his pipe and enveloped himself in a cloud of smoke." Later a slight earthquake tremor at Tuckabatchee caused many simple warriors to regard Tecumseh as a man of supernatural, mystic powers, wise in council and infallible in war.[4]

Josiah Francis, son of a Scotch trader and his Creek wife, became the most widely known of the "prophets" inspired by Tecumseh. Francis was even empowered to create subordinate prophets. High-Head Jim of Autossee was one of the Creek leaders who carried on the work of Tecumseh after his departure for the North, accompanied by Little Warrior and a party of Creek braves. High-Head Jim taught the "war dance of the lakes" to the southern Indians, and kept aflame their desire for war.

Little Warrior, returning from Canada, killed the settlers of a community near the mouth of the Ohio, and brought south as a captive Mrs. Crawley, the mother of one family slain in the attack. Benjamin Hawkins received news of the event and demanded that the guilty Creek warriors be punished. The Creek Council passed a decree of death for Little Warrior and his men, and sent William McIntosh to carry out the sentence. His posse killed five of the band in a house at Red Warrior's Bluff on the Tallapoosa, and he sent Captain Isaacs in pursuit of the other fugitives. Little Warrior himself and two of his followers were overtaken and killed in a swamp above Wetumka. Captain Isaacs was the son-in-law of Alexander McGillivray and prob-

[4] Pickett, *History of Alabama*, 514–15.

ably was a member of the original party led by Little Warrior on their journey to Canada. There is evidence that conviction was obtained in the Creek Council against Little Warrior and his men on the testimony of Isaacs, who gave the facts of the massacre on the Ohio in exchange for immunity and became an active agent of the tribe in carrying out the death sentence.

In addition to the Little Warrior murders in February, 1813, and the killing of Thomas Meredith a year earlier, there had been two other clashes between Indians and white settlers on the Creek-Seminole frontier. William Lott had been killed by a band of Tallassees, and on Duck River a family had been wiped out by a party of Hillabees. The action of the Creek Council in punishing the warriors who took part in the violence against the whites had the effect of creating two Creek parties hostile to each other, and providing a basis for the civil war that found Red Sticks serving as allies of the British while the followers of William McIntosh enlisted in the armies of Jackson and other American officers.

The Madison administration was determined to occupy the region between the Pearl and Perdido rivers, as a means of preventing secret co-operation of Spanish officials with the British and their Indian allies. General James Wilkinson was sent from New Orleans with 600 men to take Fort Charlotte on Mobile Bay. This was accomplished in the spring of 1813, and the Spanish garrison retired to Pensacola, while the Americans constructed a fortification at Mobile Point, naming it in honor of Colonel John Bowyer. Congress did not authorize President Madison to take East Florida, which he had expected to attempt. Since Andrew Jackson's Tennessee militia force of 2,000, which had been intended for the occupation of Pensacola and St. Augustine, was not needed in West Florida, the War Department ordered that the men be dismissed from the service at Natchez, where their impatient commander held them in readiness for advance upon the British, Spanish, Indians, or any other organized force that might stand in the path of westward expansion. General Jackson was so much disappointed by the order that he transported the men home to Tennessee at his own expense, out of the probable range of General Wilkinson's recruiting officers.[5]

Tustenuggee Thlocko, head chief of the Creek Nation, sent out messengers to the Indians of Alabama urging them to maintain the peace. At the junction of the Coosa and Tallapoosa rivers, his runners were killed and scalped by the Red Sticks. Between Burnt Corn and Escambia, a short time later, the mail rider for the United States was killed. Sam McNac, a Creek of mixed blood who was a partisan of Big Warrior (Tustenuggee Thlocko), deceived High-Head Jim (Jim Boy) as to his allegiance, and learned the major plans of the Red Sticks. They intended to make a sudden and concerted attack in many quarters; they hoped to kill Big Warrior, Captain Isaacs, William McIntosh, Little Prince, the Mad Dragon's son, Spoke Kange, Tallassee Fixico, and other "traitors." The Lower Creeks and the Seminoles would attack the white settlements of Georgia; the Choctaws would attack the new settlements in Mississippi Territory; the Upper Creeks and Cherokees, the settlers of Tennessee; Creeks of the Coosa, Tallapoosa, and Black Warrior regions, the settlers of the Tombigbee Valley.

Letecau, a follower of Tecumseh and a "prophet" who was but eighteen years of age, invited warriors and head men to visit him at Old Coosa Town to witness his powers of magic. A large assemblage resulted. Letecau drew a circle on the ground with his wand, and demonstrated with his followers the Dance of the Lakes. When the dancers and spectators were sufficiently warmed to the spirit of the occasion, the young "prophet" gave a sudden war whoop, and his retainers fell upon three chiefs who had been friendly with white settlers and killed them. Other visitors escaped by jumping into the river, swimming across under water, and thus eluding pursuit. Later a band of Big Warrior's men returned and killed Letecau together with other new "prophets." The followers of Tecumseh at Okfuskee, exponents of the Dance of the Lakes, were also slain by the faction that supported Big Warrior and William McIntosh—the Creek

[5] *Annals of Congress*, 12 Cong., 2 sess., 124–27; Pickett, *History of Alabama*, 516; Cotterill, *The Southern Indians*, 176–78, n. 8 and 9.

Nation that was recognized by Benjamin Hawkins. Big Warrior had collected a large supply of corn at Tuckabatchee and had built a fort there. It was not long, however, before he had to be rescued by Indian troops sent by the agent from Coweta and Cussetta. The Red Sticks were gaining control of large sections of the Creek country.[6]

Colonel James Caller, in command of an Alabama militia force, crossed the Tombigbee and Alabama rivers, traveling southeast. His purpose was to cut off a war party under Peter McQueen and High-Head Jim who were in Pensacola engaged in purchasing military supplies. On the journey to Pensacola McQueen's warriors had destroyed the house of James Cornell, a mixed-blood Creek of the Big Warrior faction. A Negro slave and a white man at the house had been beaten until they were unconscious and Cornell's wife carried away to the Pensacola slave market.

Colonel Caller, reinforced by a band of Indians under James Cornell, intercepted the returning Red Sticks at Burnt Corn Creek, and attacked. The militia and their Creek allies numbered 180 men; the Red Sticks, according to Benjamin Hawkins, were 350 strong.[7] A wild and disorganized clash resulted, with Colonel Caller's force concentrating upon the seizure of one hundred pack animals laden with ammunition, and being outmaneuvered in the process. The militia lost ground and finally lost the skirmish, although they were able to carry away a part of the plunder taken in the first rush.[8] Two Americans were killed and fifteen wounded in this engagement.

During the early part of the Creek civil war the wealthy mixed-blood Indians of the Little River area and their followers dropped down the Alabama River and constructed a fort near the house of Samuel Mims, an Indian farmer. The white population of the region co-operated in building the fortification, which was a strong, square stockade, an acre in extent. It stood

---

[6] Pickett, *History of Alabama*, 520.

[7] *American State Papers: Indian Affairs*, I, 849–50; Pickett, *History of Alabama*, 52–25; Cotterill, *The Southern Indians*, 179–80; Debo, *The Road to Disappearance*, 78, 79. The number in McQueen's party was probably exaggerated.

[8] *American State Papers: Indian Affairs*, I, 851.

about 400 yards from the boat yard on Lake Tensaw, a mile east of the Alabama River. The Red Sticks had been planning an attack upon Coweta, after the evacuation of Tuckabatchee by Big Warrior; but their main offensive was diverted to Fort Mims by the families of Creek warriors killed at the battle of Burnt Corn Creek.

Thirteen Upper Creek Towns united their forces for an attack upon the mixed-blood and white defenders of Fort Mims. A party of warriors from Autossee, Okfuskee, and Tallassee marched toward Coweta, in order to draw the attention of Agent Hawkins' Creek government away from the main Red Stick offensive, on the same day that William Weatherford (Red Eagle, or Lumhi Chati) led his force against Fort Mims, August 30, 1813. The commander at the fort was taken completely by surprise; and Weatherford's warriors in overwhelming numbers came through an open gate, quickly routed the defending soldiers, and massacred the civilians who had left their plantations to take refuge within the stockade. Less than a score of these people survived the bloody encounter, in which 107 soldiers, 160 mixed-blood and white civilians, and 100 Negro slaves were killed.[9]

The Creek war merged into the conflict between the United States and Great Britain, with the Fort Mims affair. Before that disaster the Red Sticks, brandishing their red war clubs in frenzied attacks upon the partisans of Agent Benjamin Hawkins, were primarily concerned with maintenance of old Indian customs and prevention of white settlement, which they regarded the most destructive influence against the Indian's way of life. Afterwards, the followers of Weatherford and Menawa, McQueen and High-Head Jim (Jim Boy, or Tustenuggee Emathla), Francis the Prophet, Opothle Micco, and Osceola, were fighting for the British cause in America as the foreign influence least burdensome to the Indians.[10]

Tennessee, Louisiana, and Georgia, the states nearest to

[9] *American State Papers: Indian Affairs*, I, 855; Debo, *The Road to Disappearance*, 79.

[10] *Ibid.*, 40, 59ff., 66, 75ff.; Babcock, *The Rise of American Nationality*, 130–31; Cotterill, *The Southern Indians*, 180–81.

Fort Mims, took immediate and vigorous steps for dealing with Creek hostility in the Alabama country. John Floyd marched a Georgia militia force against Artussee and was joined in the attack by the Coweta Chief, William McIntosh and the Tuckabatchees under Tustenuggee Hopoie. Artussee and Tallassee were destroyed before Floyd withdrew to Georgia. A federal expedition under Brigadier General F. L. Claiborne, accompanied by Lieutenant Colonel Pushmataha with 135 Choctaws, moved from the south against Weatherford, who held a strong position on the left bank of the Alabama River. In spite of the magic rites practiced by their prophets, the Red Sticks were defeated and driven back. Weatherford's men fought bravely and held their ground long enough to allow the women and children to cross the river and escape. Most of the Red Stick warriors, too, found safety by fading singly or in small groups into the neighboring swamps.[11]

The hardest blows against the Red Sticks were struck by General Andrew Jackson of Tennessee. Six weeks after the first call for help was received, he had marched into northern Alabama with a militia force of 2,500 ready to move into any area that was threatened by the hostile Creeks. Short terms of enlistment, mutiny among his untrained troops, desertion, and serious shortage of supplies compelled Jackson to demonstrate the courage and resourcefulness that he possessed. After a hard fight at Talledega Town, he waited at Fort Strother on the Coosa for reinforcements. His army became a powerful machine by comparison with the Indian war parties that opposed him. At its greatest strength, the number of effective soldiers in Jackson's force was about 5,000, including 600 Cherokees under Gideon Morgan, Colonel John Lowry, and Major Ridge.[12]

In the spring of 1814, Jackson marched against the principal Red Stick force, which made its stand under Chief Menawa at Horseshoe Bend on the Tallapoosa River. A log barricade erected by the Creeks across the neck of land at the bend of the river was attacked on March 27. As Jackson stormed the

[11] *Ibid.*, 185–86.
[12] *Ibid.*, 186.

breastworks, his Cherokee allies crossed the stream and attacked the Red Sticks from the rear. Of 1,000 warriors who fought under Chief Menawa, only 70 escaped to join their women and children in a hidden spot prepared in advance of the battle. Menawa, severely wounded, was forced to remain in hiding until the end of the war.

General Jackson's losses were 51 killed and 150 wounded. The prevalence of arrow wounds furnished clear proof that the Red Sticks, either as a demonstration of their reliance upon Indian customs or through necessity, fought this decisive engagement mainly with their own primitive weapons.[13]

On August 9, 1814, General Jackson signed with the Creeks a treaty by which they ceded to the United States approximately two-thirds of their territory. By the terms of the agreement thus forced upon them, the tribe was cut off from contact with Spanish territory on the south, and a new area was provided for white settlement on their west. Perhaps the most remarkable feature of the agreement was its disregard for the interests and desires of the friendly Creeks. On that subject, Agent Benjamin Hawkins wrote: "It struck me forcibly . . . that the general, . . . authorized only to retain lands conquered from the hostiles to indemnify the United States, . . . should take nearly eight million acres from the friendly Upper Creeks, giving, without consulting them, what he called an equivalent, which they did not deem such."[14]

Jackson's campaigns against the Creeks thus resulted immediately in acquisition of territory to add to the public lands of the United States, an outcome that was highly pleasing to a large number of citizens, particularly in the Southwest. The Indian wars had other results that followed more slowly, yet inevitably. Jackson became a major general in the United States army and was placed in command of the Seventh Military District, that extended westward from the Perdido across the lower Mississippi. The campaign which was fought at New Orleans in that district, against General Edward Pakenham in command of an

[13] *American State Papers: Indian Affairs*, I, 857, 858, 860; Debo, *The Road to Disappearance*, 80–82.

[14] Kappler, *Indian Affairs: Laws and Treaties*, II, 107–10; *American State Papers; Indian Affairs*, I, 493; 826–27; II, 26.

invading British force, was more than an incident in Jackson's military career, since it undoubtedly had some bearing upon his selection as a candidate for the presidency and his election to that office in 1828 and 1832.

The effect upon the Creek Indians was obvious also. Return Meigs and Agent Benjamin Hawkins witnessed the treaty, Tustenuggee Thlocko (Big Warrior) signed it for the Upper Creeks, Tustenuggee Hopoie of Tuckabatchee for the Lower Creeks, and various other Muskogee leaders signed as town chiefs: William McIntosh for Cusseta, Noble Kinnaird for Hitchitee, Timpoochee Barnard for Yuchee, John O'Kelly for Coosa, John Carr for Tuskegee, and Alexander Grayson for Hillabee. The hostile chiefs of the Upper Creeks, however, did not agree to Jackson's terms.

Menawa was still in hiding, waiting for his wounds to heal and nursing his resentment. Peter McQueen, Prophet Josiah Francis, Powell (Osceola), who was to become the most famous of all the Seminole war leaders, Savanah Jack, Hossa Yahola, and many other Red Stick head men, joined the movement southward into Florida. About one thousand of the Upper Creek warriors took refuge with the Florida Seminoles at this time, sending back a message to Benjamin Hawkins to the effect that they had no intention of surrendering.[15]

[15] Debo, *The Road to Disappearance*, 82; Cotterill, *The Southern Indians*, 188–89; *Dictionary of American Biography*, XIV, 76; *The National Cyclopedia of American Biography*, IX, 211.

CHAPTER 5

The Creek-Seminole Frontier, 1814–16

'He had a title among them which he well merited, Cap-pe-tum-nee-lox-au, *the Prince of Liars."*

BENJAMIN HAWKINS

COMMODORE WILLIAM HENRY PERCY of the British Navy landed military supplies at Pensacola in September, 1814, and Lieutenant Colonel Edward Nicholls came ashore with several companies of troops. A few weeks earlier Nicholls had issued a proclamation to the people of Louisiana and the Ohio Valley, urging them to join his cause.

"Natives of Louisiana," he wrote; "on you the first call is made, to assist in liberating from a faithless and imbecile Government your paternal soil. Spaniards, Frenchmen, Italians, and British, whether settled or residing for a time in Louisiana, on you I also call to aid me in a just cause."

Nicholls had a word of praise for the Indians and declared that they were pledged to aid the British. "Not even an enemy will an Indian put to death except resisting in arms," the English officer stated.

His appeal to Kentucky was a combination of barracks diplomacy, ignorance of the people, and sheer stupidity. "You have too long borne with grievous impositions. The whole brunt of the war has fallen on your brave sons; be imposed on no more, but either range yourselves under the standard of your forefathers, or observe a strict neutrality." He ended with a pathetic reference to Great Britain's heroic effort to save Europe from Napoleon Bonaparte, and of American tyrants' dastardly attempts to "stab Great Britain from the rear," while she was up to her neck in the blood of that sacred cause.[1]

Two days later (August 31, 1814) Nicholls wrote directly to Monsieur Jean Lafitte, the pirate who made his headquarters at Barataria south of New Orleans. "I have arrived in the Floridas for the purpose of annoying the only enemy Great Britain has in the world," the Colonel wrote to the freebooter; assuming, perhaps accurately, that no deep-seated loyalty to any country would interfere with Lafitte's choice of a patron. "As France and England are now friends, I call on you, with your brave followers, to enter the service of Great Britain, in which you shall have the rank of captain." Details of the offer were added, along with a suggestion that the bearer of the message, Captain McWilliams, and Captain Lockyer of the *Sophia*, "who carries him to you," would satisfy the pirate on any point not covered by the written offer. Lands for Lafitte and his men were promised, in proportion to rank; $30,000 in money for the pirate leader; and a full pardon for his crimes in the seizure of British ships.

Apparently Lafitte went off at once to New Orleans in the hope of obtaining a counter-proposal from the United States. But Louisiana officials were dubious about his sincerity; instead of a full pardon and a rich contract, they sent an expedition with orders to bring him back a prisoner. Lafitte escaped, however, and Captain Lockyer, returning to Barataria for a second visit, found the pirate headquarters deserted.[2]

The British officers at Pensacola invited Seminoles and Creeks to enlist for service against the United States, and about seven hundred warriors came in for the purpose of joining the British cause. Captain George Woodbine was assigned the task of making an effective military force from the Indian recruits.

From the beginning of British activities on the Gulf Coast, General Jackson was much concerned over the possibility of a military and naval attack upon New Orleans. He wrote to Gov-

[1] *Niles' Register*, Vol. VII, 134-35; *American State Papers: Foreign Relations*, IV, 548.
[2] *Ibid.*, 547; Brevard, *History of Florida*, I, 33, 34.

ernor William C. C. Claiborne in regard to defense of the city, and to the War Department concerning British-Spanish relations in Florida. Secretary John Armstrong urged Jackson to avoid a clash with Spain, but added: "If they admit, feed, arm, and co-operate with the British and hostile Indians, we must strike on the broad principle of self-preservation."[3]

Jackson occupied Mobile, garrisoned and repaired Fort Bowyer, and upon receiving word that a British naval unit was approaching the fort, sent a party of reinforcements with supplies to Major William Lawrence. Colonel Edward Nicholls landed a force of one hundred marines and three hundred of Captain Woodbine's Indians a few miles from the fort, while Commodore Percy came up with four ships and opened fire upon the fortifications. The *Hermes*, at the front of the attack, was anchored within musket range of the fort's defenders, and all of the British ships were under the fire of the batteries. A volley from the ships' guns was answered by a steady and devastating cannonade from the shore batteries. The flag of the *Hermes* was shot down and raised again by a member of the crew. The flagstaff on the fort, also, was cut by a cannon ball and quickly replaced. Captain Woodbine's Indians, acting as if on signal, attempted to rush the fortifications but were met by an effective musket fire, and failed to gain entry. The *Hermes* was disabled and drifted about still under the fort's guns. Commodore Percy removed the wounded to the *Sophia*, took off the rest of the men, and set fire to the disabled ship. All of the vessels except the *Hermes* escaped to Pensacola. The American losses were four privates killed, five wounded; British losses, thirty-two killed, forty wounded.[4]

Tennessee troops under General John Coffee arrived in Mobile to reinforce Jackson's army. By November 1, 1814, the total American force on the Gulf Coast numbered about 4,000, of whom one fourth were regular soldiers. The mounted troops, regular and militia, totaled 1,500.

[3] Quoted in *ibid.*, I, 35.
[4] *Ibid.*, I, 36, 37; Report of Inspector General A. P. Hayne, *American State Papers: Indian Affairs*, I, 860–61.

On November 6, from his headquarters near Pensacola, Jackson sent the following message to Governor Mateo González Manríque:

"The various violations of that neutrality which under existing treaties should have been faithfully maintained by you towards the United States; our declared enemy the British having been permitted to take possession of your Fortifications and fit out expeditions against us; your having given an assylum [sic] to the savages hostile to the United States, feeding and arming them to war against us, have compelled me to approach your city. I come not as the enemy of Spain but I come with a force sufficient to prevent the repetition of those acts so injurious to the United States and so inconsistent with the neutral character of Spain. To effect this object is my determination.

"I therefore demand possession of the Barancas and other Fortifications with their munitions of war. If delivered peacebly [sic] . . . the property, liberty, and laws of your citizens shall be respected. But if they are not peacebly let the blood of your subjects be upon your own head. I will not hold myself responsible for the conduct of my enraged soldiers and Indian warriors."[5]

The charge that Indians hostile to the United States had been armed and fed in Spanish territory was correct, as we have noted above; also accurate was the statement that Manríque had turned over San Carlos, St. Michael, and other fortified places for the use of British troops. Governor Manríque refused Jackson's offer to accept peaceable surrender and the American commander prepared to attack. The troops ready for action included the Third, Thirty-ninth, and Forty-seventh Infantry; a part of General Coffee's Brigade; a part of the Tennessee militia regiment; the Mississippi Dragoons; and a Choctaw Indian company. Jackson feinted with the Dragoons, west of Pensacola, but moved his main force around the rear to the east side of the town, reaching a position within a mile of the outskirts. Seven British ships in the harbor were a threat on the left, as the Americans advanced; on the opposite side was a fort of unknown strength; in front, fortifications and batteries.

5 *The Correspondence of Andrew Jackson*, II, 92.

The two-cannon battery in Pensacola did some damage in Jackson's center and a scattering of musket-fire came from the houses; but a bayonet charge led by Major William Laval silenced the battery and the regular troops quickly occupied the houses. Governor Manríque asked for terms of surrender and Jackson took over control of the town. The British force at Barancas, the harbor entrance, and on Santa Rosa Island destroyed batteries and all military supplies that could not be easily removed, withdrew on board their ships. Jackson hastened back to Mobile, where he expected an attack; but instead of moving west, the British forces landed near the mouth of the Apalachicola River and fortified a new position on Spanish soil.

Major Uriah Blue was sent against this British post in East Florida, where he was able to dislodge the garrison but unable to deal successfully with the hostile Indians. The few Indian families that were captured became prisoners at Fort Montgomery; but far greater numbers of the Seminoles simply faded into the forest and took refuge in remote hiding places.[6]

British and American peace commissioners, maneuvering to obtain the greatest possible advantages for their respective countries at Ghent, were obliged to settle terms without specific information on the campaigns of the Southwest, where preparations were under way for the greatest battle of the war. General Edward Pakenham left Jamaica on November 26 with a fleet of fifty ships bearing an army of ten thousand British veterans. Sir Samuel Gibbs, another experienced general officer of proved ability, was with the expedition. Both men had served with the Duke of Wellington in Spain, and they shared the confidence of their soldiers in the outcome of this adventure in America.

General Jackson did not arrive in New Orleans until December 2, 1814, barely a week ahead of the British invasion. The new secretary of war, James Monroe, obviously recognizing the peril of permitting the British to gain a decisive advantage in the lower valley of the great river, sent supplies in large quantities, using newly constructed river steamers for the big job of

[6] Brevard, *History of Florida*, I, 39–40.

transportation, and sending also large units of Tennessee and Mississippi militia. General Jackson became the central, driving force of the energetic preparations for the defense of New Orleans, with its population of twenty thousand and its key position on the Mississippi River.

The British fleet arrived on the coast below the city and General Pakenham took immediate steps in preparation for the coming struggle. On December 23, his advance guard of two thousand troops passed Lake Borgne and reached a point seven miles below New Orleans on the bank of the Mississippi. Next day Jackson attacked this party with a superior force, getting effective help from the *Carolina,* a schooner armed with twelve guns. The British advance guard threw up earthworks beyond the *Carolina's* range, and settled down to wait for the main army.

General Jackson made good use of the time thus allowed him for defensive measures. Five miles from the city he constructed earthworks on the border of a dry canal, in a position so strong as to impress General Pakenham with the necessity of heavy artillery for the assault. Almost a week elapsed while the British landed their heavy guns and hauled them through the mud to a position from which Jackson's earthworks could be reached. General Pakenham hoped also to silence the *Carolina's* batteries.

On January 1, 1815, Jackson's fifteen guns opened fire upon the advancing British force. Although Pakenham's heavy artillery numbered twenty-four pieces, his losses were excessive as his troops moved forward across an open space, and he decided, after his most effective cannons were disabled, to draw his party back out of range. On January 8, with solid reinforcements, General Pakenham advanced again upon Jackson's position where four thousand strongly entrenched men had already proved their steady quality and their marksmanship both with rifles and heavy guns. On one side of the American parapet the river gave protection against a flanking movement, on the other side a cypress swamp afforded the same defense. The five thousand British regulars who attempted to storm the earthworks were met by rifle and cannon fire, both terribly effective. The losses of the attacking force were 40 per cent of their total number—two thousand men killed, wounded, or missing. Three major generals, including Pakenham, were killed. The American losses were comparatively light, with a total casualty list of seventy-one.[7]

The British drew off their remaining troops and returned to their ships. On the way back to Jamaica they stopped at Mobile Bay and inflicted severe damage upon Jackson's fortifications there. On February 11, 1815, New York received the welcome news that peace terms had been agreed upon three weeks earlier by the British and American commissioners at Ghent; but the same news had not reached the southwestern frontier at the time of the final clashes of arms there.[8]

General Jackson's military command in New Orleans continued for a short time after the war, and Pensacola was returned to the Spanish authorities. Lieutenant Colonel Edward Nicholls, without official instructions from Spain and apparently without orders from his superiors in the British Army, occupied the fort that Captain Woodbine and Commodore Percy had helped him to construct on the lower Apalachicola during the war. Nicholls assumed a sort of protectorate over the Seminoles and wrote to Agent Benjamin Hawkins concerning this "runaway" branch of the Creeks, nominally under control of the Spanish authorities in Florida. On April 28, 1815, Nicholls informed Hawkins that he had sent captured slaves, "lately owned by the citizens of the United States, or Indians in hostility to the British forces," to the British colonies where they were received as free settlers.[9]

"I have had a complaint from the Seminole Chief, Bowlegs," Nicholls continued. Then came his account of a raid upon a Seminole town and the plundering of a peaceable party of Indians returning to their homes from St. Augustine. With this as a preface, Nicholls laid claim for the Creeks to territories "as they stood in 1811."

Enclosed in the Nicholls letter to Hawkins was Article Nine

[7] Babcock, *The Rise of American Nationality*, 146–48.
[8] *Ibid.*, 185.
[9] *American State Papers: Foreign Relations*, IV, 548.

of a "treaty" with the Creek Indians, which the Colonel seemed to think was binding upon the United States. The paper was signed by "Hopoy Meico, Hepoaeth Meico, Cappachimico," and other Seminoles, each with a cross mark (x), witnessed by Captain G. Woodbine and Nicholls himself. In answer to this part of the communication, Benjamin Hawkins wrote on May 24, 1815: "One of the chiefs is a Seminole of East Florida, and has never resided in the United States; and . . . neither of the three has ever attended national councils of the Creeks or is in any way a part of their Executive Government."

"I have ordered the Seminoles to stand on defense," Nicholls wrote to Hawkins, "and have sent them a large supply of arms and ammunition, and told them to put to death, without mercy, anyone molesting them; but at all times to be careful and not put a foot over the American line."

Benjamin Hawkins, a better-than-average agent, was drawn into an exchange of sharp letters with the British military man, a literary duel which the American easily won. In one of his letters Hawkins wrote: "I expected from the tenor of your orders, which I conveyed to you from Admirals Cochrane and Cockburn, on the 19th of March, that you had left the Floridas ere this with the British troops under your command, and that Spain and the United States would have no more of British interference in the management of their Indian affairs."[10]

Hawkins gave to Nicholls a brief account of another British adventurer's career among the Seminoles, that of the late William Augustus Bowles. "This gentleman, after attempting in various ways with the Seminoles to usurp the government of the Creeks without success, created himself director general of Muscogee, declared war against Spain, murdered some of his subjects, and took St. Marks. He ordered me with my assistants, in the plan of civilization, out of the Creek Nation.

"I communicated his proceedings to the national councils . . . who replied that he had a title among them which he well merited, *Cap-pe-tum-nee-lox-au*, the Prince of Liars."

[10] Hawkins to Nicholls, May 24, 1815, *ibid.*, IV, 549.

Hawkins was especially pointed in his reply to the boast that Nicholls had ordered the Indians to do violence. "On an *ex parte* hearing, you have 'armed the Seminoles, and given orders to put to death without mercy, anyone molesting them.' This is cruelty without example—scalping men, women, and children, for troubling or vexing only, and the executioners the judges! . . . You will be held responsible and your strongholds will certainly not avail. If you are really on the service of His Britannic Majesty, it is an act of hostility which will require to be speedily met, and speedily crushed. But, sir, I am satisfied you are acting for yourself, on some speculative project of your own. The sovereign of Great Britain could not, from his love of justice in time of peace, his systematic perseverance in support of legitimate sovereigns, almost to the impoverishment of his own nation, suffer any of his officers to go into a neutral country to disturb the peace."

Hawkins stated flatly that murders and thefts, committed against the Indians, would be punished. As to the status of Colonel Nicholls he added: "The treaties you have made for the Creek Nation, with the authority created by yourself for that purpose, must be a novelty. It would surprise me much to see your sovereign ratify such as you have described them to be, with a people such as I know them to be, in the territories of his Catholic Majesty. I shall communicate what has passed on the subject between us, to the officers of Spain in my neighborhood, that they may be apprized of what you are doing."[11]

That Colonel Nicholls had some information regarding a British plan to set up an Indian buffer-state on United States territory as a part of the peace terms, is clear.[12] That he received official encouragement to carry on his activities in Spanish Florida after the war, is likely. That his "diplomatic" letters to Benjamin Hawkins, stupidly arrogant in their tone and preposterous in their assumption of authority, gave him little basis for continued support either in England or Spain, is certain. His con-

11 Hawkins to Nicholls, May 28, 1815, *ibid.*, IV, 550–51.
12 Babcock, *The Rise of American Nationality*, 178.

nection with the Creeks and Seminoles promoted discord between Indians and white settlers, fanned the fires of animosity
that were smoldering, and added to the misunderstanding between two widely separated peoples, red and white, already at
odds over the interests of their respective cultures.

CHAPTER 6

The End of the Spanish Regime
in Florida

*"I think hard about the female killed at Tookabatchee,
she was a beloved woman."*

BIG WARRIOR

AS HAWKINS HAD PREDICTED, the British government
was not willing to ratify the treaty that Edward Nicholls
and George Woodbine had arranged with Indians whom they
represented as Creek leaders, and with the kinsmen of the Creeks
in Florida. The Creek warriors and chiefs who had retreated to
Florida after their disastrous campaign against General Jackson,
had been led by Nicholls to believe that they would get back
their lands in Alabama, ceded to the United States in the treaty
of August 9, 1814; and as a means of gaining the support of his
government, Nicholls took Chief Francis the Prophet and a
delegation of Seminoles with him to England in 1815. The Indians were received with honors and showered with presents,
the Prophet being given a sum of money, such valuable trinkets
as a goldplated tomahawk and a jeweled snuffbox, and a commission as brigadier general in the British Army with the uniform of that rank.

The fort on the lower Apalachicola, some sixty miles below
the United States boundary line and fifteen miles from the Gulf
Coast, was left by Nicholls in the hands of the Seminoles, who
were not especially eager to occupy it. The Negroes of the river
valley, however, maintained a garrison at the fort. Approximately 800 free Negroes, including 250 men able to carry arms,
lived on valley land north and south of the fort, a narrow strip

73

some fifty miles long containing cultivated fields and good range for livestock. This free population, many of whom were descendants of escaped slaves from the plantations of Georgia and the Carolinas, chose their own leaders and enjoyed a precarious status of self-government under Spanish authority.[1]

In some instances the Seminole leaders owned Negro slaves, who were permitted to live among the free black population and intermarry with them. The Negroes, both free and slave, were often used by the Seminoles as interpreters and as agents to conduct necessary business with people of European descent. There was no absolute prohibition of Seminole intermarriage with the Negro slaves; and the children of such mixed unions acquired the condition of free persons. The persistent tendency of new fugitive slaves to join the black population in Florida, the ready acceptance of these runaways by the Negroes and by the Seminoles, and the determination of masters in the United States to recover their property—or perhaps to take advantage of the confusion and recover additional slave property—all combined to make border diplomacy complicated. Only the weakness of Spain offered the hope of a simple solution of the entire problem, in acquisition of Florida by the United States. If Great Britain had retained Florida in 1783, or if the Indian buffer-state with England admitted to partial control had been established in 1814, the renewal of war between the United States and Great Britain would have been inevitable.

The Negro fort, a structure of earthen walls, occupied a strong position at the top of Prospect Bluff, a low but steep elevation protected in the rear by a swamp. Generally, the water of the Apalachicola River was too shallow to permit the approach of large boats with heavy guns. The fort was provided with a variety of artillery pieces: one thirty-two-pounder, three twenty-four-pounders, two nine-pounders, two six-pounders, and one brass five-and-one-half-inch howitzer.[2]

---

[1] Brevard, *History of Florida*, I, 42, 43 n.40; *Correspondence of Andrew Jackson*, II, 242. Captain Amelung described the location of the Negro Fort, "on the eastern bank of the Apalachicola River 15 miles above the mouth and 120 miles east of Pensacola."

There was violence on the Seminole-Creek frontier during 1815 and 1816. Evidence of conflict is found in the correspondence of Nicholls and Hawkins, mentioned above, and in many other contemporary sources. Big Warrior, writing to General Jackson on April 16, 1816, with the confidence of an established friend of the white people, was obviously much disturbed over the failure of the United States officers to prevent the killing of Indian citizens.

"My friend Jackson, . . . I have now to speak . . . on a subject that concerns us," Tustenuggee Thlocko wrote. "Since the treaty at Fort Jackson, there has been several murders committed above the line, by Soldiers and citizens. One in particular at the Council House, I did not think the murderer would be carried out of the country, but would be executed. Instead of that he was taken over the line. One was killed at Okmulgee Ferry, . . . one at Big Spring . . . by the militia and one by a captain of the army at Fort Jackson. I think hard about the female killed at Tookabatchee, she was a beloved woman."

General Jackson himself was deeply concerned over the presence of the Negro garrison on the Apalachicola. He warned Mauricio de Zuñiga, commandant at Pensacola, on April 23, 1816: "A Negro Fort erected during our late war with Britain . . . has been strengthened since that period and is now occupied by upwards of two hundred and fifty Negroes, many of whom have been enticed away from the service of their masters—citizens of the United States: all of whom are well clothed and disciplined. . . ." Jackson added that such a condition was likely to bring trouble between peaceful nations. Failure of Spain to control the centers of disturbance, "will compel us in self-defense to destroy them."

Captain Ferdinand Amelung, who carried Jackson's message to Pensacola, returned with Governor Zuñiga's reply and a translation of the document on June 4, 1816. The messenger gave as

[2] Brevard, *History of Florida*, I, 41–45; Giddings, *Exiles of Florida* 33–35. The fort has been described as a structure of heavy stone; but there is no evidence of rock walls, either in the defenses erected by Edward Nicholls or in Fort Gadsden which was erected on the site by order of General Andrew Jackson, after the United States came into control of the spot.

his opinion that the Spanish officer was sincere in his statement to the effect that the citizens of Pensacola suffered as much as the people across the line in the United States, from the presence of the garrison on the Apalachicola. Pensacola was without adequate defenses, Amelung said, with 80 to 100 Spanish soldiers, 150 colored troops, 150 serviceable muskets, and "not enough Gunpowder to fire a salute."[3]

Governor Zuñiga further stated that he would be proud to be commanded by General Jackson, and if the Captain General of Cuba could not furnish him the means to protect his position, he might apply for help in the United States.

In the spring of 1816, General Edmund P. Gaines constructed Fort Scott, just north of the Florida boundary and near the mouth of Flint River. The commander expected to transport supplies from New Orleans by way of the Apalachicola, which involved passing under the guns of the Negro fort. The first shipment of food and other supplies left New Orleans on June 24, 1816, and reached the mouth of the Apalachicola on July 10. Two gunboats and two schooners, commanded by Sailingmaster Jairus Loomis of the United States Navy, made up the convoy of supplies. General Gaines sent Colonel Duncan Clinch with two companies of infantry to take a position near the Negro fort, in the event that the garrison should fire upon the supply boats.[4] Information of this movement of troops was sent to Loomis, who waited at the mouth of the Apalachicola for five days before learning anything as to the intentions of the Negro garrison.

On July 15, a small boat from the convoy was fired upon by Negroes from a boat that emerged from the mouth of the river and immediately withdrew when one of the gunboats opened fire. It became necessary for the expedition to obtain fresh water; and when Midshipman Luffborough was sent out with four men to fill the kegs, his party was ambushed. One man, John Lopaz, escaped by swimming and reported the attack. About forty Negroes and Indians concealed in the bushes along the river

[3] Correspondence of Andrew Jackson, II, 241–43.
[4] James Parton, The Life of Andrew Jackson, II, 398–400.

bank had fired a volley at close range. Luffborough and two of his men fell at the first burst of shots; one man was taken prisoner, and Lopaz plunged into the river and swam under water for the opposite shore.

In the meantime Colonel Clinch marched from Fort Scott toward Prospect Bluff. On the way he was joined by a party of Seminoles who were on the warpath with the Negroes at Nicholls' Fort. The Seminole leaders agreed to act in concert with Clinch's force, and proceeded along the river bank as the soldiers from Fort Scott dropped down the stream by boat. The Indian war party seized every Negro they met; and one of their prisoners carried the fresh scalp of a white man. When he was brought before Colonel Clinch and admitted that he and his companions had ambushed a boat's crew a short time earlier, the troops from Fort Scott moved forward and took a position about one mile above Prospect Bluff. A message was sent to Sailingmaster Loomis, requesting that he bring his gunboats as near to the Negro Fort as possible.

At five o'clock on the morning of July 27, 1816, Loomis anchored within range of the fort's guns, which opened fire at once. The cannon fire from the ship's batteries had little effect upon the heavy earthen walls of the fort; but some of the balls were heated to a glowing red, and fired at such an angle as to fall within the fortification. One of the hot shots landed in the great magazine where Colonel Nicholls had stored more than seven hundred barrels of powder.

The resulting explosion, startling in its immediate effects, was a major disaster for the Negroes of the Apalachicola. Two hundred and seventy persons were killed instantly; and of the remaining sixty-four who were within the fort, over half died of their wounds. The leader of the Negro warriors, Garcon, and a Choctaw chief who was captured with him, were uninjured by the explosion; but both were turned over to the Seminoles for execution when they admitted that they had put to death, by burning, the sailor captured in the ambush of Midshipman Luffborough.[5]

[5] Parton, *Life of Andrew Jackson*, II, 403–407; Giddings, *Exiles in Florida*, 38–43; Brevard, *History of Florida*, I, 44–45; Patrick, *Florida Fiasco*, 301.

Colonel Duncan Clinch had promised his Indian allies all the small arms that might be captured in the attack on the fort, and his casual agreement was to have a serious bearing upon the events of the following months. The number of muskets and carbines was unexpectedly large—twenty-five hundred of the former and five hundred of the latter; and in addition there were five hundred swords in steel scabbards and four hundred pistols. The decision of the Seminoles to fight a war against the United States must have sprung from their new feeling of power—an unaccustomed sense of being rich in the resources of war.[6]

In the spring of 1817, a middle-aged Scottish trader named Alexander Arbuthnot brought from New Providence, a British island lying east of the Florida coast at a distance of about one hundred miles, a cargo of ammunition, guns, knives, blankets, clothing, calico, beads, and vermillion, to engage in trade with the Seminoles. He was an established merchant in Nassau, the principal town of New Providence; and the Florida venture was commercial, not political. He brought the goods in his own schooner, and expected to make an excellent profit in the exchange for corn, pelts, and beeswax of the Seminoles. The British citizens of this time in Nassau regarded Arbuthnot a man of respectable education and property, of fair intelligence and business ability, and gave him credit for being humane and public spirited.[7]

Arbuthnot's sympathy for the Seminoles, apparent from his first contacts with them, was to make him the storm-center of many disputes concerning the Florida Indians. There is ample evidence that he took their side on all questions of conflict with officials of the United States, and that he regarded arming the Indians as simply providing them with the means of self-defense.[8] Many of his letters written during the troubled period after the Negro fort was destroyed are printed in the records of the United States Congress. In a letter to the British Minister

6 Parton, *Life of Andrew Jackson,* II, 399, 407.
7 *Ibid.,* II, 411.
8 Arbuthnot to Commander at Fort Gaines, March 3, 1817, *American State Papers: Military Affairs,* I, 682; Arbuthnot to his son, April 2, 1818, *ibid.,* I, 722; Arbuthnot to the Honorable Charles Bagot, Jan. 27, 1818, *ibid.,* I, 723.

at Washington, Charles Bagot, he gave as his reason for writing, "the pressing solicitations of the chiefs of the Creek Nation, and the deplorable situation in which they are placed by the wanton aggressions of the Americans." A memorandum on the back of this letter contained the following lists, evidently referring to Indian troops and military supplies:

"King Hatchy, 1,000; Boleck, 1,500; Oso Hatjo, 500; Himashy Miso, 500; at present with Hillisajo, ——— ; at present under arms, 1,000 and more; and attacking those Americans who have made inroads on their territory.

"A quantity of gunpowder, lead, muskets, and flints, sufficient to arm one thousand or two thousand men. Muskets, 1,000; arms smaller, if possible. 10,000 flints, a proportion of rifles put up separate. 50 casks gunpowder. . . . 2,000 knives, six to nine inch blade, good quality; 1,000 tomahawks. 1,000 pounds vermilion. 2,000 pounds lead, independent of ball for musket." In view of this letter and other messages written by Arbuthnot, the suggestion that he was free from all intention of starting a war between the Seminoles and American border settlers is untenable.

A "talk" by General Edmund P. Gaines to the Indian chiefs, Hatchy and Boleck, as translated by the English interpreter for the Seminoles was included in Arbuthnot's message to Charles Bagot. "Your Seminoles are very bad people," Gaines was reported as saying; and the "talk" added specific accusations concerning theft of livestock, burning of property, and murder. "Give me the murderers," Gaines was quoted as saying, "and I will show them my law; and when that is finished and past if you will come about any of my people, you will see your friends. . . . But there is something out in the sea—a bird with a forked tongue—whip him back before he lands, for he will be the ruin of you yet. Perhaps you do not understand who or what I mean —I mean the name of Englishman."

In a final paragraph the "talk" added: "You harbor a great many of my black people among you at Sahwahnee. If you give me leave to go by you against them, I shall not hurt anything belonging to you."

King Hatchy's reply was also included. "You charge me with killing your people, stealing your cattle, and burning your houses; it is I who have just cause to complain of the Americans. . . . While one American has been justly killed, . . . stealing cattle . . . more than four Indians . . . have been murdered by these lawless freebooters. I harbor no Negroes. When the Englishmen were at war with America, some took shelter with them; and it is for you white people to settle those things among yourselves, and not trouble us with what we know nothing about. I shall use force to stop any armed Americans from passing my towns or lands."[9]

In November, 1817, the chief of Fowltown, a Seminole village in Georgia near the Florida line, warned the commandant at Fort Scott to keep his soldiers away from the Indian community. Returning to his headquarters, General Gaines learned of the warning and sent a runner to request that the belligerent chief pay him a visit.

"I have already said to the officer commanding at the fort all I have to say. I will not go," answered E-me-he-Maut-by, the Seminole leader. Upon receiving this reply General Gaines sent a force of 250 men to arrest the Seminole and his warriors. In the early dawn of November 21, 1817, a brief exchange of shots took place at Fowltown in which four Seminole warriors and one squaw were killed. The number of Indians wounded was not ascertained, since they were removed as the people abandoned Fowltown. A document signed by Robert White, in the absence of Colonel Nicholls, certifying the faithful adherence of E-me-he-Maut-by to the British cause in the late war, together with the scarlet coat and golden epaulets of a colonel's uniform, were found in the chief's house. General Gaines ordered the burning of the captured town, and the First Seminole War had begun.[10]

A letter from the Creek Indian agent, David B. Mitchell, to George Graham, who was acting as Secretary of War, clearly suggests the opinion that General Gaines had blundered into

[9] *American State Papers: Military Affairs,* I, 723–24.
[10] Gaines to Jackson, Nov. 21, 1817, *American State Papers: Military Affairs,* I, 686.

his attack upon Fowltown. The friendly Indians at Mitchell's agency "unanimously expressed much regret that hostilities should have commenced between the troops under General Gaines and the Fowltown Indians . . . because these Indians, although they did not unite with the friendly ones during the late war, neither did they join the Red Sticks, and had recently expressed a great desire to become . . . friendly." Later, to an investigating committee of the United States Senate, Mitchell made the significant statement: "Truth compels me to say, that before the attack on Fowltown, aggressions . . . were as frequent on the part of the whites as on the part of the Indians."[11]

On November 30, 1817, a party of forty soldiers under Lieutenant R. W. Scott, traveling up the Apalachicola River in a large open boat, was attacked by Seminole warriors at a point one mile below the mouth of the Flint. Seven women, the wives of soldiers, and four small children were passengers on the boat. Due to the swift current of the river at the point of attack, the craft was avoiding mid-stream and proceeding slowly along the heavily timbered shore. At the first volley from the concealed Indians, Lieutenant Scott and most of his men fell, killed or wounded. One woman was not hit by the shower of bullets and the Indians quickly made her a prisoner. Of the six soldiers who escaped into the river, only two reached Fort Scott uninjured to report the disaster. The children and members of the party who had been wounded were speedily killed and scalped.

Major Muhlenburgh, attempting to ascend the river a few days later with three boatloads of military supplies, was fired upon and forced to anchor in mid-stream. Here he waited for a rescue party from Fort Scott, keeping his men out of the reach of Seminole bullets and caring for those who were wounded in the initial attack. The rescue was made with great difficulty.

On December 16, 1817, Secretary of War John C. Calhoun wrote to General Gaines: "Should the Seminole Indians still refuse to make reparations for their outrages . . . it is the wish of the President that you consider yourself at liberty to march

[11] Mitchell to Graham, Dec. 14, 1817, *ibid.*, I, 688; Parton, *Life of Andrew Jackson*, II, 429–30.

across the Florida line and to attack them within its limits, . . . unless they should shelter themselves under a Spanish post. In the last event, you will immediately notify this Department."[12]

Ten days after the Secretary of War had authorized the invasion of Spanish territory for the purpose of attacking the Seminole Indians, he sent another order to General Gaines, directing him to "repair to Amelia Island"; and at the same time he ordered General Andrew Jackson to Fort Scott. About 800 regular soldiers were stationed at the Fort and 1,000 of the Georgia militia had been called into the national service. General Gaines estimated the total number of Seminole warriors at 2,700. "Should you be of the opinion that your numbers are too small to beat the enemy, you will call on the Executives of adjacent States for such an additional militia force as you may deem requisite," Calhoun instructed General Jackson.[13]

At about this time President James Monroe received a letter from General Jackson which expressed the basic view of the Tennessee leader, and for all practical purposes the attitude of the entire southwestern frontier regarding United States relations with Spanish Florida. "Let it be signified to me through any channel (say Mr. J. Rhea)," Jackson wrote, "that the possession of the Floridas would be desirable to the United States, and in sixty days it will be accomplished."[14] That Jackson believed he was authorized to march his military force into Florida by the President's order is clear; and it is possible that he regarded his instructions sufficiently explicit to justify his entire course of conduct in Florida.

General Jackson marched his available troops, numbering more than one thousand, from Tennessee to Fort Scott covering the distance of 450 miles in forty-six days. Heavy rains made the roads very bad—impassable for baggage wagons in some places. The force reached the junction of the Flint and Chattahoochee

[12] Gaines to the Secretary of War, Dec. 2, 1817, *American State Papers: Military Affairs*, I, 687–89; Calhoun to Gaines, Dec. 16, 1817, *ibid.*, I, 689; Parton, *Life of Andrew Jackson*, II, 430–31.

[13] Calhoun to Gaines, Dec. 26, 1817; Calhoun to Jackson, Dec. 26, 1817, *American State Papers: Military Affairs*, I, 689, 690.

[14] Thomas Hart Benton, *Thirty Years' View*, I, 170.

rivers, without supplies, on March 9, 1818. Provisions were so low at Fort Scott that the Commandant had recently been compelled to appeal for help, and a small party from Fort Early had started down the Flint with a boat load of supplies. When General Jackson reached Fort Scott the relief boat had not been heard from.

The new commander was faced with a hard choice: to wait with his hungry troops at Fort Scott, hoping for relief; or to proceed down the Apalachicola River to meet the supply vessels from New Orleans, promised in February by Quartermaster General George Gibson. Two sloops laden with provisions had been reported in the bay at the mouth of the river, and a large keel boat had been sent down to bring back a part of the much-needed cargo.[15] On the morning of March 10, 1818, all of the available cattle and swine were slaughtered and issued to the men. The combined forces numbered 2,000, and each man received three meat rations and one quart of corn, thus exhausting the food supply.

Riding low in the water with its cargo of food from Apalachicola Bay, the keel boat was met by Jackson's men as they advanced along the river; and the weary troops, on short rations for three weeks since Jackson had passed Fort Early, had the satisfaction of a full meal. The soldiers marched forward with renewed vigor, and after five days reached the site of the Negro fort on Prospect Bluff. Lieutenant James Gadsden of the engineers was given the task of building a temporary fort for the protection of supplies that were expected from New Orleans.

While Jackson was marching into Florida, his Creek allies under General William McIntosh were carrying on hostilities against remnants of the Red Sticks in Georgia. In messages to Jackson, the Indian officer complained of being hampered by high water in the streams, but reported minor actions resulting in the capture of some Lower Creek prisoners. Couchatee Micco with 30 warriors eluded McIntosh's party, but 53 Red Sticks with arms were captured along with 180 women and children.

[15] *American State Papers: Military Affairs*, I, 697–98; Parton, *Life of Andrew Jackson*, II, 442–43.

On April 8, 1818, General Jackson made an extensive report of his activities in Florida, addressing his communication to the War Department. He had advanced from the fortification on Prospect Bluff, which he named Fort Gadsden, toward the heart of the Seminole country. Six days later, on April 1, he was joined by his Creek allies under General McIntosh and by a party of Tennessee volunteers under Colonel Elliott. After one light skirmish, the Seminoles were driven back through the Mikasuki towns, where three hundred houses were burned, and a large supply of grain was taken along with a herd of Indian cattle. A red pole, emblem of the hostile Red Sticks, was found in the center of the public square of Kenhagee's Town; and hanging from the pole were fifty fresh scalps which were identified as belonging to Lieutenant R. W. Scott with the soldiers and civilians of his party.

As the Seminoles fell back, a part of them took refuge in St. Marks. General Jackson learned that a combined Indian and Negro force had demanded admission to the fortifications there, and that the Spanish garrison was too weak to deny them. He also became convinced, in the words of his report, "that, if not instigated by the Spanish authorities, the Indians had received the means of carrying on the war from that quarter; foreign agents, who have long been practicing their intrigues and villanies in this country, had free access into the fort; St. Marks was necessary, as a depot, to ensure the success of my operations. These considerations determined me to occupy it with an American force."

Jackson added that he had made an inventory of munitions and other goods after taking over the Spanish fort, respected all property rights, and furnished the commandant and the garrison with transportation to Pensacola. "Success depends upon the rapidity of my movements," he explained; "tomorrow I shall march for the Suwanee river, the destroying of the establishments on which will, in my opinion, put a . . . close to this savage war."

In a final paragraph, Jackson revealed that Captain Mc-Keever, a naval officer co-operating with his force, had captured

Francis the Prophet, or Hillis Hadjo, together with the old Red
Stick chief, Hornattlemied (Himollemico). Duncan McKrimmon, who had been a prisoner in the hands of Chief Francis
early in the war, was instrumental in his capture, since he informed Captain McKeever that the Prophet was in St. Marks,
and that he probably would be deceived by the display of the
British colors from the American ship. The romantic incident
of McKrimmon's rescue by the pleading of young Milly Francis,
daughter of the Seminole Chief, the story of which was repeated
in many versions through the years, gave a touch of irony to
the capture of Hillis Hadjo.

"This is what I get for saving your life," said Francis to Mc-
Krimmon, when he saw that his former prisoner was among his
American captors. "It is to your daughter Milly that I owe my
life; and I will do anything that I can for your deliverance,"
answered McKrimmon.

Alexander Arbuthnot, the Scottish trader, had been picked
up at St. Marks. "He is in confinement," wrote Jackson, "until
evidence of his guilt can be collected."[16] After his journey to the
Suwanee, where he captured another British subject named
Robert Ambrister, who was suspected of inciting the Seminoles
to war, General Jackson returned to St. Marks and ordered a
court martial for the two "foreign agents." With Major General
Edmund P. Gaines presiding over twelve officers selected by
Jackson from the regular troops, Tennessee Volunteers, Kentucky Volunteers, and Georgia militia, the special military court
found A. Arbuthnot guilty of "exciting and stirring up the Creek
Indians to war against the United States," and sentenced him
to be "suspended by the neck until he is dead." The court also
found Robert C. Ambrister guilty of "aiding, abetting, and com-
forting the enemy, supplying them with the means of war, . . .
and of leading the Lower Creek Indians in carrying on a war
against the United States. Ambrister was sentenced to be shot;
but upon reconsideration of his case, the court ruled that he
should be punished "with fifty stripes on his bare back, and be

[16] *American State Papers: Military Affairs*, I, 699–700; Parton, *Life of Andrew Jackson*, II, 431–32; 454–58.

confined with a ball and chain to hard labor for twelve calendar months." General Jackson approved the sentence of Alexander Arbuthnot and the original sentence of Robert Ambrister. He disapproved the reconsideration of Ambrister's case, and ordered the execution of the two prisoners. Accordingly, Arbuthnot was suspended by the neck from the yard-arm of his trading vessel, and Ambrister was shot. Chief Francis the Prophet and Himollemico, the Indians whom General Jackson called the "prime instigators of the war," were also put to death.[17]

Pensacola was the next objective of the triumphant American leader. After a few days of rest at Fort Gadsden, Jackson commenced his march through West Florida at the head of 1,200 men, regular soldiers and Tennessee Volunteers. On the way he learned that a Georgia militia force under Captain Obed Wright had attacked the Lower Creek town, Chehaw, and massacred seven of the people, including a head man named Howard, who was an uncle of General William McIntosh. Five other men and one woman were killed and their houses burned.

General Jackson entered into an angry correspondence with Governor William Rabun over this incident, after the General ordered Wright's arrest and the state authorities denied his official power to handle the case. Eventually the militia officer was tried and acquitted by the state of Georgia, and the Chehaw Indians received $8,000 as compensation for the destruction of their property and the killing of their citizens. The incident was an atrocity of peculiar magnitude, because this Indian band had fed Jackson's hungry troops as they marched southward to Fort Scott, and nearly all of the warriors were in the service of the United States at the time of the massacre.[18]

On May 24, 1818, Jackson's troops marched into Pensacola. The Spanish Governor had fled to Fort Carlos de Barancas, where he prepared to defend his position. Jackson sent a demand for surrender of the fort, which Governor José Masot denied; whereupon the Americans moved upon the Barancas, with one

[17] *American State Papers: Military Affairs*, I, 721–34; 700; Parton, *Life of Andrew Jackson*, II, 454–78.
[18] *Ibid.*, II, 488–97.

nine-pound gun and five eight-inch howitzers. The fort's guns opened fire, Jackson's men "returned it spiritedly," and presently the garrison asked for terms of surrender.[19]

After nine months of campaigning, the United States military force was practically in control of Spanish Florida. Without a declaration of war upon Spain, an officer of the United States Army had ousted Spanish officials, punished the Spanish Indians, and executed British subjects. The diplomatic maneuvers which followed were closely connected with the domestic policies of southwestern settlers of the frontier and the slaveholding citizens of the entire South. Their basic purposes centered upon the expulsion of Spanish authority from Florida and removal of the Florida Indians to some part of Louisiana Territory. A treaty was signed at Washington on February 22, 1819, by Secretary of State John Quincy Adams for the United States, and Luis de Onís for Spain, by the terms of which Florida was ceded to the United States and the Spanish boundary was defined from the mouth of the Sabine River on the Gulf of Mexico to the Pacific Ocean at the forty-second parallel.

The event marked the beginning of a new era for the Seminole Indians: unhappily, a period of continued injustice and brutal warfare, under a new master.

[19] Account written by General Jackson in a letter to George W. Campbell of Tennessee, quoted by Parton, *Life of Andrew Jackson*, II, 499–501.

CHAPTER 7

The Treaty of Camp Moultrie

*"Don't tell my people I said the Governor
can build his house here."*

NEAMATHLA

ACQUISITION OF FLORIDA by the Adams-Onis Treaty in 1819 transferred responsibility for the Indians of the province from the weak hands of the distant Spanish monarchy to the relatively vigorous, and almost entirely unscrupulous, control of the United States. Although the young republic had established the precedent of making formal Indian treaties, there was a sharp distinction between the status of a tribe and that of a foreign nation. In an oration delivered in 1802, John Quincy Adams expressed an opinion which was, in effect, the permanent view of the American nation regarding the Indian's title to his native land.

"Their cultivated fields; their constructed habitations; a space . . . for their subsistence . . . was undoubtedly by the laws of nature theirs. But what is the right of the huntsman to the forest of a thousand miles over which he has accidentally ranged in quest of prey? Shall the liberal bounties of Providence be claimed by a few hundreds? Shall the lordly savage not only disdain the virtues and enjoyments of civilization himself, but shall he control the civilization of the world?"[1] In his plea before the United States Supreme Court in the case of *Fletcher* v. *Peck*, Adams stated in sharper terms the attitude of Americans descended from European stock.

[1] Jedidiah Morse, *Report to the Secretary of War on Indian Affairs*, 282.

"What is the Indian title? It is mere occupancy for the purpose of hunting. It is not like our tenures; they have no idea of a title to the soil itself. It is overrun by them, rather than inhabited. It is not a true and legal possession."[2] The opinion of the United States Supreme Court itself was firm support for the distinguished attorney's statement. "The nature of the Indian Title," ran the Court's opinion, "which is certainly to be respected by all courts, until it be legitimately extinguished, is not such as to be absolutely repugnant to seisin in fee on the part of the State." The American commissioners at Ghent, in 1814, added the weight of their opinion in these words: "The recognition of a boundary gives up to the nation in whose behalf it was made, all the Indian tribes and countries within that boundary."[3]

American citizens in general, and particularly the people of states and territories adjacent to Florida, regarded acquisition of the Spanish province simply as a necessary step in the removal of Seminole Indians to the West. The First Seminole War (1817–18), before the Adams-Onis Treaty, had been an outgrowth of violence between Indians and the white settlers of Georgia and Alabama. Closely connected with friction along the border was the long-continued dispute over the recovery of fugitive slaves. When Jackson withdrew his victorious army from Florida in 1818, he negotiated no treaty with the Seminoles. The Monroe administration was still trying to hold the Creeks responsible for their Florida relatives, and in 1821, John C. Calhoun, secretary of war, sent General Thomas Flournoy of Georgia and Colonel Andrew Pickens of South Carolina to reopen "talks" with the Creek Indians. The state of Georgia also sent commissioners to the meeting, and brought so much pressure upon Flournoy and Pickens in regard to the return of fugitive slaves that both resigned. In reply to the complaints of General Flournoy concerning the attitude of the Georgia commissioners, Secretary Calhoun wrote:

"The President has directed that your resignation be ac-

[2] *Ibid.*, 283; *Fletcher* v. *Peck*, 6 Cranch 87.
[3] Morse, *Report*, 284.

cepted; and General David Meriwether has been appointed as commissioner in your place. The President regrets that you should have taken such a view of your instructions . . . as to induce you to tender your resignation. When the instructions were given, the difficulty which has since taken place between the commissioners of the United States and those of the State of Georgia was not anticipated. The latter instructions grew out of that difficulty, which it was their object to remove. . . . They had the same common object, so to conduct the negotiations as to give satisfaction to the State of Georgia. In fact, as the negotiation was commenced wholly for the benefit of that State, the President was solicitous to conduct it in perfect harmony with its local authority. . . ."[4]

The Georgia commissioners were insisting upon the return of fugitive slaves, as provided in the agreements made at Augusta, Galphinton, Shoulderbone, New York, and Colerain, some of which were concluded without the approval of the Creek council, and all of which were entered into without the authority of the Seminole tribe. In a "talk" delivered to the Creek chiefs on December 29, 1820, the Georgia commissioners said:

"Brothers: As to the Negroes now remaining among the Seminoles, belonging to the white people, we consider these people (the Seminoles) a part of the Creek Nation; and we look to the chiefs of the Creek Nation to cause the people there, as well as the people of the Upper Towns, to do justice."[5]

The Creek chiefs answered in a "talk" by General William McIntosh, who stated that Alexander McGillivray, after the Treaty of New York, had delivered all the black prisoners he could collect to Major Seagrove, then United States Indian agent. McIntosh further reminded the commissioners that he had taken a part in the Florida campaign under General Duncan Clinch, in which the Negro fort was destroyed and a large part of its occupants were slaughtered. The Negroes who were taken alive had been surrendered to General Clinch, to be returned

---

[4] American State Papers: Indian Affairs, II, 251; Giddings, The Exiles of Florida, 60, 61.
[5] American State Papers: Indian Affairs, II, 253.

to their masters. Other Negro captives had been turned over to Colonel Hawkins for their owners.

"If the President admits that country (Florida) to belong to the Creek nation," McIntosh stated, "I will go down with my warriors and bring back all the Negroes I can get, and deliver them up." The Chief added that when all claims and counter claims were exhibited and examined, he did not think there would be much difference of opinion between the Georgians and the Creeks.[6]

The Treaty of Indian Springs, laid before the United States Senate by President James Monroe on January 26, 1821, provided a cession of about 5,000,000 acres of the best Creek land, between the Flint and the Chattahoochee rivers, and contained a special clause reserving the village of Buzzard Roost for the Creek Nation; and one thousand acres "to be laid off in a square so as to include the Indian Spring in the center thereof; as also six hundred and forty acres on the western bank of the Oakmulgee River, so as to include the improvements at present in the possession of the Indian chief, General McIntosh."

The United States, in consideration for the land cession, agreed to pay the Creek Nation $10,000 in cash; $40,000 "as soon as practicable after the ratification of the convention; $5,000 annually for two years thereafter; $16,000 annually, for five years thereafter; and $10,000 annually, for six years thereafter," in money or goods, at the option of the Creek Nation. The United States agreed, "as a further consideration for said cession," to pay to the state of Georgia whatever balance may be found due by the Creek Nation to the citizens of the said state "to be paid in five annual installments, without interest, providing the same shall not exceed the sum of $250,000; the commissioners of Georgia executing to the Creek Nation a full and final relinquishment of all the claims of the citizens of Georgia against the Creek Nation, for property taken or destroyed prior to the Act of Congress of 1802, regulating the intercourse with the Indian tribes."[7]

[6] *Ibid.*, II, 252–53.
[7] *Ibid.*, II, 248–49.

The greater part of the claims thus assumed by the United States were for slaves who escaped from their masters during the American Revolution and prior to the year 1802. Commissioners who settled the claims fixed the value of 92 slaves and all other property lost to the Creeks by Georgians, between 1775 and 1802, at $119,000. William Wirt, representing the interests of the United States, declared that the price paid for the slaves was from two to three times their value.[8] In cash and goods the Indians received about four cents an acre for their land; including the dubious claims for escaped slaves and stolen property, the bargain was reached at about seven cents an acre.

During the last months of the Madison administration and the early years of James Monroe's period in the chief executive office, Congress had before it many problems of organic law for the new provinces, and enabling legislation for new states. Louisiana had become a state in 1812, and the territories north of Kentucky and south of Tennessee were ready for statehood. During a span of three years (1816–19), Indiana, Mississippi, Illinois, and Alabama were admitted to statehood. West of the Mississippi River, Missouri was clamoring for admission to the Union; and on the northern frontier of New England, the territory of Maine had more than the population required for setting up a congressional district. Between Louisiana and Missouri, the Arkansas country was filling up with settlers. The boundaries of Arkansas Territory extended far to the west of the present limits of the state.

As governor of Florida, General Jackson formally received the surrender of the Territory from Spain in a ceremony at Pensacola on July 17, 1821, and military government was brought to a close less than a year later.[9] Jackson's brief career as governor was vigorous, to say the least. To serve with the first governor, President Monroe appointed two district judges, two attorneys, two secretaries, three collectors, and a marshal. Colonel George Walton became secretary of West Florida, W. G. T. Worthing-

[8] Giddings, *The Exiles of Florida*, 68 (quoting from *Opinions of the Attorney General*, 1822).

[9] Parton, *Life of Andrew Jackson*, II, 594–603; Brevard, *History of Florida*, I, 71.

ton, secretary of East Florida, and Elijius Fromentin, United States judge for the western district. William P. Duval, who was later to serve for more than a decade as territorial governor of Florida, became the first judge of the Eastern District. Before provision was made by act of Congress for a territorial delegate, Judge Duval made a trip to Washington with a report for President Monroe on conditions in the Eastern Judicial District.

Governor Andrew Jackson had been commissioned by the President to "exercise all the powers and authorities heretofore exercised by the governor and captain general and intendant of Cuba, and by the governors of East and West Florida; provided, however, that the said Andrew Jackson, or any person acting under him, or in the said territories, shall have no power or authority to lay or collect any new or additional taxes, or to grant or confirm to any person or persons, . . . any title or claims to land within the same."

The Governor appointed mayors, aldermen, justices of the peace, and other local officers. He was keenly disappointed because President Monroe did not place within his powers the appointment of major territorial officers, as a means for the General to reward his friends. The taxes levied by the American town officials were in harmony with the fees collected under Spanish authority. In St. Augustine the mayor and aldermen levied a real estate tax of 2.5 mills, a tax of one dollar per year upon each slave over seven years of age, 7.5 per cent upon auction sales, two dollars per year on each dog, and fees of twenty-four dollars per year on dram shops, fifty dollars on each billiard table, and ten dollars on each carriage. A Sabbath closing law was imposed upon theatres and gambling houses—probably through the influence of the Governor's energetic wife, Mrs. Rachel Jackson.[10]

The Governor quarreled with the former Spanish executive, José Callava, over various problems connected with the transfer of authority from Spain to the United States, finally reaching a climax of executive ineptitude in sending the foreign officer to jail, and ordering federal Judge Elijius Fromentin to appear at

[10] *Ibid.*, I, 64; Parton, *Life of Andrew Jackson*, II, 607.

the Governor's office and explain why he had attempted to interfere by means of a writ of habeas corpus for the release of Callava.

In September, 1821, Jackson wrote to his friend John Donelson of Tennessee that he hoped to start for Nashville by the first of October, and that he expected to resign his office as governor, "the moment Congress meets." He reached the Hermitage on November 3, and there received friendly letters from President Monroe and Secretary John Quincy Adams in regard to his controversy with José Callava and Judge Fromentin.

The territorial government provided by Congress for Florida, placed the executive authority in the hands of a governor, appointed by the President to serve for three years, and a secretary who was also deputy governor, chosen by the President for a four-year term. The function of law-making was placed in the hands of the governor and a council of thirteen members appointed annually by the President. Residents of Florida were eligible for appointment to the council. Two superior courts were provided, with authority vested in the council to establish the lower courts.

William P. Duval was appointed by President Monroe to follow Jackson as governor. Judge Duval had been keenly interested in the affairs of the new territory from the beginning of occupation by the United States, and had added the function of serving as a sort of unofficial delegate in Washington to his duties as federal judge, as noted above. The career of Duval, like that of Andrew Jackson, had a deep and permanent effect upon the lives of the Seminole Indians in Florida.

Governor Duval was the son of a Revolutionary soldier and a native of Virginia. His life was spent mainly on the frontier, first in the state of his birth, then in Kentucky, and finally in Florida. A story of his boyhood gives more than a clue to the willful nature of young Duval. When he was sixteen, his stern father rebuked him for idleness as he sent him out for a log to feed into the fireplace. William walked to the stable, saddled a horse, and rode west to Kentucky. After an absence of twenty years he rode back to his Virginia home, hitched his horse, and carried in a log. "There is the log you sent me for father," he said.

"You were long enough getting it," answered the head of the house, speaking his line as if it had been rehearsed. In Kentucky, young Duval had studied law, practiced in the frontier courts of the new state, and won a seat in Congress. Washington Irving, who made a stagecoach journey in company with Duval the statesman, was impressed with his genial wit and ability to tell a story. The Indians in Florida also had a good word for Governor Duval: he never "spoke with a forked tongue," they said.[11]

At the time of the acquisition of Florida by the United States, studies of the North American Indians were generally lacking in the essential quality of accurate observation. Travelers, biologists, and others had written about the Indians, and the sum of their findings was large; but wide variations appear in their accounts with respect to tribal population, tribal characteristics, and chieftans. Names of towns and persons were recorded by Spanish, French, English, and American observers, with spelling based upon the sound of the word as pronounced by the Indians. The results were dissimilar to an astonishing degree.

An official survey made under authority of President Monroe after the signing of the Adams-Onis Treaty, gave an estimate of 5,000 for the total Indian population of Florida.[12] Reverend Jedidiah Morse, who made an extensive study of the Indians in the United States and Canada in the interest of Christian missions and who reported his findings in some detail, thought that 1,200 "pure-blooded Seminoles" lived in East Florida, and in the same area "a number of Creeks and other tribes." Later students generally gave up the idea of a Seminole tribe based strictly upon blood relationship, and regarded the Florida Indians a mixed group largely descended from the Creeks, who were also a tribe of mixed parentage. The Muskhogean language of Jedidiah Morse's "pure-blooded Seminoles," combined with colonial records of Creek invasions, indicate that northern addi-

---

[11] Brevard, *History of Florida*, I, 73.

[12] Morse, *Report*, 33, 308. Morse's estimates were based upon the report of Captain John H. Bell, U. S. Indian agent for Florida in 1820. M. Penieres, sub-agent for the Florida Indians, reported in 1822: "Indians, over 5,000; Negro slaves held by them, 40; fugitive Negroes, impossible to estimate."

tions to the stock of the Florida Indians after the War of 1812 were closely related to a movement that had been going on for a century.

Five hundred or more mulattoes, "maroons who live wild in the woods, . . . in a state of half slavery to the Indians," were mentioned in Agent Bell's letter to a committee of Congress in 1820; and reference was made to the slaves of Seminole chieftains, the influence exerted by the Negroes over their Indian masters, and the even greater influence of the "maroons."

Red Town, Oc-lac-o-na-yahe, O-po-nay's Town, and Tots-ta-la-hoeets-ka, or "Watermelon Town," all in the vicinity of Tampa Bay, were villages of Upper Creeks who fled to Florida after the War of 1812. Ah-ha-pop-la, back of Mosquito Inlet, Low-Walta Village, Waw-ka-sau-su, and McQueen's Village were inhabited by warriors and their families who followed Francis the Prophet and McQueen from the Coosa to the east side of Tampa Bay, and by other Creeks who had recently joined the Florida Indians. Wa-cissa-talofa, in the upper valley of the St. Marks, had an Upper Creek population from the Chattahoochee; and "Old Suwany Town" on the Suwannee River was composed of Upper Creeks from the Tallapoosa. A-la-pa-ha-talofa, west of the Suwannee, was a town that had just lost its old chief, Ocmulgee; Santa-fee-talofa, at the east fork of the Suwannee, recognized Lock-taw-me-coocky as its chief; and Took-a-sa-moth-lay was the chief of a numerous band on the Alachuan Plains.

The people of Willa-noucha-talofa, near the head of St. Marks and west of Wa-cissa-talofa, were natives of Florida; and the inhabitants of Tallahassee, on the waters of Miccosukee Pond, had lived in the country a long time. On the other hand, Top-ke-gal-ga and We-thoe-cuchy-talofa, near the O-clock-ney River, contained "very few natives of the land."[13]

On the Apalachicola River, Chief Cothrin's town (O-chuce-ulga) on the east side and Choco-nickla Village on the west side, were peopled by Indians "who were raised there." Top-hulga, adjacent to Choco-nickla, contained natives of East Florida. The sixty warriors of Choco-nickla recognized Nea-thock-o-motla as

[13] Morse, *Report*, 306–307.

their chief, with Mulatto King as *tustenuggee* (second in command). Ten miles above the junction of the Flint with the Chattahoochee, and west of that stream, was a band of Creeks who had moved south from Red Ground.

Tock-to-eth-la, on East Florida Point, was the residence of thirty Upper Creek warriors and a large number of women and children. Pe-lac-le-ka-ha, the residence of Principal Chief Micanopy of the Seminole tribe, was situated 120 miles south of Alachua, Chu-ku-chatta was 20 miles farther south, and Hitch-a-pue-susse 20 miles beyond it. The "Big Hammock" settlement was west of Hitch-a-pue-susse and north of Tampa Bay. Other Seminole towns were Oc-la-wa-haw, west of the St. Johns; Mulatto Girls' Town, south of Caskawilla Lake; Bucker Woman's Town, east of the Big Hammock; King Heijah's Town, south of Alachua; and King Payne's Negro Town, in Alachua, with a population of 300 slaves belonging to the Seminoles.

West of Payne's Town was a settlement of Mikasuki Indians called John Hicks' Town. South of Okefenokee Swamp lived a band of Cowetas, at Beech Creek a settlement of Cheehaws, and at Spring Garden above Lake George, Chief Billy's Uchees. A small settlement of Choctaws occupied a portion of the west coast near Charlotte's Bay.

Reverend Jedidiah Morse was one of the American citizens who recommended a reservation for the Seminoles removed from the seacoast—"for whilst there," he wrote, "their settlements will be the resort of pirates, smugglers, &c . . . who will keep up a communication between the islands and Cuba, excite disaffection, violate our laws, and escape with impunity from the country. And our refugee slaves aim for their settlements, with a view of escaping to the neighboring islands."[14] Morse suggested that all Florida land outside the Indian reservation, be regarded as a part of the public domain and opened to white settlement.

Many of the Seminoles, including the Creeks who had joined them since the end of the War of 1812, lived in frame houses. The Indian women dressed in a "petticoat and short gown, like

14 *Ibid.*, 308.

97

the white women." The men wore a cotton shirt "fringed down below the knee," with a belt. Jedidiah Morse said of them, "They have none of the Indian fondness for ornaments and finery. They are honest, speak the truth, and are attached to the British and Americans." He added that the McIntosh war and other conflicts, and depradations of the whites upon the Seminoles, "have destroyed their confidence in the Americans." That confidence may be restored, he said, by kindness and justice; but did not state whether or not he regarded a reservation of inferior land, cut off from the sea, an essential part of justice and kind treatment.

Most influential chief of the Creeks who came to Florida after the Red Stick war was Neamathla. Sub-chief at Tallahassee was Chefixico Hadjo; and at Mikasuki, northeast of Tallahassee on the lake named for the tribe, the town chief was Tokas-a-mathla.

On December 15, 1823, President Monroe sent to the United States Senate the text of the Treaty of Camp Moultrie that had been negotiated by Governor Duval, James Gadsden, and Bernardo Segui with some of the Seminole chiefs and warriors. The Florida Indians who were induced to sign the document probably were not a representative group of leaders, although six chiefs of the Apalachicola region finally gave their consent when they were offered an attractive allotment of land in the region formerly held by the Negroes killed in the fort at Prospect Bluff on July 27, 1816.[15] The Seminole Indians were to accept as their home a restricted area, with its boundaries fifteen miles from the Gulf Coast and not less than twenty miles from the Atlantic Coast. The Indians agreed to permit any citizen of the United States to pass and repass through their reservation for lawful purposes without toll or hindrance.

The United States made a covenant to protect the Florida Indians "against all persons whatsoever, provided they conform to the laws of the United States, and refrain from making war or giving insult to any foreign nation without having first obtained the permission and consent of the United States." It was also agreed that the United States would distribute among the

[15] *American State Papers: Indian Affairs*, II, 429–31; Giddings, *The Exiles of Florida*, 72, 73.

Old Seminole cemetery near Wewoka, Oklahoma.

Fort Gibson in 1868, where muster rolls were made of surviving
Seminoles as they arrived in the West.

From the Art Collection of
Edward Eberstadt & Sons, New York

Seminole Council House near Wewoka, Oklahoma.

tribes, "as soon as concentrated, under the direction of their agent," farming implements and livestock to the amount of $6,000, and an annuity of $5,000 for twenty years. Further obligations assumed by the government included the sum of $2,000 for the purpose of assisting in migration to the restricted area; rations of corn, meat and salt for twelve months; $1,000 per year for twenty years for the support of a school; and an equal amount for the support of a blacksmith and gunsmith.

The compact bound the chiefs and warriors to be "active and vigilant" in the return of fugitive slaves and fugitives from justice who might pass through the Indian district, and they were promised compensation for each absconding slave delivered to their agent. Article Nine of the Treaty of Camp Moultrie provided that the northern line of the Indian lands might be moved farther north, to "embrace a sufficient quantity of good tillable land to subsist them," if upon examination by the Indian Agent, the original district appeared to be inadequate. Article Ten provided a gift of one square mile, embracing the improvements of Neamathla at Tallahassee, for Colonel Gad Humphreys, Seminole Agent; and one square mile for the interpreter, Stephen Richards, both to be conveyed in fee simple.

As an especial favor to six of the Apalachicola chiefs, in consideration for their friendly disposition and past services to the United States and as a means for obtaining their support for the treaty—it was agreed in an additional article that the six chiefs should remain with their followers in the region already occupied by them. Reservations were provided as follows: (1) for the use of Neamathla and his connections, two square miles, embracing Tuphulga Village on Rocky Comfort Creek; (2) for Blount and Tuski Hadjo, an area extending four miles along the Apalachicola River, two miles wide, embracing Tuski Hadjo's improvements; (3) for Mulatto King and Emathlochee, an area on the river one mile wide and four miles long, embracing Yellow Hair's improvements; and (4) for Econchatimicco, a strip one mile wide, extending four miles along the river, and embracing his house. These grants of land, twenty square miles in their total extent, do not seem unduly generous when it is considered that followers of the six chieftains included 214 men.[16]

In support of their treaty, the commissioners wrote to Secretary John C. Calhoun: "It was a misfortune to Florida, as a frontier territory, and with her maritime exposure, to have any tribes of Indians within her boundaries. . . . To remove them seems to have been impracticable." The message added that military posts would be required to place the Indians under control in a restricted area cut off from the coasts. "It is scarcely necessary to state to you, that a majority of the Indians now inhabiting Florida . . . are warriors, if not refugees from the southern Indians. Many of them are of the old Red Stick party, whose feelings of hostility have only been suppressed, not eradicated; and even the native Seminoles have ever been of a most eratic disposition. These Indians are now scattered over the whole face of Florida; but a small portion of them having any settled residence, a majority wandering about for such precarious subsistence as the esculent roots of the woods, or the misfortunes of our navigators on the Florida Keys, may afford." The commissioners recommended that Gad Humphreys, Seminole Agent, and the interpreter, Mr. Richards, be allowed extra funds for their efforts and expense in assembling the Indians at the treaty grounds.

In a "talk" to the commissioners, Neamathla "stated that the Florida Indians had determined to incorporate with their tribes the fugitive Creeks and the Red Sticks who were among them." An attempt to make an accurate report on the number of Indians in Florida was included. "It appears the total amount is 4,833 souls," the commissioners wrote; but were forced to add that Neamathla "objected to stating the number of Negroes in the nation."[17]

The Florida Council considered the problem of selecting a site for the capital of the Territory, naming Dr. William H. Simmons of St. Augustine and John Lee Williams of Pensacola to do the work of finding the most suitable place. With the idea of

16 *Ibid.*, II, 431.
17 *Ibid.*, II, 438–41.

placing the capital on middle ground, the commissioners visited Neamathla at New Tallahassee Village. The Chief agreed reluctantly to an investigation by the commissioners, and entertained them with a ball game and dance. A variation of the Choctaw game *ishtaboli,* the match was held on a circular field, with a goal-post in the center. The men, using their regular bat-sticks, played against the women who caught and threw the ball with their hands. Enough advantages were obtained by the women in the rules to enable them to win the game.

On the following day, Neamathla came to Dr. Simmons and Mr. Williams with an interpreter to ask for a definite statement of their aims. After listening closely while they explained the need of the white men to find a site for the governor's council house, Neamathla gave permission for their investigation, but added: "Don't tell my people I said the Governor can build his house here."

The commissioners paid for the feeding of their horses, and proceeded to explore the area for twenty miles around with no interference from the Seminoles. At Old Tallahassee, however, Chefixico was clearly displeased with the prospect of having the Florida capital in Seminole territory on space carved from the Indians' diminishing ground. "Is that my land?" he asked, holding out a handful of earth that he snatched up to emphasize his point.[18]

In spite of Chefixico's belligerent attitude and the secret but determined opposition which Neamathla assumed, the commissioners agreed upon a site about one mile southwest of the Old Tallahassee fields. Governor Duval, eager to have the question of the capital's location settled, ordered that the next meeting of the Council should be held at the new site. Congress confirmed the choice of the commissioners and governor by an act passed on May 24, 1824.

[18] Brevard, *History of Florida,* I, 86.

CHAPTER 8

Difficulties of Enforcing
the Treaty

*"There are bad men among all people, the white
as well as the red."*

CHIEF JOHN HICKS

PERHAPS THE ablest leader of the Seminole Indians, at
the time when Governor Duval took office in the territory
of Florida, was Chief Neamathla. As officials of the United States
prepared to remove the Indians to the region specified by the
Treaty of Camp Moultrie, the governor and his aides offered a
wide range of opinions concerning the character, ability, and
reliability of the Chief as a friend of the government. In April,
1824, Colonel Gad Humphreys was urging Governor Duval to
buy Neamathla's property, and induce him to move south as
the most influential leader of the Florida Indians.

"I cannot close this communication without repeating the
sentiments I gave you on a former occasion in regard to Neamathla, the principal chief of the Florida Indians. By the terms
of the treaty, he is located upon a reservation very remote from
the main body of the nation. The offer of this arrangement, designed to gratify and soothe the feelings of this aged and respectable man, was wise and judicious, as calculated to have a beneficial effect upon the pending negotiations; but I cannot consider
the consummation of it less than unfortunate, inasmuch as it
removes from the immediate government of the nation the only
individual in it who possesses a perfect and undisputed authority over a people, some of whom are often troublesome to man-
age. The promptitude with which Neamathla has uniformly,

since the war, punished the offences of his people, particularly those against the white inhabitants of the country, has excited in the Indians an awe and respect for his character, and given him unbounded influence over them, and at the same time, furnishes the surest proof of the strength of his desire to be on terms of amity with the United States. . . .

"I have reason to believe that, were Neamathla permitted to sell his reservation, by means of which he might procure a valuable stock . . . he might be induced to take up his residence within the limits assigned to the Indians in the south."

Shortly afterward, Duval was forwarding to the secretary of war a copy of this letter and urging that Neamathla be permitted to visit Washington at the expense of the government. "Neamathla is a most uncommon man," wrote the Governor. "This chief you will find, perhaps, the greatest man you have ever seen among the Indians. He can, if he chooses to do so, control his warriors with as much ease as a colonel could a regiment of regular soldiers: they love and fear him. . . . . If Congress should allow him to sell his reservation of land, and direct the money to be laid out in cattle for him, it will awaken his gratitude to the Government, and render him of essential service in commanding the nation.

"This chief should be seen by you, and then you can judge of the force and energy of his mind and character. Neamathla, and the chiefs who go with him to the city, have never seen the interior of the United States, and have no precise knowledge of the strength and power of our country." Evidently John C. Calhoun was not so deeply impressed by the reports on Neamathla as were the men who worked in his vicinity, for the requested visit was not arranged.[1]

Some of the Indians discovered at once the advantages of having government funds spent in their area. The first of the buildings erected for use of the territorial government was a log structure on which a few Indian workers were employed. Seminole hunters supplied laborers and settlers with game. The

---

[1] G. Humphreys to Duval, inc., April 7, 1824; Duval to Calhoun, April 11, 1824, *American State Papers: Indian Affairs*, II, 616–17.

white population took up residence in hastily constructed frame houses, crude bark huts, or tents. The legislative council, meeting at Tallahassee, received news from Governor Duval of the Camp Moultrie Treaty, by which the Indians had agreed to live in a reservation set back from the seacoast. When the governor removed his family from St. Marks to Tallahassee, his new neighbors were Indians as well as whites. His children played in the woods with Indian boys, and the acquaintances thus formed helped to build confidence between the two races. Through friendly Seminoles, Duval learned that Neamathla was planning an uprising, and determined upon a bold course, somewhat perilous at the stage of understanding then existing with the Indians, but quite effective. He went into a council of three hundred Seminole warriors, alone except for his interpreter who disobeyed instructions by following him, with the comment, "I know we will both be killed."

Neamathla was in the midst of a speech, urging upon the fighting men of the tribe the necessity of taking up arms to protect their land. The governor walked up to the platform, seized the speaker by the throat, and rushed him out of the room. He then addressed the warriors, telling them that Neamathla had forfeited his right to hold office as principal chief, and that John Hicks was his successor; furthermore, Florida Indians who delayed removal to their reservation would be taken by force. Neamathla, unable to build up a war party for immediate action, went back to his former home in Georgia, and John Hicks supervised the settlement of the Florida Indians on their reservation, using St. Marks as a concentration point.[2]

During 1824 the Florida Indians were removed to the reservation defined in the Treaty of Camp Moultrie. In their new location the Indians found strange and difficult conditions for gaining a livelihood, and the leaders were keenly dissatisfied with the original boundaries of the reservation. Despite treaty provisions for the distribution of a fund to aid the Indians during migration, there was a great deal of hardship, even starvation, connected with removal. There was some evidence of sympa-

[2] *Ibid.*, I, 89, 90.

thetic concern on the part of Florida officials and agents of the United States Indian Office; but in many particulars, the interests of Indians and white citizens were in sharp conflict. Governor Duval, who was a slaveholder, was quite active in the pursuit of Negroes who took refuge among the Seminoles. On the other hand, as superintendent of Indian Affairs in the territory of Florida, he gave solid support to the demands of Indian leaders for enlarging the reservation, and in other ways proved his desire to promote justice.

Raids were made by the Apalachicola Indians, not caused primarily by the selection of Tallahassee as the territorial capital, but by failure of the United States to pay annuities. Payment was withheld on the charge that slaves claimed by white settlers had been given a place of refuge by the Indians. All the members of a white family were slain by the Indians twenty miles from Tallahassee, and murders of whites by the Seminoles were reported in other areas. A militia force from Leon and Gadsden counties was assembled and drilled, but no arrests of Indians were made.[3]

While removals to the Seminole reservation were going on in Florida, and some evidence of bloody conflict was appearing as a result of the controversy over fugitive slaves, together with general discontent connected with the new order, President John Quincy Adams took office, and had his turn at executive direction of Indian affairs. Adams was inclined to retain all officials of the previous administration, and made removals only for cause. William P. Duval continued to serve as governor of Florida Territory and superintendent of Indian affairs there; Gad Humphreys, appointed in 1822, remained as Indian agent.

Legal methods of the territory were such as to favor the client in all controversies between Indians and white settlers over return of fugitive slaves. There is ample evidence that Negroes whose families had been free for generations were captured and returned to the servile labor of their ancestors. Governor Duval withheld from the Seminole annuity the price of a Negro claimed by Mrs. Cook, although Indian leaders met with the

[3] Brevard, *History of Florida*, I, 90; Giddings, *The Exiles of Florida*, 75–80.

Agent and maintained firmly that the Negro in question had been born among the Seminoles and had never been out of the country.[4]

The attitude of Governor Duval toward the Indians of Florida is shown in his report of the elevation of John Hicks to the office of principal chief. "I had good reasons to believe that Neamathla . . . was determined . . . to raise some serious difficulties with the white people. This he was near doing during the summer of 1824, but my presence prevented it. I broke the head chief, and he removed to the Creek Nation, where he belonged. . . . It would not be amiss for you and the President to give the title of 'governor of the red men' to Hicks, as he has been elected its chief by the unanimous voice of the nation."

Duval was high-handed, self-confident, courageous, and able. His repeated acts of friendship for the Seminoles cannot be regarded simply as the humane policy of an enlightened government; for on many occasions it was Duval who spoke out plainly in favor of the Indian interest. But he had little regard for the deep-rooted customs of the people, if their customs interfered with his executive program in the Territory. He "broke" a principal chief as he would have ordered the chevrons removed from the jacket of a corporal, and had his successor named by the "unanimous voice of the nation." He was dealing with a people who were able to fight a desperate, costly war against the United States, and who could be goaded into such a conflict. Duval underestimated the pride and dignity of the Seminoles and their fierce attachment to their homes.

He was shrewd enough and straight enough to veto a contract of bad odor entered into by the agent, Gad Humphreys; but he did not see the necessity of cutting off Major Benjamin Chaires, the principal offender in a shady deal, from all part in the Seminole contracts. In directing Governor Duval to investigate thoroughly the charges made by Mr. Pindar against the contractor, Major Chaires, Superintendent Thomas L. McKenney wrote. "I am directed by the Secretary . . . to state . . . that he received . . . certain communications relating to the issuing

[4] 24 Cong., 1 sess., *Ex. Doc. 271.*

of rations, . . . and a copy of one from Charles Pindar to Colonel Walton, the complexion of which, taken altogether, was not satisfactory."[5] The governor was strongly biased in favor of the white settlers, on all claims involving Negroes in the Indian country. As an owner of slaves, Duval had grown into an attitude that was characteristic of his class; he had little regard for the desires of black people, or for the claims of Indians who held slaves in an easy relation involving payment of tribute, combined with virtual liberty for the Negroes.

On December 15, 1825, Superintendent McKenney sent an official letter which questioned sharply the methods used by the commissioners in obtaining the Treaty of Camp Moultrie, and an order to Governor Duval to "report the facts in this case, and state, explicitly, whether any resort was had to means . . . tending to force upon those Indians a compliance with the terms of said treaty."

Five days later, Lieutenant G. M. Brooke, in a report to his commanding officer on the condition of the Florida Indians, stated: "You will perceive by the ration returns for this month that more rations have been issued to the Indians than usual. This has been occasioned by a number of Indians (say from six to seven hundred) who were obliged to come to the sub-agency, near the cantonment, for the purpose of receiving their presents from the Government, agreeably to the treaty; most of them had traveled from eighty to one hundred miles, and were entirely without subsistence. The issuing of rations to the Indians under the treaty expired on the 10th of October. The major part of the nation are, and have been, suffering for some time in extreme want. Some have died from *starvation*, and many have lived upon the roots of the sweetbriar, as a substitute for bread. This is owing to several causes: 1st. The continued droughts, for two months, whilst their corn was tasseling; 2d. Those who removed within the new boundary line had to cultivate new lands which will not produce the first year of planting; and 3rd. Many did not come in until it was too late to plant.

[5] McKenney to Duval, Dec. 26, 1825, *American State Papers: Indian Affairs*, II, 642–43.

"I can assure you they are in the most miserable situation; and unless the Government assists them, many of them must starve, and others will depredate on the property of the whites in the Alachua and St. John's settlements. It is impossible for me, or any other officer who possesses the smallest feelings of humanity, to resist affording some relief to men, women, and children, who are actually dying for the want of something to eat.

"I therefore wish that an additional allowance of rations may be made for the post; and I trust that, on your representation to the Secretary of War, partial rations may be given generally, through the Indian Agent."[6]

The depredations which the army officer predicted were already appearing, in serious proportions. On December 16, 1825, Governor Duval reported: "I regret to state that about three hundred Indians have returned from the country assigned to them, and have crossed the Suwannee River. Complaints are daily made to me by the citizens against the Indians. They continue to kill cattle and steal corn from the settlers, who are now ready to take up arms, and repel the intrusion and outrages of these unfortunate people. I have sent orders to Alachua, to the commanding officer of the militia, not to permit any attack to be made on the Indians for killing cattle; and I hope you will recommend to Congress to make some provision to indemnify the citizens for their losses. I have every reason to believe that many of the Indians are in a starving condition. I have not heard from the agent on the subject of the withdrawal of the Indians from his agency. I fear he has lost all influence over them, and now nothing short of force can restrain them.

"If I had the command of two hundred regulars, and were permitted to employ two of the Apalachicola chiefs, who were once under General Jackson, with a few of their men, I could, without the danger of bloodshed, make all the Indians return to their boundary. These people have great confidence in me, yet they fear me as they should; with this force, I pledge myself that the treaty should be carried into complete execution in peace, and to your satisfaction.

6 Brooke to Col. George Gibson, Dec. 20, 1825, *ibid.*, II, 655.

"The Indians who have recrossed the Suwannee I have ordered to be furnished with twenty days' rations, and directed them immediately to return back to their lands."[7]

In January, 1826, Governor Duval was directed by Thomas L. McKenney, general superintendent of Indian affairs, to employ Major John Phagan as subagent for the Florida Indians, at a salary of five hundred dollars a year. Later in the month, Duval answered various letters from the Superintendent, some of which had been written to George Walton, secretary and acting governor of Florida. The main topics of Governor Duval's correspondence in this period are the grievances, discontent, and misery of the Seminoles, and the actual danger from the desperate natives to white settlers in the Territory.

On January 23, the Governor wrote: "I assure you that no extension of the Indian boundary will keep them from starving until their next crops come in. The Apalachicola Indians are in a deplorable state. Three times last year were their corn fields and fences swept away by the uncommon rise of the river. All these Indians live on the river, and, until now, they have never solicited the aid of the Government for provisions.

"The old chiefs Blunt and Tuski Haijo have just left me; they have given me a gloomy picture of the distress now prevailing for want of food. These chiefs and their warriors served with General Jackson during the Seminole War.

"In order to prevent the Indians from starving, the strictest economy must be pursued; and to do this, corn and salt only will be purchased for them, unless the Department should authorize some pork and beef now and then to be distributed. Small portions of either would be a blessing to these poor improvident people.

"The Indians have continued to fall back on the settlements, and have lately acted violently in Alachua, by driving a family from their farm, and taking all the provisions, and destroying part of their houses.

"I must still say that a military post ought to be established on the south frontier of Alachua. I hope, by my presence among

[7] Duval to the Secretary of War, James Barbour, Dec. 16, 1825, *ibid.*, I, 642.

the Indians, to settle . . . the causes of difference that exist between them and the citizens of Alachua. I consider a military post in that quarter as essential to the protection of the Indians as of the citizens. It would check in the bud any improper design from either party.

"The rations which were received by the agent at Tampa Bay were not all issued to the Indians; but, as they have been received, and must be lost to the Government unless they are disposed of, I have directed Colonel Humphreys to issue them to the emigrant Indians, in the most economical manner, to subsist them. These rations are the same that Colonel Walton mentioned in his last letter . . . to you, as having accumulated at Tampa Bay &c. . . .

"A very small amount of actual cash has been turned over to me by the late acting Governor. I am, therefore, without funds to meet my accounts that have been presented. . . .

"The complaints that have been made to me by the citizens of this Territory, on account of alleged losses in cattle and other property taken and destroyed by the Indians, have determined me to attend and take legal proof of these losses, and submit them to the War Department. I do believe that many who complain loudly have sustained no loss, and that the actual loss will be trifling. By taking this step, all clamor against the Indians will be silenced; and I hope the Secretary of War will approve of the measure. No evil, and much good, may result from this proceeding. Those who have just claims for indemnity will be heard in a formal manner, and all who complain will have a fair opportunity of proving the injury they have sustained. . . ."[8]

Governor Duval had to consider, from the beginning of his term, the problem of contracts for furnishing the Seminole Indians with rations of beef, corn, salt, and other articles. As in the delivery of supplies to other Indians of the Five Civilized Tribes, cases of irregularity, evasion, and outright fraud appeared in the Seminole contracts.

Major Benjamin Chaires, on May 29, 1824, offered to furnish rations for the Seminoles at "eighteen cents and one quarter of

[8] Duval to McKenney, Jan. 23, 1826, *ibid.*, II, 686.

a cent per entire ration, or beef for eight cents per ration, or as much lower as any other person will, provided the price is not lower than six cents and seven eighths of a cent per ration." Colonel Gad Humphreys published the advertisement for proposals, and after receiving a number of them, endorsed Major Chaires' bid as follows: "accepted, the security being satisfactory, and terms offered more advantageous than any other with sufficient security." Mr. Charles Pindar, who had come to Tallahassee with the intention of offering a bid on the Seminole supplies came to a private agreement with Major Chaires to make no proposal of price to the government, in return for $500 in cash, to be paid when the contract should be made and completed by Major Chaires. The governor of Florida had the final decision on contracts for supplies, and Duval rejected the Chaires bid on the ground that the price was too high. Further bids were solicited by advertisement in Florida, Charleston, New Orleans, and elsewhere. Governor Clark of Georgia came to Tallahassee in person, and submitted a bid of fourteen cents per ration. But Major Chaires submitted the lowest bid, and a contract was made with him. The deal between the successful bidder and Mr. Charles Pindar, to limit the bidding, was revealed when Chaires refused to pay the $500 he had promised, in writing, to Pindar. In view of later revelations concerning Colonel Gad Humphreys' private finances, it seems quite possible that he, as well as Major Chaires and Mr. Pindar, was in line for a substantial profit on the bidding arrangement by which an unreasonable price was obtained.

The agreement between Benjamin Chaires and Charles Pindar, on May 30, 1824, was as follows: "I promise to pay Mr. Charles Pindar, on order, the sum of five hundred dollars, on my obtaining (and completing) the contract for furnishing the Indians with beef, &c., as per the proposals requested by Colonel Gad Humphreys, Indian Agent, published in the Pensacola Gazette under date of 22d May, 1824, in consideration of the said Charles Pindar withdrawing his proposal.[9]

[9] Duval to McKenney, Jan. 24, 1826; inc. Chaires to Pindar, May 30, 1824, *ibid.*, II, 687–88.

On March 2, 1826, Governor Duval made two requests of Secretary of War James Barbour concerning Chief John Hicks: first, that he be permitted to visit Washington with a Seminole delegation of six chiefs; and second, that President Adams name him "governor of the red men in Florida."[10]

The Office of Indian Affairs objected to the visit of the Seminole delegation, and refused to grant the title of governor to Chief Hicks; but Superintendent McKenney proposed instead, "He will be distinguished by a great medal, and acknowledged as the chief of his people." A comment upon Duval's position as the government's Indian officer in Florida, and specifically upon his clash with Neamathla, showed some disapproval in the War Department.

"The Secretary approved of your talk to the Indians in the main, but thinks it proper to guard you, as the official organ of the General Government, against committing yourself in matters pertaining to the internal affairs of the Indians. . . . The making and unmaking of chiefs must be left to the Indians themselves, as also all that relates to their own regulations for their own government."

The superintendent was equally plain in his attitude on Seminole relations with the Negroes. "No buying or selling of slaves will be permitted by the agent or the agency. If the Indians own slaves, they are their property; if they secrete runaway slaves, they must give them up to their rightful owners. If the whites take theirs, the law of intercourse must be resorted to."[11]

On February 22, 1826, the Governor wrote to Superintendent McKenney a detailed account of his visit to the Seminole Reservation. "The Long Swamp, . . . is the first land near the present northern line deserving any attention. The swamp is near six miles long, very narrow, and entirely too wet for cultivation, except thirty or forty acres at its southern extremity, which is inhabited by a family of Indians; I consider it of little value. Okihumkey, signifying in our language, *one pond,* is an Indian town; the land is too poor for cultivation, and there is very little

[10] Duval to Barbour, Mar. 2, 1826, *ibid.,* II, 689.
[11] McKenney to Duval, May 8, 1826, *ibid.,* II, 698.

good land in its neighborhood. Pelacklakaha is a town occupied by the Indian Negroes; its name signifies Scattered Hammock; there is but little land fit for cultivation about it, and in the rainy season the best of it is under water. Chucuchatty, or *Red House*, is an Indian town on the margin of a large pond; it appears to be an ancient settlement. All the good lands have been exhausted by cultivation, and it is now poor, unhealthy, and has no water near it that is fit to drink. The Big Hammock is situated near this town. I spent some days in examining it, and was much disappointed in its fertility, extent, and supposed advantages. The Big Hammock is much lower than the adjoining land, which is poor, pine, sandy hills, wholly unfit for cultivation. There is a large pond in the center of this hammock, with several drains; in the wet season, it is the greater part under water; in the dry season there is no water except in this large pond. The soil, from its growth of timber, would induce a passing observer to believe it very fertile; but I found, on examining the land in many places, that it is a light mould two or three inches deep, based on white sand, and would, if cultivated, in three years become a bed of sand. The whole extent of this hammock would not make more than a township. There is but one small Indian settlement in it, and, take it altogether, I feel confident it has been vastly overrated. I think that a man who is a judge of land would not give more than one dollar per acre for the best of it above high water mark, which would be but a small part of the whole hammock. I traveled but a small distance, in going south, on the military road. I left it near Okihumky, and examined the whole country on the right of the road as far as Tampa Bay. I visited every spot where land was spoken of as being good, and I can say with truth, I have not seen three hundred acres of good land in my whole route, after leaving the agency. The lands on the Big and Little Withlecoucha are poor, and the lands on Hillsborough river, within the Indian boundary, are of so little value that there is not one Indian settlement on any one of them. I did not visit Peas Creek; I had suffered so much from drinking water alive with insects, from mosquitoes, and from intolerable hot weather, and my horses were so much reduced by the journey and the swarms of horseflies, that I determined to leave that point unexplored, having received satisfactory information that there is but a small tract of good land in that quarter. I have never seen a more wretched tract of country than that which I entered five or six miles south of Chucuchatty; the sand hills rise very high, and the Indian trail winds over an extensive sand ridge, for eight or nine miles; the whole of the timber for this distance, as far as the eye can survey, has been killed by fire; the burnt and blackened pines, without a leaf, added to the dreary poverty of the land, present the most miserable and gloomy prospect I ever beheld. After descending the southern extremity of this ridge, I entered a low, wet, piney country, spotted with numerous ponds. I had much difficulty to pass through them, although the season has been uncommonly dry; had much rain fallen, I never could have reached Tampa Bay in that direction. So low was the whole country as far as the Indian boundary extended toward Tampa Bay, that, after riding all day and until eleven o'clock at night, in the hope that I would find a dry spot to sleep upon, I was compelled to take up my lodging on a low wet place for the night. No settlement can ever be made in this region, and there is no land in it worth cultivation. The best of the Indian lands are worth but little; nineteen-twentieths of their whole country within the present boundary is by far the poorest and most miserable region I ever beheld. I have therefore to advise, as my duty demands, and the honor and humanity of my country require, that the Big Swamp be also given to the Indians, and that the northern line be fixed five miles north of the Big Swamp, and extended to the Okelawaha river east, and so far west as to include the Big Hammock; this line will take in no good land but the Big Swamp, of any consequence; but, by extending it into the pine barren five miles, it will keep off settlers from the Indian boundary, who would otherwise crowd near the line, and sell whiskey to the Indians. The pine Barren between the south end of Alachua and the Big Swamp is poor, and never can be cultivated; the distance is about twenty-five miles. The Big Swamp is six miles long and is about two miles wide, and is healthy, high, rich land."[12]

In a "talk" delivered to the Seminole chiefs by William Duval early in 1826, statements were made in the name of the Great Father at Washington, which sharply contradicted the Governor's report to Thomas McKenney, given in part above.

"How is it, my red children, that many of you act wrong and very bad, that you kill the hogs and cattle of the white people, and that you take their potatoes and corn, and burn their houses? Do you not expect such bad actions will occasion war? Beware, in time, of your danger; for if you sit still, and let your bad people continue such conduct, mighty evils will soon fall on the whole of your nation." It will be recalled that the Governor reported his doubts concerning bad conduct of the Indians.

"Listen to your great father, my red children; you have good hunting ground to the south. . . . You must not go into the white settlements to hunt. . . . I wish you to do good, and then you will be happy. . . ." But the Seminole's chances for happiness were indeed slender under conditions such as Duval had described, in the "unhealthy, poor, low, wet, miserable" region of his tour through Seminole lands, where insects swarmed, and good water to drink was not available.

"Make fields, and raise corn and provisions," the great father's talk directed them. "The best of the Indian lands are worth but little," the Governor's candid report stated.

"Chiefs, headmen, and warriors: If your bad men are not kept under, your annuity will be taken from you to pay the white people for the damage they have done. I give no corn to my white children; they are obliged to raise their own provisions; you see I have been kinder to you than to them." The irony of this statement must have been apparent, even to the Great Father, John Quincy Adams, who had never been in Florida; as to Duval, it is hard to understand why he did not choke on this portion of the "talk."

"Chiefs and warriors: You hold Negroes in your nation that belong to the white people. By the treaty, you are bound to deliver all the Negroes that do not belong to the Indians to the agent; this you have not done, although you have promised in

[12] Duval to McKenney, Feb. 22, 1826, *ibid.*, II, 688–89.

our talks to do so; you are now called upon to fulfill the treaty. You are not to mind what the Negroes say; they will lie, and lead you astray, in the hope to escape from their rightful owners, and that you will give them refuge and hide them: do your duty, and give them up. They care nothing for you, further than to make use of you to keep out of the hands of their masters. . . . Your conduct in this matter is cause of loud, constant, and just complaint on the part of the white people, who are thus deprived of their slaves." The accusation in this part of the "talk" should be compared with statements made by territorial officials concerning the guilt of white citizens in claims for fugitive slaves, and the countercharges made by the Seminoles. The suggestion that the Negroes were using the Indians for their own selfish interest is presumptuous when it is understood that these Seminoles, for many years, had been giving refuge to the runaway slaves through sympathy and a desire to aid the blacks; and that the Negroes, by alliance in war and friendship at other times, had made themselves the valued and trusted neighbors of the Indians. To be sure, there were exceptions to the general rule of understanding and confidence between the two peoples. In many instances outbreaks of hostility against the whites were traceable to the efforts of some adventurer who was in the business of promoting trouble for his own interest. Under the Spanish regime, it was men such as William Augustus Bowles or Colonel Edward Nicholls; after 1819, it was the speculator in land or the sharp dealer in Negroes of the Seminole country.

John Hicks, Duval's own choice for the office of Seminole principal chief, replied to the "talk" of the Great Father, and addressed his words to the governor whom he knew personally. The reply was conciliatory, but that did not signify agreement of the Seminoles in the policy that was behind the biased statement and the threats pronounced by Duval. The desperate struggle for existence that was to break out ten years later, in which the Seminoles demonstrated hardihood and courage not often found among people of any race, was not the result of sudden determination by a lawless people to engage in war. Rather, it was the outcome of a deep sense of injustice, built up through years of experience with Europeans bent upon possessing the Indian country. The government of the United States was not at the peak of its generosity and understanding in the great father's "talk," delivered to the Seminole Indians by the Great Father's agent, Governor Duval.

"Your talk is right, and we will keep it in mind," Hicks said in reply; but he added, "It is not my fault that my nation is poor and has lost its land." The chief agreed to bring in runaway Negroes, but said: "The white people have got some of our Negroes, which we expect they will be made to give up."

The Indian leader also charged, "Some of our people have had cattle and hogs killed by the whites; we hope justice will be done to us and that you will keep the bad white men from doing us any more mischief." His observations concerning bad citizens were wiser and more diplomatic than the references to such characters by Duval.

"There are bad men among all people, the white as well as the red," said Chief Hicks.[13]

13 *Ibid.*, II, 690–91.

CHAPTER 9

Agitation for Indian Removal, 1826–34

"These people are strongly attached to Major Phagan."

S. C. STAMBAUGH

THE SECRETARY OF WAR, John C. Calhoun, reported to President Monroe in January, 1825, on the subject of Indian removal to the West. He gave 97,000 as the number of Indians within the United States and its territories, excluding the "portion . . . west of Lake Michigan and north of the State of Illinois." The extent of the Indian lands, Calhoun revealed, —was 77,000,000 acres, or about 800 acres per capita. At that time the nation contained about 100 acres of land per capita for the entire population.

The Seminoles and their neighbors, recently acquired in the purchase of territory from Spain, were estimated at 5,000, and Calhoun dismissed them with this brief statement: "It is believed that immediate measures need not be taken with regard to the Indians of Florida. By the treaty of September 18, 1823, they ceded the whole northern portion of Florida, with the exception of a few small reservations, and have had allotted to them the southern part of the peninsula; and it is probable that no inconvenience will be felt for many years, either by the inhabitants of Florida, or the Indians, under the present arrangement."[1] In our glimpse of the actual operation of the Moultrie Treaty in the previous chapter, a considerable amount of "inconvenience"

[1] Calhoun to Monroe, Jan. 24, 1825; Monroe to the Senate of the United States, Jan. 27, 1825, *American State Papers: Indian Affairs*, II, 541-44.

118

was found among the hungry Seminoles who recrossed the Suwannee and engaged in hunting the cattle of white settlers; and among the scattered Indian villagers where death by starvation overtook Seminole citizens. Isolated white planters, too, were obviously outside of Secretary Calhoun's view of the subject, when their houses became the object of attack by desperate Indian bands. Many War Department reports on the Seminole Indians were based upon meager information; but this statement by the great South Carolina politician combined sheer stupidity with the customary ignorance.

In December, 1825, Calhoun's successor in the War Department, James Barbour, sent to President John Quincy Adams a gloomy report on the Seminoles by Lieutenant G. M. Brooke, and the President forwarded the correspondence to Congress. Secretary Barbour suggested their removal westward. "It is hoped they may accede to the proposition," Barbour wrote. "Meantime, however, humanity demands that they should be kept from starving. . . . Connecting the object of the removal of those Indians with that of their immediate relief, I would suggest that the sum of fifty thousand dollars be appropriated, with a view to both."

Less restricted by lack of information, and not quite so smug as the earlier opinion of Secretary Calhoun, the statement by the new head of the War Department was still far from showing the knowledge and imagination necessary for dealing with the complicated Seminole problem. On its economic side, a land exchange of vast extent was involved, together with large values in chattels. The removal of a reluctant people from their homes, twice within a decade, was not to be undertaken lightly. Secretary Barbour, like his predecessor, was offering a tragically small estimate of a great task. He was basing his proposal upon an underestimate of Seminole resources, will, and courage. He had no adequate grasp, even of the monetary cost of removal, or the potential values in property that the Indians were being asked to surrender. Particularly, he had no concept of the dangers of war from the blundering of officials assigned to duty with the Seminoles, and from belligerent white neighbors of the tribe in Florida and adjacent states.

As settlers poured into Florida along the Georgia frontier, pressure for removal of the Indians grew steadily on both sides of the line. In 1821, at Indian Springs, the Creeks ceded to the United States a tract of land on the Chattahoochee; and in 1825, the tribal leaders who advocated removal signed a second Treaty of Indian Springs by which land was ceded without the consent of the Council, in defiance of Creek law. For this unwarranted assumption of power, the Coweta chieftain, William McIntosh, and a part of his followers were executed, after the death sentence was passed by the Council.[2] During the following year, the Adams administration repudiated the Treaty of Indian Springs and negotiated an agreement more favorable to the Creeks than the McIntosh treaty.

In the Florida lands recently vacated by the Seminoles, development of towns and plantations was rapid. At Tallahassee, streets were laid out in squares and given names—Washington, Adams, Greene, Jackson, Bronaugh, McCarthy, Gaines, Gadsden, and Call—although the plots extended much farther than cleared land. The first flimsy houses were replaced by dwellings of hewn logs, and in 1826 the first wing of the statehouse was completed. Several churches, a masonic lodge, and housing for an agricultural society had been built by that time, and ten stores were in operation. Florida elected as its first delegates to Congress, Joseph M. Hernandez and Richard K. Call.[3]

One of the nation's early railroads, chartered in 1834, was carrying passengers and goods from Tallahassee to St. Marks, and within a few years to Port Leon. The mule cars first used were replaced later by locomotives. Congress had made provision for a post road from Pensacola to St. Augustine, and Colonel John Bellamy obtained the contract for building it. Other roads were constructed from principal communities in northern Florida across the Georgia line to older settlements, and from the St. Mary's River to Tampa. Virgin forest still covered the greater part of the land in the north, and the Seminole

[2] *Ibid.*, II, 249, 563–84; Wright, *Guide to the Indian Tribes of Oklahoma*, 133; Debo, *The Road to Disappearance*, 86.
[3] Brevard, *History of Florida*, I, 91, 102.

country east of Tampa Bay was practically untouched by the white man's civilization.

The planters in Florida produced corn, rice, sugar cane, and cotton. Cattle, hogs, and horses flourished throughout the farming area, and an ample supply of timber was found for local use. In the Euchee Valley of West Florida, an unusual settlement grew up under the leadership of Neil McLendon, who first came to the region on foot from North Carolina in 1820. The Euchee chief, Sam Story, welcomed McLendon and permitted him to bring in his family and a little settlement of Scotch Presbyterian friends, including the McKinnon, McKaskell, and McLeod families. A friendly relation grew up between these settlers and the Euchee Indians. Livestock, grain, cotton, and sugar cane were produced; a cotton gin was run by the McKinnons and a saw mill and a grist mill by Alexander McLeod.

The Euchee Indians, like the other natives of Florida, felt the pressure of white settlement as new immigrants arrived in steadily increasing numbers. Sam Story considered removal of his people to the West, but finally decided to settle in the everglades of Florida. The Chief's white friends were invited to join him in the removal but no general agreement was reached.[4] The McKinnon family remained in the region which became Walton County, Florida, while some of McLendon's followers moved to west Texas.

One of the most remarkable settlers in Florida Territory was the nephew of Napoleon Bonaparte, Achille Murat. He was the son of Marshal Joachim Murat and his wife Caroline, sister of the Emperor Napoleon. He was twenty-four when he arrived at St. Augustine in company with President Thomas Cooper of South Carolina College, in the year 1825. Young Murat had lived under a great variety of conditions before he came to America, and it is safe to say that his life in Florida was not only different from anything that had gone before, but was in many respects more interesting and useful. At the age of five, he had been Duke of Berg and Cleves; at seven, crown prince of Naples; at fourteen, a royal exile; and at twenty-one an immigrant to the United States, the relative of a former emperor.

[4] *Ibid.*, I, 107–11.

Kate Murat, the wife whom he married a year after he came to Florida, was the great grandniece of George Washington.

Murat traveled west from St. Augustine on the old Spanish trail, carrying with him his chattels—household goods, slaves, one hundred head of cattle, and a "pet owl." On the road, the party subsisted largely upon wild game. He met James Gadsden, who had come to Florida as an aid-de-camp to General Jackson in 1818, and in civil life had become a surveyor and road builder.[5]

Achille Murat and Gadsden became partners in the management of a plantation which they called Warcissa, situated fifteen miles west of the territorial capital. Richard Keith Call, who had opened a land office in Tallahassee, became a business acquaintance of Murat and Gadsden. Murat came into possession of an estate which he called Lipona, where he and his beautiful wife became famous for their entertainment of distinguished visitors. In a letter to a friend in Europe, Achille drew a sharp word picture of a visit by Governor William P. Duval to James Gadsden, in the rough setting of the primitive American territory. "What would you say," wrote Murat, "if you saw a man wearing a tattered straw hat, deerskin trousers, blue stockings, shoes covered with mud, riding a raw-boned horse, arriving to consult another man dressed in much the same way, about a treaty with the Indians?"[6]

The presidency of Andrew Jackson was distinguished by growing hostility of settlers against the southern Indians, a pressure that was reflected in the Removal Act passed by Congress in 1830, and in the attitude of Indian agents and special commissioners. In 1832, Jackson's secretary of war, Lewis Cass, appointed Colonel James Gadsden of Tallahassee to negotiate with the Seminoles concerning removal from Florida to the West. It was the young surveyor's task to convince Seminole leaders that they ought to do two things, both against their better judgment, which had become twin ideas in the minds of Georgia and Florida people: to remove westward, and to reunite with the Creek tribe.

[5] A. J. Hanna, *A Prince in their Midst*, 89–105.
[6] *Ibid.*, 112.

The officials of Florida Territory succeeded in assembling Seminole delegates at Payne's Landing on the Ocklawaha River in the spring of 1832. On May 9, a treaty was signed by Gadsden for the United States, and by a few Seminole chiefs for the Florida Indians. The preamble, which contained a clause that was not explicit, became the subject of endless controversy. The disputed portion of the document contained the following provisions:

"The Seminole Indians . . . are willing that their confidential chiefs, Jumper, Fuch-a-lusti-hadjo, Charley Emartla, Coi-hadjo, Holati-Emartla, Ya-ha-hadjo, Sam Jones, accompanied by their agent, Major Phagan, and their faithful interpreter, Abraham, should be sent at the expense of the United States, as early as convenient, to examine the country assigned to the Creeks west of the Mississippi River; and should they be satisfied with the character of that country, and of the favorable disposition of the Creeks to reunite with the Seminoles as one people, the articles of the compact and agreement, herein stipulated at Payne's Landing on the Ocklawaha River, this ninth day of May, one thousand eight hundred and thirty-two, between James Gadsden, for and in behalf of the Government of the United States, and the undersigned chiefs and head men, for and in behalf of the Seminole Indians, shall be binding on the respective parties."[7]

Seven articles followed, stipulating that the Seminoles should give up their lands in Florida and emigrate to the Creek country west of the Mississippi; that the United States should pay the Seminoles $15,400 for their real improvements in Florida upon their arrival in the Creek country (of which Abraham and Cudjo were to receive $200 each); that the United States should distribute, as the Seminoles arrived in their new homes, a blanket and a homespun frock to each of the warriors, women, and children; and extend the annuity for support of a blacksmith ten years beyond the date set by the Treaty of Camp Moultrie; and in addition to other annuities secured under that treaty,

[7] *Compilation of All the Treaties Between the United States and the Indian Tribes*, 807–808.

to pay the tribe $3,000 per year for fifteen years; to pay the owners of cattle for their losses; and liquidate all claims against the Seminoles for slaves and other property provided the total amount, after investigation, should not exceed $7,000.

Article Seven contained a clause with a time limit, which the United States failed to meet. Had justice to the Indians been regarded a basic consideration, the government, because of this failure, would have reopened the entire negotiation instead of adopting the arrogant view which Jackson's appointees felt obliged to take. The Seventh Article contained the following provisions:

"The Seminole Indians will remove within three years after the ratification of this agreement, . . . the emigration to commence as early as practicable in the year eighteen hundred and thirty-three (1833), and with those Indians occupying the Big Swamp, and other parts of the country beyond the limits as defined in the second article of the treaty concluded at Camp Moultrie Creek, so that the whole of that proportion of the Seminoles may be removed within the year aforesaid, and the remainder of the tribe in about equal proportions during the subsequent years of eighteen hundred and thirty-four and five (1834 and 1835)."[8]

Seminole explorers with their agent and interpreters made the journey to the Creek country which extended north from the lower Canadian across the Arkansas River about twenty-five miles, and westward to the limits of the United States. The Seminole party traveled by boat to New Orleans and by river steamer up the Mississippi and the Arkansas, to a point some two hundred miles below Fort Gibson. For the last stage of the journey and the exploration of the Creek lands, the chiefs and their companions were supplied with horses to ride. They reached Fort Gibson in November, 1832, spent about five weeks in the examination of their proposed new home, and assembled with Major Phagan at Fort Gibson to confer with the Montfort Stokes Commission, sent west by President Jackson to deal with

8 *Ibid.*, 808.

a great variety of Indian problems. On March 28, 1833, the Seminoles were induced to give reluctant and partial approval to a document which government authorities prepared for completion of the Payne's Landing Treaty. The agreement thus imposed upon the delegates stated that the character of the country they had explored was satisfactory.[9]

The Stokes Commission had reached an agreement with the Creeks on February 14, 1833, which defined the boundaries of the Creek Nation, provided for removal of the Seminole tribe to Creek lands, and for the Seminoles to become a constituent part of the Creek Nation. The language of the Seminole agreement, with names of the Seminole delegation affixed by means of cross marks, is significant for its legal form, explicit phrasing, and evasive intent. The purpose was to clear the way for removal of the Seminoles, with or without their consent; but under such forms of negotiation and agreement as to leave the impression that the Indians, without coercion, had signed a treaty to remove.

"Whereas, the Seminole Indians . . . entered into certain articles of agreement with James Gadsden, . . ." this portion of the document ran; and the article of the Payne's Landing Treaty, providing cession of all their land in Florida after certain conditions had been met, was quoted. The Creeks had agreed to the terms, the Seminole delegates were satisfied, and the commissioners were ready, "by virtue of the power and authority vested in them" to assign a definite tract of Creek land to the Seminole Indians. The country assigned was the land extending west from the junction of North Fork with the Canadian to a line extending from north to south between these two streams, and crossing the forks of Little River.

For the United States, the three members of the Stokes Commission signed the agreement; and the following names of the Seminole chiefs were affixed, each with a cross mark; Holahti Emathla, Ouschmatche (Jumper), Charley Emathla, Ya-ha-hadjo (Mad Wolf), Ne-hath-clo, Fuch-a-lusti-hadjo (Black Dirt), and Coi-hadjo. The name Arpeika (Sam Jones) mentioned in the

---

[9] Kappler, *Indian Affairs: Laws and Treaties*, II, 394; *Compilation of All the Treaties* . . . , 809.

THE SEMINOLES

preamble of the Payne's Landing Treaty, does not appear on the Fort Gibson agreement.[10]

The Fort Gibson document made a slight change in the words taken from the preamble of the Treaty of Payne's Landing. Instead of, "and should *they* be satisfied," the later agreement substituted, "and should *this delegation* be satisfied." The pronoun *they* in Gadsden's treaty was the word which made the instrument, in a most important provision, ambiguous. The evidence is strong that all members of the exploring party regarded their agreement at Fort Gibson simply an expression of their favorable opinion of the country between the Canadian and its north branch.

On April 3, 1833, the secretary of the Stokes Commission at Fort Gibson, S. C. Stambaugh, wrote to the secretary of war, Lewis Cass, that Major Phagan was about ready to go back to Florida. The writer noted that the Seminole chiefs, after thirty-two days of exploring the Little River country, "appeared to be much pleased." He also had a good word for the Agent: "These people are strongly attached to Major Phagan, and he appears to have their interests and welfare deeply at heart, without losing sight of the interests of the gov't. Gov. Stokes, the old, excellent, and steady friend of us all, wrote a letter a few days ago on this subject in which I heartily concur."[11]

James Gadsden, Major Phagan, and James D. Westcott, Jr., the acting governor of Florida, were all eager to see the end of negotiation and the beginning of Seminole removal. Nearly all of Phagan's acquaintances in the Indian Service seemed to be impressed with his fitness for the job of supervising the removal; but unfortunately, irregularities appeared in his financial accounts which could not be explained satisfactorily, and he was

[10] *Compilation of All the Treaties* . . . , 807–10; Kappler, *Indian Affairs: Laws and Treaties*, II, 394. Apparently, Ne-hath-clo had been sent as a substitute for Sam Jones. Other Seminoles accompanied the party. One of these was Tulkee-Emathla who was recommended by James Gadsden because he had two sons and two uncles in the West, which would influence the delegates in favor of emigration. (Gadsden to Cass, June 29, 1832, O.I.A.: Seminoles.)

[11] Stambaugh to Cass, Apr. 3, 1833; Westcott to Bellamy (Com. of Ind. Aff.,) Feb. 2, 1832; Gadsden to Cass, Dec. 4, 1833, O.I.A.: Seminoles–Emigration.

discharged from office before actual removal began. Whether or not Phagan could have managed the task of removal better than his successor, Wiley Thompson, who was to forfeit his life trying to do the job, is a question on which we can only speculate. It is certain, however, that Phagan was guilty of gross misconduct in his handling of funds, and it is probable that the better informed Indians knew it and despised him. On the other hand, there is evidence that the tribe as a whole had a very real affection for the man.[12]

The time element in the Treaty of Payne's Landing, violated by the United States, is one item that was never explained away, even by those contemporary officials who were insistent upon holding the Indians to the letter of their agreement, ignoring the customs of the tribe and violating the fiduciary relation that was supposed to exist between them and the government. It is strange indeed to find a treaty of the United States ratified by the Senate with solemn constitutional formality and proclaimed by the President as being in effect on April 12, 1834, and to find in the final clause of that treaty an important obligation of the United States to be performed in the year 1833. The Jackson administration did not get the Seminole treaties ratified soon enough to enable officers of the government to live up to their side of the two treaties. Thomas L. McKenney, former chief of the Bureau of Indian Affairs, broke sharply with Jackson on the Seminole documents that were drawn up at Payne's Landing and Fort Gibson.

"Not only did this delay in ratification occur," McKenney wrote in his *Memoirs,* "but it was not for some time after, that means were appropriated to carry it into effect. It . . . therefore had lost every spark of its vitality . . . and was called by the Indians, in derision, 'A white man's treaty.'" Yet Jackson had the effrontery to tell the Seminoles: "I have directed your friend, General Thompson," to remove one-third of the tribe during 1835, *"as provided for in the treaty."* McKenney added, "The

---

[12] Com. of Ind. Aff. to Major John Phagan, Jan. 24, 1832; J. Nollner to Lewis Cass, Aug. 16, 1833; Henry M. Moffit to Lewis Cass, Aug. 22, 1833, *ibid.;* Wright, *Guide to the Indian Tribes of Oklahoma,* 231.

treaty provided for no such thing. It provided for such removal in 1833, the Indians ratifying it, but not in 1835."[13]

Jackson's "talk" then notified the Seminoles that, in the event of their refusal to go quietly and voluntarily, the commanding officer had been directed to remove them by force. Regardless of the interpretation placed upon the preamble to Gadsden's treaty —whether the *delegates* of the exploring party, or the *Seminole Tribe* had to agree that they were satisfied with the conditions of removal to make the cession of Florida land binding—the decision to hold the Indians to a narrow view of the two documents, contrary to their well established custom, was a major blunder. Such mistakes cannot be laid at the door of one official —Duval, Humphreys, or Phagan; Henry Barbour, Lewis Cass, or John Eaton; nor even at the door of President Andrew Jackson who was not only the leader of Indian policies that were shortsighted and unwise, but also the product of an age in which popular demand was for quick, temporary expedients—blundering, hasty action. The nation supported Jackson's Indian policies, or accepted them without much reluctance. The Seminoles were the victims of a growing, turbulent, dynamic society in which justice had to give way to the vigorous surge in favor of material development.

When the Seminole exploring party returned to Florida in 1833, the tribal leaders asked for a general council to consider their report. Agent John Phagan, already under the scrutiny of his superiors with regard to his accounts, took the position that there was no question of removal to be settled by the tribe, and refused to call the council.

Phagan's successor as Seminole agent in September, 1833, was General Wiley Thompson of Georgia. Thompson was a native of Virginia and a resident of Georgia for many years. A man of more than ordinary ability, he was fifty-two, and inclined to ill health. He had served as a militia officer in the War of 1812, rising to the rank of major general. After two years he was elected for six consecutive terms to the United States House of Representatives, where he supported President Jack-

[13] Thomas L. McKenney, *Memoirs, Official and Personal*, 274–76.

son's policy of Indian removal. Elbert Herring, also a Jackson man and a strong advocate of Indian removal, became commissioner of Indian affairs.

As secretary of war, Lewis Cass received many complaints about Major Phagan's drafts upon the War Department. The Honorable Joseph M. White, member of the United States House of Representatives, sent charges supported by affidavits against Major Phagan to Cass and to President Jackson. On January 24, 1832, Secretary Cass replied as follows: "The President has referred to this Dept. your letter to him . . . concerning Major Phagan, the Indian Agent of Florida.

"Copies of these papers will be immediately forwarded to Major Phagan, and he will be called upon for such explanation as he may wish to make."

A draft for $500 cashed by the Tallahassee Mercantile Company, and dishonored, became the object of inquiry by G. W. Harris, another member of Congress, who hoped to recover the amount of the draft "to be paid out of his (Phagan's) accruing salary." But the War Department had already settled with the Seminole Agent, and his creditors complained: "The Major drew upon the Department knowing at the time that nothing was due him in order to obtain money without intending its payment."[14]

A separate treaty had been made at Tallahassee with the Indians of the Apalachicola on October 11, 1832, by which it was provided that Chiefs Blount and Davy with their followers, together with the warriors and families belonging to the band of Tuski Hadjo (deceased), a total of 256 persons, should remove beyond the limits of the United States not later than November 1, 1834. Other treaties provided a choice for Valcapasacy (Mulatto King), Tustenuggy Hadjo, and Econchatimico, of remain-

---

[14] See Laverty Cantly and Co., correspondence, also, J. Nollier to Cass, Aug. 16, 1833; and J. B. Thornton, Second Comptroller's Office, to Lewis Cass, Aug. 29, 1833, O. I. A.: Seminoles—Emigration, 1833. Thornton wrote: "Of the vouchers exhibited by Major Phagan, twelve were found to have been so altered as to increase their aggregate amount." For Joseph M. White's correspondence, see Cass to White, Jan. 24, 1832; Cass to White, Jan. 25, 1832; Herring to Phagan, Jan. 27, 1832, O. I. A. Letters Sent, No. 8, 1832.

ing in Florida Territory, subject to the government and laws thereof, or of migrating to "a country of their choice." The United States agreed to pay Blount and Davy $13,000 for the surrender of their lands; and offered to pay Mulatto King and Tustenuggy Hadjo $3,000 for their land, provided those leaders elected to remove under the provisions of the Treaty of Payne's Landing; and offered the same amount to Econchatimico with the same condition. Annuities in the amount of $5,000 were to be continued to these Indians of the Apalachicola during the time that they remained in Florida.[15]

Wiley Thompson, the new Seminole agent, received his first letter of instructions written on November 23, 1833, by Governor William P. Duval. "You will proceed from this place (Tallahassee) to the Agency immediately, and take possession of the same, and all the books, papers, &c., in relation to Indian affairs." Duval urged the new agent to prepare the Seminole chiefs for removal, to order back young Indians who were visiting at a distance from their towns, and to report for further instructions after attending to removal of the Apalachicola bands. The Governor warned Thompson that his expenses away from the agency were not to exceed $3 per day.[16]

The situation of Chief Blount on the Apalachicola was a difficult one. He had an exploring party in the Trinity Valley of Texas looking for a suitable place to settle his band. Some of his young men were reluctant to go west, and were hiding out in the Seminole reservation. Violent attacks had been made upon his town, the details of which were related to Governor Duval by the subagent, D. M. Sheffield. Hugh Robinson, Silas Wood, and Jackson Wood had come down from Alabama with a small party of Indians, claimed Chief Cochran's widow and three children as their kindred, and snatched them away, together with their movable goods such as cattle and hogs. Blount was severely beaten. Warrants were issued and some arrests resulted. Philip Oaks and George Stafford were caught and charged with

[15] *Compilation of All the Treaties* . . . , 1–6; Coe, *Red Patriots*, 260–62.

[16] *American State Papers: Military Affairs*, VI, 457 Duval to Thompson, Nov. 23, 1833, *American State Papers: Military Affairs*, VI, 457. The name of the chief at Iola was spelled in two ways, *Blunt* and *Blount*, in the official records.

being parties to the outrage, but escaped. Acting Governor James B. Westcott, Jr., offered $100 to any person who would give information leading to the arrest and conviction of Oaks and Stafford.

Preparations for removing to Texas were delayed by the necessity of returning boys of Blount's band from Choctaw Academy, a boarding school founded by Richard M. Johnson in Kentucky. On November 29, 1833, Governor Duval explained to Commissioner Elbert Herring the situation on the Apalachicola. Duval had advanced $300 to send out an exploring party; and subsequently, acting Governor Westcott had advanced to Blount and Davy Elliot $1,500 of the $13,000 due the Indians for their land, after removal. Evidence in regard to the robbery of Blount was being collected, and the Governor stated, "I am satisfied, from what Mr. Westcott says, no delay will take place on that ground. I trust the arrival of the Indian boys will not be delayed."

To guarantee speedy delivery of the school boys, Wiley Thompson started for Kentucky to fetch them; but other steps had been taken for their return, and they arrived in Tallahassee on January 13, 1834. Five other Indian boys were returned from Kentucky shortly afterward. In his letters to Duval about the boys from Choctaw Academy, Wiley Thompson reported his early impressions of the Florida Indians. "That there are collections of runaway slaves, and Indians who are outlaws from their nation, there can be no doubt," he stated. "The slaves belonging to the Indians have a controlling influence over their masters, and are utterly opposed to any change of residence." General Thompson suggested that more troops would be needed at Fort Brooke on Tampa Bay, if the Indians were to be removed. He complained that unlicensed traders were a disturbing factor, and added that the outlaw bands would have to be broken up, "for as long as they are permitted to remain, every Indian who is unwilling to emigrate will seek their protection and support."[17]

The problems of Wiley Thompson's early months as agent

[17] Duval to Herring, Nov. 29, 1833; Jan. 20, 1834, *ibid.*, VI, 457–58.

are revealed in his official reports. He feared that lawless white men or Indians would rob Chief Blount as he attempted to leave the country with the large cash payment he had received.

Of the 256 Indians stipulated for removal with this band, General Thompson reported, "Some have died, some have fled to the Creek and Seminole Nations, while there are some, I fear, who will give us trouble before we get them off."

White claimants of slaves held by the Indians were a principal source of disorder. While Judge Cameron's court was considering the evidence in these claims, white men tried to take the slaves by force, and the Indians of Econchatimico's band, supported by the Negroes, took up arms and prepared to resist. Thompson approved the order of D. M. Sheffield that the Indians should protect their property by force, but warned them "to be very cautious not to commit any wanton aggression." The Agent reported attempts to bribe steamboat captains on the Apalachicola to seize Negroes. A court decision for the Indian claimant, thought General Thompson, would not give him permanent protection.[18]

Wiley Thompson reported that he had found young warriors from Blount's town on a hunting expedition with the Seminole chief, Fuch-a-lusti-hadjo, who was reluctant to order the Apalachicola boys back to their own towns. The Chew Cochatta and Peas Creek Indians, the Agent said, were in favor of removal; many others opposed. Old Micanopy, principal chief of the Seminoles, a descendant of Oconee leaders, and hereditary ruler of his people, was personally against removal. His reasons for opposition were: fear of the union with the Creeks who would control a united national council, and fear that the Seminoles would be compelled to give up their slave property.[19] Thompson deplored the influence of traders, whiskey dealers, and swindlers. "hovering on and all around the Indian border," and shrewdly opposed to Seminole removal. The whiskey dealers encouraged degeneracy and bought cow hides with the brands cut out. "Their grasping avarice, and the convenience of pond water, tempted

18 Thompson to Duval, Jan. 20, 1834, *ibid.*, VI, 451.
19 *Ibid.*, VI, 453; Wright, *Guide to the Indian Tribes of Oklahoma*, 231.

them to make two barrels of whiskey out of one. They are thus reaping a golden harvest which will be blasted by the removal of the Indians."

General Thompson took particular notice of an island settlement southeast of Charlotte Harbor on the Gulf Coast. The population was composed of Negroes, Indians, and Spaniards—"a lawless, motley crew." A kindred settlement on the mainland added their influence against Seminole removal. These settlements on the southwest coast gave the Indians contact with the "clandestine Spanish trader."

The long connection of General Thompson with the politics of Georgia is reflected in some parts of his report. In a reference to claims allowed the citizens of Georgia under the first Treaty of Indian Springs, in 1821, he wrote: "As a representative of that State, I have often urged, and still think, that a part of the Georgia claims were improperly rejected." Since Georgia, in the treaty, gave up all claims against the Creeks for property destroyed or captured prior to the year 1802, the citizens who claimed losses could receive compensation only from the United States. The President had rejected all claims for interest, property destroyed, and increase of slave property. A balance of nearly $150,000 remained in the fund, and any public man who could get a substantial part of it for the state would undoubtedly better his standing with Georgia voters. General Thompson wanted to link removal legislation with a federal law on the settlement of claims, "so as to operate as an additional inducement" to removal.

Creek claims on Seminole Negroes, free and slave, added confusion to a problem already complicated. For example, John Winslett, who described himself as a "citizen of the Creek Nation west of the Mississippi," presented a demand for Negroes held by the Seminoles. The commissioner of Indian affairs, Elbert Herring, wrote to Governor Duval, "It would seem that the demand is well founded in equity." Of the same case, Wiley Thompson reported to Duval: "The Creek Indians cannot be supposed to have a fair claim to the Negroes."

The United States had paid the citizens of Georgia for the

Negroes in question, out of money allowed the Creek Nation for lands ceded under terms of the treaty of January 8, 1821. But some of the slaves had their own solution for the problem. In December, 1833, John Winslett signed a statement to the effect that he had pursued three runaway Negroes from Georgia to Florida, and lost them in the vicinity of Tampa Bay. He feared to go farther because of the settlements of desperate men near Charlotte Harbor.[20]

As a new agent, Wiley Thompson asked two questions concerning the extent of his powers: (1) "Does the agent have the power to order white persons out of the Indian country for misconduct? and (2) Does he have the power to order out free persons of color?" Governor Duval found legal ground for expulsion of whiskey peddlers, but none for ordering out law-abiding persons of color.

The removal of Blount's Apalachicola band brought new troubles for the chief and continued the hardships his followers had suffered in Florida. While the Indians were assembled at Apalachicola Bay, before taking a boat for New Orleans, demands were made upon Blount by an Alabama man named Price, accompanied by his attorney, for payment of an alleged debt. The claim, which the Agent said was for no more than three or four hundred dollars, was denied by Wiley Thompson who referred Price to the War Department for settlement. The claimants agreed, but Thompson suspected that they intended to follow Blount beyond the protection of the United States.

The Agent accompanied the emigrants to New Orleans, landing them below the city in an effort to elude Price; but the Indians, in possession of cash received for their land, loitered in New Orleans after Thompson had gone back to Florida, and were charged in court by the Alabama claimants with avoiding debts and running away with mortgaged slaves in the amount of $2,000. Chief Blount paid the amount, took a receipt, and supposed the matter settled; but the Indians still had cash and Negroes, which was a challenge to the men who had followed them. Other charges were trumped up, and Chief Blount was

[20] *American State Papers: Military Affairs*, VI, 453, 459.

placed in jail along with Osia Hadjo (Davy Elliott), "until they should give security to pay such judgment as the court might render upon a final determination of the case."

An attorney named William Beattie was now pressing charges against Blount and Davy in behalf of Chief Cochrane of the Apalachicola Indians for recovery of the sum of $6,500. The case is reported in the records of the District Court of New Orleans under the title, *Coa Thlocko, alias Cochrane* v. *John Blunt.* This was in April, 1834. Since the court would not be in session during the summer months, and time would be required to obtain evidence with which to fight the charges, Blount and Davy decided to settle out of court, if possible. They raised $2,000 in cash, and delivered two slaves, valued at $1,000 in settlement of Cochrane's claims. The Indians then proceeded up the Mississippi and to Opelonsas toward the Texas border.[21]

In 1834, President Jackson appointed John Eaton to take the place of William P. Duval as governor of Florida. Governor Duval did not get out of office without being touched by the suspicion of fraud that was so common in the Indian service— and unfortunately, was so often based upon sordid fact. Commissioner Elbert Herring wrote as follows to the Governor on April 10, 1834: "I have received your letter of the 26th ult. enclosing 2 from Thompson to yourself with an account of William G. Porter for provisions furnished the emigrating Apalachicolas, and an estimate of the sums due to persons employed in your superintendency.

"You must furnish evidence—and authority upon which this expense was incurred. The treaty provided that $13,000 should be paid to these Indians in full consideration for the land ceded, and for the expenses of an exploring party. . . . The obvious intent was that no additional expense should be incurred by the Government.

"Your Excellency will permit me to remind you of the immediate necessity of your attention to my letter of the 4th of Nov.

---

[21] Sheffield to Thompson, May 16, 1834; Thompson to Herring, June 10, 1834; Thompson to Herring, July 15, 1834; H. Lockett, Dist. Attorney's Office, New Orleans, to Lewis Cass, July 22, 1834, O. I. A.: Apalachicolas—Emigration.

last. It appears that no account has been rendered by you subsequent to the 31st. Dec. 1832. This . . . must be communicated to Congress, and will oblige the Dept. to withhold your personal compensation until the provisions of the act of 31st Jan. 1833 are complied with."[22]

Eaton was a native of North Carolina, a resident of Tennessee, and a close friend of the President. He had served as Jackson's secretary of war from 1829 to 1831, and his experience in Indian affairs was wide. The controversies over the social status of Mrs. Peggy Eaton at Washington had been a major cause of Jackson's early cabinet changes, and at Tallahassee her life was not pleasant. It was said that she found relief from boredom only at the races, which she attended as often as possible. The Governor, too, felt some opposition in the Florida capital, occasioned perhaps by the President's appointment of a nonresident. Even the Indians, according to a current report, were not impressed either with the person or the record of the new Governor. The Tallahassee chief, Thlocko Tustenuggee (Tiger Tail), is said to have followed Eaton into the governor's office the first time he appeared there. The Indian stood for a short time with his arms folded, regarding the Governor intently and in silence. Then he turned and stalked out, still without saying a word.[23]

[22] Herring to Duval, April 10, 1834, O. I. A.: Letter Book Twelve. Apalachicolas.
[23] Brevard, *History of Florida*, I, 119–21.

CHAPTER 10

Prelude to War, 1834–35

"The Indian is considered in a state of pupilage and incapable of protecting himself against the acts and wiles of civilized man."

WILEY THOMPSON

T HE FLORIDA CAPITAL was a raw frontier town when John Eaton and his wife, Peggy, came to make it their home in 1834. The land in the vicinity of Tallahassee was just over a decade removed from actual occupation and local control by the Seminoles; and during the next decade it was to be the scene of agitation by citizens' committees for new measures of Seminole control, news reports of Indian outrages, and troop mobilization for war against the Indians.

The new Governor's lady was thirty-eight, her husband forty-four. Peggy's career had been interesting and varied, though it was filled with discouragement and contained some tragedy. The daughter of a Washington tavern keeper, and beautiful as a child, Peggy O'Neale had been spoiled by some of her father's distinguished guests. Her mother was Rhoda Howell, who, Peggy said, was the sister of a New Jersey Governor, Richard Howell. At an early age, Peggy was married to John B. Timberlake, a young purser in the Navy. He died suddenly while on a cruise in the Mediterranean, and it was rumored that he took his own life. This rumor was coupled with another—that Senator John Eaton of Tennessee, who had his quarters at the O'Neale Tavern, was on very familiar terms with Mrs. Timberlake. Eaton had been appointed to fill an unexpired term in the Senate in 1818, and with the election of Andrew Jackson to the

Presidency in 1828, the Tennessee senator became at once a prominent figure among those mentioned for cabinet posts.

Before his appointment to the Senate in 1818, Eaton had published a dull, stupidly partisan *Life of Andrew Jackson* which, badly written though it was, caught the attention of a public that was eager for material on the frontier general. In Europe as well as America, this book was widely demanded. Eaton's first wife and her sister, who married Major William B. Lewis, were Jackson's wards; and the husbands of the sisters both became powerful in Tennessee politics and ardent supporters of Jackson for President. After seeking the advice of his friend Jackson, John Eaton asked the widow of Purser Timberlake to marry him and she agreed. The wedding ceremony was planned for January 1, 1829, two months before the new administration was installed. Jackson appointed John Eaton to his cabinet as secretary of war, and undertook the task of gaining a place for Mrs. Eaton in Washington society.

Jackson had first-hand acquaintance with ugly rumors, and he quickly withdrew his confidence from persons who spread or accepted unproved attacks upon his friends. But more than the President's support was needed to obtain social acceptance of Mrs. Eaton against the determined snobbery of Mrs. John C. Calhoun. In 1831, Eaton resigned to clear the way for Jackson's reorganization of his cabinet. In 1833, he was defeated in his effort to regain his seat in the United States Senate; and early in 1834, the President named him governor of Florida Territory. William P. Duval was notified of the change on April 12; but Eaton was slow in taking over his new post, and George K. Walker acted as temporary chief executive.

The people of Florida were offended by the appointment of a nonresident governor, and the rustic first families of Tallahassee society were determined that Mrs. John C. Calhoun, even with the definite flavor of New England codfish in her aristocratic bearing, should not out-snub them. They succeeded in making Peggy Eaton feel that she was not wanted, and the Governor's lady tossed her curls, dressed herself in a green velvet gown that displayed to advantage her vivid beauty, added the striking touch of a bonnet with white ostrich plumes, and took herself to the races.[1]

The horse races at Tallahassee in this period attracted large crowds. Races were run in heats, each horse running two or more mile trials with a brief period of rest between. In spite of two short sections of deep sand in the circular track of the Marion course, the winning mare in 1834, *Queen Adalaide,* owned by a Virginian named J. J. Harrison, ran her first heat in one minute and fifty-nine seconds, and her second in two minutes flat. The owner received a purse of $250 for *Queen Adalaide's* sharp performance.[2] There were races at Quincy, Marianna, and Pensacola; and a few years later jockey clubs had been formed at St. Joseph and Apalachicola. Peggy Eaton, bored with the meager attention she received in Tallahassee, made trips to Pensacola and elsewhere, sometimes with her children, frequently with a black maid.

Governor Eaton worked steadily at his job, and during his brief term won the respect of many citizens including his successor, Richard K. Call. A letter from the Governor to Lewis Cass shows the trend of his thinking on the Seminole problem; and it may also furnish a clue to the fact that President Jackson quickly found an attractive diplomatic post far away from Florida for his old friend, John Eaton. He pointed out the fact that the Payne's Landing Treaty, providing partial removal of the Seminoles in 1833, was not ratified until 1834. "I pray you, does not this circumstance raise a doubt whether . . . the treaty can be considered valid and binding?" Eaton wrote. "The Indian question of removal is one that should be managed with great caution and care. . . . Tread then cautiously! The people here want their lands on which they reside." Land speculators, the governor thought, were the source of greatest conflict; he advised force only as a last resort, and no use of the militia under any circumstances. "They will breed mischief," he declared,

---

[1] Brevard, *History of Florida,* I, 119–21; *Dictionary of American Biography,* V, 609–10; XIV, 41–42 (articles on John Eaton and Peggy O'Neale by Thomas P. Abernathy).

[2] Dorothy Dodd, "Horse Racing in Middle Florida," *Apalachee* (1950), 2–29.

"The employing of a military force is an act of war, and the Indians will embody and fight in their defence."[3]

Wiley Thompson, in a report to the Commissioner of Indian Affairs, made the general assertion that the Seminole Negroes were in danger of enslavement by the Creeks if moved to Indian Territory, and in danger of enslavement by white people if they remained in Florida. Governor Eaton agreed with the statement; and in view of Creek determination to thwart the Seminole desire for separate territory, the first half of the proposition would seem to be established. The other half is proved by the violent attacks upon John Blount and Davy Elliott, and the later raids upon Econchatimicco, to mention just a few of the demonstrations of danger to Negroes in Florida.

On June 18, 1834, a delegation of Creeks visited Secretary Lewis Cass and addressed a "talk" to him which shows clearly the attitude of the western Creeks toward integration of the Seminoles. The request was as strong as the Creek leaders could make it. They did not want to be divided into "separate clans and divisions. . . . If we are to live there as one people we may be happy; if we be cut up into separate clans, then we shall be unhappy." Signers of this "talk" were Roly McIntosh and Fos hutchee Micco, who made their X marks, and Chilly McIntosh.[4]

Wiley Thompson had not been in Florida many months before he understood the temper of the Seminoles better than the officials in Washington who had only indirect contact with them. In answer to Commissioner Herring's letter directing him to prepare the Florida Indians for emigration, Thompson expressed some doubts. He would do his utmost to carry out plans of the Indian Office; but the Seminole Indians would not accept, without resistance, a union with the Creeks; claims of the Creeks upon Seminole slaves was the cause of keenest discontent; union of the councils would enable the Creeks to obtain the slaves by majority vote under process of law and would reduce Seminole

[3] Eaton to Cass, Mar. 8, 1835, O. I. A.: Seminoles—Emigration; quoted in part by Brevard, *History of Florida*, I, 121; and by John T. Sprague; *The Origin, Progress, and Conclusion of the Florida War*, 82.

[4] Creek Delegation to Hon. Lewis Cass, June 18, 1834, O. I. A.: Seminoles.

chiefs "to privates and subject them and their slaves more certainly to control of the Creeks."

Wiley Thompson then made a suggestion of low duplicity; he thought the Seminoles should certainly not be informed of the plan to unite them with the Creeks, until they "shall have . . . arrived at, or in the neighberhood [*sic*] of their new home: then the proposition could be made without the risk of perplexing consequences, and . . . would probably meet with success, especially if a Treaty could be effected by which the Slaves and honorary distinctions would be secured to the Seminoles."[5] The Stokes Commission had designated a portion of the Creek nation as the home of the Seminoles, to meet specific demands of the exploring party; and any attempt to defeat the purpose of separation was certain to breed trouble. Without attempting to rationalize the action, President Jackson in removing the Seminoles simply ignored the treaty guarantee of separate territory.[6]

Wiley Thompson's difficulties were increased by his lack of experience, the old governor's removal, and the slow transfer of the Florida superintendency to Governor John Eaton. Thompson's questions and comments to Commissioner Elbert Herring indicate some lack of confidence on the part of the agent. He was undecided as to presenting the removal program to the Seminoles. Should the Indians be assembled, or "will a convocation of the Chiefs suffice?" How good was the Negro Cudjoe as an interpreter? Stephen Richards was the best he had found, but his expenses "would perhaps be considerable, as he lives near 300 miles from the Agency." Where should sub-agent Sheffield reside—at Tallahassee, where Governor Duval placed him, or at the agency?

In a talk delivered to the Florida Indians at Fort King on October 23, 1834, Agent Wiley Thompson assured them that the President would defend them and their Negro property against all persons. Should any of the Negroes be so foolish as to object to removal, he added, the President "would compel them to go, even in irons, if necessary."[7]

---

[5] Thompson to Herring, July 15, 1834, Grant Foreman Transcripts, VI, 25–28.
[6] *Compilation of all the Treaties . . .* , 809.
[7] *American State Papers: Military Affairs*, VI, 64–66.

On the following day the Indian leaders who had explored the western lands and signed the document for John Phagan and the Stokes Commission, had a chance to give their views of the Gibson agreement. The principal chief, Micanopy, also made a brief statement:

"When they were at Camp Moultrie they made a treaty, and was to be paid their annuity for twenty years. That is all I have to say."

Onselmatche (Jumper): "The land is very good. I saw it and I was very glad to see it. . . . The neighbors there are very bad people; they did not like them bad Indians (the Pawnees). . . . Your talk seems always good, but we do not feel disposed to go west."

Holahti Emathla: "We told the agent that the people were bad there—the land was good. When we went there we saw Indians bring in scalps to the garrison. . . . I am sick. I cannot say all I want to say."

Charley Emathla: "I am no half-breed, and do not lean on one side. If they tell me to go after the seven years (that the Moultrie Treaty had to run) I say nothing; . . . until the seven years are out, I give no answer."

On the following day, October 25, 1834, Holatter Micco (Billy Bolek) stated his determination to stay in Florida until the time stipulated in the Camp Moultrie Treaty had expired. "I never gave my consent to go west," he said; "the whites may say so, but I never gave my consent." Charley Emathla spoke again and said among other things: "At Payne's Landing the white people forced us into a treaty. I was there; I agreed to go west and did go west; I went in a vessel and it made me sick. . . . We wish to hear the Agent's views and opinions on the matter."

Wiley Thompson spoke words of conciliation; but taking the stand demanded by the Jackson administration and the people of Florida, he was unable to avoid deep offense to the Seminole chiefs. "You have told me you want to talk the matter over calmly, and in good humor," he said. "I am not mad: I am your friend; I feel here that I am, and that it is my official duty to be so." The Agent used the words "foolish" and "unreasonable" in regard to the talk of these proud men and added: "You know you had the right to make that treaty. You did make it, and you know and feel that you are all bound by it. . . ."[8]

As the crisis in regard to Seminole removal rapidly moved upon him, Wiley Thompson was obliged to deal with routine problems of his administration, and with details unfinished by his predecessors. He was puzzled to learn that John Phagan had paid the interpreter, Cudjoe, only $175 in a period of three years and had carried him in the Agency accounts at $480 to $500 per year.[9] He had to consider the claim of former Agent Gad Humphreys to two Negro slaves who were in possession of a Seminole woman, Culckeeshowa. Humphreys had seized the slave boys while Wiley Thompson was absent from the agency; but they had run away and come back to the Indians. When Thompson demanded that the slaves be turned over to Colonel Humphreys, the Seminole chiefs declared that Culckeeshowa had never sold the boys, their mother Caty, or her two daughters and their children, but that they had passed out of her possession through a pretended purchase. A trader named Dexter on the St. Johns River had given relatives of Culckeeshowa a trifling amount of whiskey for the Negroes. Col. Humphreys had gone to St. Augustine for the "professed purpose of claiming the Negroes for Culcheeshowa." But he stated that he had been compelled to purchase them, "to prevent them from being carried off to Charleston." He still held the woman Caty, her two daughters, and their children. In his report to Lewis Cass, Agent Thompson stated that Dexter's swindling practices were notorious, and that the President had some knowledge of the trader's character "obtained while in military command in this country."[10]

Early in January, 1835, Wiley Thompson wrote a confidential message to Governor John Eaton, which shows something of the connection between Florida territorial politics and the Indian agent's problems.

[8] *Ibid.*, VI, 65–68.
[9] Thompson to Herring, March 3, 1835, O. I. A.: Seminole.
[10] Thompson to Cass, July 19, 1835, O. I. A.: Seminoles.

"It has been suggested to me," Thompson began, "that an attempt (perhaps a determined effort) will be made during the pending session of the Legislative Council of Florida to subject the Seminole Indians to the jurisdiction of the Territory." Fraud in connection with the natives was the object of the move, he believed. Claims of white imposters would be upheld by the Florida courts. "Hence the effort . . . to subject these people to territorial jurisdiction." Thompson charged that territorial papers were withheld from him, to keep him in the dark concerning the relations of the Territory with the Indians. He asked that Eaton "exercise the Executive Prerogative, in the event that legislation were passed, to extend the jurisdiction of Florida over the Seminoles."[11]

The question raised by Governor John Eaton on the validity of the removal treaty with the Seminoles was submitted by the secretary of war to Attorney General B. F. Butler. The official reply admitted that there was "great force in the suggestions made by Governor Eaton." Butler said the United States was found to make no claims "which are not authorized by the Treaty's sense and spirit." However, he regarded the Treaty valid. "The United States," he wrote, "is necessarily obliged to become, for all practical purposes, its own interpreter and judge." Hence, the government had the right to remove the Indians in the later span of three years not specifically provided by the treaty.[12]

In a sense, this was simply a statement of the sovereignty of the United States, and its legal right to violate the obligation of contract. Justice for the Indian tribe had no weight in this opinion; but in Eaton's view justice is recognized along with the practical matter of Seminole propensity for war. Acceptance of Butler's interpretation over Governor Eaton's was to cost the United States 1,500 lives in military personnel, to which must be added some hundreds of civilians. In property, the Seminole War cost at least $30,000,000—a sum large enough to carry on several years of peaceable negotiation—even to employ a few

[11] Thompson to Eaton, Jan. 10, 1835, O. I. A.: Seminoles.
[12] Butler to Cass, March 26, 1835, O. I. A.: Seminoles.

Seminole men, women, and children on porch, photographed
in the Oklahoma Seminole Nation, possibly at the Agency
building in Wewoka.

Seminole Council House and Governor's Residence, Seminole
Nation, circa 1890.

Western History Collections
University of Oklahoma Library

extra blacksmiths, a few teachers, and to furnish additional rations at 14¢. It should be remembered, too, that in the future the Seminoles were to become citizens of the United States; hence their warriors killed in battle were national losses. The number of Indians who died was kept secret, and there are no records which reveal the total with accuracy.

In a council at Fort King in April, 1835, Jumper, the "sense bearer" of Chief Micanopy, spoke for the tribe and declared that the Seminole people would not move west. Wiley Thompson was provoked out of his usual diplomatic manner, and proceeded to rebuke the Indian chiefs as if they were wrongheaded school boys. He charged them with bad faith in regard to the treaty, which brought an angry reply from Jumper and Arpeika. General Duncan Clinch then spoke and told the assembled chiefs that the United States would be obliged to use force if the Indians did not comply with their treaty. Upon reconsideration, eight of the chiefs agreed to go west; but five of the most influential leaders refused to change their position. Whereupon, Wiley Thompson declared that the five—Micanopy, Onselmatche (Jumper), Halpatter-Tustenuggee (Alligator), Fuch-a-lusti-hadjo (Black Dirt), and Arpeika (Sam Jones)—were deposed as chiefs.

Thompson's report of this development brought a sharp reply from the acting secretary of war, C. W. Harris. The President approved General Clinch's threat of removal by force, but not the deposing of five chiefs by General Thompson. "Such a proceeding has hitherto been unknown in our intercourse with the Indians, and it is an interference with their internal concerns," Harris wrote. While the immediate effect might seem beneficial, it was feared that the Indian reaction would be injurious. The hereditary position of some chiefs, and the rise of others to power in the field or in council, was an influence not easily broken, Harris believed. They would be excited to take a determined stand against emigration; the Negroes would furnish means for their opposition, and the character of the country would make the project of removing them by force a dangerous and difficult matter.[13] The President suggested, Secretary Harris asserted,

[13] Harris to General Clinch and Wiley Thompson, May 20, 1835, O.I.A.: Seminole–Emigration.

that the matter of deposing chiefs should be submitted to the chiefs, or to the Indians assembled in council.

The meeting at Fort King brought to the attention of Wiley Thompson an Indian whose name had not appeared to any extent in the reports from Florida. Not having the rank of chief, Osceola was not expected to voice his opinions in the council; but when the Agent offered to the assembled Indian leaders an opportunity to sign a document agreeing upon removal, and the chiefs were divided on the issue, he protested vigorously against surrender of Seminole rights. There is a tradition (probably a dramatized version of his indignant opposition to removal) that Osceola stalked to the front of the room and plunged his knife through the paper tendered by Wiley Thompson to the chiefs for their signatures.[14]

Osceola was born on the Tallapoosa, in the Creek country of Georgia. His mother was the daughter of a former Creek who had achieved the position of Tustenuggee, or town chief, among the Seminoles. Probably the father of Osceola was a Scotch trader named Powell—though some contemporaries, including the painter, George Catlin, spoke of him as a full blood Indian. Recent research has brought to light evidence which seems to prove that his mother was of mixed ancestry—Creek and European—and that Osceola, like John Ross and Alexander McGillivray, was less than half Indian. He fought against the United States in the War of 1812, probably taking part in the battle at Horseshoe Bend. He had moved to Florida and was living in the vicinity of Fort King while Governor Duval was trying to hold the Seminoles to the narrow confines of their land reserved under the Treaty of Camp Moultrie. Apparently, Osceola served

[14] *Dictionary of American Biography,* XIV, 76 (article on Osceola by Katherine Elizabeth Crane); Coe, *The Red Patriots,* 119; Giddings, *The Exiles of Florida,* 98; Brevard, *History of Florida,* I, 118, 123–26, 167; Kenneth W. Porter, "The Episode of Osceola's Wife, Fact or Fiction?" *Florida Historical Quarterly,* Vol. XXVI, 92; Sprague, *The Florida War,* 96, 101, 105; Welch, *Osceola Nikkanochee,* 29. Mark Boyd has called attention to a break in the copy of the Treaty of Fort Gibson in the National Archives, and an attached note which describes the "lateral crack or tear" as the "mark of Osceola's knife." Obviously, great confusion exists concerning this episode. The writers who relate the story are not agreed on the document that was supposed to have been knifed, or upon the time of the alleged incident.

under Duval as a scout, helping to capture Indians who strayed beyond their border.

Osceola married Che-cho-ter, the daughter of a Seminole sub-chief. Many stories, based upon the spectacular and tragic career of the great Seminole warrior have gained wide acceptance by means of repetition in a variety of printed materials. One of these accounts which is not supported by historical data, concerns Che-cho-ter. Joshua Giddings states that the mother of Che-cho-ter was a Negro fugitive slave, that the young wife herself was captured, while on a visit to Fort King for the purpose of trading, and was sold into slavery. According to this account, Osceola became an implacable foe of white men because of Che-cho-ter's treatment.

In official reports and letters to friends, Wiley Thompson stated that Osceola had come to his office and insulted him on several occasions. Finally, the Agent felt obliged to imprison him, and informed the belligerent Indian that he must remain in confinement until he could give security for his better behavior. Friendly chiefs interceded, and Thompson released him on his promise to come back with his followers in five days and to acknowledge the removal treaty. Osceola did return with seventy-nine men, women, and children; he would have brought more, but many were out hunting. The Agent was elated, and wrote: "I now have no doubt of his sincerity, and as little that the greatest difficulty is surmounted."[15]

Wiley Thompson was placed in charge of emigration, and was directed by the Indian Office to submit a general plan of operations for removal. On August 27, 1835, his plan was ready. He proposed to assemble the Indians at the Seminole Agency and at a point to be selected at Tampa or Hillsborough Bay. They would travel chiefly by water, and the main route would be Tampa to New Orleans, thence by river boat to Rock Roe on the White River. He planned to establish a general camp at the point of embarkation with issuing houses and cattle pens, and a depot of provisions; and to transport the emigrants from the agency to the general camp in wagons. Places of encamp-

[15] Thompson to Gibson, June 3, 1835, O. I. A.: Seminole–Emigration.

ment with cattle pens were to be established from twelve to eighteen miles apart.

For the passage by sea large schooners were obtained, "seaworthy and every way prepared and arranged with a view to the convenience, comfort, and safety of the emigrants." A time schedule was attached which provided assemblage at the Agency by the first party on January 1, 1836; embarkation for the Belize on January 20; transfer to river boats on January 31, and arrival at Rock Roe on February 15th. "Emigrants should reach their new home by March 9 or 10," the Agent wrote.

Rations were to consist of "Bread Stuffs: principally corn which is considered most wholesome for Indians, and the most economical. A small portion of wheat flour for a change and for the sick.

"Meat Ration: Fresh Beef in camp and on the march, to be supplied from the cattle to be received by the United States from the Indians. Salt pork on board the Transports."

Thompson planned to use one physician, "with a suitable supply of medicines;" one interpreter and one laborer for 500 Indians; one assistant special agent; one assistant disbursing agent; and also conductors, drivers, and assistant conductors. The general plan stated that the disbursing agent was responsible for providing against transports parting company, and for a suitable allowance of wood and water, arrangements for cooking, privies, and "an efficient polisce [sic] on board each transport." As superintendent of emigration, Thompson proposed to exclude all intoxicants, "except for medical purposes strictly."

Wiley Thompson believed that military force would be required for removal. He estimated that twelve days might be required "to collect the disaffected and stragling [sic] Indians."[16] In this prediction he has never been charged with exaggeration or unfounded fears.

While the Seminoles gradually reached their determination to fight rather than be dispossessed of their homeland, while former officers of the government and other citizens schemed to gain possession of Indian land or chattels, and while the Agent

[16] Grant Foreman Transcripts, VI, 73–79.

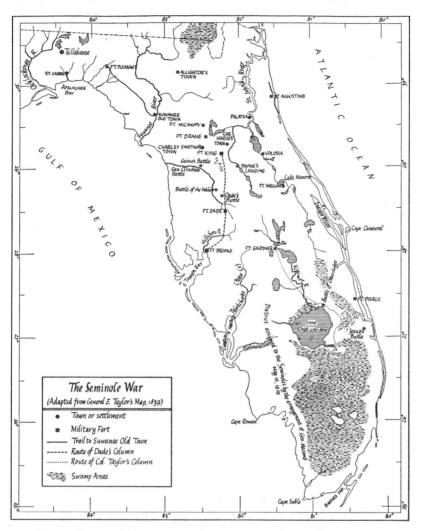

The Seminole War
(Adapted from General Z. Taylor's Map, 1839)
• Town or settlement
■ Military Fort
— Trail to Suwanee Old Town
----- Route of Dade's Column
······· Route of Col. Taylor's Column
🌿 Swamp Areas

reluctantly came to the conclusion that "disaffected" natives would be a tough people to dispossess by military force, the territory of Florida moved through several changes in its executive staff. After Duval's term as governor, and the brief interim of acting Governor George K. Walker, John Eaton held the job for more than a year. He had some grasp of the broad principles, at least, of United States relations with Indians. But Eaton was ambitious, Peggy was dissatisfied, and the people of Florida had pecuniary interests that were likely to be checked by Eaton's theories of justice to the Seminoles. They had exactly the man to look after their relations with the Indians in Richard Keith Call of Pensacola, more lately of Tallahassee. General Call's peculiar interest in the Seminole problem is indicated by a message that he sent to President Jackson on March 22, 1835.

"I have letters from some of my friends in Tallahassee, . . . requesting me, if possible, to obtain permission from the Government to purchase the Indian right to certain Negroes residing among the Seminoles, and supposed to belong to the Indians." Call assumed that no objection could be made to the purchase and gave as his opinion that sales of Negroes would greatly help in removal of the Seminoles. "The Negroes have great influence among the Indians," he wrote. "They are better aggriculturists [sic] and inferior huntsmen to the Indians, and are violently opposed to leaving the country. If the Indians are permitted to convert them into specie, one great obsticle [sic] in the way of removal may be overcome." General Call requested specifically that Robert W. Williams and William Bailey be authorized under approval of the agent to purchase 150 Negroes. "I shall be greatly obliged by having the permission sought for forwarded at Tallahassee, for which place I set out tomorrow.[17]

Wiley Thompson's reaction to the proposal is stated in his prompt letter to the secretary of war. "The intercourse laws prohibit the purchase of an Indian Poney [sic] by a member of civilized society, without permission of the Agent; and why, but because the Indian is considered in a state of pupilage, and incapable of protecting himself against the arts and wiles of civilized man." Attention was called to the relative values of slaves and ponies, and the added necessity of protection in slave property. Thompson agreed with Call in regard to Negro influence among the Seminoles and called attention to the wealth accumulated by the slaves in the form of livestock and to the relative liberty enjoyed by the servile class, by comparison with slaves on plantations owned by white citizens. "They live in

[17] Call to President Jackson, March 22, 1835, O. I. A.: Seminole.

villages seperate [*sic*] and in many cases remote from their owners, enjoying equal liberty with their owners, with the single exception that the slave supplies his owner, annually . . . with corn . . . in no instance exceeding ten bushels." The Agent asserted that an Indian would almost as soon sell his child as his slave, except when under the influence of intoxicating liquor.

At the conference that resulted in the Treaty of Payne's Landing, Thompson recalled, both Indians and Negroes were assured that their present relations would be continued. That agreement was a great advantage in persuading them to remove. "I have given them a pledge that I will do everything in my power, consistent with the rights of others, to save Blacks from worse bondage . . . and that I will not permit a sale of any slave unless it be clearly dictated by Humanity."

Malcontented Indians were whispering that Thompson was trying to get control of the Negroes for himself; and at the worst possible time, a party of citizens arrived at the agency with permission from the War Department to purchase slaves from the Indians. The Agent put them off, and explained that their visit was a source of great danger. He added that he should "feel that he was accessory to the enslaving of a free man" if he should permit the sale of one or more Negroes to persons intent only upon profits. "With the most respectful deference to the Department, I should consider any other [course] an abandonment of the principles of the Treaty and Humanity." If it should become generally known that the War Department approved sales of the Seminole Negroes, Thompson feared a rush of speculators into the Indian country. "Should this happen and be tolerated, God only knows what the consequences will be."

This long and earnest letter, giving to the Jackson Administration the benefit of Wiley Thompson's brief experience in Florida and, of more importance, the liberal thought of the best agent who had been sent to the Seminoles, was answered by the acting secretary of war.

"The President approves the decision communicated to General Call," Harris wrote. He then explained that the law did not contain provisions designed to secure slave property for the

Indians; that protection of their means of procuring "subsistence" by hunting or tilling the soil was intended. False reports as to Thompson's personal interest in the slaves would be silenced, "by your publication of the views of the department on the subject, and interposing no further obstacles to the purchase of these slaves, than may be necessary to secure their owners a fair equivalent."[18]

The signs of Seminole hostility accumulated. In October, 1834, a sharp increase in the sales of arms and ammunition to Indians was noted, and Wiley Thompson ordered that the sales be suspended. On December 28, the Agent made an optimistic report on the attitude of the Indian leaders, but a month later he gave the opinion that a large part of the Seminoles were opposed to removal as the result of "being tampered with by designing persons, until some projects of speculation or some fraudulent claims for slaves could be prosecuted."

On June 19, 1835, an armed clash outside of the Indian boundaries between Seminole hunters and white men resulted in several casualties—three whites wounded, one Indian killed, one wounded. Thompson demanded surrender of the Indians who took part in the conflict, and the chiefs immediately caused the arrest of six men for trial. In October, 1835, the express rider from Tampa Bay to Fort King was killed. Attacks on plantations were reported more frequently than ever before, and it was clear that the Indians were collecting stores of war materials. Osceola boasted that he had 150 kegs of good powder and he would not leave Florida until that was used up.

News from the Seminole country grew steadily more depressing. On November 30, 1835, Wiley Thompson wrote to General George Gibson that five chiefs with four or five hundred followers had fled to Fort Brooke for protection against the war party. Charley Emarthla, friendly to removal, was murdered "by the treachery of Powell [Osceola] who professed to be and was considered friendly. The consiquences [sic] resulting from this murder leave no doubt that actual force must be resorted to for the purpose of effecting removal, as it has produced a

[18] Thompson to Harris; Harris to Thompson, May 22, 1835, O. I. A. Seminole.

general defection." The Indians in camp near Fort Brooke were in deplorable condition without hope of immediate relief in necessary food supplies. The Agent feared that they would rejoin the hostile forces. At this time Wiley Thompson was in favor of a determined effort to remove the Indians who were willing to go.[19]

At about midafternoon on December 28, 1835, Wiley Thompson and Lieutenant Constantine Smyth, who had just had dinner with the Agent, walked into the woods near the agency. They were not more than three hundred yards from the office when a party of Indians, who had been hidden within sight of Fort King, arose from ambush and fired upon them. Both men fell, Wiley Thompson with fourteen bullet wounds, Smyth with two. The Indians took their scalps, then ran quickly to the house of Erastus Rogers, the sutler, and killed him along with his two clerks. The Negroes in the sutler's house escaped.

The troops stationed at Fort King, except Captain Landrum's company, were absent on an expedition to Lang Synne Plantation. The sutler had moved his goods inside the fort, but, with the clerks, had meals at his house outside of the area protected by walls. Captain Landrum, without knowing five men were absent from the fort, supposed when he heard the firing that a large party of Indians had approached his position and fired a volley to bring him out. Pursuit was attempted later; but the Seminoles had disappeared, leaving corpses and smoking ruins behind them.

During the attack, friendly Indians at Fort King recognized the shrill, piercing war whoop of Osceola; so it was known at once that he had led the hostile party. Lieutenant J. W. Harris, reporting the death of Thompson and his companions, gave such information as he had been able to gather. "All the Upper Indians . . . have gone over to the War Party. Micanopy, the Head Chief, is opposed to hostile measures though still objecting to emigrate, and has ordered all his people to remain neutral."[20]

[19] Thompson to Gibson, Nov. 30, 1835, O. I. A.: Seminole–Emigration; *Niles' Register*, Jan. 24, 1835.

[20] Harris to Gibson, Dec. 30, 1835, Grant Foreman Transcripts, VI, 91–99.

From three hundred to five hundred of Micanopy's people were at Tampa; all the rest, thought Lieutenant Harris, would take the warpath.

On the morning of that day, December 28, a large party of warriors under Micanopy, Jumper, and Alligator lay in wait for Major Francis L. Dade, who was marching with two companies and a six-pound cannon from Fort Brooke to Fort King. It has been asserted that Major Dade's Negro guide, Luis Fatio (or Luis Pacheco), was secretly in touch with the Seminoles; but probably Luis disclosed no secrets. It was not difficult, without a spy in Dade's marching force, for the Indians to keep themselves informed as to the route followed by the soldiers, and their location at a given time.

At a narrow passage where the road was bordered by palmettos, the Indians sprang their trap. Half of Dade's men—more than fifty—fell at the first volley. The concealed Indians were firing at a distance of thirty or forty yards, and they were in a position to take deliberate aim. It is said that Micanopy leveled his gun at Major Dade, who was riding in the advance guard, Jumper took aim at Captain U. S. Frazer, and both officers fell dead at the first Seminole volley. In the words of George A. McCall, who accompanied General Gaines on an inspection of the battlefield two months later, Major Dade was "shot probably through the heart, as I should judge by the bullet-hole in his side."

Captain G. W. Gardiner rallied his men and when the Seminoles returned to the attack they found the little party barricaded within a flimsy pine-log shelter. Lieutenant W. E. Basinger fired the six-pounder until all the men about him fell. The Indians rushed in and completed the work of destruction. Of the one hundred and two soldiers in Major Dade's party, only three were alive when the shooting ended. Two of them died of their wounds at Fort Brooke; the third, Private Ransom Clark, died of his wounds five years afterward. The eight officers all died in the battle. The Indians lost three killed and five wounded. Luis Pacheco (Fatio) was taken prisoner—his life was spared because he was a Negro. He was removed to the West with Coacoochee and returned after fifty years, when he told his story to Mrs.

John Claude Engle, daughter of the original owner of Luis, Francis Philip Fatio.[21]

Osceola returned to Wahoo Swamp from Fort King to take part in the celebration of his exploit and the destruction of Dade's force by Jumper and Alligator. A scalp dance was arranged by the medicine chief, Hillis Higher Hadjo. A supply of liquor had been captured from the white men, and in the safety of their hiding place, the Seminoles passed around the firewater and spent the night in revelry. Mock addresses were delivered to the scalp of Wiley Thompson, with mimicry of his manner of speech and gestures. "The Indians who do not go peaceably, the Great Father will remove by force," the speaker said; and the Seminoles roared with laughter.[22]

One of the great tragedies of Seminole relations with the United States was bound up in this grotesque comedy. The Indian war leader had selected one of the best friends of the Seminoles among the white men for death; and the Indian funmakers had picked upon the most familiar of the dead men, their little father, for the greatest laugh of the season. No one present understood clearly that the powerful government which had employed Wiley Thompson, and sometimes reproached his best efforts, was great enough to blunder many times and still crush the Seminole Indians and dispossess them. And, it may be added, few people in Florida or in Washington realized the terrible price that would be exacted by the Seminole Indians. The report of Thompson's death and the ambush of Dade's troops swept across Florida like a tidal wave, leaving terror and wild exaggeration in its wake.

It was the responsibility of General Clinch to regain control of the Seminole country and protect the plantations. He was joined by General Robert Keith Call, commander of the Florida Volunteers, who marched immediately from Tallahassee with three hundred mounted men, picked up en route nearly two

---

[21] Mark Boyd, *Florida Aflame,* 105–107; Kenneth W. Porter, "The Early Life of Luis Pacheco née Fatio," *The Negro History Bulletin,* Vol. VII (1943), 52; Maj. Gen. George A. McCall, *Letters from the Frontier,* 299–303; G. R. Fairbanks, *History of Florida,* 283–93; Sprague, *The Florida War,* 90–91.

[22] Sprague, *The Florida War,* 90–91.

hundred more, and placed his force in position to co-operate with General Clinch.

Learning from the Seminole scouts that two white military parties were approaching the Withlacoochee, Osceola and Halpatter Tustenuggee (Alligator) with 250 warriors, including some 30 Negroes, moved to cut them off. At noon on the last day of the year 1835, General Clinch reached the river, and his guides began looking for a ford which they believed to be in the vicinity. No passable ford was discovered, and the deep, rapid current proved to be a serious obstacle until an old canoe was found which would carry six or eight men. Lieutenant Colonel A. C. W. Fanning succeeded in crossing about 200 regular troops, and Brigadier General Call was in the process of taking his force across, when Osceola and Alligator attacked. The Seminoles were in a strong position, protected by scrub timber along the south bank and in the bordering swamp. Call's Florida Volunteers were spectators of the skirmish, but could lend little aid, since the regulars were between them and the Seminoles. Call himself crossed, and twenty-seven of the Volunteers, led by Colonel Warren and Lieutenant Colonel Mills, managed to get into the fighting.

The shooting continued for more than an hour, when General Clinch ordered a bayonet charge. The Seminoles scattered, but took a new position a short distance back. A second charge and a third followed. During the heat of the conflict, an Indian bullet cut through General Clinch's cap, and another struck the sleeve of his jacket. Captain William M. Graham was wounded in the leg. After the third charge, the Seminoles retired into the swamp, and no pursuit was attempted. The fight had begun about four o'clock in the afternoon, and General Clinch determined to recross the river before dark. Osceola returned to his original position and gave to Clinch's maneuver the appearance of retreat. General Call reported the crossing of the Withlacoochee to Governor Eaton as a project of considerable risk in which his forces played a creditable part.[23]

[23] Carolyn Mays Brevard, "Richard Keith Call," *Florida Historical Society Quarterly*, Vol. I, No. 3, pp. 9–10; Sprague, *Florida War*, 92–93.

General Clinch reported losses as follows: regulars, 4 killed, 25 wounded; Volunteers, 15 wounded. Later, it was learned that the casualties were considerably higher. Losses of the Seminoles cannot be determined accurately, since they removed both dead and wounded. It is probable that the early reports in Tallahassee of their casualties were greatly exaggerated and that the Indians themselves gave, in their later account of the affair, a low estimate. Call reported that "nearly one-third of their number had been cut down." Osceola was said to be hit in the arm by a rifle ball during this engagement; Alligator seemed to think that the wound received by their leader was the cause of their retreat. In any event, the Seminoles had out-maneuvered the army of General Clinch, and held their own against a force somewhat more than twice the number of the Indian warriors. Lieutenant George A. McCall, in a letter to his father, observed that he did not agree with those who thought the war would be over quickly; it was more likely to be a seven years' war, he thought. McCall added that the war had been brought on by "huge blundering, or by unfair dealings on the part of the Government Agents."[24]

General Edmund P. Gaines, commander of the western military department, was in New Orleans when the news from Florida came to him. He left New Orleans on February 3, 1836, with six companies of the Fourth United States Infantry under Lieutenant Colonel D. E. Twiggs, and a regiment of Louisiana Volunteers under Colonel P. F. Smith. In all, Gaines brought some 1,100 soldiers into the campaign, arriving at Fort Brooke on February 10.

On March 16, 1836, President Jackson named Richard K. Call to take John Eaton's place as governor of Florida. Support was strong in the territory for appointment of a Florida man, and Jackson himself thought highly of his friend who commanded the Florida Volunteers. As a young staff officer under General Jackson, Call had been entertained at the Hermitage, along with William O. Butler, James Gadsden, Sam Houston, and other soldiers who were marked for promotion.[25]

[24] McCall, *Letters from the Frontier,* 299.

[25] An account of R. K. Call's career appears in two installments in the *Florida Historical Society Quarterly,* Vol. I, Nos. 1 and 3 (July and October, 1908), entitled "Richard Keith Call," by Carolyn Mays Brevard.

When John Eaton was given his appointment as United States minister to Spain, President Jackson accomplished more than one object. Eaton certainly deserved consideration in the payment of political debt; but as governor of Florida he was showing a strong tendency toward support of Wiley Thompson, who still had weight with the electorate of Georgia and could not be ignored or pushed around. But the views of Thompson in regard to justice for the Seminoles and for the Negroes among them were running counter to the dominant political forces in the territory and to Jackson's own views.

In Madrid, Peggy Eaton, no longer judged by a court of public opinion in which gossip was the principal witness, was to enjoy the happiest years of her life from 1836 to 1840.[26]

[26] *The Autobiography of Peggy Eaton,* left in the hands of Rev. Charles F. Deems, was published at New York in 1926.

CHAPTER 11

Removal by Force:
Seminole Trail of Tears

*"About half the party have been and are still sick. Many continue
very low and must die. Three died yesterday, three this morning."*

LIEUTENANT J. VAN HORNE

A SLIGHT DIVERGENCE from the clear intention of the
Payne's Landing Treaty and the agreement at Fort Gibson
had been all that was needed to bring about a bloody war.
Departure from the agreements by President Jackson and his
advisers was narrow enough to confuse many American citizens,
even those who had power over Indian relations; so that these
good persons during the rest of their lives accused the Indians
of duplicity; but it was wide enough to convince a majority of
the Seminole Indians that the officers of the United States Government were treacherous in the extreme, that a white man's
word was of no value. The Indians adopted a desperate attitude
of willingness to fight to the death; and the result was a struggle
that cost many hundreds of lives, and an expenditure of money
far greater than the probable cost of a reasonable policy of negotiation and education.

Tribal leaders and officials of the United States commonly
misunderstood each other. Congressmen and other persons who
helped to make Indian policy regularly underestimated the
resources, determination, and courage of the Seminoles. Few
white persons realized fully the deep attachment of the Indian
to his native land. Of course, most of the Seminoles had a limited
concept of the white man's resources for making war and the
strength of his urge to possess the Indian's property.

In some respects Seminole removal was like that of the other Southern tribes. There was reluctance to go west, even violent opposition to removal, in all of the Five Civilized Tribes. Cherokees and Creeks maintained internal strife over removal for many years. Even the Choctaws and Chickasaws occasionally found, in their contests with white men over property rights connected with removal, a subject for deadly combat. But the Seminoles as a tribe followed leadership that was opposed to removal; they challenged the United States of America to put them out of their homeland—even the least valuable portions to which they had been restricted.

The immediate task of restoring order in Florida was attempted by territorial officials and the portion of the army commanded by General Duncan L. Clinch. A contest over authority resulted in the choice of Winfield Scott, over Clinch and General Edmund P. Gaines, as commander. Another rivalry that lasted throughout removal was that of the Territorial governor with the army. In general, Florida officials were eager to recognize the enormity of Indian outrages, and to hustle the Indians out of their homes at any cost—especially if the cost could be made to fall most heavily upon federal troops and the United States Treasury.

The awkward process of treaty-making, with evasive intentions, was at the bottom of the trouble; the delay involved in negotiations with the Seminoles from 1832 to 1834 probably cut off one chance for peaceable removal. On this point, Dr. Mark Boyd has written: "It is likely, had the government been prepared to move swiftly in 1833, the entire project could have been realized in that year with the sullen compliance of the Indians. The government, however, took no steps to this end until after the belated ratification of 1834. The injustice of holding the Indians to the Fort Gibson agreement, without regarding the United States strictly bound by its terms, is shown by a glance at their situation. A season of poor crops, followed by one in which many Indians neglected to plant, expecting daily to be called up for emigration, determined for the Seminole country a food supply that was tragically short. Indians raided white settlements in order to feed their starving children. Frustration and hunger aroused their resentment, in particular that of the Mikasukies."[1] Conflict between the governor and the military officers is apparent in the official reports. Major General Macomb commented on the fight at the Withlacoochee crossing with a blunt claim that regular soldiers "bore the brunt of the action." He pointed out that fifty-seven of the two hundred troops who crossed the river with General Clinch were killed or wounded while only three officers and twenty-seven men of the Volunteers took any part in the battle. "Why so many remained out of the action is not explained." Alexander Macomb thought that the war might have terminated in that battle if the whole force had displayed "the same zeal and bravery as was evinced by the regular troops."[2]

General Call of the Florida Volunteers contradicted the Macomb report in several important particulars. He gave himself principal credit for the orderly retreat; he discovered better means of re-crossing the river than was used by Clinch in getting the men over. Call also recognized the bravery and coolness of the officers who crossed with him and stated that his men took a valiant part in the action.

Actually, the Seminole chiefs determined the plan of the battle. With an old canoe as bait for crossing, they caught their enemies divided into three parts: two hundred on the south side of the stream, two hundred in the process of making the crossing, and three hundred on the north bank where they could watch the fight but could not engage in it. The Indians inflicted heavy damage on the troops engaged, and caused the whole force, more than twice their number, to retreat. Reports of this encounter must have caused President Jackson some loss of confidence in the leaders of his armies in Florida.

"I should be highly gratified to command the army," wrote General Call, and I believe I could soon bring the war to a close.

---

[1] Mark Boyd, "Asi-Yahola or Osceola," reprint from *Florida Historical Quarterly*, Vol. XXXIII, Nos. 3 and 4 (Jan.-Apr., 1955), 26.
[2] *American State Papers: Military Affairs*, VI, 817.

I fear, however, this I cannot do without injustice to General Clinch; he is a brave and good man, but I fear he is too slow . . . to conduct a war against the Indians."[3]

While General Gaines was making arrangements to move his troops to Tampa Bay, General Clinch was strengthening his position at Fort King, and General Call was laying his plans for political advancement. The question of command was settled on January 21, 1836, by the appointment of Winfield Scott, and a few weeks later Gaines landed at Tampa Bay. His march to Fort King and return to Fort Brooke were of little significance in the military picture, except as the young officers and men of his command gained firsthand information on the subject of fighting the Seminoles in Florida. General Scott had reached Picolata on the St. Johns River, about one hundred miles north of Fort King, where he expressed surprise and displeasure at the news of Gaines' advance into Florida.

Meager supplies were obtained by the troops on their way back to Fort Brooke, but at the crossing of the Withlacoochee the Seminoles again gave battle. Lieutenant Izard was killed and General Gaines wounded in the first exchange of shots. Gaines ordered the erection of a log barricade and sent messages to Scott and Clinch, asking for supplies and proposing a counter-attack upon the Indians. Scott ignored the suggestion and ordered Clinch not to send provisions. General Gaines' wound, caused by a bullet through his lower lip, proved to be painful but not so dangerous as to put him out of action. "It was mean of the redskins to knock out my teeth, when I have so few," he remarked to Captain Hitchcock.[4]

On March 1, 1836, Jumper, Alligator, and Osceola attacked the improvised fort at "Camp Izard," and were driven off after a sharp skirmish. Provisions had run so low that the daily ration of corn was one pint. On March 3, Gaines ordered the slaughter of a horse for food; and before relief arrived, the men had consumed all of their horses. In defiance of Scott's orders, General Clinch sent James Gadsden with forty head of cattle to relieve

[3] 26 Cong., 1 sess., *Senate Doc. No. 278*, 25ff.
[4] Ethan Allen Hitchcock, *Fifty Years in Camp and Field*, 93.

the starving condition at Camp Izard. In the meantime the Semi-nole chiefs had proposed a peace parley through the Negro interpreter, Abraham.[5] A conference was arranged, Jumper speaking for the Indians and Captain Hitchcock for the army. "Enough men have been killed," Chief Jumper said; "we do not want to lose more." Hitchcock told them, "Five thousand men are coming—you must yield or all be killed." Jumper re-peated his theme, "Enough men have been killed," and Osceola added, "I am satisfied."

"They listened very attentively to my talk, and their appear-ance indicated their entire sincerity," Captain Hitchcock re-called later in his account of the meeting.[6] The best of the con-temporary authorities are inclined to agree with this judgment, even with respect to the good intentions of Osceola.[7] As the con-ference between Captain Hitchcock and the Indians was closing, the advance guard of Clinch's relief party arrived and opened fire upon the line of Indians who were waiting for the results of the peace talk. The Seminoles scattered, and without doubt many of them left the place with the impression that they had been tricked. General Gaines had proposed that the Indians should wait south of the Withlacoochee for General Scott's ar-rival, since the new commander would have authority to make terms with them.

Gaines and Scott met at Fort Drane and the conference was confined strictly to cold formalities, after which General Gaines and Captain Hitchcock departed for the West. Scott's plan for ending the war consisted of three main parts: (1) an advance into the Seminole country from Fort Drane; (2) a similar ad-vance from Volusia on the St. Johns; and (3) an expedition from Tampa Bay to the forks of the Withlacoochee, where the three forces would join and crush the remnants of the Seminole Na-tion. With the command in Florida, General Scott had been

---

[5] *Ibid.*, 93. The authorities do not agree upon the identity of the messenger. Brevard, *History of Florida*, I, 131, states that the sentry was hailed by Caesar, an old slave of Micanopy.

[6] Hitchcock, *Fifty Years in Camp and Field*, 94, 95.

[7] Boyd, "Asi-Yahola or Osceola," reprint from *Florida Historical Quarterly*, Vol. XXXIII (1955), 42.

given authority to recruit troops in Georgia, Alabama, and South Carolina. His volunteers, together with regular soldiers and the Florida militia, gave him command of a larger force than any previously seen in the Florida war.

Through April and May, 1836, General Scott tried to put his plan into operation with these adequate forces. The Indians avoided battle, raided behind his marching armies, and again brought panic to the settlers of Florida. Fort Drane was attacked on the night of April 20, and Captain Landrum's small force held the place with great difficulty. St. Augustine was in danger of attack due to the absence of able-bodied citizens in the volunteer army, and the presence of many slaves who were familiar with the Seminole Negroes and perhaps in some instances related to them by the ties of kinship and marriage. Two companies of South Carolina militia finally arrived for the protection of St. Augustine.[8]

After two months of the active operation of Scott's program, under his direction, little progress had been made and the hot weather was due in Florida. When General Scott was ordered to take over the campaign against the Creeks in Alabama, command in Florida was offered to General Clinch; but he was on the point of resigning his commission in the army, and he refused to accept the promotion. Governor Call was eager to fight a summer campaign against the Seminoles, and the opportunity was apparently within his grasp; but the War Department limited his appointment as acting commander with the proviso that General Thomas S. Jesup should take charge upon his arrival in Florida. Call's independent command was not a spectacular success, as many of his friends expected it to be. Shortage of supplies, lack of experienced troops, and the indisputable skill of the Seminoles in conducting any campaign in Florida, summer or otherwise, combined to bring about his disappointment. By comparison with Jesup, Call was an amateur.

Governor Call defeated Seminole war parties in the vicinity of Wahoo Swamp, but also suffered reverses. When he advanced

[8] Brevard, *History of Florida*, I, 132–34; Brevard, "Richard Keith Call," *Florida Historical Society Quarterly*, Vol. I, No. 3, 11–15.

to Suwannee Old Town and then to Fort Drane, Osceola and most of his warriors fell back, turning the cattle into their corn fields before withdrawing. One of the tasks Governor Call had undertaken was to search out "coves" where Seminole women and children raised crops for their warriors. He surprised a camp four miles from the Withlacoochee, where he killed eleven warriors and captured twelve women and children. At Fort Drane he was joined by a party of 750 Creeks. When the combined force crossed the Withlacoochee, they found Indian and Negro towns recently abandoned.[9] The action of November 1, 1836, in which General Call led more than 1,000 soldiers into the Great Wahoo Swamp, was called by Joshua Giddings a "severe defeat for the white troops."[10]

On December 8, 1836, General Jesup took command of all the United States forces in Florida, and Governor Call returned to Tallahassee to devote his full time to the duties of chief executive. He persisted in advocating a summer campaign for the following year; but before that time he had been removed from the governorship by President Martin Van Buren. "It is a thankless matter and perilous to one's advancement to call attention of those in power to the inefficiency of their measures," wrote Call's biographer.[11] Perhaps the new President, who was not an old comrade-in-arms with Governor Call, did not approve his activities on the slave market for Seminole Negroes, and was not impressed with his record in removing the Indians by force.

General Thomas Sidney Jesup was forty-eight years old when he came to Florida as commander. He was born in Virginia, removed as a youth to Ohio, and was commissioned a second lieutenant in the Army at the age of twenty. He served on General William Hull's staff in 1812 and advanced rapidly in rank during the war. After Lundy's Lane, where he was wounded, he became brevet colonel "for gallant conduct and distinguished skill." After the war he became quartermaster-general of the army and in 1828 attained the rank of major gen-

---

[9] Brevard, *History of Florida*, I, 140–42.
[10] Giddings, *The Exiles of Florida*, 131–33.
[11] Brevard, "Richard Keith Call," *Florida Hist. Soc. Quarterly*, Vol. I, 3–17.

eral. Just before coming to Florida, he was commander of the United States forces against the Creeks in Georgia and Alabama. His appointment to the Florida command was the result of his record as a fighting officer. He was to have many disappointments in the Seminole campaign, but none through personal failure. He was to become a friend of the Seminole Indians, like Wiley Thompson, through acquaintance with the people.[12]

His combined army was the most formidable that had been assembled in the territory up to this time. A large part of his eight thousand soldiers were trained in the hard task of fighting the Seminole Indians. Jesup marched toward Fort Brooke on December 12, establishing new fortified posts at strategic points: Fort Armstrong at the site of the Dade Massacre, and Camp Dade at the crossing of the Withlacoochee. He was making use of the enlistment time remaining for his Tennessee Volunteers and some other experienced men whose time was running out.

A few prisoners were captured, including sixteen Negroes of Osceola's band who were taken on January 10, 1837. Primus, a Negro who had been with Osceola since General Gaines' ordeal at Camp Izard in the spring of 1836, told Jesup that the great Seminole chieftain had been sick and had fled recently from a Negro camp near the Withlacoochee, upon the approach of white soldiers. Only his family and three warriors were with him at the time of his escape, but Primus believed that he could raise 100 warriors. Another captive told Jesup a few weeks later that Osceola was in the region of the Oklawaha.[13]

On January 22, 1837, Jesup marched his troops from Fort Armstrong toward Lake Ahapopka, where Micanopy, Onselmatche (Jumper), and Halpatter Tustenuggee (Alligator) had concentrated their forces. Near Lake Ahapopka, Colonel D. A. Caulfield attacked a settlement in which both Seminole and Negro warriors were found. Chief Osarchee, his son, and two other warriors were killed; nine Negro warriors were captured together with their women and children. On January 26, Colonel

---

[12] *Dictionary of American Biography*, X, 62, 63 (article by R. C. Cotton).
[13] Boyd, "Asi-Yahola or Osceola," reprint from *Florida Historical Quarterly*, Vol. XXXIII, Nos. 3 and 4 (Jan.-Apr., 1955), 47, 48.

Archibald Henderson attacked an Indian war party on Hatch-e-lus-kee Creek and drove them into the neighboring swamp. Twenty-three Negroes were captured, together with the party's baggage and more than one hundred ponies.

On January 27 the main body of Seminole warriors was over-taken near the Great Cypress Swamp, and General Jesup ordered an attack. After a sharp skirmish the Seminoles retreated into the swamp with soldiers in close pursuit. Twenty-five prisoners were captured—mostly women and children, both Indian and Negro. On the following day one of the Negro captives was sent with an offer of amnesty to the Seminole chiefs, provided the removal treaties were carried out. Negotiations followed, painfully slow because of distrust on both sides, with Abraham the Negro interpreter taking a prominent part in delivering the messages and making them understood. On February 3, 1837, the pacific exchanges had progressed so far that Abraham, Jumper, and Alligator agreed to a general peace conference, with hostilities suspended pending its outcome, on February 18.

General Jesup and his party returned to Fort Armstrong, and the Seminoles with their Negro allies proceeded in their own way to decide how the white leader's offer should be met. Without doubt Abraham was using his influence for peace including emigration of Indians and Negroes. Micanopy and Hal-patter Tustenuggee, also, were committed to a policy of peace.

That the Seminole Indians, for the purpose of treaty-making, were not a closely organized unit, was clear during the interval of peace. On February 8, King Philip and Coacoochee, probably with Luis Pacheco (Fatio) a member of their party, led two hundred warriors against Fort Mellon. Colonel A. C. W. Fanning's soldiers, aided by a Lake Monroe steamer armed with a small cannon, drove the Seminoles off, but only after Captain Charles Mellon was killed and 17 defenders wounded.[14] On the day agreed upon for the peace conference at Fort Dade, the Seminole leaders did not appear; but a week later Halpatter and Holatoochee (Davy), the nephew of Chief Micanopy, re-

---

[14] *American State Papers: Military Affairs*, VII, 831; Sprague, *The Florida War*, 168–69; Giddings, *The Exiles of Florida*, 136.

ported to General Jesup that Seminole hunting parties were widely separated in the southern peninsula, remote from the ordinary trails and waters, thus making more time necessary for collecting the warriors and chiefs. March 4 was set as the new date for the meeting at Fort Dade. General Jesup stipulated that no peace talk would be held without Micanopy, and that no permanent peace could be arranged on other grounds than emigration. Twelve hostages were left as security for the good intentions of the Seminoles.[15]

Unable to travel, Chief Micanopy authorized Onselmatche and Yaholoochee to act for him. On March 6, 1837, these Seminole head men signed an agreement which General Jesup regarded as the final step in the Seminole war. Hostilities were to end at once, the Indians agreed to go west with their Negroes, and while they were preparing for the long journey, to withdraw south of the Hillsborough River. The chiefs agreed to assemble their people by April 10 at a camp near Tampa Bay, for emigration. The commander signed the following compact: "Major General Jesup, in behalf of the United States, agrees that the Seminoles and their allies, who come in and emigrate West, shall be secure in their lives and property; that their Negroes, . . . shall also accompany them West; and that their cattle and ponies shall be paid for by the United States."[16]

On March 18, 1837, from army headquarters at Fort Dade, Jesup sent a jubilant report to the adjutant general at Washington. Micanopy had come in to approve the agreement signed by Alligator and Jumper, and he had heard favorable news from Arpeika (Sam Jones) and Osceola (Powell). General Jesup was confident the trouble was over, but he warned that "imprudent violence" on the part of citizens could renew it. "Should they attempt to scize any of the Indians, either as criminals or as debtors," the results would be disastrous, and he should not hesitate to declare martial law in order to protect his prisoners.

His troops were in position to advance rapidly in any direc-

[15] *American State Papers: Military Affairs*, 827–29, 833, 865; Boyd, "Asi-Yahola or Osceola," reprint from *Florida Historical Quarterly*, Vol. XXXIII (1955), 48, 49.

[16] *Ibid.*, VII, 834; 25 Cong., 3 sess., *Ex. Doc. No. 225.*

tion, in the event that the Indians were not acting in good faith. He enclosed a copy of the document signed by the Principal Chief, which ran as follows: "I, Micanopy, . . . having had read and fully explained to me certain 'Articles of Capitulation' entered into on the sixth day of March, 1837 at Fort Dade, Florida, between Major General Jesup of the United States Army, for and on the part of the United States, and Hoethle Ma-tee (Onselmatche, or Jumper), Holatoochee (Davy), Yaholoochee (Cloud), Halpatah Hajo (Halpatter, or Alligator), &c. my representatives, do hereby fully acknowledge and confirm every Article of the same." The Chief signed by means of a cross-mark, and the document was witnessed by L. Churchill, inspector general; I. A. Chambers, acting adjutant general; T. B. Linnard, A. D. C.; and William M. Graham, captain and battalion major, acting agent for the Seminoles.[17]

While Wiley Thompson, Governor Call, and the generals in succession had met the problem of removal by force, a beginning had been made in the administration of emigration. On October 21, 1835, before the death of Thompson, Lieutenant Joseph W. Harris, disbursing agent, had written to General George Gibson that he was much embarrassed by the disposition of contractors in New York to combine, to "withdraw the lower in favor of the higher bids," and to reject contracts "upon the eve of Signature." He observed that the price of corn quoted to him in New York was $1.12 per bushel; and that the grain might be purchased from St. Marks traders at a "saving of $600 to $1,000."[18]

Lieutenant Harris was back at Fort King in December, and his report to General George Gibson on the death of Wiley Thompson contained a recommendation for David M. Sheffield as superintendent of emigration to succeed him. The suggestion was not followed, however. "Until further notice," Gibson wrote to Harris, "you will consider yourself as Superintendent of the Emigration of the Seminole Indians & will be governed by the

---

[17] Jesup to Adj. Gen. Roger Jones, Mar. 18, 1837, O. I. A.: Seminoles—Emigration.
[18] Harris to Gibson, Oct. 21, 1835, *ibid.*

orders of the General commanding in Florida." The order was written on April 14, 1836; but Harris had departed for Arkansas with a band of emigrants and did not receive the notice of his promotion for three months.

On April 25, he reported from New Orleans on the band he was taking west. Fifty-five of the 512 Indians had died before they reached Tampa Bay. The muster roll at Fort Brooke contained 399 names, but one child died on the night before they embarked. Over half of the party were stricken with severe illness before they reached New Orleans. Since this was the last band to be moved during the season, Harris expected to conduct them all the way to Little Rock, where they would be turned over to Captain Jacob Brown, principal disbursing agent for the West. On the journey up the Mississippi the conductor was so sick that he was unable to leave a coherent account at all stages of the trip. He arrived in Arkansas deeply discouraged and anxious only to be relieved of his band. He went to Hot Springs where he rested for a few weeks, hoping to regain his health. On July 14, he received General Gibson's letter announcing his promotion in the emigration service; but he answered on a somewhat petulant note and started for White Sulphur Springs, Virginia.

In spite of his illness and bad temper—his resentment of the treatment given him seemed to be directed against Congress more than the War Department or the Seminole Indians—Harris proposed measures which indicated his strong sympathy for the native people whom he was helping to dispossess. Among other measures advocated were these: payment of $1,500 for livestock losses and back pay to Cudjoe, the interpreter; $4,175.50 to the friendly Seminoles for property losses; regular army pay for Seminole warriors who served under General Gaines; and for other Seminoles, $1,120 for 28 horses at $40; $900 for 150 cattle at $6; $300 for 100 hogs at $3; and $680 for losses of provisions. Less than a year later Harris resigned from the service, and before the end of the year 1837, he was dead, at the age of thirty-two.[19]

[19] Harris to Gibson, June 4, 1836; Harris to Commissioner C. A. Harris,

In addition to Captain Jacob Brown, Lieutenant George G. Meade and Lieutenant J. Van Horne were engaged in transporting Indians west of Rock Roe in Arkansas. The cost of transportation by land was high, as Brown explained, because owners of teams and wagons had no guarantee of employment, due to the uncertainty of Seminole emigration. A contract sent to the Indian Office in 1836 shows the general character of the agreements. James Erwin and Daniel Greathouse agreed to have in readiness for twenty-one days such number of wagons "as shall be required—not exceeding Sixty, at Rock Roe on the south bank of White River." Each unit was to be a "Good and substantial Five Horse or Six Ox Wagon," capable of handling a 3000 pound load. The teams were to be in good condition. The rate of pay was to be $4 per day in the service of transporting Indian baggage and "such Indians as cannot walk; and $1.50 for each wagon and team not actually employed in transportation—but ready at Rock Roe for such service."

Lieutenant Van Horne's Journal for Holati Emathla's band and his official reports to Captain Brown, George Gibson, and Commissioner Harris give a vivid and in some parts a gruesome picture of the Seminole "Trail of Tears." On May 14, 1836, he relieved Lieutenant George G. Meade of a band of emigrants at Titsworth, one hundred miles east of the Seminole country. Meade had provided eleven wagons, but there was not enough room in them for the Indian goods and the seventy-eight sick travelers whom Van Horne found on his hands. "I still find it necessary to leave here with Mr. Titsworth three bales of blankets, which it is very desirable should be shipped to the Seminole country, as early as practicable," he wrote to Captain Brown. An entry in the journal for May 14 complained that the Seminoles would not obey the doctor who accompanied the party, but insisted upon bathing the sick in the cold waters of the river. The people of Arkansas protested destruction of their timber by the Indians—and Van Horne tried to solve the problem

Mar. 3, Apr. 1, 1837, O. I. A.: Seminoles—Emigration. From Portsmouth, N. H. he wrote, "My disease, become obstinately chronic from an ill-judged treatment, etc."

by moving along. "Issued 4 days' rations of corn, & started west. 4 miles. Had to go back after 4 wagon-loads of corn & meat, of which there was a surplus, because of sick Indians—and dead Indians.

"May 17—Indians wanted to camp until sick got well. Tried to get more teams but without success. A principal man very low, they begged me to let them stay till he died and was buried. He died and was buried. . . .

"May 19—Rain. Hotulge Yohola, Indian doctor and principal man, dying. Indians insisted on staying until he died and was buried. Roads deep in mire. Wagons had to be hauled for miles through deep mire, ten yoke of oxen to each. . . .

"May 22—Started at nine o'clock. Made ten miles to Poteau River. Road boggy. Poteau not fordable. . . . An axletree gave way. . . . After dark a Choctaw introduced a gallon of whiskey into camp, which I took from him."[20]

On May 23, 1836, Lieutenant Van Horne reported to General Gibson from the Choctaw Agency, near the site of present day Skullyville: "Since my last re. have made only about 70 miles to this place. We have had every difficulty to contend with. A constant scene of vexation and toil. About half the party have been and are still sick. Many continue very low and must die. Three died yesterday, three this morning. It has rained powerfully every day flooding the streams and making the roads deep and miery. . . ."

The contacts of Lieutenant Van Horne with Colonel William Armstrong, superintendent at Skullyville, were not altogether satisfactory as the reports disclose without actual complaint of the colonel's interference. "The Supt. told me on my arrival . . . that he had postponed his departure to the Red River a day or two to have an interview with the Sem. It had been my design to have gone four miles beyond here last evening. . . . However I encamped here to afford him an interview. This morning they availed themselves of this pretext, and could by no means be restrained from a talk with him. The Wife and

---

[20] Brown to Gibson, Jan. 1, 1836; Van Horne's Journal, Holati Emathla's Band, O. I. A.: Seminoles—Emigration.

daughter of Black Dirt, 2d chief, and Tustenuggee's principal warrior have just died." The Seminoles wanted to stay for the rest of the day, and Van Horne reluctantly consented. "In the after part of the day it rained powerfully," he added.[21]

Vehicles dragged through mud by doubling teams, broken wagons, impassable streams; "numbers very low and dying;" the journal is a dreary record of misery. "From one, two, and three deaths per diem, we now have four. The effluvia and pestilential atmosphere of the waggons, where some twenty sick or dying lay in their own filth, and even the tainted air of their camps is almost unsupportable."[22] Holati Emathla died during the night of June 3. He was buried by his people the following morning, "on a handsome eminence . . . one and a half miles from the Canadian. His body and effects were encased in a strongly built wooden pile, built to the height of five feet above the surface of the earth. The neighboring ground was carefully cleared of grass and leaves, and a fire left burning near his head."

On June 5, Van Horne and the survivors of his party reached a point on the Canadian that was opposite land assigned to the Seminoles. Unable to cross the stream with wagons, he discharged the teamsters and crossed in boats. Two months afterward he was able to report that the Indians had become quite healthy, but he added: "Notwithstanding the good opportunity they now have of building houses and living comfortable and happily, I regret to say they seem not disposed to exert themselves. They are exceedingly dissipated, idle, and reckless."[23]

In Florida, the optimism of General Thomas Jesup continued for two months after his armistice with Micanopy and the lesser chiefs at Fort Dade. By the eighth of May, he still expressed confidence, but was beginning to consider elements of danger in the situation; and on June 5, 1837, he wrote the most pessimistic report of his entire career. The events which caused that reversal of opinion will be considered in the next chapter.

[21] Van Horne to Gibson, May 23, 1836, O. I. A.: Seminoles–Emigration.
[22] Van Horne's Journal, O. I. A.: Seminoles–Emigration.
[23] Van Horne to Gibson, Aug. 23, 1836, O. I. A.: Seminoles–Emigration.

CHAPTER 12

Seminole Guile

*"No Seminole proves false to his country, nor has a single instance
ever occurred of a first rate warrior having surrendered."*

GENERAL THOMAS JESUP

O N MARCH 8, 1837, General Jesup was at the climax of his most successful year in Florida. The tone of his letter on that date to the commissioner of Indian affairs reflects his expansive, dominating mood. Possibly, Jesup saw himself, during a brief span of weeks, as a great man—a commander engaged in a tremendously important job that no one else could do. He had received the commissioner's various letters, but had been too busy to answer them. He wrote:

"There is a . . . fair prospect of removing a part, at least, of the Seminoles in the course of the next two months: in that event I will detail an officer to make the disbursements; and as I do not wish to be embarrassed with accounts, I would prefer to make drafts on the department in his favour letting him be held accountable for the sums drawn. The hope that Lieut. Harris would join before any movement of the Indians could possibly take place has prevented me from designating an officer. . . ."[1]

In a report to Secretary of War Joel Poinsett on April 8, 1837, Jesup expressed the belief that the war was over. "Should, however," he hastened to add, "any attempt be made to seize the

[1] Jesup to C. A. Harris, Com. of Ind. Aff., Mar. 8, 1837, O.I.A.: Seminoles—Emigration. On March 3, Lieutenant J. W. Harris had resigned, on account of ill health, from his post as disbursing agent; he had insisted on permanent resignation on April 1; but on July 18, 1837, it was Joseph W. Harris, acting superintendent, Florida Indians, who certified Lieutenant Casey's claims of that date.

Indian Negroes, or to arrest any of the chiefs or warriors, either as criminals or debtors, an immediate resort to arms would be the consequence."

Near Jesup's headquarters, several prominent chiefs of the Seminoles were encamped with detachments of their followers. Micanopy, Holatoochee, Yaholoochee (Cloud), Coacoochee (Wild Cat) were among them. The Negro chieftain, John Coheia (Cowiya, or Gopher John), was in camp. General Jesup was strongly impressed with Coacoochee, whom he regarded the most talented of the Seminoles. "He should and no doubt will, be the principal chief of the nation."

Wild Cat promised that Arpeika and his Mikasuki followers would come in, and that when he had collected his cattle on the St. Johns, he would return with his father and all his people to the emigrating camp. The chiefs agreed to surrender all Negroes taken during the war; they were to be delivered to the military posts on the St. Johns.

To control the "strolling vagabonds" whom he expected to linger after the emigration of the main body of Indians, Jesup proposed to re-establish Fort King, to keep a garrison at Fort Drane until early June, and to build a new post between Fort Drane and the Suwanee. He suggested that expenditure of a few thousand dollars, "judiciously applied as compensation to the chiefs of energy and influence," would aid greatly in the tedious work of removal. Here perhaps was the least accurate estimate Jesup was to put in writing concerning the Seminoles: a serious underestimate of their love of Florida, attachment to their Negro allies, and ability to take the punishment of a destructive war.

In the middle of April, writing to Commissioner C. A. Harris, Jesup reported that the Indians had begun delivery of their cattle and horses. "The emigration will be tedious and expensive," he wrote; "but I think it will certainly take place. The Seminoles, however, have less regard for their promises than any other In dians I have ever known." He also complained of the influence of Indian women who were wives or mistresses of the Spanish fishermen. He did not agree with General Scott, that these women might be permitted to remain with their husbands. "This is contrary to the custom among the Indians," Jesup observed; "with them the family belongs to and always accompanies the wife's relations."

Captain John Page, superintendent of emigration in the spring of 1837, gave interesting reports on the Indians at Tampa Bay. He talked to the chiefs and learned their views on the war. They were willing to tell him about the battles in which they had taken part, and to give the number of Indians killed in action. "I cannot make out fifty they have lost, counting the number missing in each town." The chiefs also revealed that the Seminoles were not hard-pressed for food. Most of the cattle taken by Jesup's soldiers belonged to the white people. "To see them come in driving their cattle and horses before them, it does not look much like starvation; they readily admit that was their least trouble."

On May 8, two months after his triumphant meeting with Micanopy's people at Fort Dade, Jesup reported to the secretary of war that most of the Indians were concentrated in the vicinity of Fort Mellon on Lake Monroe. Evidently, the General did not suspect Osceola of duplicity at this time. "Powell will be highly useful in bringing the Indians in, and in hastening embarkation." One thing only, he feared—the "imprudence" of Florida citizens and "officious interference."

From newspapers, Jesup said he had learned "that certain citizens of Florida, who, I presume are unwilling to trust their persons nearer to the Seminoles than Charleston, are denouncing me. . . . I can have no agency in converting the Army into Negro catchers, particularly for . . . those who are afraid to undertake the recapture of their property themselves."[2]

Colonel William S. Harney reported from Fort Mellon to General Jesup at army headquarters on Tampa Bay early in May, 1837. With Osceola, Coacoochee, and Co-e-hadjo in camp, Harney was confident that emigration would proceed smoothly, if the leaders were "indulged a little longer." Time was required

[2] Jesup to Poinsett, Apr. 9, 1837; Jesup to C. A. Harris, Apr. 15, 1837; Jesup to Poinsett, May 8, 1837; Page to Harris, Apr. 20, 1837, O. I. A.: Seminoles—Emigration.

John Chupco (seated, center), the council,
and light-horse police.

Missionary party to the Florida Seminoles in 1909. Standing, left to right: Dan Long, A. J. Brown, John Wesley, George Scott, Sissy Long; seated, Mrs. A. J. Brown, Mrs. Alice B. Davis, Lizzie Bruner, Irene Davis (later Mrs. W. S. Key), Lucy Brown (later Mrs. Barney McKellop), Mrs. George Scott.

Oklahoma Historical Society

Below: Site of Fort King, near Ocala, Florida.

to get the scattered hunters together, dispose of their livestock, and make all necessary arrangements. As he wrote his report, the officer learned that Arpeika (Sam Jones) had arrived in camp the previous night in time to take part in the council. "Co-e-hadjo and Powell (Osceola) are with me now; Powell slept in my tent last night with me, and they both say they are almost sure that it will not be more than a week before they are all on the road to Tampa Bay."

General Jesup had directed that no trade be permitted between the Indians and the sutler at Fort Mellon. "This placed me in a very awkward situation," wrote Harney, ". . . as they are literally naked, many of them." After hearing the chiefs and consulting with the officers, it was decided to permit a limited amount of trade. The commander at Fort Mellon, after some inquiry among the chiefs, learned that there were in his vicinity some 2,500 Indian warriors, "good warriors, and not including lads &c, or Negroes, who fight as well as the best of them." The chiefs did not tell Colonel Harney how many slaves they owned, or how many free Negroes there were among them. Furthermore they did not wish to surrender Negroes belonging to the whites, until the Indians were ready to move, on the ground that many of them would hide in the swamps before they could be brought in.

On June 1, 1837, Captain Page sent a report to Commissioner Harris from Tampa Bay in which definite suspicion was shown that the calm was deceptive. "I have been encamped with the Seminole Indians twelve miles from this place," he began. He had pretended illness, in order to be in a position to watch the Mikasukies, who "had been passing backwards and forwards" in a manner described by Captain Page as "mysterious conduct." The Captain trusted Jumper and Micanopy, but not the Mikasukies. "In four or five days it will be readily ascertained whether the treaty will be complied with or the war to commence again. If the latter it must [be] a war of extermination."[3]

On June 5, 1837, General Jesup reported to Commissioner

[3] Harney to Jesup, May, 1837, copy enclosed in report, Jesup to Commissioner C. A. Harris, May 8, 1837; Page to Harris, June 1, 1837, O. I. A.: Seminoles—Emigration.

Harris the sudden change of his fortunes in the removal project. "I have now to acquaint you with the entire failure of the scheme of emigration," he wrote. Micanopy, Jumper, and Cloud, with their families were secured and carried off by a party of warriors on the night of the 2d inst. It is stated that the warriors have degraded Micanopy, and have placed Sam Jones, the Mikasuki chief, at the head of the Nation. I believe the emigration of the Seminoles to be impracticable under any circumstances. Those who removed last year were Upper Creeks, not Seminoles. The country can be rid of them only by exterminating them. I have sent a few Indian and Negro prisoners to New Orleans, and I shall immediately discharge the vessels which have been employed to carry the Indians off, and shall deposit to the credit of the Treasurer of the United States, the sums placed to my credit in the Branch of the Bank of Alabama, and the Union Bank of Louisiana at New Orleans."

Captain Page's report on the abduction of Micanopy added but few details. The band of Mikasukies numbered about two hundred. Sam Jones and Osceola had ordered that no white man was to be harmed in the raid, but no dissent was to be permitted their own people. "Micanopy refused . . . saying he had signed a treaty. . . . They told him his blood would be spilt if he did not go. He threw his bosom open and told them to kill him and do it quickly. They then forced him on his horse and guarded him off." Captain Page regarded Jumper and Micanopy sincere; Cloud he believed to be in harmony with Osceola and Arpeika.

General Jesup explained the situation to Secretary of War Joel Poinsett, in a detailed report. The military campaign had been completely successful, he wrote; but the emigration failed. He pointed out that the Indians had been driven from all of their strongholds north of Tampa Bay and Ahpopka Lake. Hostilities had ceased, and travel in Florida was safe. It must be admitted that Jesup had given the most effective display of military power that had been shown in Florida since the active days of General Andrew Jackson.

But in the complicated problem of representing the United States as the commander of its army, with tactful handling of the territorial officials and due regard for voters of Florida and the states, he had failed as miserably as Duval, Wiley Thompson, Gaines, Scott, and Call before him. Florida ground was in great demand by its owners, the Seminole Indians, and by white settlers who wanted to dispossess them. Fugitive slaves in Florida were greatly desired by owners; unscrupulous men saw in the confusion surrounding Seminole slaves and free Negroes an invitation to fraud. An administrator in Florida who tried to protect treaty rights of Indians, immediately clashed with powerful interests of influential citizens. As long as Andrew Jackson was President, the United States could be depended upon to place property rights of voters ahead of treaty rights of American Indians. But the Seminoles were not inclined to submit tamely to long-continued injustices.

General Jesup did his best to explain away his failure to take the Seminoles out. "Soon after the Indians had begun to assemble in this neighborhood [army headquarters on Tampa Bay] the measles, which had prevailed in the Army during the winter, broke out among them, after which very few came in—the Indian Negroes had been alarmed by the arrival in camp of individuals who had lost their slaves during the war—most of them fled, and but few could be prevailed upon to return. This was the state of things when, as I have already reported to the Adjutant-General, a party of armed warriors seized the Chiefs Micanopy, Jumper, and Cloud in their camp about eight miles from this place on the evening of the 2d instant, and hurried them off to the swamps of the interior. I had received through the Principal Creek Chief on the morning of the 1st inst., intimation that an attempt would be made in a few days by a party of Mikasukies and a small band of Seminoles to kill or abduct those chiefs—I ordered Major Graham who was stationed with a mounted company and a hundred and twenty Creek warriors four miles from Micanopy's camp, to send out spies at night and observe the movements of the Indians. The Major sent two Indians into the Seminole camp on the night of the 1st and though he ordered them to go out again on the night of the second they either disobeyed the order or failed to report. The mounted force here and at Major Graham's camp was held in readiness to move at a moment's warning, but it was not until the morning of the 3rd that the flight of the Indians was known. They had twelve hours start, and in the state of the country, and the extreme heat of the weather, pursuit would have been useless." In view of the many charges that have been made against General Jesup as a violator of truce pacts, his statement on this incident is enlightening. "The principal chiefs met me in council on the 1st instant and I might have seized them and captured their camps, but such an act would have been an infraction of the treaty." He added that the capture of a few hundred warriors would have been "poor compensation for a violation of the national faith— the Indians now have no faith in our promises." He also thought that Chief Micanopy and Jumper would be valuable assets to the United States as counterweights to Sam Jones (Arpeika), leader of the hostile Mikasukies.

General Jesup was ready to call the policy of Seminole removal a failure. "One month ago I could have made a treaty with them as permanent as that with Great Britain and have restricted them to any limits I might have assigned them." In all other removals, he said, acute pressure of white population had preceded actual emigration. This was the first time an attempt had been made to "transfer Indians from one wilderness to another." He thought it impossible to get all the Indians out of Florida without exterminating them; he doubted that public opinion would sustain extermination, involving use of northern Indians and bloodhounds.

Jesup predicted that the Mikasukies would renew the war and he was ready to meet them. He left the way open for appointment of his successor, without prejudice, by recommending the establishment of supply depots for the next campaign, and suggesting that troops should be in the field by the first of October. "The officer who is to be charged with the operations of the next campaign should be at once placed in command of the Army in order to make timely arrangements for the service."[4]

[4] Jesup to Com. C. A. Harris, June 5, 1837; Jesup to Sec. Joel Poinsett, June 7, 1837; Page to Harris, June 6, 1837, O. I. A.: Seminoles—Emigration.

On June 10, 1837, Jesup reported to Joel Poinsett that he had called upon the governor of Florida for three hundred men east of the Suwanee and four hundred men west of that river, mounted militia to take the place of Florida troops recently discharged. Regular troops, he thought, should be kept quiet during the hot weather, in order to be ready for the autumn campaign. Florida militia could best handle the summer assignments. For the fall campaign he advised:

"Regiments should be placed upon the war establishment of at least a hundred men to the company, and the ranks should be filled as soon as possible, in addition to which there should be an auxiliary Indian force employed to be here by the 1st of September. Shawnees, Miamis, and Delawares would be preferable to Creeks. The troops and all officers below the rank of Major-General, should receive double pay while serving in Florida. . . . If the war be carried on it must necessarily be one of extermination. We have, at no former period in our history, had to contend with so formidable an enemy. No Seminole proves false to his country, nor has a single instance ever occurred of a first rate warrior having surrendered."

It was clear that Thomas Jesup, the soldier, thoroughly respected the fighting qualities of his adversaries. On June 16, he advised the Secretary of War on the subject of permanent solution of the Seminole problem. He believed, like Wiley Thompson before him, that the Indians had been "tampered with by interested white men." He stated as his opinion that the chiefs had not enough influence to remove their people, and that the Seminoles could not be removed, so long as they were able to obtain ammunition. He pointed out that the Negroes and Indians of Florida had a strong disposition toward identity of interests and feelings, and believed that Indians remaining in Florida would always have among them Negroes who "will form a rallying point" for runaway slaves. "And should they remove," he added, "the fastnesses of the country would be immediately occupied by Negroes. I am very sure they could be confined to a smaller district near Florida Point, and would accept peace and the smaller district referred to as the condition for surrender of all runaway Negroes." Then Jesup made a statement which seemed to indicate a touch of modesty—perhaps the chastening influence of matching wits with Osceola and Coacoochee, through one military and one diplomatic campaign.

"I throw out these hints for the consideration of my official superiors;" he wrote, "without pretending to offer an opinion as to the propriety of adopting them."[5] Later in the summer of 1837, on July 20, Jesup sent an important report from St. Augustine, where he had established headquarters, to the adjutant general, concerning captured Negroes:

"I enclose a list of the Indian Negroes captured during the campaigns," the report began. The captives included the most influential men among these Seminole allies, and the leaderless remnant, he thought, would not be effective. He had attempted a division of the Negro prisoners, and eighty were at Camp Pike, Louisiana, on their way west with the Seminoles. Eighty-eight of the ninety-three Negroes whom he identified as belonging to white citizens, had been returned to their owners or held subject to their orders, and two others were kept on duty at Tampa Bay at the request of their owners. Two, because of their acquaintance with the Seminole country, were serving as guides for the army, and one who had been sent as a messenger to the Indians had not been permitted to return. Six of the Seminole Negroes had died at the time of this report and seventeen were still at Tampa Bay, waiting for transportation west.

"Of the Indian prisoners who have been taken and secured I shall not be able to furnish a list until my return to Tampa—they amount to between eighty and ninety," the General wrote. Twenty-three Seminole prisoners were at Camp Pike, three were held at St. Augustine, fifteen had died, and "about fifteen women and children relatives of the Creeks were allowed to accompany their relatives to Mobile Point, and to Econchatimico's Town on the Apalachicola River. The remainder were at Tampa, all except three of them with the Creek Indians."

The list of Negroes enclosed in General Jesup's report was

[5] Jesup to Poinsett, June 10, 1837; Jesup to Poinsett, June 16, 1837, O. I. A.: Seminoles—Emigration.

labeled, "Registry of Negro Prisoners captured by Thomas S. Jesup, owned (or claimed) by Indians, 1836–1837." Four pages were required for the list of 103 names, together with the General's descriptive comments, and in some instances the name of the Indian owner. Among the Negroes listed were these:

Ben   Owner, Micanopy, Age, 40. Father. [The mother and nine children follow on the list.] One of the most important and influential of the Negroes.

Inoinophen   Age, 45. Husband. Commander of Negro force on the Withlacoochee. Chief counselor among the Negroes, and the most important character. [Wife, Eliza, and two children listed.]

Ben, Jacob, &
  Mundy,   Age 22, 24, 20. Intrepid, hostile warriors.

Murray   Age 35. Owned by Colonel Crowell, and claimed by Nelly Factor. The best guide in the Nation.

Dick   John Hicks Town. Said to be the property of Colonel Gad Humphreys.

Toney Barnet   Age, 36. Claims to be free. Said to be a good soldier and an intrepid leader. He is the most cunning and intelligent Negro we have seen. He is married to the widow of the former chief.

Polly Barnet   Age, 36. Claims to be free.

Abraham   Age, 50. Claims to be free. The principal Negro chief. Supposed to be friendly to the whites.

A few of the 103 Negro prisoners listed by General Jesup as belonging to the Seminoles were wounded before their capture, and a few died on their way to Louisiana.[6]

By September the commander had moved his headquarters from St. Augustine to Tampa Bay, and was preparing to conduct his next campaign against the Seminoles. His message to Major W. G. Freeman in regard to discharge of the Creek regiment has in it some important evidence that has been generally neglected concerning his attitude toward the American Indian.

[6] Jesup to Adj. Gen. R. Jones, July 20, 1837, O.I.A.: Seminoles—Emigration.

The correspondence is a part of Jesup's record; without it, an accurate estimate of his total influence would be impossible.

"You will proceed with the last detachment of Creek warriors on board the *Tomochichi* to Pass Christian, where you will make arrangements to discharge the regiment," he directed Major Freeman. There followed a detailed order as to pay for the troops, their comfort and convenience under contract with the transportation company, and as to their being "put in motion to the West without unnecessary delay."

Major Freeman and Captain Boyd were directed to help the Indians with the transaction of their business in New Orleans. "They will desire to make many purchases for themselves and their families," Jesup suggested; "and they should be advised not to waste their money, but to purchase such articles only as shall be really useful; they should be told of the necessity of providing against cold weather which they will have to encounter before they arrive at their new homes; and I wish you and Captain Boyd to assist them in their purchases, so as to prevent imposition being practiced upon them."

In the event that the contractors were not bound to furnish sufficient accommodations for the "sick and infirm," and all articles necessary for their comfort, the General wrote, "You are authorized to direct Mr. Reynolds or who-so-ever may be charged with superintending the emigration, to make the necessary provisions for those purposes."

Freeman was ordered to keep accurate records of Creek Indians killed and those who had died in the service of the United States—one copy for the War Department, one for General Jesup. The warriors were to be instructed that they were not obliged to take discount upon their paper money. "Advise them to retain the same notes they receive and to part with none but for such necessary articles as they may require." The chiefs and warriors of the second Creek battalion, whose families were already in the West, were to be given preference in transportation. "Should the second battalion move separately," the General added, "and you think it advisable, or the Indians desire it, Captain Boyd may be continued in service and accompany that battalion west. In that event he will be instructed to proceed to Washington, on completing that service, for the settlement of his public accounts."

Jesup's confidence in Major Freeman was clear in the order to exercise "a judicious discretion" in any case not covered by specific instructions, and to report to the General for further special duties, upon the completion of the assignment. An extract from a letter written by General Jesup on the same day to Lieutenant F. Searle, acting assistant inspector general, Army of the South, has in it significant data with respect to auxiliary Indian troops in the Seminole War. Lieutenant Searle was ordered to muster the Creek regiment out of service and honorably discharge them. Then, at New Orleans, he would "obtain funds to pay the Creeks for the captured Negroes." Explicit directions were given as to paying the Creek participants in the catching of Negroes.

"The chiefs and warriors who were actually in the field and present at and aiding in the capture of the Negroes are alone to receive any part of the sum allowed—those who remained in camp and did not march are to receive nothing. Eight thousand dollars will be paid to the captors for the Seminole Negroes and twenty dollars each for those the property of citizens. The amount allowed for the Seminole Negroes will be apportioned as follows, viz: to the first battalion, five thousand, seven hundred dollars; to the second battalion, two thousand dollars; and to the spy battalion, three hundred dollars."

Searle was instructed to examine the prisoners at Camp Pike, and to make a careful description of each Negro, "specifying their names, ages, height, sex, and such other particulars as you may think important." The prisoners were to be comfortably clothed by the assistant quartermaster, housed in the barracks, and used as laborers, under guard, if the officer in charge desired to employ them.

"Bowlegs will be taken on and placed with the prisoners at Fort Pike," Jesup stated. In his letter to Lieutenant Searle a list of thirty-five Negroes belonging to citizens was included, along with the record of their capture by the first and second Creek battalions. Searle, like Freeman, was ordered to report directly to Jesup, upon completion of his special duty.

To the Secretary of War, General Jesup gave an account of his agreement with the Creeks as follows:

"The Creek Indians have been promised a reward for the captures they should make of Negroes belonging to the citizens of the United States. Had compensation not been promised they would have taken no prisoners, but would have put all to death. I compromised with them by allowing twenty dollars for each slave captured." They had been promised, before they entered the service, all Seminole property captured by them, including Negro slaves. "To end all difficulty on that subject, I have purchased the Negroes from them on account of the public, for eight thousand dollars." About eighty Negroes were included not counting Abraham, the guide, and his family, who were free. Some of these prisoners, Jesup added, "may be found on investigation to be the property of citizens. I respectfully request that the purchase be sanctioned." The suggestion that money for paying the Creeks might be charged to the Seminole annuity, was an obvious effort to gain official support for his purchase, and the General added other arguments.

"It is highly important to the slaveholding states that these Negroes be sent out of the country; and I would strongly recommend that they be sent to one of our colonies in Africa. The sum paid to the Indians is entirely satisfactory to them though it is far less than the value of the Negroes."

To the Commissioner of Indian Affairs, Jesup repeated information given to the Secretary of War, and added an interesting item. "The Seminole Negro prisoners are now all the property of the public," he stated. "I have promised Abraham the freedom of his family if he be faithful to us, and I shall certainly hang him if he be not faithful." Abraham was used as an interpreter, and was also one of the best guides in the Seminole country.[7]

In his attempt to settle the matter of the Seminole Negroes,

[7] Jesup to Freeman, Sept. 9, 1837; Jesup to Searle, Sept. 9, 1837; Jesup to Poinsett, Sept. 22, 1837; Jesup to Harris, Sept. 24, 1837, O.I.A.: Seminoles—Emigration.

it must be admitted that General Jesup was not able to make use of his best talents and most extensive training. The Creeks were involved, the Seminoles were not satisfied, the Negroes suffered some of the worst of their long succession of abuses, and the United States became a dealer in slave property. The last mentioned item gave Joshua Giddings and other antislavery men a choice morsel for attack upon the government's fugitive slave policy, and the trade in human chattels.[8]

It had been Jesup's intention to keep military and removal operations unhampered by the problem of runaway Negroes. He instructed the commander at Fort Armstrong to refuse permission to Colonel Dill of Florida to search for escaped slaves among the Seminole captives. The General was completely sincere when he agreed that the emigrants should take their Negroes west with them, and he understood thoroughly the danger of injustice in permitting local court processes to determine questions of disputed ownership. He also saw clearly the peril of renewal of war in the Negro question. His instructions to Lieutenant Colonel Miller at Tampa Bay on March 27, 1837, show his attitude at that time. "I have . . . been informed that Mr. Cooley's business at Tampa Bay is to look after Negroes. If that be so, he must be sent away; a trifling circumstance would light up the war again. Any interference with the Negroes which would produce alarm on their part would inevitably deprive us of all the advantages we have gained. I sympathize with Mr. Cooley in his afflictions and losses, but responsible as I am for the peace of the country, I cannot and will not permit that peace to be jeopardized by his imprudence."

Co-e-hadjo, in April, 1837, came to a conference with General Jesup at Fort King and agreed that Seminole Negroes captured during the war, and perhaps others belonging to white masters, should be surrendered. The means by which this break was made in the Seminole case for removal of their Negroes is not clear. Co-e-hadjo had no authority to speak for the Indians who had signed articles of capitulation; his lack of personal interest in the Negro question perhaps made him indifferent; and a bribe

[8] Giddings, *The Exiles of Florida*, 146–55.

for his agreement is not to be ruled out. On April 29, 1837, Jesup wrote to Colonel Brown of St. Augustine, "I have made arrangements with the Indians for the delivery of Negroes captured during the war. . . . The Indians are not bound to surrender runaway Negroes. They must and shall give up those taken during the war; at all events, they shall not take them out of the country. Further than that, I shall not interfere."

Two days earlier the General had written to Judge J. L. Smith, also a citizen of Florida. "I received . . . your letter . . . with a list of the slaves you claim. Ansel is the only one of the three who has been taken. I have him employed . . . as an interpreter." Few Negroes could be expected to come in, Jesup believed; and he regarded the slaves a major factor in preventing surrender of the Indians for migration. Haste on the part of citizens to recover slaves was a serious obstacle to the army's efforts. "More than thirty Negro men were in and near my camp, when some of the citizens who had lost Negroes, came to demand them. The Indian Negroes immediately disappeared, and have not been heard of since."

In the language of General Jesup's reports and correspondence with citizens, there is much ambiguity. He made no distinction between Negroes "captured during the war," and those who sought refuge with the Seminoles, sometimes joining their relatives in the Seminole country during the war. His slight change of attitude on the debatable question as to what made a person of African descent a "Seminole Negro" opened the way for a multitude of claims from adjoining states, as well as Florida Territory. The Legislative Council added its influence to the general confusion by a resolution that recognized the right of masters to go into the Indian country and recover their own slaves. Bold citizens, armed and ready to fight for recovery of their fugitive slaves or their livestock, ranged the Seminole lands in company with desperate men who were simply willing to risk their lives in the effort to obtain Negroes for the slave market.

General Jesup understood the danger, but lacked the knowledge of politics and political leaders to apply the remedy. With Van Buren in the chief executive's office after March 4, 1837, firm adherence on the part of the General to the terms of Seminole capitulation would have been possible in Florida. At times, Jesup was inclined to overestimate the greatness of his military achievement; but he was prone to underestimate the political strength that his military campaign gave him.

The seizure of eighty-six Negro prisoners at Tampa Bay for shipment to New Orleans was strictly in accord with Jesup's agreement with the Seminole chiefs; but the precipitate manner in which the maneuver was carried out frightened the Seminole slaves who were still at large. The capture of fugitives and their return to white masters could not be accomplished without alarm to all the Negroes. Jesup wrote to Governor R. K. Call, that thirty Seminole Negroes in camp near the Withlacoochee River had vanished into the forest upon the approach of Florida citizens searching for their slaves. In breaking the news of the *coup* by Osceola and Arpeika to James Gadsden, General Jesup wrote on June 14: "All is lost, and principally, I fear, by the influence of the Negroes."[9]

Renewal of the war, made inevitable by the Mikasuki *coup* of June 2, 1837, was due mainly to the deviation of United States authorities from the spirit and the letter of General Jesup's agreement at Fort Dade. Political pressure upon the General was directly responsible for his shifting policy. The attitude of the Legislative Council in Florida, newspaper critics in all parts of the South, citizens' assemblies at St. Augustine and elsewhere, with demands that owners of escaped slaves be permitted to look for their property under protection of their government, all combined to force upon General Jesup a modification of his stand concerning the Negroes. Resentment against the Seminoles, whom he had regarded a defeated people, contributed to his rationalization of his own surrender to misguided public opinion.

While General Jesup was enjoying his greatest victories and suffering his worst defeat in East Florida, the Indians of the Apalachicola were under the care of the subagent, Archibald Smith, Jr. In spite of obvious weaknesses in grammar and literary

---

[9] Jesup to Gadsden, June 14, 1837; Jesup to Jones, July 20, 1837, O.I.A.: Seminoles—Emigration; Giddings, *The Exiles of Florida*, 152–55.

style, Archibald was a voluminous letter writer, and his reports to the Commissioner of Indian Affairs gave a fairly complete record of the year in his area. Smith had a keen interest in the welfare of his charges, and possibly, as he claimed for himself, a deep insight in regard to Indian character.

He reported on January 5, 1837, "I wrote you a few short lines in reply to your kind letters of the 1st, 2nd, and 18th Nov. in which I promised at a more leisure [sic] moment to write you more fully but of that leisure moment I have been deprived by sickness in my family until now." He was busy with the affairs of the Apalachicola Indians: food for their immediate needs; attention to the welfare of sick, aged, and helpless Indians; regard for the future of warriors engaged in fighting the Seminoles, and for their wives and children.[10]

Ten days later Archibald Smith again found it necessary to "take up his pen and write a few hurried lines." He had received a bulletin from the territorial governor, charging Seminole Indians with the murder of several persons west of the Suwannee. Smith reported a strange band of Indians encamped near the mouth of Black Water Bay, Santa Rosa Sound. Eighty warriors and their families was the strength of the party, said to be rebels who had recently fled from the Creek country to avoid removal west of the Mississippi. The region in which they had pitched camp, Smith said, was "an entire wilderness without any inhabitants. abounding in large swamps and morasses. . . . Report says the inhabitants of West Florida are afraid to go to their camps or speak to them (May God forbid that ever such should be the case with me) for of an Indian I hope never to be afraid." He added that, should his government require it, he could with an honest interpreter remove the band to any point in the United States. "There is a certain manner in which the Indian race can be led without coercion, I have unfortunately for myself been raised on the frontiers. Since I was 9 years of age am now in my 42nd year, hence my knowledge of the Indian character must be

[10] Archibald Smith, Jr., to Com. C. A. Harris, Jan. 5, 1837, O. I. A.: Seminoles—Emigration.

perfect. for further particulars on this subject I will refer you to Hon. Jos. M. White now in Congress who has known me for a number of years." Smith thought it likely that the size of the fugitive band had been "exajjorated;" but, regardless of their number, he was willing to have them added to his subagency on the Apalachicola.[11]

By the middle of February, Smith was writing to the Office of Indian Affairs on the subject of distress among his people. The bands of Econchatimicco and John Walker, who had been robbed of their slaves and pushed out of their reservations during the previous year, had planted little as a result. The young men were in the armies of the United States, and the older men, women, and children on their reservations were in want. Smith stated that they were good Indians, "having known them personally for the last 16 years." He added that new raids were threatened, with "trifling vagabond white men lurking around their towns, making mischief. it gives me much trouble and uneasiness. and not able to suppress it. by no means whatever."

The agent believed these people were about ready to make a reluctant journey to the West. They would go if Smith could accompany them as their emigration agent. Joe Riley, a very able young Indian and grandson of Chief Econchatimicco, had expressed his willingness to remove with about one hundred followers. Sale of Joe Riley's property to the United States, control of a band of invading Creeks, the sale of Seminole Negroes in Georgia, unpaid annuities of the Apalachicola Indians, his own illness with "Billious fever," and many other items were included in Smith's letters to the Commissioner.

On November 3, 1837, he wrote a "hasty line or two" in four pages, giving an account of Joe Riley's capture of hostile Creeks and Smith's disposition of them. Generally Commissioner C. A. Harris wrote stiff, officially formal replies to the Agent's newsy letters; but the impression persists in the correspondence that the Indian Office was frequently at fault, that gross neglect of the Indians was not at all uncommon, and that the semiliterate

[11] Smith to Harris, Jan. 15, 1837, O. I. A.: Seminoles—Emigration.

Archibald Smith was aware of the flaws and able to make a shrewd guess as to their origin.[12] A touch of the ludicrous appeared in every report, almost every line, from the Apalachicola Agency; but running through all of Smith's letters were accounts of affairs that were deeply serious: hungry, discontented Indians, who had good reason to be resentful toward government officials and white men in general; laws of the Tallahassee government, openly violated by citizens whose representatives wrote the laws; tragedies that resulted from broken promises and principles of justice ignored—these were the items that must have been the most offensive to the men who administered Indian affairs.

[12] Smith to Harris, Feb. 19, Mar. 12, July 27, Nov. 3, 1837; Harris to Smith, May 5, 1837; Harris to Call, May 4, Harris to Pres. of Agricultural Bank, May 4, Harris to Call, June 1, Harris to Collins, May 6, Harris to Brown, May 6, 1837, O. I. A.: Seminoles—Emigration.

CHAPTER 13

General Jesup's Second Campaign

"I was in hopes I should be killed in battle,
but a bullet never touched me."

COACOOCHEE (WILD CAT)

WHEN HIS SUPERIOR officers showed no disposition to replace him in Florida, General Jesup entered vigorously into preparations for the autumn campaign of 1837. The War Department followed his suggestion in ordering enlistment of northern Indians to replace the Creeks. Secretary Joel Poinsett took into the service during the summer about eight hundred Indians—Shawnees, Sauk and Fox, Kickapoos, and Delawares. About two hundred Choctaw guides were enlisted also.

General Jesup did not expect major pitched battles, and the Seminole chiefs avoided coming to grips. A prisoner at Tampa revealed that they were waiting for the army's next move. During the second week of September, General Joseph M. Hernandez, operating from St. Augustine, captured King Philip and Uchee Billy with their followers and held them prisoners in Fort Marion. Philip sent news of the capture to his relatives, and his son Coacoochee (Wild Cat) came back with the messenger to offer surrender of his band, together with all livestock, Negroes, and other chattels recently acquired. On October 17, Coacoochee, who had been free for two weeks in consultation with his people on the problem of removal, returned to General Hernandez and announced that Osceola, with one hundred followers, was ready for a conference. As evidence of his good intentions, Osceola sent to the General a neatly beaded peace pipe and a white plume. Co-e-hadjo also sent presents, and General Jesup, who had returned to St. Augustine, directed Hernandez to send presents to Osceola which were carried by Coacoochee.[1]

In the course of the negotiations that followed, Osceola proposed that General Hernandez come to his camp near Fort Peyton without a military escort for a talk. General Jesup directed Hernandez to take an escort strong enough to meet any surprise attack, and to regard Osceola as being on probation. General Hernandez, accordingly, rode to Osceola's camp followed by an escort of two hundred mounted men, and the conference began. Osceola stood under a white flag, indicating that he regarded the meeting a truce, not a surrender. Hernandez carried a paper, prepared by General Jesup, with a list of seven questions to be put to the Seminole chiefs, Co-e-hadjo and Osceola. If their answers were not satisfactory, they were to be made prisoners.

Among the questions were these: "Are you prepared at once to deliver up the Negroes taken from citizens? Why have you not surrendered them already, as promised by Co-e-hadjo at Fort King? Have the chiefs of the Nation held a council on this subject? Why have the chiefs of the Nation not come themselves to the conference? Have they sent a message, and if so, what is their message?"

Co-e-hadjo, speaking for the Seminoles, said that Micanopy, Yaholoochee (Cloud), and Onselmatche (Jumper) all had measles and would come later for a talk. The answers to the other questions were unsatisfactory, and General Hernandez gave the signal for his mounted escort to seize the Seminoles.[2]

There were ninety-five persons in Osceola's party: twelve chiefs in addition to Co-e-hadjo and Osceola; seventy-one warriors, six women, and four Negroes. Forty-seven rifles, loaded and ready for use were within their reach, but the warriors had

[1] *American State Papers: Military Affairs,* VII, 848; Boyd, "Asi-Yahola or Osceola," reprint from *Florida Historical Quarterly,* Vol. XXXIII (1955), 52–54; Giddings, *The Exiles of Florida,* 164–67; Brevard, *History of Florida,* I, 147.

[2] Boyd, "Asi-Yahola or Osceola," reprint from *Florida Historical Quarterly,* Vol. XXXIII (1955), 54, 55; *Niles' Register,* Vol. LIII, 263; 25 Cong., 2 sess., *House Doc. No. 327,* 410–11; Giddings, *The Exiles of Florida,* 166–67; Brevard, *History of Florida,* I, 147.

no opportunity to bring them into action. The soldiers with their weapons leveled would have wiped the party out. These Indians were Mikasukies, and it has been asserted that the hostile intention of the party was proved by the fact that few women and no children accompanied them. General Jesup believed that it was Osceola's intention to obtain the release of Philip, either by seizing some officer to exchange for him, or by an assault upon Fort Marion. General Hernandez ordered the captives marched to St. Augustine under close guard. Osceola, who had the appearance of being ill, and two others of the party were supplied with mounts; the rest were required to walk.

At the end of November, Captain Pitcairn Morrison, in charge of emigration at St. Augustine, held 137 prisoners: warriors, 88; women, 32; children, 15; and Negro slaves of Seminole Indians, 2. Two of the warriors had been assigned to duty with the army. King Philip and Osceola were in Fort Marion also; but Coacoochee and Talmus Hadjo were not there. On the previous night they had escaped with sixteen warriors and two of the Seminole women. The escape of Wild Cat, one of the most daring exploits in a war that was filled with heroic deeds on both sides, had in it more than dramatic significance. Probably this chief was the only Seminole who had the personal ability and prestige as a war leader to keep alive the spirit of resistance among his people. It is certain that Arpeika (Sam Jones) and Halpatter Tustenuggee (Alligator), each with a strong following of warriors, joined with Coacoochee in the final major conflict of the war. And it is likely that the chief who risked his life in the spectacular escape was ready, at the time of his imprisonment, to co-operate in the removal. The detention of Coacoochee at St. Augustine must rank as one of the major blunders of the war.[3]

On December 3, 1837, Captain Morrison wrote to Commissioner Harris for funds to carry on his work. He had just received three Seminole warriors, along with twenty women and children, as prisoners. They had been sent from Fort Mellon, half-starved

---

[3] Morrison to Harris, Nov. 30, 1837, O. I. A.: Seminoles—Emigration; Brevard, *History of Florida*, I, 148–49; Kenneth Porter, "Seminole Flight from Fort Marion," *Florida Historical Quarterly*, Vol. XXII, 113–33.

and in need of clothing. "I shall purchase some articles for their health and comfort." Morrison said that the funds handed over to him by Lieutenant Searle, in the form of Louisiana bank notes, were of no use in St. Augustine; and added, "I shall have to request that Ten Thousand dollars in South Carolina notes be placed to my credit in one of the Banks of Charleston, as their [sic] may be many expenditures at this place on account of Seminole emigration, that is if a principle [sic] part of the emigration takes place from the city of St. Augustine."

Two weeks later Morrison reported that General Jesup had sent Micanopy, "principle chief," twenty-eight warriors, and forty-three women and children, "in a very destitute condition." He stated that the measles had broken out among the prisoners, and "carried off some Fifteen men, women and children since the first of the month." He thought the high mortality was due to "improvident habits and want of care of themselves." Morrison feared that no more Indians would come in voluntarily, "as they have already commenced their . . . constant disregard of their promises, I have no faith or confidence in any of them, their whole object appears to be to gain time."

Unfortunately, Captain Morrison's concept of Indian character and the relations between the United States and its Indian wards was fairly typical of the men who had first hand contact with the natives. Especially unfortunate was the fact that this view seemed to reflect, fairly, the opinions of many officials who were his superiors. None of the men in the field, however, was too ignorant to recognize the possibilities of $10,000 placed in his hands for expenditure on the needs of the Indians, in an outpost where rigid accounting was almost impossible.

On December 20, 1837, Captain Morrison reported to the secretary of war, Joel Poinsett, that General Jesup had ordered the prisoners to be sent from St. Augustine, either to Savannah or to Charleston. After consultation with Colonel Fanning, Morrison had decided upon Charleston. "The whole number here are about Two Hundred, amongst them the principle [sic] Chief Micanopi, Coa Hajo, and a few sub-chiefs. I beg leave respectfully to recommend that they be sent as early as practicable to

Arkansaw [*sic*] as a number of them still have a hope to be left in the country."[4]

He reported at the same time the list of persons serving under him in the work of moving the captured Seminoles and their Negro allies to the West:

C. S. Lovell, Assistant Superintendent,
    on duty at Fort Brooke _____$4.00   per day.
Abraham, Principle [*sic*] Interpreter _____$2.50   "   "
Toney (Negro)   "   _____ 1.00   "   "
Billy   "   _____ 1.00   "   "
Pompey (Negro)   "   _____ 1.00   "   "

At the suggestion of Colonel John H. Sherburne, who had some acquaintance with the Cherokee Indians, the aid of that tribe's leaders was sought by the War Department in obtaining the consent of the Seminoles to removal. John Ross, principal chief of the Cherokees, got in touch with the Secretary of War, and agreed to the scheme. Ross appointed Hair Conrad, Jesse Bushyhead, Thomas Woodward, and Richard Fields with Major Pole Cat as their interpreter; and the party came to St. Augustine in November, 1837.[5]

General Jesup wrote to the Cherokee commissioners, "When I received your note today, I was too much engaged to reply in writing, but I desired . . . Lieut. Chambers to inform you that I would see you immediately." The General declared himself greatly pleased with his first interview, and added: "I appreciate fully the benevolent and humane motives which have impelled your Chief to order, and you to undertake, the perilous enterprise in which you propose to engage."

Co-e-hadjo and Osceola were permitted to send messengers inviting their people to surrender, "with the assurance of protection for the future and oblivion for the past." He asked the commissioners for certified copies of their instructions.

---

[4] Morrison to Harris, Dec. 3, 1837; Morrison to Harris, Dec. 18, 1837; Morrison to Poinsett, Dec. 20, 1837, O. I. A.: Seminoles—Emigration.

[5] Jesup to Cherokee Commissioners, Nov. 13, 1837, Grant Foreman Transcripts, Vol. VI, O. I. A.: Florida, File R-1, Supplemental; *American State Papers: Military Affairs*, VII, 816.

At this early stage of Cherokee diplomacy in Florida, John Ross wrote to the Secretary of War that he was much pleased with the prospects of peace. The great Cherokee chief expressed the hope that perfect understanding would be maintained between the Indian commissioners and the army officers in Florida. Success of the mission would depend, he thought, "upon a judicious, liberal, just, and prompt action in the course to be adopted."[6]

General Jesup arranged for a meeting between the Cherokee commissioners and the prisoners in St. Augustine. Osceola was sick; but he talked to Richard Fields and declared that he was ready to take his people west to their new home. A messenger was sent from the Cherokees to Micanopy, Arpeika, and Halpatter Tustenuggee. John Ross's commissioners, accompanied by Co-e-hadjo, traveled south from St. Augustine to Lake Monroe, where they hoped to meet leaders of the hostile Seminoles. At Fort Mellon a messenger from Micanopy informed the Cherokees that he would meet them for a talk at Chickasawhatchee Creek, about forty miles from Fort Mellon, and near the outlet of Lake Poinsett. After a conference with the Cherokees, Micanopy and twelve chiefs agreed to go back with them to Fort Mellon.[7]

In the meantime, Osceola's family and his personal following surrendered to General Jesup at Fort Mellon. Their number had been thirty when reported by Abraham to Lieutenant Casey on July 18, but had probably been reduced slightly since that time. Che-cho-ter and another wife of Osceola, his sister, and two of his children were in the party, which contained also four or five warriors.

Micanopy, Co-e-hadjo, Yaholoochee (Cloud), Nocose Yohola, and Tuskegee, the nephew of Arpeika, came in with the Cherokee Commissioners to Fort Mellon. Again, a difference of opinion arose between General Jesup and the Seminole chiefs as to the status of the Indians during the conference. The Chero-

[6] Jesup to Commissioners, Nov. 13, 1837; John Ross to Joel Poinsett, Nov. 29, 1837, Foreman Transcripts, VI.
[7] Boyd, "Asi-Yahola or Osceola," reprint from *Florida Historical Quarterly*, Vol. XXXIII (1955), 56–59; *American State Papers: Military Affairs*, VII, 886–91.

kees maintained, with the Seminoles, that Micanopy and his people came in under a white flag of truce; General Jesup regarded the mission a surrender. On December 5, 1837, a conference was held in which the Seminole leaders and the Cherokee commissioners met with General Jesup and his staff. The General, through the interpreter Abraham, addressed his blunt question to Micanopy. "What do you expect from me?"

"We are ready to go west; we want no more war," answered Micanopy.

"The Seminoles have deceived the officers of the United States many times," said Jesup. "Are you ready to surrender your families, at St. Augustine?"

"Our families and our Negroes will go west with us," replied Micanopy.

"Can you obtain the surrender of Sam Jones, and all the Mikasukies in this part of the Territory, within four days?"

"Yes, Arpeika will come in with his people," said the Chief.

"You will have ten days in which to make good these promises," declared General Jesup.

The chiefs remained as hostages while messengers were sent to their followers with a report on the conference, and to Arpeika and Halpatter Tustenuggee. The Cherokee commissioners accompanied the messengers to continue their work of persuading the Seminoles to lay down their arms. One great obstacle existed to the maturity of the plans for peace. Coacoochee, who felt that his confidence had been betrayed and who was burning with desire for revenge, was at large. Undoubtedly, in the week since his escape from Fort Marion, he had found it possible to get in touch with Arpeika and Halpatter. The boldest and most resourceful war chief of the Seminoles, with the added prestige of imprisonment by the white general and escape from his stronghold, was now to combine his forces with the implacable Mikasukies under Arpeika and those of the shrewd and cunning Halpatter Tustenuggee for a last desperate battle. Coacoochee with Talmus Hadjo had made his way down from St. Augustine to the Tomoka River, east of the St. Johns, where the chief's band was waiting for him. It was reported that Arpeika (Sam Jones) was on his way to Fort Mellon to surrender for emigration when he met Coacoochee. After a conference of the chiefs, Arpeika put the question before his warriors—should they go to Fort Mellon and enroll for the journey west, or go deeper into the swamps and continue the struggle. The Mikasuki warriors voted solidly for war. The attitude of Coacoochee (Wild Cat) at this time is shown in his statement, reported by John T. Sprague: "I was in hopes I should be killed in battle, but a bullet never touched me. I would rather be killed by a white man in Florida than die in Arkansas."[8]

As General Jesup had feared, the Cherokee commissioners returned on December 14, 1837, without Sam Jones or any of his Mikasuki warriors. The General then made prisoners of the Indians who had come in and were encamped near Fort Mellon, and sent them on a steamer to St. Augustine. As noted above, Captain Morrison reported them as including, in addition to Micanopy and the subchiefs, twenty-eight warriors and forty-three women and children. The Cherokees regarded General Jesup's seizure of the Seminoles at Fort Mellon a violation of the spirit of the agreements that were reached with Micanopy and his followers before they came in. Richard Fields and his associates were not fully aware of Jesup's experience in matching his guile against that of Osceola, Arpeika, Halpatter and Coacoochee. Perhaps it was too much to expect that the soldier should suddenly become a statesman and act in the "judicious, prompt, and liberal" manner John Ross hoped for.

Zachary Taylor was fifty-three when he was directed to take charge of the field troops in Florida in the summer of 1837. His military career of thirty-one years was varied, with service in the War of 1812, which earned for him the rank of brevet major, and active duty on the frontier of Wisconsin and Louisiana. In 1833, Colonel Taylor sent the Indian chief, Black Hawk, a prisoner to Jefferson Barracks in charge of Lieutenant Jefferson Davis. Two years later Davis resigned from the army, married Miss Knox Taylor, the Colonel's daughter, and settled down as a cotton planter in Mississippi. Colonel Taylor was sent to Florida

[8] Sprague, The Florida War, 327.

on July 31, 1837. He landed at Tampa Bay, and by December his force of 1,100 men was ready to march into the Seminole country. General Jesup's instructions left Taylor free to plan his own campaign, but carried one explicit order: to destroy or capture the Seminole Indians.

Colonel Taylor marched from Fort Gardiner on December 19, 1837, toward the Kissimmee River where the Mikasukies under Arpeika were reported to be gathered in force. On the march, Taylor's Indian scouts learned that Onselmatche (Jumper) and a small band of warriors with their families and a few Negro slaves were encamped near the trail. Captain Parks, the Indian leader of the Delawares and Shawnees attached to Taylor's army, was sent to talk with Onselmatche; and after a short exchange of peace vows, the Seminole agreed to give up his band for emigration. The company of Shawnees conducted Jumper and his party to Fort Gardiner.[9]

Colonel Taylor's force marched beyond Lake Istopoga toward Lake Okeechobee where the Mikasukies were preparing to make a final stand. As the soldiers advanced, Arpeika and Coacoochee fell back, refusing to give battle on ground where mounted troops could maneuver freely. On Christmas morning, 1837, Arpeika took his position in a hammock where the dense growth of timber gave excellent protection, and the attacking force would be compelled to advance through a swamp in which saw grass stood four or five feet high. Arpeika and his Mikasukies, supported by Otalke Thlocko (Prophet), formed the Indian right wing. In the center stood the warriors of Halpatter Tustenuggee, and on the left, Coacoochee with eighty fighting men. The total Indian force, according to figures given later by Alligator, numbered less than four hundred.

Zachary Taylor placed Colonel Gentry's Volunteers, together with his Indian troops and Morgan's Spies, in the front line. Back of them were the regulars of the Fourth and Sixth Infantry regiments, and held in reserve a third line made up of the First Infantry. Here, on a battleground selected by the wiliest

[9] Brevard, *A History of Florida*, I, 149–50; Giddings, *The Exiles of Florida*, 172–74.

of the Seminole leaders and between forces vastly unequal in their firing power, the hardest battle of the Seminole War was fought. Like the seven-year contest as a whole, the situation of the Indians at Lake Okeechobee was hopeless; they were overwhelmed by the power of their opponents.

Leaving their horses and baggage under adequate guard, Taylor's first-line troops advanced on foot at noon through the grass-covered swamp. They were met by a blast of destructive fire. Coacoochee's warriors, Seminole and Negro, were hidden in the timber beyond a stream that wound its sluggish course through the swamp. Colonel Gentry fell at the first volley; and as the front line steadily advanced, other valued men of Taylor's command went down—Major Sconce, Captain Childs, Lieutenant Flanagan, Rogers, Hare, Gordon—in all, twenty-four men.

The Volunteers and Morgan's Spies were thrown into confusion and fell back. The Fourth Infantry advanced, and Lieutenant Colonel Thompson moved up with five companies of the Sixth Infantry, receiving the full weight of Seminole fire along the entire line. Efforts were made to spread the superior numbers of Thompson's force in such manner as to outflank the hidden Indians; but an impassable marsh was found on the left and on the right. Thompson fell, mortally wounded. His adjutant, Lieutenant Center was killed. Throughout Taylor's forces, officer mortality was high. Colonel Taylor reported that one company lost all of its commissioned officers, and had but four men who were not hit.

After the battle had continued for three hours, Lieutenant Colonel Foster of the Fourth Infantry gathered the remnants of six companies, a total of 150 men, for a bayonet charge. The Seminoles and their Negro allies were dislodged and the field was won, but Taylor's army had lost 26 killed and 112 wounded. Nine dead Seminoles were left on the field, and one Negro. Soldiers of the Fourth and Sixth Infantry, reinforced by fresh troops from the reserves, pursued the retreating Seminoles until darkness turned them back. Colonel Taylor buried his dead, and on the following morning was ready to march back to the Withlacoochee, which he reached on the last day of the year, 1837.

The United States Army had found another competent soldier to lead its field forces in Florida and to replace General Jesup, who was exhausted by his campaigns against the Seminoles. On January 24, 1838, Jesup was wounded in a skirmish at Jupiter Inlet, and four months later was sent back to his post as quarter-master general at Washington. Taylor was given the rank of brevet brigadier general, and placed in command of the troops in Florida.[10]

As in the problems connected with interpretation of the Seminole treaties of 1832 and 1834, endless disputes have arisen over Jesup's course in dealing with Seminole prisoners in 1837. For those who have accused the General of breaking faith with his Indian adversaries, a reminder may be in order that Osceola had deceived Wiley Thompson at the end of 1835, in regard to his peaceful intentions, with results fatal to the Agent; and that the Seminole leaders had misled Jesup himself as to the tribe's acceptance of the removal treaty in February, 1837, which resulted in a new outbreak of the war. General Jesup was responsible for carrying out a specific policy dictated by his government, and he was dealing with chiefs who regarded any form of deception justifiable if it would save their people from disaster or relieve them of burdens imposed by former contacts with the whites. It was not General Jesup who worked injustices upon the Seminoles or their Negro allies; it was the decisions of the United States, of Florida Territory and the neighboring states, reached by the imperfect processes of more or less popular governments, and put into effect by the warped pressure of interests that were not thoroughly democratic.

The Cherokee commissioners and their tribe took a view that was identical with that of the articulate Seminoles.[11] That is, when Osceola agreed to a conference with General Hernandez at Fort Peyton, he was making a concession, thereby saving the agents of the United States the expense of coming into the swamps after him. In return he expected, after the conference

[10] Sprague, *The Florida War*, 203–13; Giddings, *The Exiles of Florida*, 174–78; Brevard, *History of Florida*, I, 149–50.
[11] George Catlin, *The North American Indians*, II, 247.

under a white flag of truce, to have a free choice of surrender for emigrating or resuming the war. Dr. Mark Boyd, in his discussion of the events which led to making Osceola a prisoner, headed the topic "Guile against Guile," and wrote of the General's decision, "It would be difficult to understand how, given the opportunity, Jesup could have done otherwise than to seize Osceola and the other Indians, and not have been derelict to his duty."[12]

General Jesup, in a report to the Secretary of War, defended his action on three main grounds. (1) Osceola had been a persistent leader of hostility while pretending friendship for the whites and aquiescence in removal. Osceola's messenger, the Negro subchief John Coheia (Cavallo), had violated his parole in May, 1836. It was reported that Osceola's followers had killed a white man just before his proposal to talk peace; and that a Mikasuki-Tallahassee war party had gone on a raid to the Alachua frontier even as Osceola and Co-e-hadjo had started for the conference at Fort Peyton. Co-e-hadjo and Osceola had drawn subsistence for their bands the previous year, and Osceola, by "force and threats," had prevented Co-e-hadjo from carrying out his agreement to emigrate. (2) Osceola had tried to kill Yahola Hadjo, Jesup's messenger to Co-e-hadjo and Noscose Yahola. (3) "As I had informed the chiefs at Fort King that I would hold no communication with the Seminoles, unless they should determine to emigrate; as I had permitted no Indian to come in for any other purpose but to remain; as they were all prisoners of war or hostages who had violated their parole; as many of them had violated the truce entered into at Fort King . . . and as the white flag had been allowed for no other purpose than to enable them to communicate . . . without danger of attack from our parties, it became my duty to secure them, on being satisfied . . . that they intended to return to their fastnesses. . . . I directed that they should be treated with every kindness, and have every accommodation consistent with their security."

It has been charged that General Jesup shifted his position

12 Boyd, "Asi-Yahola or Osceola," reprint from *Florida Historical Quarterly*, Vol. XXXIII (1955), 52, 55.

in regard to the capture of Negroes from the Seminoles, and that his resulting change of policy broke promises made to the Indian leaders, and specifically violated his agreement made at Fort Dade on March 6, 1837. Actually, he shifted his position but little, and that change was to meet the positive demands of his government. There is much evidence in Jesup's official correspondence that he made a strong effort during his command in Florida to prevent any slave-hunting that would defeat the main objective of the war—removal of the Seminoles. It is certain, too, that he promised the Indians continued possession of their slave property, and compensation for livestock that could not be transported west. As will be shown later, he was still trying to secure for them the rights that he had promised to the Seminoles long after he was transferred to Washington.[13]

The Cherokee commissioners reported to John Ross in Washington. They were disappointed in the results of their contacts with Jesup, for the relatively simple reason that they wanted one result, while he wanted another. Jesup was trying to convince the Seminoles that their only chance for survival was in submission—full acceptance of the removal treaties. That was the policy his government was determined to put into effect, and he was the agent of its enforcement. The Cherokees were taking a stand with the United States and its officials in favor of Seminole removal; but with full recognition of the Indian's reluctance to be pushed from his native land, of the differences that prevented full tribal unity in making and enforcing treaties, and of the sly persistence with which certain chiefs and warriors would put off the day of actual removal. The Cherokees understood and sympathized with the Seminoles; but they did not know the contents of Jesup's orders, and the pressure that would get the orders obeyed through one commander or another.

Furthermore, because of General Jesup's on-the-spot authority as commander, they failed to grasp fully the limitations upon his individual power. John Ross understood the situation more broadly than any of his agents, but he hoped for states-

---

[13] Jesup to Jones, Mar. 18, 1837, O. I. A.: Seminoles—Emigration; 25 Cong., 3 sess., *Ex. Doc. No. 225*; Giddings, *The Exiles of Florida*, 146–51.

manlike decisions which could not come out of Washington on
the problem of the American Indian in the time of the Seminole
War. Within the limited scope of his authority, General Jesup
was unable to assert a power of leadership great enough to carry
the nation along with him, but he did prove that he was "a firm
friend of the red man." In the course of time he was to prove
his complete sincerity in the promises he made to the Indians
and his willingness to make a personal fight for Seminole rights.[14]

Following the report of the commissioners, John Ross placed
a formal protest before the Secretary of War concerning the imprisonment of Seminoles under what they regarded a flag of
truce. General Jesup became the object of much public criticism
and of an official investigation by the United States Senate.
Thomas Hart Benton of Missouri conducted his defense, and
the General was cleared of all charges.

General Jesup's reputation has suffered from an accumula-
tion of causes. His course in Florida ran counter to the wishes
of many local politicians who had influence. He would not engage the army in the work of catching runaway slaves, but only
the Negroes who were allies of the hostile Seminoles. He did
not lend his influence to the fraudulent seizure of Negro prisoners on claims of doubtful validity. But, as the responsible military
agent of the United States, he attempted to carry out the policy
of removal by force, and quite naturally failed to gain the good
will of the Seminoles. His very effectiveness as a soldier made
enemies for him among those who had strong sympathy for the
Indians. The need of thoughtless persons to find a scapegoat for
the failure of American society and American government in
dealing with the Seminoles, has led a great many critics to heap
blame upon the shoulders of Thomas Sidney Jesup.

General Jesup placed before the War Department a plan to
end the war on the basis of a permanent Seminole reservation in
southern Florida. While he waited for Joel Poinsett to answer his
letter, various bands of Seminoles contacted previously by his
messengers waited in nearby camps to learn the decision of the

[14] "Report of the Cherokee Deputation into Florida," with footnotes by
Grant Foreman, *Chronicles of Oklahoma*, Vol. IX, 423–38.

government at Washington. When Jesup received his answer to the effect that the Seminoles would be obliged to move west, he seized as many Indians and Negroes as possible, and hurried them off to Fort Brooke as the first step in their journey to the valley of the Canadian.

On March 1, 1838, Lieutenant W. G. Freeman, who had been placed in charge of the camp for Seminoles and Negroes near Fort Jupiter, East Florida, reported to Commissioner Harris a list of persons assembled for emigration. In camp, there were 197, including women and children, with small bands coming in daily. On March 24, 1838, the total number of prisoners reported at Fort Jupiter was 527 Indians, 152 Indian-Negroes, and 14 fugitive slaves. After their capture, 16 of the Indians escaped.[15] It was possible to charge that Jesup violated the confidence of Halleck Hadjo, Tuskegee, and other Seminole leaders by his action in securing them before he notified them of President Van Buren's decision, and the charge was made. But to General Jesup, the war was not a sporting proposition in which the underdog was to be given every opportunity to kill and be killed before being brought under control. His idea was to carry out his orders by removing the Indians before Seminole bullets and swarming insects had brought further losses to his men; and before the overwhelming power of his army had completed destruction of the Seminole Tribe.

[15] W. G. Freeman, Lt. on emigration duty, to Commissioner C. A. Harris, Mar. 1, 1838 and Mar. 24, 1838, Foreman Transcripts, I, 163; Boyd, "Asi-Yahola or Osceola," reprinted from *Florida Historical Quarterly*, Vol. XXXIII (1955), 60, 61.

CHAPTER 14

Removal for Profit, 1838–41

"Sir, I have seen 2,000 Indians drunk at the North Fork of the Canadian in one day."

A. J. RAINES

WHILE THE CHEROKEE commissioners were work-ing out the final moves of their gesture toward peace, the tragedy of Osceola was unfolding to capture the attention of the American public and make his name the best known of all the Florida Indians. As noted above, General Jesup had or-dered Captain P. Morrison to send the prisoners from Fort Marion to Savannah or to Charleston before the end of 1837; and the Captain had elected to send them to Charleston.[1] In-cluded in the party of 203 were Micanopy, Osceola, Philip, Co-e-hadjo, Yaholoochee (Cloud), 116 warriors, and 82 women and children.[2] The *Poinsett* reached Charleston on January 1, 1838, and the prisoners were taken to Fort Moultrie on Sullivan Island, which was regarded a more secure place for their imprisonment than Castillo de San Marcos (Fort Marion), the old Spanish stronghold at St. Augustine.

The Indians at Fort Moultrie were given freedom within the enclosure for the benefit of their health, and the chiefs were taken to the Charleston theatre on January 6 to see the perform-ance of the play *Honey-moon*. In the case of Osceola, health precautions were somewhat late. He had suffered from a chronic

[1] Morrison to Harris, Dec. 20, 1837, O. I. A.: Seminoles–Emigration.
[2] Boyd, "Asi-Yahola or Osceola," reprinted from *Florida Historical Quarterly*, XXXIII (1955), 61.

malaria infection since the summer of 1836 when his party of Mikasukies occupied Fort Drane, after Captain Merchant had withdrawn his troops from that unhealthful post. Evacuation of Fort Drane by the white troops had been ordered after more than one-third of the garrison there had become ill of malaria and their commander, Major Julius Heileman, had died of the disease. As Dr. Mark Boyd has pointed out, reports of Osceola's illness were frequent after his band occupied Fort Drane. "The rampant illness could hardly have been anything else than malaria, and the intensity of the epidemic must have permitted the infection of a large portion of the anopheline mosquitoes thereabout, which were certainly abundant." The writer states further that Osceola's appearance, after the late summer of 1836, was such as "one would expect to observe in a sufferer from chronic malaria."[3]

At Fort Moultrie, Osceola and the other chiefs permitted the artist George Catlin to paint their portraits. During the sittings Osceola developed a severe attack of sore throat which was especially dangerous because of lowered vitality incident to his chronic malaria. The post surgeon, Dr. Weedon, had informed Catlin that the Indian probably would not live through the winter. On January 27, 1838, Osceola was so ill that his new friends, George Catlin and some of the officers, sat up with him all night. He had refused, after his final acute attack of quinsy, to allow Dr. Weedon to treat him and accepted only the care of an Indian doctor. It is possible that Osceola had discovered that Dr. Weedon was the brother-in-law of Wiley Thompson, and that the Indian regarded his life not entirely safe in the hands of the late agent's relative.

Osceola lived through the night of January 27, and Catlin left Charleston two days later with the impression that he had a chance for recovery. His strength rapidly declined, however, and he died on the following day. He insisted upon being dressed in his ceremonial costume during his last hours. With him at the time of his death were his two wives and two of his children.

[3] *Ibid.*, 44, 45, 56, 61. Dr. Boyd's views on the subject of Osceola's illness are of peculiar interest and value because of his knowledge as a doctor of medicine, his acquaintance with the topography of Florida, and his familiarity with its insect life.

Zachary Taylor's first twelve months of active campaigning in Florida was the largest single year of Seminole removal. After the fight near the shore of Lake Okeechobee on December 25, 1837, there were no major battles; but a steady stream of prisoners moved toward Tampa Bay, and the transportation of Seminoles and Negroes to New Orleans and up the Mississippi was one of the main projects of the War Department. Captain P. Morrison at Fort Moultrie was instructed by the Commissioner of Indian Affairs to send such prisoners as would not, in his judgment, make trouble, by way of New Orleans.

On March 12, 1838, the Office of Indian Affairs applied to General Jesup for military support in removal of the band of Creeks held by Archibald Smith near the Apalachicola Agency. There were 150 Indians in the party, and Daniel Boyd of Washington had been chosen as their conductor to the west. After explaining the tendency of this band toward violence, the commissioner ended his letter as follows: "I have to request that, if it be compatible with the present state of the war in Florida, and other engagements, you will furnish with all possible dispatch the military force required."[4]

On April 30, 1838, Major Isaac Clark, assistant quartermaster at New Orleans, reported 1,150 Indians and Negroes at New Barracks—"half of them sick . . . no agent here to attend to anything . . . the duty, devolves on me and I have not a dollar of their funds."

During May and June nearly 1,600 emigrants left Florida on the sea voyage to the lower Mississippi. Marine Lieutenant John G. Reynolds, assigned to the hazardous task of conducting Indians and their slaves from Tampa Bay to the West, found himself in the midst of a contest over valuable slave property. Three factors contributed to the complexity of his job: orders from superior officers in the military service; his peculiar status with respect to the Indian Office; and the pressure exerted by fugitive-slave owners, traders in fugitive slaves, and adventurers fishing for profit in the muddy waters of disorder. Lieutenant Reyn-

[4] Smith to Harris, Jan. 4; Harris to Jesup, Mar. 12, 1838, O. I. A. Letterbook, XXIII.

olds was not well educated in the liberal arts; but he was a man who understood the purpose of his orders and the justice back of that purpose.

He conducted parties of emigrants to New Orleans, gave sharp attention to contracts for transportation, moved Indians and Negroes up the river with such speed and efficiency as to confuse the slave-traders and their attorneys, and defended his course, when necessary, with forceful though inelegant arguments. On May 15, 1838, he reported: "Arrangements are made for embarkment of the party with the exception of 67 negroes who are claimed by persons from Georgia. . . . The strength of the emigrating party will be about 1,160 Indians and negroes, I have been obliged in consequence of the increase to appoint additional assistance." A week later he changed his plans and sent 500 emigrants north under Captain R. D. C. Collins, reporting, "I done this as Collins is perfectly acquainted with their country." Supported by General Gaines in the legal battles over slaves, and advised by District Attorney John Slidell, Reynolds kept the Negroes with their Indian masters unless prevented by court orders which he could not ignore.

It may be recalled that General Jesup had ordered that the Creek warriors should be paid the sum of $8,000 for their claims on Negroes they had captured. Because of a higher offer from private claimants, the Creeks refused to accept this money when it was offered to them by Jesup's inspector general at New Orleans. The tangled problem of Seminole Negro ownership gave the Indians and government officials more trouble than any other factor of emigration. It was an obstacle to settlement of the Seminoles on the lands assigned to them for many years; and some lawless members of the Creek Tribe were known to seize free Negroes in the Seminole Nation as late as 1854.[5]

The army's attitude in support of General Jesup is suggested in Special Order No. 4, issued by Edmund P. Gaines on March 21, 1838: "Major Zanziger will on receipt hereof, deliver to Lieu-

[5] Jesup to Searle, Sept. 9, 1837; Reynolds to Harris, May 15, 1838; May 21, 1838, O. I. A.: Florida–Emigration; Harris to Cooper, May 9, 1838, O. I. A. Letterbook, Vol. 24; S. A. Worcester to Sec. of War Jefferson Davis, Sept. 6, 1854, Foreman Transcripts, VI, 173–74; VII, 66.

tenant Reynolds all Slaves . . . belonging to . . . the Seminole
Indians, to be conducted by him . . . to the Arkansas River, where
the said Indians and their slaves are to be permanently settled."
The struggle of Lieutenant Reynolds to carry out this order, over
what appeared to be the determined opposition of the Indian
Office supported by the secretary of war, cannot be presented in
detail here. The stature of General Jesup and all the officers who
recognized the humane justice of his removal program, and attempted to carry out his orders, is increased by the evidence of
the official reports. Commissioner C. A. Harris, on the other hand,
emerges in the role of a public official working to obtain property
for men of political influence at the expense of the Indians and
to the detriment of the slaves. Even Secretary of War Joel Poinsett was advising citizens of Georgia to bid on Seminole Negroes
as a means of gaining quick profits.[6]

On June 18, 1838, Lieutenant Reynolds reached Fort Gibson
and reported the condition of his two emigrant parties. Of 1,127
Indians and Negroes who started up the Mississippi in two boats,
54 had died on the journey, including King Philip who was
buried sixty miles east of Fort Gibson. In Florida, General Zachary Taylor refused to take a personal stand on the disputes aris-
ing over Jesup's orders, but stated emphatically: "I shall do the
utmost in my power to get the Indians and their Negroes out
of Florida, as well as to remove them to their new homes west
of the Mississippi."

James C. Watson of Georgia, on the advice of Joel Poinsett,
had offered the Creek warriors $14,338 for 67 of the Negroes
claimed by them. Watson's brother-in-law, Nathaniel P. Collins,
had been made his agent for recovering the Negroes. Commissioner C. A. Harris wrote a sharp rebuke to Lieutenant Reynolds
for his failure to turn over these Negroes to Mr. Collins. "So far
as may be in your power you will please give all proper aid in
carrying out the directions to deliver them to the Creeks," he
ordered, in conclusion.

Reynolds answered that it was very doubtful whether the
Creeks would have obtained them, "as there were very many

[6] Foreman Transcripts, VI, 161.

persons (I am informed) ready with claims . . . is why they were forthwith dispatched in order to prevent further difficulty. . . . It is certain the negroes could not be identified as those taken by the Creek warriors, and again, if the Comr. will have the goodness to refer to my orriginal [*sic*] instructions in relations to those negroes, he will observe, that I was enjoined to incur *no expense* in turning them over, which certainly could not be avoided, in the absence of proper persons to receive them. . . . In dispatching them westward I was under the full conviction of having performed my duty."

The personal clash between Reynolds and Commissioner Harris resulted more satisfactorily than might have been expected. "I was surprised at being called upon to answer for my 'conduct' toward Mr. Collins, as also the Department for disregarding its orders." Reynolds added that he would offer no defense to the "alligations" in the Commissioner's letter. He did, however, enclose letters from a sheriff, an attorney, and from Major Clark, which might have been regarded as evidence that the Lieutenant was ready to fight, if charges were filed against him. On October 30, 1838, it was reported that Reynolds was bedfast with a fever in New Orleans; and before his recovery, T. Hartley Crawford, who replaced Harris as commissioner of Indian affairs, wrote that the explanation sent by Reynolds regarding shipment of the Negroes west was a "full and satisfactory vindication" of his management of that business. The policy of the Indian Office had been elevated to the standard set by the generals, by Major Isaac Clark, and by the marine lieutenant, John G. Reynolds.

T. Hartley Crawford sent another message which reveals a measure of respect for Lieutenant Reynolds in the Indian Office. "Agreeable to your request, . . . you are hereby relieved from further service in the Department of Indian Affairs, and will consider yourself at liberty to report to . . . your proper command in the Marine Corps. As to . . . your recall to settle your accounts, I have to say that they have, thus far, been rendered in a manner so satisfactory that it does not appear that your presence here is, or will be, necessary for their adjustment."

General Arbuckle reported in September that the Seminoles who arrived during the summer of 1838 were still encamped about Fort Gibson. They had no tools with which to build cabins, they were destitute of clothing, blankets, transportation, and all necessities. Arbuckle recommended to the Adjutant General the appointment of an agent for the Seminoles.[7]

Early in 1838, the Apalachicola agent, Archibald Smith, Jr., was removed from office by the Department of Indian Affairs. On March 28 the chiefs sent a joint protest against the removal. The style of their letter was unmistakable—Smith wrote it for them. No other person, white or red, could have written it.

"We are informed that our worthy friend Mr. Smith whom we have lived near for 17 years past is no longer our agent. this is the worst news that ever came to our towns. we are now told that a Mr. Walker a Lawyer from Pensacola is our principal agent, that Mr. Richards and Mr. Face, a Yankee merchant in the Town of Chattahoochee are sub-agents and that a Mr. Boyd from Washington. that those gentlemen in company with other villains who have been trying to frighten & run us off for several years and did succeed in taking 20 odd negroes from us on the 10th day of March 1836 when all our warriors were in the Seminole Nation assisting the white people this is the manner in which we were paid for our help to the U.S. our warriors have been kept in the woods in West Florida since June last. by the entreaties of Gov. Call in searching the swamps for the hostile Creek Indians until they are naked for clothing & Blankets. and not the first cent of money yet. . . ." The message urged that Smith be kept as agent, that a party of explorers be sent west to seek out a new home, that their slaves be returned to them, and that Walker, Richards, Face, and Boyd be kept far away from them. The letter was signed by the use of the X mark, by Econchatimicco, John Walker, Joe Riley, Wasea Hadjo, Fos Emathla, Echoela-Hadjo, Bill Umka, and seven others. Mr. Boyd took the band west. Archibald Smith had officially "taken up his pen to write a few hurried lines" for the last time.

---

[7] Arbuckle to Jones, Sept. 11, 1838; Reynolds to Harris, Oct. 30, 1838; Crawford to Reynolds, Nov. 8, 1838, Foreman Transcripts, VI.

On October 28, 1838, Boyd reported from Pensacola Bay that the "whole tribe of Apalachicola Indians and 34 Creeks from Dog Island," had embarked for New Orleans, on the steamer *Rodney,* and two schooners, the *Vespar* and the *Octavia.* Several Indians were sick as the voyage began, and Boyd stated that he would employ a physician at New Orleans if the condition of the party seemed to warrant it. The amount added to the expense of the voyage by the use of the two schooners was $450 for the *Vespar* to the mouth of the Mississippi and $600 for the *Octavia* to New Orleans.

John P. Duval, acting governor of Florida, wrote to Joel Poinsett on November 6, 1838, that the smooth exit of the large party of Apalachicola Indians was due to General Taylor's presence with a military force, and to the "indefatigable exertions of the Agent, Mr. Boyd." Two weeks after the journey began, Boyd reported the Arkansas River so low that his prospect of getting farther than Little Rock was slender, and even reaching that point was doubtful. "I will . . . go as far as I can by Steam Boat and then take wagons."[8]

With the increase of Seminole emigration in 1838, along with the growing problem of subsistence for the Indians of other tribes in the West, corruption in the purchase and disbursement of supplies grew enormously. A. J. Raines, writing to Commissioner Harris on June 4, 1838, revealed much of the inner working of Indian contracts, and furnished material for later investigations. Raines accused persons in high positions; and although he disclaimed hostility toward any of them, his revelations might have been inspired by malice. "It is to correct evils that are springing up to an alarming extent," he claimed as his motive. His language, though crude and slightly bombastic in places, was convincing as to his knowledge and sincerity.

Samuel Mackay, according to Raines's statement, had taken a contract to feed the Creeks when he came west. Mackay was honest. He might have "speculated on the gov't," but instead he

8 Smith to Harris, Jan. 4, 1838; Apalachicola Chiefs to Harris, Mar. 24, 1838; Foreman Transcripts, VI, 153, 154, 164–66; Boyd to Harris, Oct. 28, 1838; Duval to Poinsett, Nov. 6, 1838; Boyd to Harris, Nov. 13, 1838, O. I. A.: Seminoles– Emigration.

discharged his bond and sold his remaining goods to the disbursing agents at cost. Then a contract was made with James Glasgow, James Harrison, Thomas T. Tunstall, James W. Breedlove, who was collector at New Orleans, and Governor James S. Conway of Arkansas. The rate agreed upon was 9½ cents per ration. Raines, the letter writer, and Samuel Mackay were named by the partners as agents to handle the goods.

The letter is long: instances of peculation were multiplied with detailed figures. A scheme of the contractors to "corner" all the produce in the country, pay their bond forfeiture of $40,000, and then sell to the government at their own price, was set forth. "Sir, I was called in Council with these dark and desining [sic] men and therefore am acquainted with all their secret springs." Raines suggests, rather vaguely, that he was responsible for cargoes of goods being sent to break up the monopoly of Glasgow and Harrison, thus saving the Government a large amount of money—perhaps $500,000. He paints a dark picture of the effects of fraud upon the Indians. "Out of the 16,200 persons, not one half of them have a *mouthful* of provisions. The $20,000 paid by the Contractors for their Corn enabled them to buy that amount of Whiskey. Sir, I have seen 2,000 Indians drunk at the North Fork of the Canadian . . . in one day. . . . and these poor people was made the instruments of enriching a few unprincipaled [sic] and wicked Contractors."

Then comes a proposal which has in it just a delicate suggestion of personal interest on the part of A. J. Raines. "Justice can be done to the Indians, if you would appoint some man (none of your milk and Cider city ruffle shirt men) to superintend all issues made to these people. . . . Let him be well paid, let him be a man, that has no price for his honor, but is above price. . . ."

The writer warned Commissioner Harris against the possibility of renewed Indian war in the West, reminded him of the terrible cost of the Florida War, and suggested again that the government should "give some honest, industrious man a good price, and he will put things in order." Raines had practically admitted that he was an honest, industrious man, and his experience would seem to indicate that he was not a "milk and Cider city ruffle shirt man." What better superintendent of disbursement could have been found by the Indian Office than A. J. Raines himself?

A letter from J. S. Conway, of Arkansas, to Commissioner Harris on July 14, 1838, gives in brief another side of the charges by Raines. "You having allowed me to paruse [sic] communication . . . I deem it my duty . . . to say to you that Mr. Raines is a man without character & I believe that all the material complaints are without foundation. He acted for some months as agent for the company & Mr. Harrison informed me that he found Raines so great a "scamp" that it was a discredit to the company to retain such a man as Agent. Consequently he was discharged."[9]

There were other complaints against Harrison, Glasgow, and their associates. For example, Mr. J. Jones wrote to the Honorable L. T. Lynn that "rascally frauds" were being practiced upon the government and the Indians by the fur company, and that the greatest of all the frauds was that perpetrated by Harrison and Glasgow. Captain R. D. C. Collins of Little Rock was accused, along with the company of contractors, in a swindle that resulted in $500,000 gain on a single Indian contract. "He the said Collins is to have one sixth of this enormous proffit [sic] the contract barres [sic] fraud on its very face." Jones urged that Captain Collins be investigated thoroughly. His own information, he said, was from a private source, a "plain honest troothful man," but he was not at liberty to give his name. "All of these partys are Whigs," the writer stated; "I can assure you these men are using their money verry lavishly to brake our party down, . . ."[10]

While settlement of Indians in the land west of Arkansas was providing many citizens with employment or profit, and in some instances with opportunities for illicit gains, the actual process of removal by force was continuing in Florida. The procedure adopted by General Taylor for completing the Seminole con-

[9] Raines to Harris, June 4, 1838; Conway to Harris, July 14, 1838, Foreman Transcripts, I, 142–52, 168.
[10] Jones to Lynn, Nov. 20, 1838, *ibid.*, 281.

quest and removing the rest of the Indians and their allies was similar to the plan outlined by General Winfield Scott. It is true that Scott, in his brief period of command, showed little promise of completing the task. The Seminole campaign called for ability to meet unexpected turns of events, and Scott seemed bewildered by the rapid movement of Indian war parties.[11]

President Jackson recorded his own impressions of the military campaigns in Florida. In a letter to James Gadsden early in the war he commented: "It is true that the whole Florida war from the first to the present time has been a succession of blunders and misfortune."[12] This letter was written in November, 1836, and the President put General Jesup in command of the operations in Florida on December 8, less than a month later. In a memorandum on the Florida campaign, written after his second term as President, Jackson wrote a pointed criticism of General Scott's tactics against the Creeks in Georgia. "If Jessups [sic] command had not struck them and put an end to the war and a bleeding frontier he, Genl Scott and the whole army must have been disgraced. ?[Why] hesitate to strike, for what, to let the Indians scatter and flee, and then to persue when the scientific plan of campaign was mature."[13]

General Taylor's method was to divide the area known to contain hostile Seminoles into small districts, to set up new military posts at frequent intervals, and to patrol the entire region thoroughly. He established 53 new posts, and set his men to building wagon roads for the hauling of military supplies. By February 25, 1839, he had a party of 196 Indians and Negroes ready for removal. Florida was relatively peaceful, and there was little resistance to Taylor's efforts to gather Seminoles for emigration. The commander regarded both the Indians and their Negro allies as prisoners of war, and discarded General Jesup's policy of capturing fugitive slaves for the purpose of returning them to their masters.[14]

[11] Correspondence of Andrew Jackson, V, 468–71.
[12] Jackson to Gadsden, Nov. 1836, A. J. Donelson Papers, Library of Congress.
[13] Correspondence of Andrew Jackson, V, 469.
[14] Sprague, The Florida War, 225; Giddings, The Exiles of Florida, 251–57; Brevard, History of Florida, I, 151–52.

While Taylor, prior to his appointment as commander, had been engaged in penetrating the heart of the Seminole country and winning the costly victory over Arpeika and Coacoochee at Lake Okeechobee, General Jesup was conducting a tedious campaign east of the St. Johns. Results were meager in Indians captured for emigration, until the engagement at Lake Hotchee was fought late in January, 1838. Tuskegee and Halleck Hadjo were driven from their position with severe losses. Jesup lost seven killed and twenty-nine wounded, the General himself receiving a painful wound from a bullet that struck him in the face.

As noted above, the Indian leaders were willing to consider terms of peace after this battle, and the General made his bid for ending the war short of complete conquest, with a large Seminole reservation south of Pease Creek. Jesup's enemies said that he betrayed the trust of Tuskegee and Halleck Hadjo when he made them and their followers prisoners; the General said that these Seminole leaders surrendered their Negroes without condition, and that he immediately sent them west. Then, when President Van Buren refused to follow Jesup's suggestion to settle all remaining Seminoles on a Florida reservation, Tuskegee announced that he and his people would follow their Negroes to the Canadian.

About a year later, General Alexander Macomb came to Florida with instructions to carry out, in effect, the proposal of Thomas S. Jesup and Zachary Taylor: that is, to make peace with the Seminoles on the basis of their remaining in Florida. The agreement was reached after a month of negotiation, and on May 18, 1839, General Macomb announced that the war was over.[15] In July, however, a band of 250 Indians who had no part in the peace pact made a surprise attack upon a party led by Colonel William S. Harney, on the Caloosahatchee River south of Charlotte Harbor. Harney and seven of his soldiers escaped; twenty-two soldiers and two traders were killed; and the two Negro interpreters were made prisoners. One of them was executed the next day. The commander at Fort Mellon, ignoring the fact that the Spanish Indians of the southwest coast had not

[15] Brevard, *History of Florida*, I, 152; Foreman, *Indian Removal*, 371-72.

been included in General Macomb's agreements at Fort King, regarded the Seminole promises violated and seized forty-five peaceful Indians who came in to obtain rations. General Taylor's soldiers built roads, established new posts, and tried to protect the citizens against hostile Seminoles.

A new party of Seminole delegates, selected by Captain John Page, came back from the West to Florida in the summer of 1840, to help with emigration. Holatoochee headed the commission of eleven; Primus and Tony (Sharp Bullet) acted as their interpreters. Colonel W. J. Worth used them with skill, and with their aid collected a party of 220 emigrants at Tampa Bay on March 21, 1841. They were landed by Major William G. Belknap opposite the mouth of Grand River in the western Indian country on April 19, and from that point traveled overland to the Deep Fork.[16]

Lieutenant LeGrand Capers embarked with a party of about 200 Indians and Negroes at Tampa Bay on May 7 and reached New Orleans on May 13. Major Isaac Clark hurried them aboard the *John Jay* and gave Captain H. McKavett strict orders concerning their delivery in the West, as a means of preventing fraudulent seizures of the Negroes. No person was to be allowed to come on board as the *John Jay* traveled up to the party's destination.[17] McKavett landed them at Choctaw Agency on the Arkansas, June 13, 1841, and obtained wagons for their transportation to Deep Fork.

Under C. A. Harris, the business of the Office of Indian Affairs had fallen into a deplorable condition of dust and cobwebs. While the broom of Commissioner T. Hartley Crawford was new, he proceeded to do some cleaning up. Early in the year 1839, he wrote to Captain Pitcairn Morrison, superintendent at Fort Brooke: "This office is wholly destitute of information in relation to the operation and progress of the Seminole removal." He called upon Morrison to give promptly the information provided by the regulations; and inquired sharply concerning a

---

[16] Poinsett to Page, May 29, 1840, O.I.A. Letterbook, XXVIII; Foreman, *Indian Removal*, 375–78.

[17] Clarke to Crawford, May 16, 1841, O.I.A.: Seminoles–Emigration.

lot of Indian livestock for which disbursement of funds had been made. "I wish to know what has become of those horses and cattle. . . . I hope to receive from you a full and satisfactory statement upon this subject."

In a later message Crawford made pointed inquiries into Morrison's accounts with a Negro interpreter. "J. W. Harris . . . transmitted $225.00 to Fort Drane for the payment of King Cudjoe accounts which it appears by the receipt of King Cudjoe now in this office was paid over to him, being his claim in full to the close of the second quarter, 1835. A claim is now presented . . . in favor of King Cudjoe for the whole sum of $420. . . . According to the adjustment of his accounts as above stated, $195 will be paid."

To Captain R. D. C. Collins, Crawford wrote on May 22, 1839: "I have to remind you that no accounts of your disbursements have been received in this office for any later period than the 3rd quarter of 1838." A message from the War Department to Captain Collins on August 31 ran as follows: "Your letter tendering your resignation as an officer in the Army has been received and in answer I transmit to you a report from the Commissioner of Indian Affairs respecting the state of your accounts which you are requested at once to settle. Until they are squared with the Government your resignation cannot be accepted."

When members of Congress were involved in the settlement of claims, spurious or genuine, the difficulties of the Indian Office were increased. To an inquiry by the Hon. D. H. Lewis of Alabama in regard to claims of Opothle Yahola and Jim Boy for Negroes, Crawford answered that the receipt of the two Indians for $2,322.39 was filed with the report of the settlement; and suggested mildly, "This doubtless was the transaction to which you refer."[18]

Contests over slave property were frequent in the Seminole country. Siah Hardigan of the Creek Nation wrote a bitter and incoherent complaint to William Armstrong over his failure to

[18] Crawford to Morrison, Feb. 14 and Mar. 22; Crawford to Collins, May 22; Poinsett to Collins, Aug. 31, 1839; Poinsett to Lewis, Jan. 11; Crawford to Mitchell, Feb. 6; Crawford to Mitchell, July 24, 1840, O. I. A. Letterbook, XXVI, XXVII, XXVIII.

recover slave property purchased from "the right and lawful owners." The agent and the Seminole chief would not give him a satisfactory answer. "I have proved that those Negroes having nothing to do with the Watson claim and were not taken prisoners by the party [Jim Boys]," Siah wrote. He added that he had seen a letter of Colonel Logan, Creek agent, to the Seminole Chief "Micco Napper" [Micanopy], "stating too him if Stinson came to take any property . . . by force, it was their own fault and not let them do it." This was bad advice, Siah thought. It encouraged the Negroes to fight and made it difficult for the Hardigan brothers to round up their livestock, "which we have scattered all over the country around them." The writer ended his message, "All I want is justice between both partys, and done in a friendly manner."[19]

On December 23, 1839, the steamboat *Orleans* arrived at Fort Gibson with 48 Seminole emigrants. They were mustered by Aaron Barling, assistant agent, and started on their way to Deep Fork in wagons. "Captain Logan being absent, I issued to them Blankets, Linsey and hunting shirts, agreeably to the Seminole Treaty," Barling reported to William Armstrong. Nocose Tustenuggee, Osiah Harjo, and Long Snake were members of this party. Armstrong's muster roll for the final quarter of 1839 showed 491 subsisted, not including the party that had just landed.[20]

Captain Page had a complaint to make in regard to the handling of Seminole Negroes. Six persons, headed by a man named Brown, had appeared at Tampa Bay with authority from Secretary Joel Poinsett to interview the visiting Indians from the West. The delegates refused to meet them, and advised that they be sent away. They had come to look for Negroes, and if they were allowed to remain the slaves who were out with the hostile Seminoles would prevent their coming in. General Armistead, after consulting with Captain Page, decided to send Brown and his associates out of the area. "It was a great error in Mr. Poinsett appointing and authorizing such people to come here,"

19 Hardigan to Armstrong, Dec. 8, 1839, O. I. A.: Seminoles—Emigration.
20 Barling to Armstrong, Dec. 31, 1839, *ibid.*

Page wrote to Commissioner Crawford, "and surely a want of confidence in those engaged in the negotiation. During their stay here, three days, they were making affidavits before a justice of the peace, relative to the Negroes now here."

As a veteran in the Indian service, with five years of experience in Florida, the disbursing agent was obviously qualified to criticize. Coosa Tustenuggee was on the point of coming in for emigration, Page reported in another message to the Commissioner, when Captain Kerr and his troops suddenly descended upon the band and carried them as prisoners to Fort King. Furthermore, the runners who were sent to Halleck Tustenuggee, "notwithstanding they all had passes from General Armistead," were seized and imprisoned. All of this, thought Captain Page, was extremely bad management.[21]

Waxe Hadjo, a subchief of the Coosa Tustenuggee band, was an opponent of removal and an enemy of all white citizens who attempted to occupy any part of his native land. On May 2, 1841, Le Grand Capers reported that the express rider from Fort King to the agency on Tampa Bay had been killed. The mailbags were scattered about and the rider's belongings were found near the spot where his body had been burned. Captain Beall's dragoons came to the spot promptly and after a hard pursuit captured Waxe Hadjo, whose name had been mentioned often in connection with recent depredations. The captured Indian leader was executed by hanging.[22]

The Seminole chieftain most wanted for removal in the summer of 1841 was Wild Cat (Coacoochee). Rumors to the effect that he was about to come in were persistent, but Captain Page remained doubtful. "Some have confidence in his coming," he wrote to Commissioner Crawford; "but I see little to encourage that belief." At Fort Pierce on Indian River, northeast of Lake Okeechobee, Major Thomas Childs was constantly on the alert for news of Coacoochee, and was ready to act when the first message from the chief arrived.

[21] Page to Crawford, Mar. 3, Mar. 14, and Apr. 30, 1841, O. I. A.: Seminoles —Emigration; Foreman, *Indian Removal*, 80, 93, 126, 146, 153, 183, 346, 374.
[22] Capers to Crawford, Apr. 20, May 2, and May 7, 1841, O. I. A.: Seminoles —Emigration.

Three Indians approached the fort one day, accompanied by a Negro interpreter named Joe, and asked to see the commander. The officer of the day conducted them to Major Childs, and they told him that they had been sent by Coacoochee. They then handed him a piece of paper signed by Colonel Worth at Tampa Bay, which authorized Coacoochee to come to Fort Pierce for supplies while collecting his band for emigration.

"Where is Coacoochee?" inquired Major Childs.

"Close by," answered Joe, who then explained that the Chief wanted to know whether the paper signed by Colonel Worth was "all right." Childs assured Joe that the paper would be respected, and detailed Lieutenant William Tecumseh Sherman with an escort of ten mounted men to accompany the interpreter and one of the Indians back to Coacoochee. Sherman left a description of the incident in his *Memoirs*.

"We continued to ride for five or six miles when I began to suspect treachery, of which I had heard so much in former years, and had been specially cautioned against by the older officers; but Joe always answered, 'Only a little way.'" As the party approached a hammock, "standing like an island in the interminable pine forest, with a pond of water near it," a few Indians could be seen standing about. "This is the place," said Joe.

Sherman halted the escort, ordered the sergeant to keep a sharp watch, and rode forward with Joe and the Seminole guide. As they reached the border of the hammock, a dozen Indian warriors stood up around them. Sherman asked for the chief, and a young Indian, dressed like the others, slapped his breast and announced, "Me Coacoochee." Through the Negro interpreter, Sherman explained that Major Childs had sent the escort to conduct Coacoochee to the Fort.[23]

"He wanted me to get down and talk," Sherman recalled. "I told him that I had no talk in me, but that, on his reaching the post, he could talk as much as he pleased with the 'big chief,' Major Childs."

Sherman noticed that the guns of Coacoochee's warriors were

[23] Page to Crawford, Apr. 30, 1841, *ibid.; Memoirs of General William T. Sherman*, I, 23ff.

conveniently placed, leaning against a tree. When he ordered his escort to come up and seize the rifles, Coacoochee pretended to be very angry; but the young officer explained that it would relieve the tired warriors of carrying the additional burden for the soldiers to take them on their horses. A mount had been brought along for Wild Cat, and the little party of Indians, waiting only for their leader to dress himself for the meeting with Major Childs, proceeded to the fort. In the conference which followed, Coacoochee declared that he was tired of war, and ready to lay down his arms. He said that his people were scattered, and it would take a "moon" to gather them for emigration. He wanted rations for himself and his followers for a month. Major Childs agreed and Coacoochee promised to have his band of about 160 ready to go west in the time allotted. The chief and his warriors, after the "talk," accepted the commander's offer of refreshments and "proceeded to get regularly drunk."

During the month of waiting, messengers came to the fort several times to obtain additional supplies. Finally Coacoochee and about twenty warriors came in driving a small herd of horses. None of their women and children were with them. Convinced that Wild Cat did not intend to remove his band to the West, Major Childs arranged a council in such manner as to make seizure of the party an easy matter. Coacoochee and his uncle were invited to a separate room, "to take some good brandy instead of the common commissary whiskey." The plan was carried out and the entire party became prisoners. Coacoochee admitted that, for a month, he had been engaged in removing the women and children toward Lake Okeechobee, and that he had intended to follow them after one last visit to the fort. Major Childs sent out a cavalry force to capture the rest of Coacoochee's band, but they were not found. The wily chief and his warriors were placed on a schooner, bound for New Orleans; but General Worth stopped them at Tampa Bay, and sent Coacoochee to gather up the women and children of the band.

The few hundred warriors and their families who remained in Florida, well concealed in remote swamps and hammocks, Sherman thought would have no difficulty in obtaining food.

"Deer and wild turkey were abundant, and as for fish there was no end to them. Indeed, Florida was the Indian's paradise, was of little value to us, and it was a great pity to remove the Seminoles at all, for we could have collected there all the Choctaws, Creeks, Cherokees, and Chickasaws, in addition to the Seminoles. They would have thrived in the Peninsula, whereas they now occupy lands that are very valuable, which are coveted by their white neighbors on all sides, while . . . Florida still remains with a population less than should make a great state."[24]

The emigration party with which Coacoochee came west, numbering about 200, reached Fort Gibson early in November, 1841. He promised to move on to the Deep Fork promptly; but due to circumstances which will be explained in the following chapter, his plans were changed. He and his followers, like the band that recognized Halpatter Tustenuggee as their chief, settled temporarily in the vicinity of Fort Gibson. It was not until March, 1843, that he did lead his people to the land assigned to them. His career in the new Indian Territory was to be turbulent, as it had been in Florida. He was to serve as his tribe's delegate on a mission to Washington; to lead a colony bound for Mexico; to travel west and undertake an extensive trade with the Plains Indians. In every year of Coacoochee's life there was conflict, action, and a great deal of personal danger.

[24] Sherman *Memoirs*, I, 23ff.

CHAPTER 15

End of the War:
More Removals for Profit

*"It appears that Mr. McKee intends to make money off every
person employed by the Gov. in his agency."*

CHARLES A. BAILEY

THE VIGOROUS administration of T. Hartley Crawford
in the Indian Office continued to bring salutary results. Lieutenant Capers became disbursing agent at Tampa Bay in February, 1841, and during the following months was praised for
work well done, reminded of discrepancies, and sharply rebuked
for items of omission in his reports. Crawford was pleased with
favorable news on removals, he sometimes questioned the need
of additional funds, he urged upon Capers "the strictest adherence to the Regulations" in making disbursements and rendering
accounts, and on receiving a muster roll and expense sheet for
a party moved west, he wrote: "The price of transportation is
considered reasonable, and is much below any formerly paid . . .
on the Florida removal." In short, Crawford furnished the guid-
ance his subordinate was justified in expecting, and he had the
satisfaction of seeing improvement in the service.[1]

At Washington the Cherokee statesman, John Ross, in spite
of great disappointment in the relations of his own people with
the government of the United States, tried to aid the Seminole
Indians. To the Secretary of War he wrote: "In order that you
may be possessed of certain facts coming within my own personal
observation in relation to the Seminoles who have been removed

[1] Crawford to Capers, Feb. 6, Apr. 3, May 15, and May 28, 1841, O.I.A.
Letterbook, XXX.

west of the River Mississippi—I deem it my duty to make you this communication." Arriving with the Eastern Cherokees in their new home west of Arkansas early in 1839, Ross had found Seminole Indians encamped near Fort Gibson at various places on Cherokee lands. As he was about to start for Washington with a Cherokee delegation, he was visited by Alligator (Halpatter Tustenuggee), Seminole chief, and some of his warriors. Halpatter asked the Cherokee to convey a message to the Secretary of War, "for the ear of the President; that he may know some of the promises that were made through his officers in Florida."

Alligator said that General Jesup had promised him, specifically, new guns for his men—plows, hoes, axes, and kettles— to replace those left behind. He had also promised an agent and had stated that the new country in the West was a land abounding in game. Not one of the promises had been fulfilled. The land assigned to the Seminoles was occupied by other Indians. Game was scarce. "I have no gun to kill squirrels and birds for my children," Alligator said; "no axe to cut my firewood—no plows or hoes with which to till the soil for bread—and no agent of the United States to whom to represent my wants and grievances —in this, my peculiar condition, I am perplexed to perceive the true cause why those fair promises have not been fulfilled—or, whether they were made only to deceive me?"

In Washington, the doors of the executive departments were closed to John Ross, so he could not present Alligator's plea in person; but he hoped his letter might obtain help from Secretary John Bell on Alligator's grievances. In response to an inquiry from Bell, Commissioner Crawford stated that virtually all stipulations had been met in regard to guns, hoes, plows, kettles, etc., and that Alligator should not be indulged with goods so long as he remained on Cherokee land. Crawford recommended the appointment of a subagent for the Seminoles.

A similar inquiry from the Secretary of War to General Jesup brought this reply: "I have the honor to report that the statement of Mr. Ross is substantially correct, and I consider the public faith pledged, as far as a military commander had authority to pledge it, that the articles left by that band in Florida be replaced. The battle of Locha Hotchee . . . led to . . . immediate and positive surrender of their negroes, and the conditional surrender of their bands. . . . Several of the bands that had not surrendered, and among others Alligator's, when they found the President would not consent to their remaining in Florida on any terms, were, through the influence of the negroes and chiefs whom I employed, and the promises I made them, induced to consent to surrender and emigrate.

"The Indians had retreated before the Army from fifty to two hundred miles, and on the route had left their plows, axes, and brass kettles, and other property. Alligator sent me a message that he would surrender as soon as his people could collect their property, and the means of transporting it to Tampa Bay should be furnished. . . . I directed the messengers to say to him that new kettles, plows, hoes, &c. were better than old ones, and if he would leave his old property and bring his people immediately in, every article left should be replaced in Arkansas. I also promised him a new rifle, and all the advantages secured by the Treaty of Payne's Landing and the Capitulation at Fort Dade."

The general added, "The claim is just: but apart from its justice the highest considerations of policy demand that it be acknowledged and satisfied."[2]

Here was Thomas S. Jesup, the Florida commander, with the pressure of immediate military and political necessity removed, and free to consider justice for the Indians as the matter of first importance. It is a view of the General that has seldom been presented because the current accounts were kept by anti-slavery men, or proslavery men, or Indian haters, or the speculators in land or chattels. None of these groups found Jesup's policies quite to their liking. They seized upon his mistakes and magnified them, and they did not hesitate to misrepresent his views. Like Wiley Thompson, he was one of the outstanding friends of the Seminoles among the officers of the United States. Furthermore, while he took no stand against slavery—it would

[2] Ross to Bell, April 12, 1841; Crawford to Bell, April 28, 1841; Jesup to Bell, May 3, 1841, O. I. A.: Seminoles—Emigration.

have been remarkable if he had, considering his background—
he insisted upon the human rights of Negroes, gave full respect
to their talents as guides and interpreters, and recognized the
bravery of Negro warriors.

After receiving General Jesup's answer to the Secretary of
War concerning Seminole claims for replacement of their goods,
Commissioner Crawford wrote an account of the matter to Major
Armstrong at the Choctaw Agency, and ordered that farming
implements and other goods should be purchased for Alligator's
band. "This occasion may be taken to induce Alligator and his
people to remove and settle in the Seminole country, and on
that condition only will the articles be delivered to them."

Commissioner Crawford was keen in searching the records
for evidence of fraud. After a correspondence of five months
with Gary Hinant, of Washington, D. C., in regard to a claim
for Negroes seized by the Creek warriors in Florida, Crawford
wrote to the claimant as follows: "The letters . . . are evidence
. . . so far as to suspend all action in your favor. . . . It is, also,
represented that the claim is founded on fraud and it is considered not authorized by law as a claim on the United States."[3]

Mr. R. D. Mitchell, of Tennessee, became an applicant for
employment by the Indian Office to supplement his project for
speculating a bit in slaves while he served his country as an
officer in removing the Seminoles. As an honest Whig, from Secretary John Bell's home state, Mitchell was sure that he deserved consideration.

He combined in one letter his plea for help in obtaining
Negroes from the Indians, and the offer of his services: "I have
been here for some time trying to get some Negroes which I
have in the Creek Nation and I am afraid will take me some
time as the Agent Colonel Logan doze appear like he is not disposed to show me any favours. . . . I should like to have the contract of feeding them [the Seminoles] there is some Shawnes
and Dellewars that have been removed from the Choctaw Na-

---

[3] Crawford to Armstrong, July 17, 1841; Crawford to Hinant, Feb. 10, 1841;
March 20, 1841; June 19, 1841; July 26, 1841, O. I. A. Letterbook, XXX. See also,
Poinsett to Hinant, Feb. 6, 1841, O. I. A.: Seminoles—Emigration.

tion if they are provisioned I should like verry much to have the contract which I would do at thirteen cents the same that the Seminoles are fed at. . . . I shall take a great pride in exerting myself to accomplish what I undertake as our side must win with proper action."[4]

In addition to William T. Sherman, whose activities in Florida were described briefly above, other young officers who later achieved high military rank took part in the Seminole campaign of 1841.

During his last year as a cadet at West Point, Lieutenant George H. Thomas had read a book on *The Territory of Florida*, by John Lee Williams. Stories from the Seminole War seemed to indicate that his first active service as an officer would be in Florida; so he was keenly interested in the account by Williams, who was a resident of the territory and a thorough student of its rivers and coasts, its Indian and Spanish background, even its animal and vegetable life. After Thomas graduated and received his commission as second lieutenant, he was assigned to Company D, Third Artillery; and on November 23, 1840, he took passage with his company from New York to Savannah, Georgia, en route to the scene of war in Florida. Braxton Bragg, of the West Point class of 1837, was on the same ship.[5]

From Savannah, young Thomas traveled with his company to Lauderdale on the *Forester*. At the little military post, he entered upon a way of living far different from any he had ever experienced. Cane huts served as shelter for officers and soldiers —and all of the huts, as well as the Indian wigwams that stood near by, were infested by fleas and swarming with cockroaches. The slow current of a river separated the settlement near the beach from a jungle of tangled vines, swamp cypress, and Spanish moss. The jungle cats, alligators, owls, and other wild life of the place filled the night with noises unfamiliar to the young Virginian; but most of all his sleep was disturbed by the constant humming of mosquitoes.

[4] Mitchell to Bell, Aug. 12, 1841; Mitchell to Bell, Aug. 13, 1841, O. I. A.: Seminoles—Emigration.
[5] Freeman Cleaves, *The Rock of Chickamauga*, 14–16.

The region had its attractive features. Fish and other sea food of excellent quality and great variety made the job of furnishing supplies relatively simple for Lieutenant Thomas. It was difficult to obtain beef and pork, and he tried to satisfy the need for a change of diet by hunting deer and wild turkey. Thomas was quartermaster, adjutant, and ordnance officer for the post. While he was tied closely to his multiple duties there, other officers took parties into the Everglades to capture families of Seminoles and escort them to Tampa Bay.

At last, Lieutenant Thomas had his chance to go on a scouting expedition, as second in command under Captain Richard D. A. Wade. They surprised an inland village where eight Indians were captured. At another village of Mikasukies, all the inhabitants were made prisoners. At a third village, they found but one Indian, a small collection of empty huts, and a field of pumpkins. The raid had taken a total of fifty-five prisoners, of whom fourteen were warriors, sixteen women, and twenty-five children. Thomas's Florida duty ended in February, 1842, when he and his company were sent to New Orleans.[6]

Coacoochee's band came west in the autumn of 1841. The muster roll of the party that landed November 12, under the direction of Captain W. Seawell, was sent to Major Armstrong. There were 197 names, 3 having died on the way west. Billy and Charles, two Negro interpreters accompanied by five slaves, were members of the party. Opis Hadjo Boy, Case Yahola, and Faso Hadjo were among the heads of families. The party had been persuaded to land under the influence of Micanopy and other old settlers, and Coacoochee agreed that they would move to the Deep Fork immediately. However, the day after their arrival the weather turned cold and they refused to go any farther. Promising to move upon Seminole lands when the weather became warmer, they went into camp opposite the mouth of Grand River.[7]

In September, 1841, nine commissioners were selected from

[6] *Ibid.*, 17–21; Sherman, *Memoirs*, 27.
[7] George W. Clark to Armstrong, Nov. 16, 1841, O. I. A.: Seminoles—Emigration.

the western Seminoles to aid the United States officers, under the direction of Captain S. B. Thornton, in recruiting Indians for removal. Halpatter Tustenuggee (Alligator), Hotulke Emathla, and Waxie Emathla were the principals of this commission. At Fort Smith they were joined by Colonel John Garland with six companies of the Fourth Infantry. Through the fall and winter following, several hundred Indians and a small number of Seminole slaves were gathered at Tampa Bay and transported to the territory west of the Arkansas. The *Laurance Copeland* carried emigrants from Tampa Bay to New Orleans in the spring of 1842. Three hundred of them were taken on the steamer *President* to a point on the Arkansas sixty miles below Little Rock. After a rise in the river, they were able to reach Webber's Falls on June 1; and from this point they traveled overland to Deep Fork. Captain T. L. Alexander was in charge of this party after it left New Orleans.

The latter part of the journey was enlivened by the refusal of the Indians to march toward Deep Fork, since they preferred to join Alligator's band near Fort Gibson. Captain Alexander required the aid of five companies of soldiers from Fort Gibson to enforce his requirement that the party should march directly to their own lands.

Lieutenant E. R. S. Canby conducted a band of one hundred Seminoles and Negroes from New Orleans on July 22, 1842, on the steamer *J. B. Swan*. Lieutenant Canby put his passengers ashore six miles below Little Rock because of low water, and discharged the boat, "in consideration of the sum of $800 from the amount ($2,200) of the original contract." It was found that the price of teams—oxen, mules, horses—took a sharp rise in that part of Arkansas. Canby was forced to purchase one wagon and team in order to obtain enough transportation for the Indians who could not walk, and for the baggage. Teams were hired at the rate of $3 per day for a load of 2,000 pounds, with forage for the teams and subsistence for the drivers. For the return trip, $3 per twenty miles was allowed. The leader had been furnished with funds at New Orleans for an all-river passage; and at Little Rock he found in his possession considerably less money than was required to complete the journey by land. A Seminole Negro slave helped him solve the problem.

"Being unable to negotiate drafts, the Interpreter, John Coheia, or Gopher John, placed at my disposal the sum of $1,500, to enable me to meet my engagements on account of Transportation. To refund this, a draft for that amount was left in the hands of Captain E. B. Alexander, Assistant Q. M. at Fort Smith.

"Gopher John, in addition to being a valuable interpreter, possesses the good qualities of being a zealous friend of the whites, and a strong disposition to oblige the Agents of the Government."

Canby's party crossed the Arkansas River by ferry at Norristown, and reached the Choctaw Agency on August 26. Proceeding west, they crossed the Canadian at the Falls, reached Creek Council Ground on September 5, and on the following day reported to the Creek agent. The distance from Fort Smith to the Creek Council Ground, by their route, was one hundred miles. Lieutenant Canby reported that his party, at the end of their journey, "were generally in the enjoyment of good health and well satisfied with their condition and prospects."[8]

General Zachary Taylor, whose request to be relieved of his command in Florida had been "reluctantly granted" on April 21, 1840, had been assigned to duty at Fort Smith.[9] In the Spring of 1842, he summarized Seminole removals and locations as follows: Under Halpatter Tustenuggee (Alligator) and Holahtochee, a few miles north of Fort Gibson, 1,097; under Coacoochee (Wild Cat), a few miles south of Fort Gibson, 70; under Micanopy, from 10 to 40 miles southwest of Fort Gibson, 827; under Concharte Micco, twenty miles south of the Fort, 479; and under Fuch-a-lusti-hadjo (Black Dirt), 360 on Little River. Thus, according to General Taylor's count, there were 2,833 Seminoles, including their Negroes, in the western Indian lands. It had been proposed to John Ross of the Cherokees that the Seminoles on Cherokee land might be removed by the use of

[8] Alexander to Crawford, May 18, 1842; Canby to Crawford, Sept. 16, 1842; idem. to idem., Nov. 12, 1842, O. I. A.: Seminoles—Emigration.

[9] Dictionary of American Biography, XVIII, 349 (article by Wendell H. Stephenson).

Federal troops; but the great chief counseled patience, and refused to lend his influence to removal by force. Some of the squatters, by permission of the Cherokee government, planted grain or cotton, and were given additional time in their temporary locations until their crops were harvested. General Taylor's census was transmitted to William Armstrong, Acting Superintendent of the Western Territory, by Major George W. Clark on March 21, 1842.[10]

In Florida, the war had gradually settled down to a process of flight by families and small bands of Indians and Negroes from one hidden spot to another, pursuit by the troops, occasional surprise attacks by the soldiers, and in rare instances counter raids by the Indians. Lieutenant William T. Sherman, stationed at Fort Pierce, recorded his view of the situation in the peninsula during the summer and autumn of 1841. Chekika of the Spanish Indians had been captured and executed by General W. S. Harney. It was absurd, Sherman said, to call these raids upon Indian villages a war. On November 20, he was promoted to first lieutenant and ordered to join Company G at St. Augustine.

In a letter to Miss Ellen Boyle Ewing, Sherman wrote a description of Picolata, the post to which he was assigned as commander. "It is situated on the St. Johns River, opposite, and eighteen miles distant from St. Augustine, between which there is a good road with a military escort twice a week. Along this road many murders have been committed but none since we took Coacoochee, whose party had formerly infested the road. Now there is considered no danger and persons pass backwards and forwards constantly in parties of two and three. . . . It is a very beautiful spot indeed. Magnificent live oak trees shade the yard, enclosing my splendid quarters, and the St. Johns, a noble sheet of water, about one and a half miles broad, adds beauty to the whole."[11]

[10] Clark to Armstrong, Mar. 21, 1842, O. I. A.: Seminoles–Emigration; Foreman, *Indian Removal*, 380.
[11] William T. Sherman, *Sherman's Home Letters*, 16–19; Miss Ellen Boyle Ewing, who later married Sherman, was the sister of Thomas Ewing, secretary of the treasury under William H. Harrison. Sherman was twenty-two at the time of this letter; Miss Ewing, seventeen.

In December, 1841, Tustenuggee Chupco, a subchief, surrendered with seventy followers near the Great Cypress Swamp. They were taken to Fort Brooke for emigration. On August 14, 1842, Colonel Worth announced that the war was over, though there had been no important battles for several years, and the hostilities were not ended with his announcement. President John Tyler also commented that the war "has happily been terminated," in his second annual message.[12]

Even as Tyler's message was placed before Congress, one of the "casual outbreaks" was taking place. Chief Pascofa was accused of raiding in the Apalachicola Valley, where his band of Creeks had disturbed the peace of Florida Territory occasionally since 1838, when they broke away from the party that migrated to the West under Daniel Boyd. The people of Florida called Pascofa's band the "Ocklocknee Indians." Colonel Ethan Allen Hitchcock was assigned the task of bringing them in for emigration.

On December 12, 1842, with two companies of the Third Infantry, Colonel Hitchcock came down the Apalachicola River in the steamboat *William Gaston*. He declined to add two companies of volunteers to his force, obviously depending upon his reputation among the Indians as a reasonable man who would perform his duties with as little conflict as possible. Messengers from Colonel Hitchcock got in touch with Pascofa, and arranged for a conference. The chief was ready to emigrate, and desired only that his capitulation should be marked by some special ceremonies to emphasize the importance of the event. Colonel Hitchcock agreed, and the celebration was held. Then the *William Gaston* moved out of the Apalachicola along the coast to the mouth of the Ocklocknee, and thirty miles up that stream to the point agreed upon for the entire band to come on board. It required several days beyond the time set for departure to collect Pascofa's followers, but on January 9, 1843, they were all assembled: twenty-one warriors, nineteen women, and ten children. According to local tradition the small number of children was due to the extreme necessity of the band four years earlier,

[12] Richardson, *Messages and Papers,* IV, 198–99.

when their infants were put to death as a means of preventing the capture of the entire group.

Colonel Hitchcock issued blankets, shirts and turbans, and calico dresses to the members of the party. While waiting for them to assemble, Hitchcock learned that Thlocko Tustenuggee was a captive, and that Ochacker, a Creek chief who was classed among the hostiles, had been taken by the order of General William J. Worth at Tampa Bay. LeGrand Capers sent Thlocko Tustenuggee's band to New Orleans on the brig *Lawrence,* which he chartered from its master, Charles R. Griffith, for the sum of $700. The party consisted of ninety-one Indians and three Negro slaves.[13]

John McKee, the new subagent for the Seminoles in the West, reported to Commissioner Crawford in August, 1842: "On the arrival of the late Seminole emigrants I found it impossible to take a Muster Roll . . . in consequence of one of the Leading Chiefs of the party being dissatisfied though I find the number to be still 303 two of the delligation quit the Party one died and one born three that was left at Batten Ruch came on which makes the 303." A second report on the same day stated: "I receipted for sixty-eight tents in the possession of the Party the tents are unfit for use and I the return of Lt. Haskins will show it the are still in possession of the Indians the are unwilling to give them up you will please advise me in relation to this matter as I do not like to be Responsible." Major Armstrong wrote to Crawford on the subject of the tents as follows: "Lieut. Hoskins ought not to have asked McKee to receipt for the tents, he was unable to get them himself. McKee was ignorant of the responsibility he incurred and therefore gave the receipts. The Indians will not give up the tents willingly."[14]

Unfortunately the sub-agent John McKee had other faults, in addition to his inexperience with accounts and his meager

---

[13] Contract for the Brig *Lawrence,* O. I. A.: Seminoles–Emigration; Foreman, *Indian Removal,* 381–83; Giddings, *The Exiles of Florida,* 303–12; Brevard, *History of Florida,* I, 171–72.

[14] D. A. Kurtz to Armstrong, Oct. 8, 1841, O. I. A. Letterbook, XXXI; McKee to Crawford, Aug. 9, 1842; Armstrong to Crawford, Aug. 14, 1842, O. I. A.: Seminoles–Emigration.

schooling, which disqualified him for a successful career in the Indian service. Major G. W. Clark accused him of padding his accounts shamelessly in number of rations purchased and in many other particulars. Clark's message to William Armstrong gave details:

"The first item is for provisions furnished the Indians on their route—the beef and corn (they received no salt) cost $38.75, which he should have purchased and issued on account of the Govt. and taken receipts for, and it would have cost the Govt. only $38.75, whereas he wishes to pocket $43.75 and make the Govt. pay $82.50. . . .

"The third item is for a family that arrived between issues— he made this same issue within two miles of my house—he would not send for me—but he makes the issue at one of the contractor's depots—he purchases the provisions at $13.28 and wishes to make the contractor pay $33.11, his profit to be $19.83."

Charles A. Bailey wrote to Major Armstrong: "Mr. McKee told me he could hire a blacksmith in Louisville who would come out here and work for twelve dollars per month and board found him, and . . . he would make the difference some $300 or $400 to himself. He then proposed to employ me upon the same terms, and told me that he would employ a Negro or an Indian man as his U. S. Interpreter, and make him strike in the shop, thereby save to himself the striker's wages. I declined on the ground that I wanted the full wages and would board myself. . . . He told me at the same time that he intended to go to Kentucky and employ a teacher for $300 or $400 and board, and he could save to himself the difference in the teacher's salary. It appears that Mr. McKee intends to make money off every person employed by the Gov. in his agency. . . ."

Contracts for subsistence of the Seminoles continued as one of the leading sources of contention among officers of the United States and other interested persons. Charges of graft were common among the losers in the bidding, and in some instances the facts seemed to justify the accusers.[15]

[15] Clark to Armstrong, Aug. 1, 1842; Aug. 23, 1842; Bailey to Armstrong,

G. W. Clark wanted the Seminole parties moved directly to their own land instead of permitting them to stop at Fort Gibson, where it was their tendency to spend their money for whiskey and "become poor drunken wretches." Those who are settled, he said, raise corn, rice, beans and other products, "sufficient to subsist them, are making comfortable cabins, clearing small fields, and appear to be satisfied and contented. . . . While those who stop about this Post expend their money for whiskey, are speculated upon and cheated by bad white men and half breeds, become impoverished, dissatisfied—commence stealing in the neighborhood; and finally become the worst kind of population."

In October, 1842, the Seminole Chiefs, probably through their clerk, Thomas O'Beirne, wrote a joint letter to General Zachary Taylor. As General Jesup's successor in Florida, Taylor was regarded by Indian leaders as their best hope for fulfillment of promises. Charges against the United States were crudely phrased but they were specific: the Seminoles had been deceived in the removal treaties; Creeks were settled on the land assigned to them; there was no agent in the West to hear their grievances and give assistance; the Creeks were determined to take their slaves to satisfy the Florida war claim.

"When General Jesup left then you General Taylor took command and you always like to see us and talk to us and now we like to see you and talk with you there is a great deal of sickness among our people but if health permits the head chief and two or three others will go to see you in the course of a few days. . . ."

The signatures, each acknowledged with a cross mark, were those of Micconuppa (Micanopy), Co-e-hadjo, Cloud, Conchatti Micco, Tiger, Black Dirt, Tuste-na-con-chokne, Ni-co-si-hola, So-tal-a-hadjo, So-chi-micco, and Abraham the interpreter.[16]

While the Seminole head men were groping for help through

Sept. 15, 1842; Armstrong to Crawford, Oct. 1, 1842; Barnes to Crawford, May (?) 1842, O. I. A.: Seminoles—Emigration.

[16] Clark to Armstrong, Feb. 25, 1842; Seminole Chiefs to Taylor, Oct. 12, 1812, O. I. A.: Seminoles—Emigration.

the medium of a strange language, striving by diplomacy to protect their rights under removal treaties; while the contractors were reaching for profits, legitimate or otherwise; while humane and honorable officials were laboring for the welfare and progress of their Indian wards; and while corrupt officials were taking all possible loot from the United States Treasury and from the mistreated Indians—the old agent, John Phagan was bidding to revive old claims and create new ones. He wrote a pathetic letter to the Honorable James Graham, seeking to enlist the Congressman's support for recognition of his claim to compensation as the conductor of the Seminole exploring party in 1832–33. He stated his case with vigor, if not with accuracy.

"To send a man 2,000 miles by sea and land to resk [sic] his life through Yellow Fever and Chollerea and pay him nothing does not sound like justice to me," Phagan suggested. He claimed pay from October 1, 1832, to May 10, 1833, at the rate of $2 per day. Representative Graham enclosed his letter with a brief note to President Tyler's secretary of war, John C. Spencer.

The claims upon the Treasury, in connection with the Seminole War, were many and varied. The widow and son of John Oponey, Creek warrior killed in action against the Seminoles, claimed $750 as compensation, under treaty terms; Ne Cose Yohola, Creek chief, claimed pay at the rate of $5 per day for service under Captain Page and William Armstrong on the Seminole mission to Florida; A. J. Forrester of Tallahassee, Florida Territory, presented a claim for a slave boy, John, who was captured in one of Coacoochee's raids and taken west by his Indian master. The value placed upon John was $300—but, Mr. Forrester thought, should have been much higher.[17]

G. W. Clark, who had been instrumental in bringing about the replacement of John McKee by Thomas L. Judge, became one of the chief figures in an investigation by Lieutenant Colonel R. B. Mason. The inquiry into methods of the issuing agent was fairly conducted, with the obvious intention of improving the

[17] Phagan to Graham, June 3, 1842, encl. to Sec. of War John C. Spencer; Oponey, No-cose-yahola, Forrester claims, filed with Office of Ind. Affairs; Levy to Spencer, Apr. 10, 1842, O.I.A.: Seminoles—Emigration.

service of the Indian Office. The investigator reported that Clark signed abstracts for contractors without actually seeing the issues made—not once, but as a regular custom through the years 1841 and 1842. Clark "did not and could not know" whether or not the issues were made in good faith, of corn and other goods delivered to the Indians. "If for instance," wrote Colonel Mason, "Mr. Clark gave a party of Indians an order for fifteen bushels of corn on A and he only issued ten bushels, then the Indians were cheated and Mr. Clark knew no better. . . . I state it thus, that you may readily see how frauds may have been practiced on the Indians by the negligence of a Government Agent." Mason stated that he was convinced Clark "left the door wide open" for fraud.

"I beg leave to call your particular attention to the letter of the 26 Dec. *purporting* to be Mr. Constantine Perkins' answer to my note of the day before, the whole of that letter *signature* and all, I believe to be in the handwriting of George W. Clark, by what sort of shuffling and cutting, Clark should answer my note to Mr. Perkins and sign Perkins' name to it, must be left for them to explain, it certainly carries with it a very suspicious appearance. . . . The letter states that Mr. Clark "was generally present" . . . Now sir it can be proven by several witnesses . . . that order after order was brought to Perkins by different Indians from Clark on which issues of corn and salt was made. . . . If Mr. Perkins chose to issue short measure, how was an ignorant Indian to know it, if asked if he had got his corn, he would say, yes. . . . It was his duty to be present at the issuing place and see the issues made; . . . if he certified on the abstracts that he saw all the issues made, then he certified falsely . . . he betrayed his trust and did not guard those rights and interests."

Colonel Mason requested that the Secretary of War should have an opportunity to read his letter. Statements substantiating the charges were enclosed, from D. R. Logan, G. S. Irwin, James McKillop (a Creek Indian); John Barnwell, a merchant living at the mouth of Grand River (with whom John McKee boarded); and John McKee, late Seminole Agent, himself. The contractors most concerned were A. H. Olmstead and Colonel L. N. Clark of New Orleans.

This report was made at the beginning of January, 1843, and on February 16 following, William Armstrong wrote to the Commissioner of Indian Affairs: "The number of Seminoles now subsisting is greatly diminished. I have therefore discontinued the services of G. W. Clark as issuing commissary, and directed Thomas L. Judge, Seminole Sub-Agent, to perform the same."[18]

[18] Lt. Col. R. W. Mason to J. Hartley Crawford, Jan. 31, 1843; Armstrong to Crawford, Feb. 16, 1843, O.I.A.: Seminoles—Emigration.

CHAPTER 16

Seminole Struggle
for Adjustment in the West

"The Seminoles here have threatened the life of Gopher John."

LIEUTENANT COLONEL R. B. MASON

THE PERIOD of two decades, more or less, that lay between Indian removal and the outbreak of the American Civil War was a time of pioneer hardship and readjustment for all the Indians of the Five Civilized Tribes. It was a period in which many native people became shiftless and lacking in spirit, some became drunken wrecks, and some developed a hopelessly criminal tendency. Conditions of their removal had a great deal to do with the individual misfortunes of the Indians. Their suffering was very great in all the tribes; but the worst of the removal hardships were endured by the Seminoles. Even more detrimental to their welfare and normal development toward a new pattern of life in modern society than the physical pain of short rations and exhaustion was the uncertainty that surrounded them in their new western homes.

Three factors contributed most to their bewilderment. First of these was the status of their former slaves and of the free Negroes who had lived in the Seminole country. Next in importance and closely connected with the first, was the Seminole status in the Creek Nation—their right to land, the location of their dwellings, their rights in regard to government. Third among the conditions that worried them was the uncertainty that surrounded their contracts for subsistence, and even annuities from the United States. Instead of the economy and efficiency that should have been prime considerations in the letting of contracts and their administration, partisan politics and the narrower concerns of individual profits were often decisive. Corn, beef, and pork were brought from the port of New Orleans or from St. Louis at considerable expense, while Cherokees and Creeks, with an ample supply of livestock and grain, were in need of a market for their surplus products.[1] So often were supplies delivered tardily, that late delivery came to be expected; and unfortunately for the Indians the rations were too often reduced in quantity by the sharp practices of traders and agents of the government.

The Negro problem was a matter of peculiar significance to the Florida Indians. Many of the Negroes in the Seminole country, although descendants of fugitive slaves, had been free persons for several generations; and even the slaves of the Indians lived under conditions far less burdensome than ordinary chattel servitude. Joshua Giddings, who had ample opportunity as a member of Congress to consult the records that came before that body, and who displayed some familiarity with documents on slaves, attempted a summary of fugitives returned to slavery, Negro casualties, and emigration to the West. The absorption of Giddings in the antislavery movement colored his judgment, but probably his estimates are nearly correct, where discrimination as to Negro ownership by white claimants was not involved. He states that 12 Florida Negroes were returned to slavery under the provisions of the Treaty of Colerain in 1796; 270 were killed at Blount's Fort, and 30 taken prisoners—some seriously wounded. At the end of the Seminole War about 400 had been killed.

He estimated that, in the Second Seminole War, 75 were killed in battle and 500 reduced to slavery. After the removal of 1842, there were 150 Negroes still in the Seminole country; and eventually 300 emigrated from the Indian Territory in the West to Mexico. According to his account, Creek warriors seized 75 Seminole Negroes in 1850, after they had been offered $100 per head for them by white traders, and sold them into slavery.[2]

[1] Grant Foreman, *The Five Civilized Tribes*, 156.
[2] Giddings, *The Exiles of Florida*, 335.

The attitude of the Seminole chiefs toward union with the Creeks is clearly shown in the correspondence of Holatoochee, principal chief after the death of Micanopy, and of other head men who joined him in letters to officials of the United States. From Tampa Bay, at the time of his return to Florida, Holatoochee wrote to Thomas S. Jesup that the Creeks occupied Seminole land, that they insisted upon union of tribal governments, and that the Seminoles were encamped "within a few yards of the spot where they landed."

General Jesup repeatedly called the attention of secretaries of war and Presidents to the condition of the Seminole Negroes in the West. He explained that more than nine-tenths of the whole number of Negroes surrendered under the assurance of freedom on certain conditions. He stated that the Negroes were employed, in many instances as guides or messengers, and that several were killed in that dangerous employment. Near the end of John Tyler's administration, Jesup wrote: "I earnestly hope that the Executive will not permit the national faith thus solemnly pledged, and which as the commander of the Army I had the right to pledge, to be violated; but that all the Negroes who surrendered to me and have been sent to the West, be protected from capture by, or sale to either citizens, foreigners, or Indians, and that measures be taken to recover all who have been separated from their families and sold."[3]

Zachary Taylor, who made no effort to capture Negro slaves in Florida for white claimants, adopted the policy of inducing Seminole removal by promising the Indian leaders protection in their ownership of slave property. The difference in the plans of the two generals was more apparent than real; for the Negroes in the West, slave or free, when left to their own devices were inclined to attach themselves to an Indian chief—their old owner, if possible. The promise made to the Creek Indians, of booty in the form of slaves, threw into the complicated situation a further element of confusion; and General Jesup was not successful in his effort to simplify the problem thus created, by

[3] Holatoochee to Gen. Jesup, Sept. 23, 1838; Gen. Jesup to Sec. of War William Wilkins, May 30, 1844, O. I. A.: Seminoles—Emigration.

245

ordering payment of the Creeks for their interest in the Negroes. There was much uncertainty for a time, as to whether or not the Creek chiefs had received the $8,000 agreed upon with General Jesup in full settlement of the Creek claim; but an official report to the Commissioner of Indian Affairs stated that the Indians refused to accept payment of $8,000. As we have seen, the offer of a larger sum by James C. Watson, of Georgia, led to a contest between the military officers and the Indian Department in which General Gaines, Major Clark, Lieutenant Reynolds, and other officers succeeded generally in delivering the Negroes in the West.[4]

The fear of kidnappers who were active in pursuit of Seminole Negroes, and the dread of falling under control of the Creek Council with its pronounced stand against free Negro towns, held the majority of the Seminoles in idleness and bewildered uncertainty for many months after their arrival at Fort Gibson. There was real danger of capture and sale to white plantation owners, not only for former Seminole slaves, but for Negroes who had never been slaves. When General Jesup came to Fort Gibson in 1845 on the business of new construction there, the Negroes appealed to him for support; and the General upheld their claims to freedom. Sixty or seventy colored laborers were given employment on the new stone fort, and other Negroes were protected against seizure.[5]

Captain John Page, under the most favorable circumstances, explained to a Seminole tribal council the reasons for their land being occupied by Creeks. "I told them it [the land] was kept open for them three years, and instead of emigrating as they agreed to do, they went to war and in the meantime the Creeks took possession." Page added that there was still good land and plenty of it; and that the President would be happy to have a portion of the country marked off for them. "I have heard but very few complaints about this country; all appear very well satisfied; now and then an old woman breaks out upon me, but

---

[4] Jesup to Searle, Sept. 9, 1837; Sloan to Harris, May 6, 1838; Reynolds to Harris, May 15, 1838, O. I. A.: Seminoles—Emigration.

[5] Foreman, *The Five Civilized Tribes*, 256–57.

they did the same thing in Florida and would if they had everything they asked for. The chiefs say they are not worth noticing." As in so many other cases, with the Seminoles as well as other peoples, the old women who protested were fundamentally right. The delay of fifteen years in obtaining a separate country for the Seminoles was peculiarly detrimental to the tribe.

A letter to General Matthew Arbuckle from three Seminole chiefs, written by a trusted interpreter who was semiliterate, and signed by each Indian with a cross mark, gives the other side of the case.

"We of the Semenole tribe Cheaf and warraors Cor Comings Sir Gen Jessep Stated to the Semenoles when the did arive at the new homes that the wood live at peace with there property retern the property Ware not there own Soe we did according to orders at tampy Bay Before we left Gen Jessep which stated to us the country ware assined ware lying vacant We found it ware not the case. We doe wish to be at peace with our property in our country Assined to us allsoe we wishes for you to state to the Government we wishes to come on sea the presedent perhaps we can range our matters to our Sattisfactoin it appear we Cannot have Justice done to us With out Going our selves for we are not settled yet the Contry We are now in it doc not suit us which we doe Wish for to contend for the Contry Ware assine to us By the Government We doe Wish for you to Pas your opinion on the subject We are now on the princeple Cheaf will vissit you on tomorrow evening on this Bisnist if you can Send a lettere to the Citty of Washington fo us on the vissit to sea our Great farther as we ask the reqest to rite us A letter alsoe assine our names to the letter if you doe write for us. Nothing more your friend and Brothers." The names of "Meco-Nollee," "Nocus-Yo-holer," and "Tos-ton-nock-ko-Jugnee" were affixed to the document.[6]

Thomas Judge, the Seminole subagent, was in sympathy with his people in their misfortunes, and he gave them support and understanding that was too rare in the Indian service. In Sep-

[6] Page to Crawford, Aug. 5, 1840; Chiefs to Gen. Arbuckle, "Jully the 10th, 1840," O. I. A.: Florida–Fort Gibson.

tember, 1843, he reported in some detail to Major William Armstrong on conditions among the Seminoles. Those Indians who had moved upon their own lands, although hostile in their attitude when Judge first came among them, were now quite friendly and co-operative. Those who were camping in the Cherokee Nation, on the contrary, were suspicious and resentful. "There appears to be . . . a counter current operating on them, which keeps up a feverish excitement; their vicinity to the garrison is an unfavorable circumstance; they frequently visit there, and state their imaginary grievances to the officers, and I am sorry to say they receive too much countenance."

Thomas Judge was convinced that the Seminoles were not understood or appreciated by officers of the government. "I find them a high-minded, open, candid, and brave people. They pay more attention to the wants and comforts of their women than any tribe I am acquainted with; they keep them well clothed, and the men pay particular attention to appear in clean and appropriate costume; they appropriate most of their annuity to clothe their women and children; in this respect they set a good example to the other tribes. If these people received a tithe of the aid and assistance that other tribes are the subject of, their advances toward civilized life would be second to none." Perhaps the cost of the Seminole War, in "blood and treasure," was responsible for the neglect of the tribe; but an "equal ratio of fatherly care and protection" was due them. Wild Cat and Alligator, with their adherents, were still in the Cherokee Nation; but some of their supporters were drifting away from them, and Judge expressed the pious hope that all might do so eventually. He recommended, furthermore, that all payments of annuities be suspended for those Indians who would not "remove to their own country and give satisfactory evidence that they intend to remain there."[7]

In spite of the fact that the most desirable portions of the land assigned to the Seminoles had been occupied by the follow-

[7] Judge to Armstrong, Sept. 15, 1843, Commissioner of Indian Affairs, *Annual Report* (1843), No. 90. Since the original letters of Thomas Judge are badly written, this one was probably edited and corrected for publication.

ers of Opothle Yahola at the forks of the Canadian, and by other Creek settlers, some bands of Agent Judge's tribe found places to take root. Fuch-a-lusti-hadjo (Black Dirt) pushed westward from Deep Fork to the Little River country, and Micanopy's people settled the bottom land on Deep Fork in scattered communities. In 1842, Halpatter Tustenuggee was absent on a mission to Florida when the question of removing his followers from the Cherokee country was much discussed. Chief John Ross of the Cherokees, the Cherokee Council, and General Zachary Taylor all refused to take summary action on the removal, while Halpatter and Holatoochee were both absent.[8]

Major William Armstrong, whose financial dealings as acting superintendent were many and varied, totaling large sums of government money, was careful and accurate in his accounts, and so far as the records show, scrupulously honest. Yet he could not avoid entanglement with shady characters among the contractors; and in some instances he gave active support to men who were not worthy of trust.

Lorenzo N. Clark, with whom Major Armstrong had many business dealings, was constantly in trouble over the fulfillment of his contracts, and was often in arrears with the United States. The activities of Captain R. D. C. Collins also caused Armstrong much embarrassment, particularly in the purchasing of a lot of spoiled pork from Colonel L. N. Clark. Eventually, Armstrong disagreed with T. Hartley Crawford in regard to a new contract with Clark, and lost his argument. Commissioner Crawford wrote to the Superintendent at Fort Gibson on November 4, 1842: "It has become necessary that measures should be taken to recover from Col. Clark the balance due from him under contract for Chickasaw provisions, delivered to him by Captain Collins in 1837. You will immediately, therefore, upon receipt of this letter, cause suit to be instituted against him and his sureties for the amount due. All the evidence necessary for you to have, in the prosecution of this suit, is already in your possession."[9]

---

[8] Foreman, *The Five Civilized Tribes*, 227.
[9] Armstrong to Crawford, May 24, May 28, June 7, and September 17, 1842; Crawford to Armstrong, Nov. 4, 1842, O. I. A.: Seminoles–Emigration.

A census taken by Thomas L. Judge on July 31, 1844, placed the number of Seminole Indians at 3,136, in addition to the Negroes. More than 500 Apalachicola Indians were included in the count. There was no accurate census of the Florida Indians before the outbreak of the second Seminole War; but if the official estimates are to be credited, a decade of war and emigration had reduced their number between 35 and 40 per cent. Fuch-a-lusti-hadjo's band was reduced from about 500 to 300 in a period of six years. The Agent reported, from time to time, that the number of children in the tribe was large, but gave no detailed figures in regard to ages represented in the population. The increase of 303 in two years and four months (from 2,833 to 3,136) does not represent growth of tribal population since there were several bands of immigrants who arrived in the West during the period. It is certain that the Seminoles, like the Creeks, declined in total number during their early years in the West. The Commissioner of Indian Affairs, reporting in 1855 from the best available data, gave 2,500 as the population of the Seminoles west of Arkansas, and 500 as the number in Florida for the year 1853.

In purchases of goods for the Florida Indians, the agents and dealers sometimes discovered opportunities for personal advantage. Although the total volume of implements bought for the Indians was large, local agents made the purchases at Fort Gibson or at Fort Smith for the Seminoles, dividing the business among various dealers of the area. On March 16, 1842, five hardware stores supplied portions of a purchase for the Seminoles that totaled $463.50. No storm of protest followed the completion of this transaction—the amount involved being too small to stir up resentment of competitors; but it was not an example of efficient buying. The same dealers regularly sold goods to individual farmers at a lower rate than they charged the Indians for goods of identical quality. The largest sum paid out for Seminole hardware in this purchase was $169, to Seaborn Hill and Company.

Of necessity, some of the Indian accounts were for small sums, due to the emergencies of transportation and subsistence.

Major Clark's bill for the moving of Coacoochee's band into the Creek Nation is an example of such a record. In his report to Superintendent Armstrong, Clark suggested that the owners of "waggons" and ferries were anxious for their money: "John Lewis, ferriage, $3.00; John Drew, 3 waggons, 10 days, $5 per day, $150; Mrs. Coody, one waggon, 3 days, $15; R. Brunner, one ditto, 3 days, $15; R. Drew, 4 ditto, 10 days, $80; S. Bradey, ferriage, $65."[10]

When Coacoochee and Halpatter Tustenuggee led a Seminole delegation to Washington in 1844, they were opposed by some of the chiefs who had moved upon lands assigned to the Seminoles. Agent Thomas L. Judge also took a stand against the visit of the Indians in the national capital, on the ground that chiefs who refused to live upon their own lands, preferring to camp upon Cherokee property, were not representative of their people. Judge stated his position on the delegation in a letter to the Commissioner, and gave his views on several related problems. Settlement of the Negro question was the most pressing need of both Creeks and Seminoles, in the Agent's opinion. He declared that the Seminoles would fight before they would accept Creek law. The Chiefs, protesting against the Coacoochee mission, stated:

"We have given our agent Thomas L. Judge full power to go on to Washington and settle our business with the government, we have full confidence in him and know that he will do everything in his power to promote our interest, We know that Coacoochee alias Wild Cat has been advised by base counsellors and by those who do not look to the interest and welfare of the Seminole people." The Agent followed this message from the chiefs with a request for payment of his own expenses on a journey to Washington during his furlough. The cost he estimated at $150, for travel one way and expenses in the city. "Nothing short of the utmost necessity . . . could have induced me to have foregone the satisfaction of remaining in the Bosom of my family during the time allowed me for my furlough," he wrote.

[10] Clark to Armstrong, Feb. 6 and Apr. 15, 1842, O. I. A.: Seminoles—Emigration; Commissioner of Indian Affairs, *Annual Report* (1855), No. 122; *The Journal of Ethan Allen Hitchcock*, 113 n. 64; Foreman, *The Five Civilized Tribes*, 230–39.

In spite of the efforts of Agent Judge and the Seminole chiefs, Coacoochee made his trip to Washington and was heard by the officials there. When the delegates had voiced their opinions in the Indian Office and accepted entertainment from a variety of sources, including Reverend Orson Douglas of Philadelphia, they returned to Fort Gibson with a new view of the nation in which they were trying to solve the difficult problems of tribal adjustment. Perhaps they had helped, also, to broaden the experience of officers who administered their affairs.

Back in the Indian country, Coacoochee and his colleagues found a desolate condition that was not the result of governmental policies; the Arkansas, Verdigris, and Grand rivers were out of their banks and large areas of bottom land were heavily flooded. Crops in the fields were under water, and granaries had been washed away, which seriously depleted the surplus grain carried over from the previous year. It was necessary for the commandant at Fort Gibson, Colonel R. B. Mason, to issue emergency rations for more than two thousand persons who were directly affected by the high waters.[11]

One band of Seminoles still lived on Cherokee lands. Their leaders and many of the warriors were willing to remain permanently and add their population of more than four hundred to the Cherokee Nation. During the period when large bands of needy Indians from Florida were encamped along the Grand River and adjacent Cherokee lands on the Arkansas, their generous hosts had suffered greatly through their theft of cattle and grain, and their outbreaks of violence. Many of the Seminoles, during their most difficult time of adjustment, were idle and drunken; and they were involved in much of the illicit transportation and sale of whiskey. The Cherokee leaders met in council with the band which proposed union, and led them to understand that it would be best for all concerned for them to occupy lands assigned by agents of the government.[12]

By 1844 the Seminoles were looking forward to a new agree-

[11] Judge to Crawford, Mar. 14 and Oct. 22, 1843; Seminole Chiefs to Crawford, Apr. 20, 1844; Judge to Crawford, May 29, 1844, O. I. A.: Miscellaneous Seminole Affairs; Foreman, *The Five Civilized Tribes*, 237.

[12] *Cherokee Advocate*, Mar. 20, 1845.

ment with the Creeks whereby ground for settlement, separate from the larger tribe, might be obtained for the Florida Indians. Thomas L. Judge made himself useful in the movement. He wrote to Superintendent Armstrong that a party of Seminoles had explored the country west, between Little River and the Canadian, and that they were eager for their Agent to visit the area with them. He had agreed, and expected to be away from the Agency for about ten or twelve days.

A few months later, Judge had a murder to report: J. L. Dawson, the Creek agent who succeeded Colonel James Logan in 1842, shot and killed the trader, Seaborn Hill. Two men besides Dawson were accused: "Dock" Anderson, as an accessory before the fact, and John Baylor, Dawson's brother-in-law, who was present when the killing occurred. As Judge reported the fatal clash, "Bailor rushed in and seized Mr. Hill by the Back and held him untill Dawson drew a pistol and shot him, he fell dead." Colonel James Logan was expected to arrest Dawson and Anderson—a reward of $500 having been posted for the former, and $200 for the latter. The Agent identified Captain Dawson as "the infamous scoundrall that has been instigating some of the despicable whites in the Creek country to annoy and injure me, he commenced his operations immediately after I discharged his relative the Public Smith, for loose and immoral conduct." Of the other suspected man Judge stated: "Anderson is believed to be the Father of a counterfeiting establishment that has been in operation some time by a man in his employ as a blacksmith."

In this message the Agent included brief reports on the school opened by the young Seminole preacher, John Bemo; on the broad problem of the Seminole Negroes; and on the persistent demand for separate Seminole land. "Nothing salutary can be done untill the Negro question is settled and the Seminoles have a country by themselves," he thought.[13]

Major Ethan Allen Hitchcock, detailed by the War Department to investigate charges of fraud in the Indian Service, was

---

[13] Judge to Armstrong, February 14, and July 11, 1844, O. I. A.: Seminoles—Emigration.

impressed by the prevalence of betting on horse races and card games among the traders, contractors for subsistence of the Indians, and army officers who were responsible for the handling of money in large sums. James L. Dawson had served in the frontier army for more than a decade. He married the daughter of the army surgeon Dr. John Baylor in 1829, resigned his commission as captain at Fort Gibson in 1835, and was appointed Creek agent in 1842. Major Hitchcock stated that Dawson, like the merchant Seaborn Hill and the post sutler, Arnold Harris, was addicted to gambling. He was also involved in land speculation and many other schemes to obtain quick wealth. Mrs. Baylor, Dawson's mother-in-law, who had come to Fort Gibson to run a boarding house for officers, had long conversations with Hitchcock and without intending to contribute material for his investigation, revealed many pertinent facts that he was able to follow up. Mrs. Baylor said that she thought the Real Estate Bank of Arkansas had no right to sell her children's mortgaged Negroes. After the murder of Seaborn Hill, the trader who supplemented his excessive profits on government contracts by sales of whiskey to the Indians, Dawson escaped arrest by Indian officers and went to Texas. The governor of Arkansas made an attempt to return him for trial, but he resisted the officers who tried to arrest him in Texas and escaped again.[14]

Major Hitchcock received unfavorable reports on the gaming habits of many officials. Through diverse channels, he learned that George W. Clark, acting agent for the Seminoles, "on $3.00 a day gambles every night and bets hundreds of dollars." The contractor, Olmstead; the merchants, Fields and Drew; Colonel Wharton Rector; and Colonel John Drennan, acting superintendent of the Western Territory, were all reported as heavy gamblers. The sutler, Arnold Harris, was said to be the agent for Harrison and Glasgow in silencing with a bribe the criticism of A. J. Raines, who had made a good start at revealing the methods of the largest contractors. Harris was married to a niece of Acting Superintendent William Armstrong. Thomas C. Wilson, a resident of Fort Gibson, said that Armstrong came to the

14 *The Journal of Ethan Allen Hitchcock,* 95–98.

West under personal obligations that amounted to $20,000, and in a few years had discharged his debts and accumulated property worth $40,000—on a salary of $1,500 "while supporting an expensive family." Wilson commented that the Superintendent raised corn at the Agency which he sold at fifty cents a bushel, "but that would not support his family."

Another superintendent in the Southwest, Elias Rector, did not escape damaging charges. In the words of Annie Heloise Abel, he "had frequently been accused of irregularities and even crookedness. As touching the Seminole removal from Florida, he had much that was peculiar to explain away. Apparently he quite frequently made queer contracts, was given to making over-charges for mileage, and to favoring his friends at the expense of the Indians and of the government."[15]

The Indian frontier was still a region of direct action in the settlement of disputes. The newspapers of the time were liberally sprinkled with stories of violence, ordinary fights making way for more colorful stories of deadly combat, revenge, and vicious murder. The *Cherokee Advocate* for May 1, 1845, contained several such news items, including the clubbing of an Indian woman, with injuries probably fatal; and the murder of Alexander McDonald, a Cherokee, for which two white men were leading suspects. The same paper on October 29, 1846, reported a "bloody affray" just across the Arkansas line, in which a young Indian, armed with a rifle, and a white man armed with a bowie knife, killed each other. Also appearing in that issue was the news that Smoker Glass, in the Skin Bayou District of the Cherokee Nation, had a "hung jury" in his trial for the murder of Wildcat Baldridge; and that Tesatesky would be executed at the courthouse in Flint for the murder of Arsuhglaee. On December 9, 1847, the *Advocate* reported that one Seminole shot and killed another near Melton's Mill, and that the killer had been captured.[16] Announcement that a meeting of the Bible Society "took place last night," and another that a Temperance Meeting would

---

[15] *Ibid.*, 94; A. H. Abel, *The American Indian as a Slaveholder and Secessionist*, I, 182 n.327.

[16] *Cherokee Advocate*, May 1, 1845; Oct. 29, 1846; and Dec. 9, 1847.

be held on Thursday, November 5, printed in close proximity to the stories of sudden death and retribution, were scarcely enough to give an overall picture of refined society.

A news story of December 9, 1847, was characteristic of the time. "The trial of Kahlontolida in Canadian last week, on the charge of having sold certain free Negroes into slavery, resulted in his acquittal, as is alleged, through the refusal of one witness to answer only such questions as he saw proper. The suit will probably be brought up in another form, and against another party, and its actual merits be thus reached."[17]

John Bemo was one of the most remarkable Indians of his time. His early life was filled with adventure, and in the absence of complete and accurate records, probably cannot be reconstructed. In its main outlines, however, his story appears in the records of the Seminole missions. He was a nephew of Osceola, and belonged to an Indian family who lived in the vicinity of St. Marks. A French sailor, Jean Bemeau, picked him up when he was ten or twelve years old and took him on a sea voyage. He served as cabin boy, became a first-class sailor, and learned something of ship carpentry. As a young sailor, he came in contact with Reverend Orson Douglas, pastor of the Mariner's Church in Philadelphia. Impressed by the frank manner and bright mind of young Bemo, the minister took steps to obtain schooling for him; and in the course of his studies, the Seminole lad became convinced that he ought to devote his life to the education of his people. In 1842, Orson Douglas planned for him to be sent to the new home of the Seminoles in the West, and on November 1 of the following year, he reported to Agent Thomas L. Judge. Bemo became acquainted with Harriet Lewis, a young Creek woman who had interests similar to his own, and they were married. Perhaps no Indian teacher had a greater influence for the adjustment of native people to white men's culture than Orson Douglas's protégé, John Bemo.[18]

The Cherokee agent, Pierce M. Butler, traveled to Texas with

[17] *Cherokee Advocate*, Oct. 29, 1846; Dec. 9, 1847.
[18] Judge to Armstrong, Jan. 29, 1844, Commissioner of Indian Affairs, *Annual Report* (1844).

Coacoochee and M. G. Lewis in December, 1845, on a diplomatic mission concerning the Comanche Indians. The party was successful in making a peace pact with the tribe, and at various points of the journey the delegates from Indian Territory were much impressed with the wild game that they saw. Undoubtedly, members of the commission discussed with each other the possibilities of trade in the Southwest, a project in which Coacoochee became permanently interested. Upon returning to the Canadian Valley, he immediately organized another expedition and set off for the Southwest in company with Halleck Tustenuggee, Oktiarche, and other Seminoles.

After six weeks, Coacoochee again returned to the Little River (Chanahatcha) country. He met with the Seminoles in the summer council of 1846, and began the promotion of his scheme for an Indian and Negro colony in Mexico. He told his people of the Comanches and other tribes in the Southwest, of their eagerness to trade peltries and mules for goods that could be obtained from the posts in the Arkansas area, and even spoke earnestly on what he called their friendly attitude toward visitors—an estimate that Coacoochee was later to revise.[19]

While his plans for a Mexican colony were taking shape, Coacoochee gave his support to the formation of a new treaty, providing separate lands for the Seminole Indians. The agreement of 1845 did not provide an entirely separate government, but it was a step in that direction, and in a small degree satisfied the demands of the transplanted Florida Indians. William Armstrong, acting superintendent of the Western Territory, with three Indian agents—Pierce M. Butler, James Logan, and Thomas L. Judge—signed for the United States. Roley McIntosh headed a list of forty-two Creek chiefs and head men. Micanopy, Coacoochee, Halpatter Tustenuggee, Nocose Yahola, Halleck Tustenuggee, Ochtiarche, Pascofar, Econchatimicco, and Fuch-a-lustihadjo signed for the Seminoles, along with thirteen other head men. Among the witnesses were Major George W. Clark, Captain J. P. Davis, J. B. Luce, and the Seminole interpreter, Abraham.

---

[19] *Cherokee Advocate,* July 30, 1846; Foreman, *The Five Civilized Tribes,* 244-45.

THE SEMINOLES

The preamble indicated the reasons for making a new treaty, and a fair summary of the troubled situation. In the treaty proper the Creeks agreed that the Seminoles might settle in any part of the Creek Nation, either separately or in a body; that the Seminole Tribe should be entitled to make its own town laws, subject to the general control of the Creek Council, in which the smaller tribe was guaranteed representation; and that no distinction should be made between the two tribes, except in their pecuniary affairs, in which each was forbidden to interfere with the other. The Seminoles stipulated that all who had not removed to the Creek lands should do so immediately; and that in all disputes concerning property rights, the decision of the President of the United States should be accepted.

Rations en route were promised to all Seminoles who desired to move westward to the Little River, for settlement in a body; and subsistence for six months to the entire tribe, excepting only those who should refuse to settle upon Creek lands within six months after ratification of the treaty. In the case of Seminoles who were still in Florida, a period of twelve months was allowed for removal in order to qualify for subsistence.

"The sum of fifteen thousand four hundred dollars, provided in the . . . treaty of Payne's Landing, shall be paid . . . immediately after the emigration of those Seminoles who may remove to the Creek country is completed; also, as soon after such emigration as practicable, the annuity of three thousand dollars for fifteen years, provided in the fourth article of said treaty, and in addition thereto, for the same period, two thousand dollars per annum in goods suited to their wants, to be equally divided among all members of the tribe." As compensation for goods abandoned by the Seminoles in Florida, one thousand dollars per year, for five years, in agricultural implements, were to be furnished the tribe. The United States agreed to mark "plainly and distinctly" the northern and western limits of the Creek and Seminole lands.[20]

Upon the ratification of the treaty in 1845, President James K. Polk referred the question of Seminole Negro status to Attor-

[20] Kappler, *Indian Affairs: Laws and Treaties*, II, 550–52.

ney General Isaac Toucey; and in 1848 the opinion was returned to the President. Title to the Negroes was to be regarded as unchanged by General Jesup's promises of freedom to the Negroes. Upon receiving the President's order, based upon this opinion, General Arbuckle directed that the Negroes be delivered to their Seminole masters at Fort Gibson. On January 2, 1849, accordingly, the slaves were officially turned over to Indian owners: to Micanopy, 78;[21] to Nelly Factor, 47; to Billy Bowlegs, 46; to Echo Hadjo, 16; to Hola-too-chee, 15; to Harriet Bowlegs, 11; and to other Seminole slaveholders, 73—a total of 286 Negroes. Many of them had been the subjects of legal contests; and unfortunately, many were to be storm centers of later disputes, in court and elsewhere.

Contrary to Creek law, the Seminole Negroes proceeded to establish their towns separately from the dwelling places of their masters. General W. G. Belknap, in delivering the slaves, had advised the Seminole leaders not to part with their Negroes—a bit of counsel that was particularly superfluous, since the Seminoles did not ordinarily dispose of their slaves.

John Coheia (Gopher John), who was a freedman under Seminole law since the council had so decreed in 1843 after his service in providing transportation for Lieutenant E. R. S. Canby's party of emigrants, was looked upon as a chief by the other Negroes. He was employed with three yoke of oxen and a wagon in the removal of the Seminoles from Fort Gibson to Little River after the treaty of 1845, and he was prominent in the establishment of the Negro town in the lower valley of Little River, near the site of present day Wewoka. Gopher John was in danger from Creek Indians and whites who tried to return him to slavery, and from a few of the Seminoles who were bitter over his co-operation with United States officers in the emigration from Florida.

Lt. Col. R. B. Mason, commandant at Fort Gibson, took his case to the Adjutant General of the army. "The Seminoles here have threatened the life of Gopher John, a Negro, who was pilot or guide for the Army in Florida. . . . A Seminole . . . fired at him

[21] Actually the slaves were delivered to Micanopy's heirs, since the Chief died on the day that he came to claim them.

with a rifle and killed the horse on which he was riding. . . .
I have told John to remain at this Post, and I would furnish him
and his family (three in number besides himself), with rations
until I received instructions from Washington. John, . . . particularly desires that General Jesup may read this letter."

Thomas L. Judge called a special meeting of the Seminole
Council, which condemned the attack on Gopher John and
voted money to pay for his horse. Eight months later, however,
the Seminole Nation was not a safe place for the former guide,
and Judge wrote again to the Commissioner of Indian Affairs.
The Negro was on his way to Washington, to ask for permission
to live in Florida as a means of escaping the vengeance of emigrant Seminoles. After he had consulted with General Jesup
he made up his mind to return to the West, face his enemies, and
live among his people. He had a powerful Seminole friend in
Coacoochee.[22]

The Seminoles had their largest settlements between the
North Canadian and Little River in 1846. Their livestock was
steadily increasing, and in 1847 they produced a surplus of corn,
rice, potatoes, goober peas, beans, and pumpkins. At this time
there were twenty-five towns, or bands, belonging to the tribe;
and each town had the right of self-government, subject to acts
of the Creek Council. Each town elected a tustenuggee, the tribal
council being composed of these subchiefs under the presidency
of the Principal Chief, or King. Supervision over the towns, by
Seminole custom, belonged to the Council; and clash of authority between that body and the Creek Council, with over-
lapping functions not specifically defined by the Treaty of 1845,
was inevitable.

Micanopy was principal chief (governor or king), and was
followed in that office upon his death in January, 1849, by Mi-
conutcharsar (Jim Jumper), son of the old warrior chieftain
Onselmatche (Jumper), who surrendered to General Taylor's
army in December, 1837, and died at New Orleans on the jour-

[22] Mason to Jones, July 10, 1844; Judge to Boone, Aug. 31, 1844; Judge to
Crawford, Apr. 27, 1845, O. I. A.: Seminole File; Mason to Jones, Feb. 5, 1845,
Adjutant General's Office: Old Files Division; Foreman, *The Five Civilized
Tribes,* 258–59.

ney west. Coacoochee had become chief counselor to Micanopy, and as "sense bearer" to the Principal Chief, held a place in the "Little Council." Other members were Tussekiah, Oktiarche, Pascofar, Echomathla, and Passuckee Yahola.

With agriculture and stock-raising steadily improving, the Seminoles were beginning to enjoy the comforts of their new affluence. Regular work and a legitimate source of income gave them confidence; their neat cabins with simple furniture and an ample supply of food represented for them the best living conditions they had enjoyed under the government of the United States. Acts of violence were still not uncommon in the Seminole Country; and there were still idle, restless members of the tribe who preferred whiskey-running to honest toil; but conditions were definitely improving. Clash of interest between the Creek and Seminole tribes remained as a fundamental source of danger. The Little River reporter for the *Fort Smith Herald* wrote to his paper in 1848: "There is likely to be trouble between the Creeks and Seminoles." The news story followed: Coacoochee had punished a young Tallassee Indian, "without good cause," by cutting off his ears. A little party of Creeks had quietly attended a dance, suddenly extinguished the lights and seized an Indian whom they supposed to be Coacoochee, and before they discovered their mistake had beaten him nearly to death. "There is great excitement prevailing and no telling what will be the upshot of the matter."[23]

Coacoochee was persistent in his plans to form an Indian colony on the Río Grande. In December, 1849, he assembled a party of Seminole, Creek, and Negro warriors, with a few Cherokees and a dozen Seminole Negro families under John Coheia to make a beginning of the project. His plan was to spend the rest of the winter in Texas, to explore the possibilities of alliance with the Comanches, Kickapoos, and other tribes that might be persuaded to join with him, and to take steps toward obtaining a land grant across the Río Grande. His party followed him to the Brazos Valley and made their camp on Cow Bayou. In addition to the Seminole Negroes, some slaves of Creek and Chero-

[23] *Cherokee Advocate*, June 5, 1848 (copied from the *Fort Smith Herald*).

kee owners were members of Coacoochee's band; without doubt it was a part of his plan to invite other fugitive slaves to join his colony, with Cherokee and Creek Negroes showing the way. After the band had established a permanent camp, their leader began the work of making alliances with the Plains Indians and the Kickapoos, while the main body of his followers prepared to plant corn and other food crops.

Slave owners from Arkansas and the Cherokee Nation, disturbed by the possibility of losses through Coacoochee's scheme, combined with the Creeks to descend upon Wewoka for the recovery of Negroes. William Drew and Martin Vann led the Cherokees, Nunin McIntosh and Siah Hardage, the Creeks, and I. M. Smith the white men from western Arkansas. Gabriel Duval of Alabama, brother of the Seminole Agent, was also a member of the invading force. The Seminoles put on their war paint and prepared to defend Wewoka. Captain Frederick L. Dent was sent out from Fort Smith to prevent the clash between Creeks and Seminoles. He sent messages to Roley McIntosh and to the Seminole Agent, reminding them of their obligation to keep the peace. A joint council was called, in which the Seminoles agreed that 180 of their Negroes might be held at the Seminole Agency as a means of preventing their flight to Texas. Without doubt a considerable number of the Negroes, had they been free from restraint, would have followed Jim Bowlegs, a former slave of Chief Bowlegs in Florida, to join Coacoochee on the Mexican border.[24]

In September, 1850, Wild Cat returned to the Seminole Nation and put before the Council a proposal to move the tribe to the Southwest. The Indians were interested, but not enough to follow him in large numbers. The Creeks called out twenty-five warriors from each town to prevent the flight of their slaves; and Coacoochee, from his camp south of the Little River settlements, defied the Creek Nation. He explained to Marcellus Duval that he had a sufficient force of Kickapoo, Tawakoni,

---

[24] Foreman, *The Five Civilized Tribes*, 261–63; Kenneth Porter, "The Hawkins Negroes go to Mexico," *Chronicles of Oklahoma*, Vol. XXIV (1946), 55–58; *idem.*, "Seminole in Mexico," *Chronicles of Oklahoma*, Vol. XXIX, No. 2 (1951–52), 153–68.

Seminole, and Negro warriors to meet an attack by the Creeks—but that he wanted to avoid trouble with the white people and if possible the Upper Creeks.

Coacoochee's organization had many obvious weaknesses. His party south of the Canadian, composed largely of Indians from the Southwest, supplemented by a few Seminole warriors and about one hundred Negroes, had no principle of unity strong enough to hold them together. The Comanche leaders disagreed with his concept of an Indian state in the Southwest, perhaps as much as he was at variance with the program of Marcellus Duval. A large band of Plains Indians fell upon Coacoochee's party, during his absence, and captured the Negroes, holding them for ransom—an old Comanche practice.

A party of Creek warriors in pursuit of Coacoochee ransomed the Negroes; but when they started back to the Creek Nation with them, Jim Bowlegs led an uprising. There were casualties on both sides, and of the sixty Negroes returned to the Arkansas, some were severely wounded. Other Negroes, trying to join Coacoochee, were attacked by Comanche raiders in Texas. Every member of one band, except two girls, was killed and the survivors were mutilated by scraping their skin, an experiment designed by the Plains warriors to determine whether or not their dark color extended to parts beneath the surface. The girls lived through the torture, and later were brought back to Little River by a Delaware trader who bought them from the Comanches as a speculative enterprise.[25]

A party of restless Kickapoos numbering about five hundred, wandering from their home in Missouri, were settled for a time on Creek land along the Canadian River. Later they were removed to the region south of the Canadian and west of the 98th Meridian, where they occupied a tract near the site of Fort Arbuckle. In December, 1850, they moved south across Red River toward Eagle Pass on the Río Grande, to join Coacoochee's Mexican colony.[26]

[25] R. B. Marcy, *Thirty Years of Army Life on the Border*, 55.
[26] Marcy to Jones, Nov. 25, 1851, Adjutant General's Office: Old Files Division, 489 M 51; Porter, "Wild Cat's Death and Burial," *Chronicles of Oklahoma*, Vol. XXI, No. 1 (March, 1943), 41-43.

CHAPTER 17

A Separate Seminole Nation

*"Wild Cat is my great friend! Tell him not to come out into our
country until I send for him."*

BILLY BOWLEGS

IN JANUARY, 1849, a white man fishing on Indian River near
the east coast of Florida, encountered a party of drunken Seminole warriors. It is not supposed that Barker, the fisherman, committed any act of violence or injustice against the Indians; but
perhaps to express their resentment against white invaders, or
simply to possess the fisherman's boat and rifle, the Seminoles
killed him. The Florida legislature immediately passed a resolution calling upon the federal government for aid to put down
the Indian uprising; and enacted a law forbidding the Seminoles
to cross the border of their reservation.

Depredations by the Seminoles had always been magnified
by the people of Florida who profited by military operations
against them. When friction developed between white men and
red, there was generally reason for resentment on both sides;
and the outbreak of the "Third Seminole War" was no exception.
The bitterness of the warriors on Indian River resulted from a
long series of minor clashes along the border; and as usual, the
Indians were not the first, nor the worst offenders. Newspapers
and legislatures took the lead in building up the atrocities committed by the Seminoles. Those who were engaged in making,
buying, hauling, storing, or selling military supplies, and even
families with one or more aspirants to the federal payroll for
the duration of an Indian war, were ready listeners to exagger-

ated accounts of depredations committed by the red men. Perhaps the United States never went to war against any people with less reason than it had for resuming the struggle against the Seminoles in 1849.

It was estimated by Captain John T. Sprague, who was one of the most experienced of the military officers in dealing with the Indians of Florida, that their total number of fighting men in 1849 was 120—70 Seminole, 30 Mikasuki, 12 Creek, 4 Yuchi, and 4 Choctaw. Their principal chief was Arpeika (Sam Jones) who was approaching the age of one hundred. Their war leader was Billy Bowlegs who was about thirty-three, an Indian who was well versed in the English language, highly intelligent, and in thorough control of the warriors of his domain—the remote, inaccessible portions of the Everglades, and a few hidden fields for the production of corn and other food products. The total population of the band was not more than 360.[1]

The killing of Barker on Indian River resulted in drastic demands by the Florida legislature, as noted above; and the United States made a new effort to complete the removal of the Seminoles to the West. It also resulted in the organization of a new delegation to Florida for the purpose of persuading Billy Bowlegs and his followers to remove. The War Department ordered Colonel Joseph Plympton to conduct the Seventh Infantry from Jefferson Barracks, at St. Louis, Missouri, to Tampa Bay, and there to report to General D. E. Twiggs. Two companies of militia were added to the combined forces, and by February, 1850, Twiggs was in command of 1735 men.

On November 17, 1849, Assunwha and a party of fifty Indians came to General Twiggs and surrendered three of the five Seminoles who were accused of killing Barker. They brought the hand of a fourth Indian who had been killed resisting arrest, and promised to catch the fifth as soon as possible. When they were informed that a decision had been reached to send the rest of the Seminoles west, Assunwha answered:

"We did not expect this talk. When you began this new [removal] matter I felt as if you had shot me. . . . When a few

[1] George W. Crawford to Thomas Ewing, March 28, 1849, O. I. A.: Seminole.

bad men broke the law—a thing that can't be prevented among any people—did we not hasten to make atonement? . . . We have killed one of our people, and have brought three others to be killed by you and we will bring the fifth. . . . We have done justice and we came here confident that you would be satisfied. . . . I will not go, nor will our people. I want no time to think or talk about it, for my mind is made up."[2]

The delegation from the West traveled to Florida in charge of Marcellus Duval. They left North Fork Town on October 16, 1849, proceeded overland to Fort Smith, and by river boat to New Orleans. On November 6, they took the steamer *Ashland* for Tampa Bay. The party was headed by Halleck Tustenuggee, and among the ten delegates were Holatoochee and Nocose Yoholo. Three Negro interpreters accompanied them: Jim Bowlegs, Tony, and Tom.

Billy Bowlegs, the most powerful of the Florida chiefs, gave full support to Assunwha; the Indians of the Everglades were determined not to move west. They would take all possible precautions to keep their turbulent young men from committing outrages, they would punish their criminals with severity, but they would not give up their homes. General Twiggs held a final meeting with them on January 19, 1850, in which he placed before them the most attractive offer made by the United States up to that time to any band of Indians for westward removal. Each warrior, upon reaching the point of assembling the party for removal, would receive a gift in cash; and when he arrived in the West, he would be paid enough to bring the total amount up to $500. For each woman and child, $100 was offered; and for the head men, additional gifts of money. Billy Bowlegs was offered the sum of $10,000 for his agreement to remove and his influence with the band. Subsistence en route, all costs of transportation, and subsistence for twelve months in the West were also offered, together with pay for all livestock left in Florida, a physician for the journey west, blankets for each family, and

---

[2] Twiggs to Crawford, Feb. 2, 1850, Adjutant General's Office: Old Records Division, War Department Files, National Archives; *Indian Advocate*, December, 1849.

dresses for the women. Halleck Tustenuggee and his Western Seminoles returned to the swamps with the Florida chiefs who were still doubtful that their people would consent to remove.

Sixty Indians—men, women, and children—assembled at Fort Arbuckle for emigration. Additions were made to the party as they proceeded, and on February 28, 1850, they were put aboard the steamer *Fashion,* bound for New Orleans. Capitchuchee and Cacha Fixico were the chiefs of the band, now grown to eighty-five, which was placed under the direction of Major T. H. Holmes. The Seminole agent, Marcellus Duval, decided that the Western delegates had done everything possible in Florida, and he took passage for them also on the *Fashion,* which arrived at New Orleans on the thirteenth of March. Major William H. Garrett was sent by General Twiggs to overtake the emigrants at New Orleans, under orders to protect them against loss of their money, both in the city and on the way up the river. Garrett contracted with the owners of the steamer *Cottonplant,* to convey the party to Fort Smith. On the ship, he persuaded the Indians to put their cash in the safe; and at Fort Smith, where they arrived on April 1, the Indians still had funds.

"There was a great and sudden rise in the price of horses and ponies, as many were needed by them," reported Reverend Charles E. Pleasants, in a letter to the *New York Sun,* on the second of April. "In fact, the town has been almost drained of this kind of property. It was a perfect harvest to the pony dealers and horse jockeys. The price which the Indians, in some cases, paid for quite indifferent animals, was astonishing. The store-keepers or merchants, also, highly enjoyed themselves, obtaining in most cases, very extravagant prices for their wares."[3]

Fort Smith's people resented the news items sent out by Reverend Pleasants. Profits wrung from the Indians, they regarded legitimate; if they didn't take the money, somebody else would get it. Judge John F. Wheeler, editor of the *Fort Smith Herald,* replied to Pleasants' first article; and later, in the *New York Sun,* the minister gave more details with caustic comments

[3] Quoted in Foreman, *The Five Civilized Tribes,* 251–52, from the *Fort Smith Herald,* May 25, 1850 (copied from the *New York Sun*).

on the practices of the merchants. When the two men met on the street, Wheeler attempted to cane the meddlesome visitor who was ready for him with a derringer. He fired one shot which struck Wheeler in the breast; but a packet of mail carried by the editor in his pocket deflected the bullet and probably saved his life. To frontiersmen who had little acquaintance with the deadly power of the derringer, the incident was little more than a harmless and amusing display of temper. "He shot the judge with a toy gun," one of the citizens explained to a visitor, "but old Judge Wheeler, he slapped the bullet down with a letter from his wife."[4]

Even while the Halleck Tustenuggee delegation was on its way back to Little River, General Twiggs had in mind a new party of commissioners to attempt the task of persuading Billy Bowlegs to go west. Major W. T. H. Brooks was sent to the Seminole Nation, with instructions to organize a delegation with Coacoochee and the new principal chief, Jim Jumper, as its leaders. The situation in Florida was unfavorable for such delegations. The current *Indian Advocate* described the reactions of Billy Bowlegs when he was asked if the peace delegation from the West would be received by the Florida Indians as visitors. "He became agitated, and held his breath for a moment. He then said, with great deliberation, 'Wild Cat is my great friend! Tell him not to come out into our country, until I send for him.' "[5] Thus, the second delegation arranged by General Twiggs had little influence; the Seminoles sent word from their swamp retreats that they would shoot any person who attempted to visit them for the purpose of influencing them to remove West. The special agent, Luther Blake, who came to Florida with a new offer—$800 to each emigrating warrior and $450 to each woman and child—failed to get results, also. Blake became very sick with cholera; but there is no evidence that he was making progress before he was stricken. In 1851, there was but little emigration.[6]

[4] *Ibid.*, 252 n.8.
[5] *Indian Advocate*, Dec., 1849.
[6] Commissioner of Indian Affairs, *Annual Report* (1851).

In western Seminole settlements, the leaders made separation a primary issue, and became eloquent when they described the evils of Creek domination. Military commanders, missionaries, Indian traders, and other observers, also noted the relation between failure of these people to adjust to conditions of their new homes, and the uncertainty that surrounded them. Foremost among their grievances was arbitrary control by the Creek government, and the related hardship of Creek encroachment upon Seminole property rights by the seizure of their slaves; or in some instances, the violation of the individual right of the freed Negro to his liberty.

At a most critical period of their adjustment, it was the misfortune of the Seminoles to have assigned to them an official who was seriously lacking in sympathy and understanding. Marcellus Duval, subagent, was personally interested in slave property, to an extent that gave his decisions a warped character. His brothers, William J. and Gabriel, were actively working to obtain Seminole Negroes for themselves; and in view of the Agent's attitude, there can be little doubt that his concern was based upon the hope of profit from sale of slaves. In the contest over enforcement of promises made to the Seminoles in Florida, promises of freedom to the Negroes, contradicting those arrangements with Seminole owners, and agreements with the Creek warriors, contradicting all other promises made to Indians and Negroes, the Duval brothers were at least consistent. They wanted the ignorant owners of slaves, among the Indians, to be unrestricted in disposing of their property; and they wanted to banish forever the idea that the Negroes themselves had any personal rights.

The Agent's letter to Brigadier General W. G. Belknap, six months after the Seminole Negroes were turned over to their Indian masters, reflects his attitude. "Those acts of the Seminole Negroes . . . based on rights (!) which the negroes still assert, they derived from the Military." Duval followed with a story of pony theft by "Walking Joe," whom he described as a notorious Negro thief, of Joe's arrest by the Indian authorities, and his rescue by armed Negroes. The pony was returned to its owner;

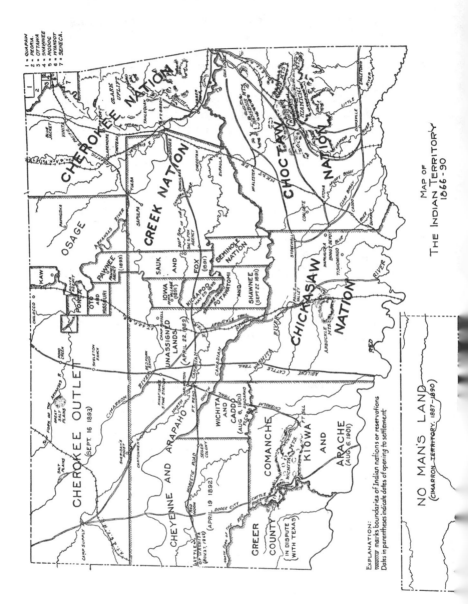

MAP OF
THE INDIAN TERRITORY
1866-90

EXPLANATION:
▨▨▨ marks boundaries of Indian nations or reservations
Dates in parentheses indicate dates of opening to settlement

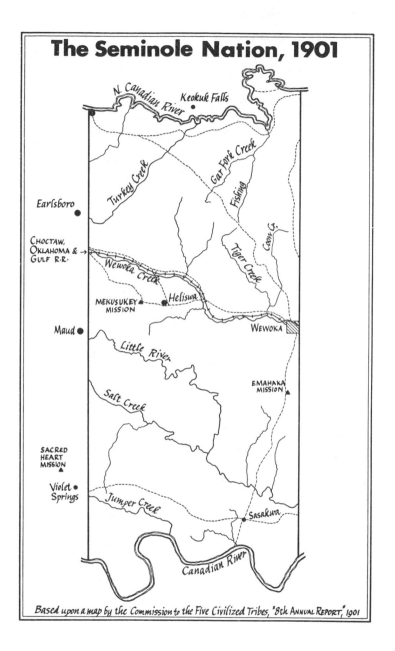

The Seminole Nation, 1901

N. Canadian River

Keokuk Falls

Turkey Creek

Gar Fork Creek

Fishing

Coon G.

Earlsboro

CHOCTAW, OKLAHOMA & GULF R·R·

Wewoka Creek

Tiger Creek

MEKUSUKEY MISSION

Heliswa

Maud

WEWOKA

Little River

EMAHAKA MISSION

Salt Creek

SACRED HEART MISSION

Violet Springs

Jumper Creek

Sasakwa

Canadian River

Based upon a map by the Commission to the Five Civilized Tribes, "8th ANNUAL REPORT," 1901

but "a messenger came from the blacks to tell the Indians how they must proceed in the future." Gopher John was involved in this affair, Duval declared, but tried to lay the blame upon the "young and unmanageable negroes."

The self-government in Negro towns that was characteristic of the Seminoles, the agent ignored; the general reputation of Gopher John for moderation and orderliness was in itself a denial of Duval's account. "They have been permitted to go so far," he wrote, "that there is no limit to their assumption of rights— . . . If I am to be held responsible for the good order in this Nation, I shall . . . insist upon the negroes being made to *obey* their owners."

Two days after this remarkable message, the Subagent wrote the Commissioner of Indian Affairs a long letter on the "errors" of General Matthew Arbuckle, in regard to the Negroes. The burden of his complaint was that Arbuckle protected the Negroes. He opposed sales of the Seminole slaves, without the approbation of the subagent, and the consent of the Negroes themselves. It may be recalled that Agent Wiley Thompson in Florida held similar views, and that every humane officer in the Indian Service had felt the necessity of protecting the uninformed natives against the sharp practices of dishonest traders.

"It has never entered my head for a moment," Marcellus Duval wrote, "that a person could own property *without the power* of disposing of it; or that a . . . gentleman of General Arbuckle's intelligence and experience, would have entertained for an instant so novel an idea, as that a slave is competent to make a contract." Clearly, the peculiar status of the slave of African descent in the Seminole country, made no impression upon this appointee. Furthermore, the responsibility of United States officials for the protection of an Indian's property interests, did not occur to him.[7]

Finally, the Agent asked that troops be sent from Fort Gibson to help in disarming the Negroes—a measure that kidnappers of slaves on the Indian frontier had favored from the beginning

---

[7] Duval to Belknap, June 7, 1849; Duval to Commissioner Wm. Medill, June 9, 1849, Foreman Transcripts, VII, 154–65.

John F. Brown, a new-model chief executive for the Seminole
tribe. He was the last principal chief before Oklahoma
statehood.

Oklahoma Historical Society

Thomas McGeisey, Seminole superintendent of public
education, father of Lincoln McGeisey.

of settlement. General Arbuckle, in a message to the Adjutant General of the United States Army, declared that he did not have sufficient troops for such an enterprise; and asked instructions from the War Department.

With officials such as Marcellus Duval in charge of their contacts with the United States and their relations with neighbors, it is not remarkable that Seminole adjustments were slow, and that the bewilderment over broken treaties and war in Florida was followed by the confusion of exploitation and conflict in the new country. In temporary camps, especially, before they had entered upon the work of building houses, clearing fields, and planting crops on new ground, their attitude was described as sullen, bitter, hopeless, desperate. When they resorted to violations of Creek law and United States law, by running flat-bottomed boats loaded with whiskey from Fort Smith to North Fork Town, the activity was in part retaliation for wrongs suffered by the Seminoles. George W. Manypenny, commissioner of Indian affairs in 1855, described their position as similar to that of the Chickasaws, whom he regarded unjustly subject to domination by the majority of the Choctaws. "The Seminoles of the West have been denationalized, and in a manner degraded, by being placed among the Creeks, and made subject to their laws. They felt the humiliation of their position, which not only discouraged them, but engendered a recklessness of disposition and conduct. . . ."[8]

In January, 1854, Archibald H. Rutherford of Fort Smith, who belonged to a prominent family of Arkansas politicians, revealed his connection with the slave trade in a letter to Daniel Boone Aspberry. "Having learned that you have succeeded in selling the Negro Claim in the Creek Nation that I gave you assistance about—it does appear that I ought to be paid for my services." Rutherford continued with a demand for a "boy or a girl worth at a fair valuation $350.00." A bill of sale in the files of the Office of Indian Affairs, indicates that some bargaining was resorted to before the sale to Rutherford was accomplished.

[8] Duval to Arbuckle, July 19, 1849; Arbuckle to Jones, July 31, 1849, *ibid.*, 166–74; Commissioner of Indian Affairs, *Annual Report* (1855).

"This Bill of Sale Witnesseth that Daniel B. Aspberry of the Creek Nation for the consideration of Two Hundred Dollars in hand paid, has this day bargained, sold and delivered, and by these presents does bargain sell and deliver to Archibald H. Rutherford of the State of Arkansas the following Negroes to wit, one slave for life, named Willie Bob, aged about 18 years and in consideration of the sum above mentioned the said Daniel B. Aspberry warrants the said Negro Willie Bob to be sound in mind and body, and binds himself his heirs, Executors and Administrators to warrant and defend the title to said Negro Willie Bob in him the said Archibald H. Rutherford his heirs and assigns forever . . . etc."[9]

Another bill of sale, given by Aspberry to C. D. Pryor accompanied by the personal note of the purchaser for the sum of $7,800, is evidence of a wider field of Aspberry's slave-trading; and a brief message from the trader to his trusted agents, R. G. Atkins and Tommy Hays, reveal the manner in which he attempted to complete his deal in the chattels of doubtful title. "As a friend, I would . . . authorize you conjointly to collect, receive, and receipt from C. D. Pryor, the money proceeding from Negro Slaves, whom C. D. Pryor purchased of me, that is the Negroes delivered to him from the Seminole Country according to the decision of the Supreme Court of the Creek Nation. The prorata calculation of $350 per heads [sic] you will know thereby the number of Negroes he gets. I also empower you to get the aid of the Light Horse Companies to arrest the Negroes and keep them in the Nation until it is paid for them that is the said C. D. Pryor have some notice to get them over the line."

Chilly McIntosh wrote to Commissioner J. W. Denver a bitter complaint about the dealings of Aspberry and Pryor in Seminole Negroes. "Aspberry him and his associates took upon themselves to dispose of Twenty three of the Negroes, sen [sic] them out of the Seminole Country into different parts of the States," McIntosh declared.[10]

[9] Rutherford to Aspberry, Jan. 27, 1854, O. I. A.: Seminole–Miscellaneous, 1854; O. I. A.: Seminole–Miscellaneous, 1857.
[10] Foreman Transcripts, VII, 44, 71, 76, 94, 95, 96.

In the summer council of 1855, Agent J. W. Washbourne worked out with the Seminole leaders a formal statement of their grievances for the consideration of the Creek Council. The Seminoles, according to this resolution, were a separate people from the Creeks. In attempting to join them with the Creeks, the officials of the United States were acting in an unjust and arbitrary manner. The laws of the Creek Nation, passed by a body in which the Seminoles had no voice, since they refused to elect members, were oppressive and unjust. Harmony and friendship between the two tribes could not be accomplished while they were joined in an artificial and undesired union. Agent Washbourne supported the Seminole request that the tribe be permitted to send delegates to Washington for the purpose of establishing a separate government.[11]

Under the leadership of Robert McClelland of Michigan, the Department of the Interior was making some progress in the reasonable solution of long-standing Indian problems. The Chickasaws were separated from the Choctaws, by the terms of a treaty which Commissioner George W. Manypenny worked out with leaders of the tribes concerned, on June 22, 1855. Seminole and Creek union was similar in many respects to that of the Chickasaws and Choctaws, with the minority group taking the lead for separation in each case. On August 7, 1856, the tripartite treaty was made at Washington by which the ties of union between Creeks and Seminoles were severed. Again it was Commissioner Manypenny who negotiated with tribal delegates the terms of the new agreement.[12] It must be admitted that the spirit of liberalism in the conduct of Indian affairs was not the sole reason for the formation of the treaty. As the Commissioner pointed out, "one of the leading objects . . . was to enable the department to overcome the chief obstacle to the removal of the Indians . . . yet remaining in Florida."[13]

In Article One the boundaries of the new Seminole Nation were defined: due north from the mouth of Pond Creek (Ock-

[11] Commissioner of Indian Affairs, *Annual Report* (1855).
[12] Kappler, *Indian Affairs: Laws and Treaties*, II, 706–14 (Choctaw-Chickasaw treaty); 756–63 (Creek-Seminole treaty).
[13] Commissioner of Indian Affairs, *Annual Report* (1856), 13.

hi-appo) to the North Fork of the Canadian; thence, up said North Fork to the southern line of the Cherokee country; thence, with that line, west, to the one hundredth meridian; thence, south to the Canadian River, and thence, down that river to the mouth of Ock-hi-appo. The area thus defined, when it had been surveyed, proved to be 2,170,000 acres in extent. The strong desire of United States officials to provide an attractive home for the Seminoles as an incentive for further removal from Florida had furnished the tribe a basis for the most favorable bargain in its history. The second article defined the Creek boundaries, and the third contained the guarantee of the United States to the Seminole Indians that no part of their cession should ever be sold without the consent of both tribes.

The United States, to settle all claims and cover losses in moving to the new location, agreed to pay the Seminoles in the West the sum of $90,000; annuities of $3,000 for ten years to support schools; $2,000 for assistance in agriculture; and $2,200 for the support of blacksmiths. It was further stipulated that the United States should invest for the Seminoles the sum of $250,000 at 5 per cent interest, the proceeds of the investment "to be regularly paid over to them *per capita* as annuity." Furthermore, an additional sum of $250,000 was to be invested "in like manner whenever the Seminoles now remaining in Florida shall have emigrated and joined their brethren in the West," the two sums to constitute a fund belonging to the united tribe for an annuity payment.

Further advantages for the Seminole people were provided: transportation and the usual twelve months of additional subsistence for emigrants from Florida; a rifle, ammunition, blankets, tobacco, and clothing for each emigrant warrior; blankets and clothing for the women and children; "and to expend for them in improvements, after they shall remove, the sum of twenty thousand dollars." It was also stipulated that the United States should expend $3,000 for the purchase of agricultural implements, axes, seeds, looms, cards, and wheels—to be proportionally distributed among emigrants and earlier settlers.

The Seminoles agreed to send a peace delegation to Florida,

the United States to pay each member "a reasonable compensation for his services." Foc-te-lus-te harjoe (Fuch-a-lusti-hadjo) or Black Dirt, was to receive $400 for his services in the Florida War. The United States agreed to build an agency and a council house for the Seminoles. George W. Manypenny, commissioner of Indian affairs, signed the document for the United States; Tuckabatchee Micco, Echo Harjo, Chilly McIntosh, Benjamin Marshall, George W. Stidham, and Daniel N. McIntosh, for the Creeks; and for the Seminoles, John Jumper, Tustenucochee, Pascofar, and James Factor.[14]

Many of the Seminoles were eager to remove to their separate lands, though some were held back for a time by fear of the wild Plains Indians, and the majority hesitated to build houses until sites were selected for the government buildings provided by the treaty. Samuel M. Rutherford, Seminole agent, reported in August, 1859, that the agency buildings were being constructed, "in a substantial and workmanlike manner," on good land, with plenty of timber and water. The location of the agency was "one mile west of the eastern boundary of the Seminole country, and about two miles north of the road recently laid out by Lieutenant Beale."[15] Henry Pope, of Arkansas, was the builder; and his contracts, including a later one for construction of the Wichita Agency, were sharply attacked by critics of the Indian Office.[16]

About one-third of the Seminoles had moved into their new district by the time the agency building was completed. Rutherford thought the prospects for crops were excellent, and that the people were well satisfied with their change of location. They were generally in good health, and on "amicable terms with the neighboring tribes." In 1860, Rutherford reported that he was encouraging all those "who exhibit a disposition to build their own houses" to do so. He also wrote that he had erected a commodious council-house, . . . thirty-six feet long by twenty feet wide, making two rooms with a fire place in each." The new

---

[14] Kappler, *Indian Affairs: Laws and Treaties*, II, 756–63.
[15] Commissioner of Indian Affairs, *Annual Report* (1859).
[16] Foreman, *The Five Civilized Tribes*, 271; Abel, *The American Indian as a Slaveholder and Secessionist*, 182n.

building, very substantial and well furnished with tables and seats, was situated about eight miles northwest of the agency, in the midst of good timber, with water and excellent range close at hand. The Seminoles were delighted with their council house and, upon its completion, enclosed it with a strong fence.[17]

Progress was made in control of Negro kidnapping, while the Seminole leaders were engaged in providing separate government. Two preachers, Cyrus Kingsbury and Samuel A. Worcester, were principally responsible for the victory. A family of free Negroes named Beams, living among the Choctaw, Seminole, and Creek Indians, were arrested upon false information and taken to Van Buren, Arkansas. As they were about to be sold to a slave dealer, Josephus Dotson, employed by Reverend Cyrus Kingsbury, instituted a suit in their favor. The Department of the Interior took part in prosecuting the case, and the verdict was for the Negroes, with full recognition of their freedom. Over forty Negroes, relatives of the Beams family, were affected by the decision. They were all the natural children or grandchildren of the original white owner, Beams; and he had freed all of them. John B. Davis of Mississippi claimed the Beams Negroes as fugitive slaves. The claim was based upon a judgment against old Beams for groceries, and an agreement with two of his legal children that they should have a part in the proceeds, if they would help Davis in obtaining possession of the Negroes.

Caleb Cushing, the United States attorney general, had written an opinion in March, 1854, which recognized the right of citizens to recover slave property within the Indian nations.[18] Probably all of the Beams Negroes would have been seized, sold back into slavery, and removed from the Indian nations to Mississippi, if Kingsbury and Worcester had not intervened.

Reverend Samuel A. Worcester wrote to Jefferson Davis, secretary of war, concerning seven of the Beams family who were captured in the Creek Nation. Gilbert, Mitchell, Lotta, Rhoda, Nancy, and Becky were all natural children of Beams,

---

[17] Rutherford to Elias Rector, Aug. 15, 1860, Commissioner of Indian Affairs, *Annual Report* (1860), 126–28.

[18] Foreman Transcripts, VII, 47–65.

Dr. Worcester declared; Martin was a grandchild. Five of the descendants of Beams were offered for sale in Tahlequah—Martin, and children of three others, and the little grandchild of one of them. All of them except Martin were free born, and he had been free for many years. "I cannot but infer that, if any document has indeed been signed by you, authorizing such sale, . . . it must have been obtained by misrepresentation."[19]

Legal procedure in the case of the Beams Negroes quickly passed the stage of simple fees and relatively honest dealing. Mr. Dotson had charged a fee of $100 when he was employed by Reverend Cyrus Kingsbury, and had incurred expenses of $213 for himself and witnesses in Van Buren. As an employee of the Indian Office, his fee was $1,000 and his expenses $500. Mr. Walker charged a fee of $750, and for expenses, $500; Mr. Spring, a fee of $500; and Mr. Raum, a fee of $300, expenses, $43.25. The total of the bill presented to the government, including a transcript of records from Mississippi, amounted to $3,624. Superintendent Dean was of the opinion that the charges were exorbitant; he pointed out, also, that $500 had already been paid to Dotson and $500 to Spring. J. W. Denver, the new commissioner of Indian affairs, recommended that Dotson and Walker should each be paid $500 and all legitimate expenses; Mr. Spring had no expenses, and had received the full amount of his fee; Mr. Raum, the sum of $75 and expenses in the amount of $43.25.[20]

Coacoochee's plans for Southwestern settlement, surrounded by conflicting reports, secrecy, and mystery, are to be understood only by considering his intense love of liberty, his ambitions as a chief, and his sympathy for free Negroes in the process of being reduced to slavery. Agent Marcellus Duval was his enemy because of the basic differences in their aims concerning Seminole Negroes. Coacoochee wanted them to be free men, and his followers; the Agent wanted them reduced to slavery and returned to one of the States—preferably by some process that would enrich his own family.

19 Worcester to Davis, Sept. 6, 1854, *ibid.*, VII, 66–68.
20 *Ibid.*, VII, 66–68, 82, 83.

Duval suggested that other officers of the government on the frontier had tried to make Coacoochee's activities appear in the nature of opposition to himself—an idea that Wild Cat also promoted. But the Indian had deeper, more sinister purposes, the Agent insisted. "He endeavored to alienate from the United States, not only his own people, but also Creeks, . . . he persuaded them to follow him, and to make Treaties with other Tribes [Prairie Inds] and Mexico; . . . he made use of a 'pass' which I gave him . . . to aid in deceiving the Indians. . . . In fact, he used every means which a cunning, designing, and intelligent Indian could use, to bring around himself a large party of active, enterprising and restless Indians, over whom he should have control—and be the supreme Head."

About twenty-five Seminole warriors followed him, and twenty Negro men and their families. Duval charged that Coacoochee would sell the Negroes in Texas if he could do so with safety. He was reported as being located for the summer with his followers on a tributary of the Brazos. A band of Kickapoos had joined him, and he was looking for a place to settle beyond the Río Grande. General Arbuckle, the Agent thought, was an "aider and abettor in Wild Cat's and Gopher John's subsequent acts." Marcellus Duval, in conclusion, recommended military action against Wild Cat, and arrest of all Negroes among his followers who could be found on United States territory. In fact, his attitude was not essentially different from that of the Florida citizens who advocated war against the Seminole Indians through the first thirty years of the tribe's control by the United States.

To the new Commissioner in September, 1850, the Seminole Agent wrote that Wild Cat's return was causing a "Sensation among the Creeks," and that his activities, if allowed to continue, would start a war between his followers and the Creeks. The Agent added that he would stand by to prevent trouble.[21] The War Department sent two officers to interview Coacoochee, and they did not find him so intractable as Duval's reports indicated. They met him at Eagle Pass, Texas, and held a long conversation

21 Duval to Brown, Sept. 21, 1850; Duval to L. Lea, Sept. 30, 1850, ibid., VII.

with him, sending a memorandum of the "talk" to Charles M. Conrad, secretary of war. Wild Cat said his plan was to find a new home for his people in Texas. His manner, according to the report, was "respectful and kind; there was no insolence, no threats, no unkind reproaches, but expressions of deep friendship."[22]

Agent Duval was correct in his surmise that Coacoochee intended to settle outside the United States. The Mexican government granted land to the Seminoles, Kickapoos, and "Mascogos," or free Negroes, in Coahuila. Wild Cat himself served the Mexican authorities in various capacities. In 1857, he was with a party of scouts keeping watch over a band of wild Plains Indians, when the dreaded smallpox swept through his followers. In camp near Musquiz, Coacoochee died with the disease. The five hundred Negroes who had settled at Nacimiento, near the headwaters of Río Sabinas in the Santa Rosa Mountains, together with his faithful Seminole band, sincerely mourned his death. After his death, the news came to Mexico that the Seminole Nation was separated from Creek control, and most of the Indians who had followed him to Mexico returned to the Little River country. A band of Kickapoos, moving south to escape the disaster of being caught between the Confederacy and the Union in 1861, settled the land thus vacated by the Seminoles.[23]

Nearly half of the Seminole Agent's report, in August, 1860, was on the subject of education. He pointed out that the people of his agency, by moving to their newly assigned lands, were placing themselves out of touch with the only school that any of their children had attended, Oak Ridge Mission, in the Creek country. He urged that more attention should be given to the problem of educating the Seminole children, and that funds should be provided for the purpose of hiring teachers, constructing suitable buildings, and obtaining necessary facilities for schooling. He predicted rapid advancement of the tribe on the basis of better education. "For," he wrote, "the Seminoles are

[22] Memorandum of Talk, Col. Cooper, Col. Temple, and Wild Cat, March 27, 1851, O. I. A.: Miscellaneous File, 1851.

[23] Kenneth W. Porter, "Wild Cat's Death and Burial," *Chronicles of Oklahoma*, Vol. XXI, No. 1 (March, 1943), 41–43.

by no means deficient in native force of character and keenness of wit."

The life of a missionary or a teacher in any one of the mission schools of the Indian frontier was sure to be filled with hardship and adventure. Mary Ann Lilley, who started from Philadelphia for the Creek Nation with her husband, Reverend John Lilley, and their four children in November, 1845, reached Coweta, on the Arkansas River, three months later.[24] The journey was made by railroad only to Cumberland, Maryland. Then the family and their missionary companion, John Bemo, took a six-horse stagecoach with space for nine passengers, and twelve on board. A quiet, sedate passenger; a lively fellow, who, after a rough mile of new road, "could not state which were his own legs, there were so many"; a politician from Pittsburgh; rain and hail in the mountains—these were some of the memoirs of the journey that Mrs. Lilley carried through her long and busy life.

The party traveled by boat from Wheeling to "Cinnati," where they went home with Augustus Lilley, John's brother; then down to Louisville, where they were delayed by boat repairs; and on to the Mississippi. At Montgomerie's Point, above the mouth of the Arkansas, they remained for a time in a big, gloomy frame hotel, which was painted "dark blue, inside."

Mary Ann met her first Indian woman, the beautiful and well dressed sister of a Cherokee judge, on an Arkansas River boat; and was surprised by the contrast between her appearance and that of two dowdy frontier women who were passengers. A party of one hundred Creek Indians, en route from Alabama to the Creek Nation, boarded the *Della* at Little Rock. Their agent was very sick, and asked John Bemo, the Seminole missionary, to take charge of the emigrants. John agreed, and had his hands full for the rest of the journey.

At Fort Smith the party began their overland journey in wagons. John Bemo and the Creek emigrants by ox-teams, the Lilley family in a light wagon pulled by a pair of mules. Mary Ann and her family made five muddy miles the first day on the

[24] "The Autobiography of Mary Ann Lilley," Seminole Miscellaneous Documents, Oklahoma Historical Society Archives.

wrong road; returned to Fort Smith, and slept in the wagon. Next day they traveled fourteen miles on the right road, and stopped over night with John Drew, the son-in-law of Roley McIntosh, "who had a Creek wife and a Cherokee wife."

The weather was cold, food was scarce, and various expedients were used to keep the party in provisions and to keep them warm. In one place, Mary Ann recorded, "Mr. Bemo went out and got some corn;" in another "Mr. Lilley had bought a ham;" and in another place, "Mr. Bemo shot a hog." The Lilley family made the acquaintance of *sofkee*, a Seminole staple food made of corn. At the crossing of Grand River, Reverend Lilley came near being drowned. Later, John Bemo's party took a separate trail and the Lilley family had to proceed alone.

The "tenderfoot" preacher's efforts to drive a team of mules across Indian country, along a road that gradually became a dim trail, revealed characteristics of the Lilley family, the country, and the mules. At the bottom of a deep gully, the mules just "stopped and began eating and would not pull a bit." The minister got out and whipped them, "but they just kicked up their heels." After he had tried everything he could think of to make the mules pull, without success, John Lilley climbed a tree and saw some smoke in the distance. "He took one of the mules and left me and the children all alone. I felt pretty bad then, felt almost like giving up. . . ."

But the children cried, and Mary Ann had to be brave. The Indian whom Mr. Lilley found could not understand English; but as they tried to make themselves understood, Mr. Loughridge and Mr. Winslett came up. They soon brought oxen and pulled the wagon out of the ravine. "After a long time," the party arrived at Coweta Mission, north of the Arkansas.

When John Lilley and Mary Ann had worked two years in the school at Coweta, some changes of teachers were made, and they were assigned to teach the Seminoles at a place seventy-five miles farther southwest. John Bemo, who owned carpenter's tools and had some skill in their use, was sent ahead by Mr. Lilley to build a house. The new mission was located about five miles east of the site of Holdenville. The crude cabin that young Bemo built, hastily, and with little help of any kind, was a single room, sixteen by eighteen feet. Mary Ann Lilley curtained off tiny bedrooms for her family and for Bemo and his wife, which left very little space for cooking, washing, entertaining visitors, study and recreation.

While John Lilley and his assistant went back to the Arkansas to bring in a supply of hogs bought from the Perrymans, the house that Bemo built caught fire from the wooden chimney; and the two women, with the help of Mr. Willis, the interpreter, had some difficulty in putting out the blaze. After a hard fight, using snow scooped up in buckets, the fire was extinguished, with only minor damage. "I felt a little better with my . . . log house after that, after having come so near losing it that season of the year," wrote Mary Ann.

During the following spring, John Bemo and Mr. Willis built a new house, one and a half stories high, with two large rooms and a hall between them on the ground floor, and "quite a room" above. Two stone chimneys, a steep "Swiss roof," a painted mantel, brass door knobs, and numerous other improvements over their former dwelling, brought from Mary Ann the comment, "So we were very high-toned."

Among the first pupils at Lilley's Mission were three Creek boys, grandsons of Mr. Edwards who ran the store on Little River, opposite Fort Holmes. A little girl named Mabel, a relative of Chief John Jumper, soon entered. A boy of twelve appeared; Mrs. Lilley cut down a pair of the preacher's pants to fit the lad, and also made him a vest. He wore the "new" garments home, and brought back his little brother. Eliza Chupco, after two years of hesitation, brought her little boy to school and became an active member of the mission. She married a Florida Seminole, taught him to read, brought him to the mission, and introduced him to a new world of ideas. He became a member and an elder in the Lilley Mission.

Mary Jumper, who later married Thomas Cloud, came to the school with her sister, Jane. Little Nancy Thompson Lilley died in 1851. John Bemo constructed a tiny coffin, and trimmed it with black cloth. After a sermon by the child's father, the

284

little Indian girls of the mission carried the coffin and the corpse of Nancy to the grave. The Indian mothers administered "medicine" to their children to keep off bad spirits; and Mrs. Lilley had to explain to them that no harm would come to the little Indian girls as a result of serving as pall-bearers. Soon afterwards, an Indian woman asked that, when her time came to be laid to rest, it should be done in the white fashion instead of the hollow tree burial used by the early Seminoles in the West.

Mary Ann Lilley's story is filled with life of the frontier, with humor and pathos, trivial observations, fundamental facts, and sometimes raw tragedy. The minute revelations of motives and hopes, and the limited but expanding view of people—red, white, and black—tell us more, perhaps, than Mary Ann deliberately intended to express.[25]

Reverend John Lilley gave an account of the funds expended at Oak Ridge Mission from October, 1848, to May, 1859, which totaled $20,864. Some additional expenditures had been made in New York in the purchase of clothing, groceries, farming implements, and other supplies, for which no itemized account had been made to the school head. John Lilley estimated that the supplies thus furnished would raise the entire cost, since opening the school, to about $35,000. Twenty-two Seminole children were in attendance in 1859—thirteen boys and nine girls. "The government has done nothing in regard to the Seminole school in the new country," Lilley explained, but he was full of plans for continuing his work.[26]

The Indians of the Plains were a menace to the Seminoles in the Little River country, and this threat to their peace and safety without doubt retarded migration. The conditions of life were still so rough and uncertain in both the new and the older settlements as to place a positive check upon the birth rate of the tribe. Agent J. W. Washbourne in 1857 reported a census count of 1,907—about 900 males and 1,000 females. Two years later, Sam-

---

[25] "Autobiography"; Indian-Pioneer Papers, VI, 213–15; XXIV, 40–42; CIV, 193–96.
[26] Lilley to Rutherford, Aug. 25, 1859, Commissioner of Indian Affairs, *Annual Report* (1859); Rutherford to Rector, Aug. 15, 1860, *Annual Report* (1860).

uel Rutherford placed the number, "including the Florida and Mexican emigrants," at 2,253, of whom 1,009 were female and 1,244 male. The actual change in two years cannot be determined accurately because figures on the Seminoles returning from Mexico are not available; but without including the emigrants the census of 1859 probably would have shown a slight decrease. It is certain that a decline of about 40 per cent had resulted from four decades of rule by the United States, including warfare, removal by force, unjust treaty provisions, and corrupt administration of treaties. The story of Seminole relations after 1819, though containing some bright spots, cannot be called a truly excellent colonial record.

J. W. Washbourne left the Indian Service under serious charges by Superintendent Elias Rector, who asked his immediate removal. Washbourne, in handling the $90,000 stipulated in the treaty of 1856 to assist in the removal and to pay for Seminole losses, was accused of making a corrupt bargain with the principal chiefs. Rector said that Washbourne received about $13,000 "in consideration of his permitting the chiefs to appropriate certain portions . . . to their own use and benefit."[27]

Samuel Rutherford, who was to follow Washbourne as agent of the Seminoles, accompanied Rector and the Creek agent, William H. Garrett, on a mission to Florida in January, 1858. Colonel Rector assembled his council on the West Coast, south of Fort Myers on March 15, 1858. He was authorized to make attractive terms with the chiefs and warriors who would agree to emigrate, and use their influence in favor of complete removal of the remaining Indians. Many of the leaders quickly gave their support to the movement when they found that Billy Bowlegs was about to agree upon terms. Other head men surrendered for emigration or were taken prisoners during the next two months: Assunwha, Nocose Emathla, Foos Hadjo, Nocus Hadjo, and Fuchutchee Emathla. The steamer *Grey Cloud* carried a party of 125 from Fort Myers, west of Lake Okeechobee, to Fort Dade on Egmont Key at the entrance of Tampa Bay, where the Florida Volunteers had concentrated some forty Indians for safe keep-

27 Rector to Thompson, Oct. 1, 1859, O. I. A.: Rector's Letter Book.

ing. The entire party of 165 consisted of 39 warriors and 126 women and children. Arpeika (Sam Jones) was still alive, probably more than one hundred years of age, but was too feeble to travel. Ten of his Mikasukies were included in the emigrants, but twelve warriors remained in Florida with their old chief. The party of peace commissioners returned on the boat with Billy Bowlegs and his followers to New Orleans. Colonel Rector then took charge of the emigrant Seminoles, and traveled up the river on the steamer *Quapaw*, reaching Fort Smith on May 26, 1858. William H. Garrett, Samuel Rutherford, and the Indian peace delegation arrived at Fort Smith two days later on the steamer *Arkansas*. The rest of the journey was made by wagon road, and the party of emigrants buried four members along the way. It rained almost continuously, streams were out of their banks, and thirteen days were required to travel from Fort Smith to Little River. Other members of the band sickened and died after their arrival in the Seminole Nation, probably from typhoid fever.

Another commission of friendly Seminoles was needed in Florida. Elias Rector bargained with Bowlegs, who agreed to head a small group of Indians and venture into the Everglades on a short tour for which he was to receive $200 in cash. In December, Colonel Rector and his party of eight Seminoles were back in Florida. In addition to the long-sought Boat Indians, who were the principal object of their search, they found the hiding place of Black Warrior and his followers, who were known to the people of Florida only through wild and improbable stories of their speed in handling boats, their implacable hatred of the whites, and the primitive savagery of their customs. Even Billy Bowlegs had not been certain that Black Warrior and his small band were still alive in the heart of the swamp.[28] A total of seventy-five Seminoles were persuaded to join the emigrants, and the party took passage for New Orleans on February 15, 1859—the final gesture of a costly and unwise policy.

[28] Rector to Denver, Jan. 22, and Feb. 15, 1859; Rector to Charles E. Mix, March 29, 1859, O. I. A.: Rector's Letter Book; Foreman, *The Five Civilized Tribes,* 274.

Almost incessant strife had been the lot of the Seminoles under the sovereignty of the United States. Torn from their native land, under conditions of bloody warfare, against an enemy that possessed many times their power, they had scarcely known the contentment that arises from security in the rearing of their families. The tough fiber and undaunted courage of an exceptional race had finally won for them a fair bargain, in the treaty of 1856, with the powerful nation that asserted its authority over them; but before they had an opportunity to adjust to their new and better situation, they were to find themselves overwhelmed by another war, a civil struggle in which their people had the misfortune to be divided into hostile camps.

CHAPTER 18

The Seminoles
in the American Civil War

*"I was very much pleased with the conduct
of the whole Indian force."*

COLONEL WILLIAM A. PHILLIPS

THE WAR BETWEEN North and South, 1861 to 1865, was the greatest misfortune of all for the Indians of the Five Civilized Tribes. Failure of the Federal Union to solve differences of interest between the two sections was not the fault of any Indian tribe; yet the people of the Cherokee, Creek, and Seminole Nations suffered more terrible losses than white citizens in any part of the country. The Choctaws and Chickasaws, with relatively little internal strife, were not completely demoralized; but the Indians who lived north of the Canadian were the victims of unendurable pressure from both sides and devastating violence in all stages of the war. Indian leaders would have preferred neutrality to active participation in the conflict; yet all of the tribes were involved. Losses of the Seminoles, Creeks, and Cherokees were heavier in percentage of total population than the losses of any southern or northern state.

Early in the war, the Indians began to lean toward the Confederate side. Removal of federal troops from the forts of Indian Territory, failure of federal annuity payments, the presence of trusted Indian agents who were committed to support of the Confederacy, and active Confederate diplomacy among the Indians, all worked in favor of the South.

Removal of federal troops from the Indian country at the outset of the Civil War, was one of the maneuvers that threw the Five Civilized Tribes into Confederate hands. The all-important problem in the South was to find the best means for winning independence; in the North, the long-range need was to discover the strength for binding the states together in a perpetual union. The relative value of the Indian country, by comparison with the portion of Virginia that was in the Ohio Valley, or by comparison with St. Louis, Louisville, Baltimore, or the District of Columbia, was a matter of judgment. Also, the question of the amount of force required for taking the places mentioned above, and many others on the border of seceding states, had to be considered.

The Indian Territory, with its sparse population and relatively small production of food crops, was rated very low on the scale of values by the federal government; and because of its position, it was regarded more highly by the Confederacy.

The Union government, which could have held the Indian tribes with a minimum of effort, did not take the necessary steps to hold them. The Confederacy, which could not spare the power to control the area during the latter part of the war, did make its occupation very costly for the Union. The Indians were divided: in the early part of the war, the Confederacy had the support of the Choctaws, Chickasaws, more than half of the Seminoles, and about half of the Creeks and Cherokees. Later, a considerable number of Creeks and Cherokees changed sides, giving the federal armies the advantage in recruits.

The reasons for Confederate diplomatic success among the Indians are not hard to discover. All of the principal officials of the United States in the Indian country were southern men, and in sympathy with secession. Elias Rector of Arkansas, superintendent of the southern Indians; William H. Garrett of Alabama, the Creek agent; Douglas H. Cooper, agent for the Choctaws and Chickasaws; P. M. Butler, agent for the Cherokees; and Samuel Rutherford, the Seminole agent, were all strong advocates of secession. Albert Pike, principal diplomatic representative of the Confederacy in the Indian country, was shrewd and effective. Furthermore, Pike was convinced that it was important to gain control of the Indians for the Confederate cause. "A force invading Texas from the North cannot leave us in its rear," Pike wrote to President Jefferson Davis. When the Kiowas, Comanches, and other Indians west of the Five Civilized Tribes sent messengers asking Pike's permission to attack wagon trains from the Missouri River to Santa Fe, he replied that he had no objection. "To go on the warpath somewhere else is the best way to keep them from troubling Texas," he wrote in his report.[1]

At the beginning of actual secession, that of South Carolina on December 20, 1860, federal troops occupied three posts in the Washita Valley: Fort Washita, near the eastern border of the Chickasaw Nation; Fort Arbuckle, fifty miles to the northwest; and Fort Cobb, twenty miles beyond the western limits of the Chickasaws. In the panic that descended upon some federal officials after the bombardment of Fort Sumter, a drive was launched to reach as many United States troops as possible for protection of the national capital. The soldiers stationed in the Indian country were sent at first to Fort Leavenworth, 150 miles north of the Cherokee boundary.

Secretary of the Interior Caleb B. Smith, impressed by the need of organized protection for the Indians during their time of decision for the Union or against it, sent an inquiry to the Secretary of War concerning the armed forces west of Arkansas. Simon Cameron answered on May 10, 1861: "In answer to your letter of the 4th inst., I have the honor to state that on the 17th of April instructions were issued by this Department to remove the troops stationed at Forts Cobb, Arbuckle, Washita, and Smith, to Fort Leavenworth, leaving it to the discretion of the Commanding Officer to replace them or not, by Arkansas Volunteers." Cameron then closed the door upon further requests. "The exigencies of the service will not admit of any change in these orders."[2]

With the removal of troops, the presence of Confederate Indian agents, the memories of unfulfilled pledges, and the actual failure of the federal government to pay annuities for 1860, came active and effective diplomacy, and co-operation for the

---

[1] *Official Records, The War of the Rebellion,* Series I, Vol. XIII, 822–23.
[2] Simon Cameron to Caleb Smith, May 10, 1861, O. I. A.: Secretary of War, 1861.

Southern cause by neighboring citizens of Arkansas and Texas. The attitude of the Indians, like that of Southern citizens of the United States, was roughly dependent upon latitude. There was a "Deep South" in the Indian country, and a "Border Area," as there was among the slave states farther east. There was never a chance that Choctaws and Chickasaws would take other tribal action than alliance with the Confederacy; and the neutrality of tribes farther north was similar, in many respects, to that of Kentucky. Chief John Ross of the Cherokees at first asserted the neutrality of his tribe; and a band of Creeks, supported by "loyal" Seminoles, Algonquians from the Grand River country above the Cherokees, and a party of Plains warriors, all under the leadership of Opothle Yahola, an old and respected Creek chieftain, maintained their neutral stand for a time.

The Seminoles, composed in a large measure of fullblood Indians, were conservative by nature and not inclined to break old ties and join the new Confederacy. C. H. Carruth reported to Major General D. Hunter on November 26, 1861, that the Seminoles, at the intertribal council on March 10, had opposed a treaty with the Confederacy. The tribe did not appoint delegates to meet with Albert Pike who negotiated unofficially and secretly with John Jumper. After the Seminole leader yielded to Pike's persuasion and raised forty-six men, he was promised six hundred rangers from Fort Cobb to crush out Union sentiment in the tribe.

"The Indians will make no further resistance to the South until help is furnished them, while a little aid would thoroughly arouse the union feeling," Carruth wrote. "Before spring they must be either our enemies or friends."[3]

As Opothle Yahola was gathering his "Loyal Indians" for testing the possibilities of a neutral stand, Colonel Douglas H. Cooper, Choctaw agent and one of the trusted representatives of the Southern Confederacy among the Five Civilized Tribes, made a final bid for Creek and Seminole support. He came to the Creek Council Ground, northwest of Opothle Yahola's camp near the mouth of Deep Fork, and sent messengers to the old

[3] Commissioner of Indian Affairs, *Annual Report* (1861), 46-49.

Creek leader. However, Opothle Yahola had made up his mind; he carried a letter from Abraham Lincoln, in which the President pointed out that a clash between the North and South was not an Indian war, not being concerned primarily with Indian interests. The letter urged Creek neutrality; and Opothle Yahola had it read by an interpreter to three hundred of his followers who were assembled at Roro-Culka on the North Canadian River fifty miles above North Fork Town.[4]

Support for the fullblood chief's neutral stand was found largely in the western parts of the Creek Nation—Greenleaf Town between the North Canadian and Deep Fork and the southwestern corner of Wewoka District near the site of present day Holdenville. Across the border in Little River Valley, practically all of the Seminole population would have remained neutral if they had received official encouragement and the gesture of federal military aid.

In addition to the camp on Deep Fork above North Fork Town, and at Roro-Culka, the followers of Opothle Yahola gathered at other points. Runners were sent with oral messages from one camp to another, according to Indian custom, and thus the "Loyal Indians" were kept informed of plans for concerted action. One party went into camp on Hillabee Creek, a tributary of Deep Fork, northwest of present day Boley. "We were joined by other groups and we in turn joined other larger groups," one of the Indians recalled three-quarters of a century later, as he tried to give an account of a little boy's part in the dangerous activities of the time.[5]

When negotiations between Douglas Cooper and Opothle Yahola failed to bring agreement, the Confederate commander determined to challenge the right of these "Loyal Indians" to maintain their neutral stand. With an armed force of some 1,400 Indians and whites—Choctaws and Chickasaws supported by a Texas cavalry unit—Colonel Cooper advanced rapidly upon the principal camp of the Creek leader. He reached North Fork

---

[4] Orpha Russell, "Ekvn-hvlwuce, Site of Oklahoma's first Civil War Battle," *Chronicles of Oklahoma*, Vol. XXIX, No. 4, 401–407.

[5] Interview with James Scott, Indian Pioneer Papers, LXXXI, 78–82.

Town on November 15, 1861, and learned that Opothle Yahola had departed hastily with all of his people. Before this movement of the southern military force, Opothle Yahola had been little concerned over the organization of a Confederate infantry company under James M. C. Smith at North Fork Town. His own warriors, in the various camps, numbered about 2,000; and when the parties were united, his followers—men, women, and children—were nearly 9,000.

The exact route followed by Opothle Yahola's band is not a matter of complete agreement among historians of the Indian phase of the war. Reasons for the variety of opinions are not hard to find. Official records, notably that of Colonel Douglas H. Cooper, gave little in the way of geographical data. Special Agent John T. Cox sent a map of the route to the Indian Office in the spring of 1864, but the conditions under which the map was made do not suggest complete information or accuracy. In fact, the rough sketch is so far from the facts of river courses and locations of Indian tribes as to be almost worthless as a means of tracing the route of Opothle Yahola's march. The maps produced for the War Department for the *Official Records* are inaccurate in many respects—not entirely reliable in regard to details of streams, hills, missions, trails and other landmarks.

There is a considerable volume of first hand information— such as interviews with persons who followed Opothle Yahola to Kansas—which is too vague to be regarded as conclusive, particularly since it is in parts contradictory. A little boy of nine or ten, getting a series of impressions from experiences that were filled with shock and tragedy, might well remember some incidents to the end of a long life; but it would probably be very difficult for him, after the lapse of years, to separate hearsay from his first impressions. As a result, one observer who honestly tried to recall what he saw in that distant past, reported: "They had no wagons, and very few had ponies;" while another said, "He rode the length of the wagon train, issuing these orders;" and in another place, "Our women, children, and some of the men were sent on with the wagons, teams, and cattle."[6]

The point is important to historians, since pieces of broken wagons found on a possible battle ground of Opothle Yahola's warriors have been regarded as important bits of evidence in locating the site of the battle. There is no generally accepted view of the matter, and the nature of the basic sources is such as to discourage positive assertions. As Dr. Angie Debo suggests, more complete evidence may yet be found to give certainty to the location of the route.[7]

Probably the various elements of Opothle Yahola's following moved toward Kansas from their camps on the North Canadian, Deep Fork, and elsewhere, timing their departure to enable them to meet at the Indian Marker on the trail at the site of Sapulpa.[8] For those who came from the vicinity of North Fork Town, that would involve traveling northwest; from Rora-Culka, Hillabee Creek, and Edwards' Store (Talasi), northeast.

The account given by James Scott in an interview when he was seventy-six years of age did, without attempting to locate the trail north, suggest a route that was fairly direct toward the mouth of Red Fork. "I did not fully realize or understand why I was given orders to round up the cattle," Scott said. "I wondered at the vast amount of cattle being killed and the meat being dried, the pork being cooked down, and all the numerous preparations. At all the houses of the neighbors, I saw all sorts of preparations with little knowledge of its meaning." His people gathered at Hillabee Creek where they were joined by other bands of Indians; and as the united parties moved toward Kansas, they "joined other larger groups."

These were Indians collected at the junction of Deep Fork and the North Canadian by Opothle Yahola, "near the present town of Eufaula, and consisted almost exclusively of the Mus-

---

[6] *Chronicles of Oklahoma*, Vol. XXVII, No. 2, 187–206; Vol. XXIX, No. 4, 401–407; Interview with James Scott, Indian Pioneer Papers, LXXXI, 78–82.

[7] One of the fairest discussions of the topic is that of Angie Debo in *Chronicles of Oklahoma*, Vol. XXVII, No. 2, 187–206. Miss Debo is impressed with source materials collected by the Payne County Historical Association under the direction of B. B. Chapman, which seem to indicate Twin Mounds west of Yale as the probable location of "Round Mountain" often mentioned in the earlier accounts.

[8] Orpha Russell, "Ekvn-hvlwuce," *Chronicles of Oklahoma*, Vol. XXIX, No. 4, 401–407.

kogee faction of which he was the recognized grand old man who had led them a few years before over the Trail of Tears from their homes on the Coosa and Tallapoosa. . . .

"My family consisted of a mother, Larney Scott; father, Artuss Yahola; and a sister, Lizzie. My mother never returned from this trip but was buried in Kansas. My father died after his return to this country.

"The first command to halt was brought by a McIntosh Negro slave, a messenger commanding us to halt. . . . Many of our men answered, 'We are not going to stop; we are on our way. . . . Seeing that we could not be detained, our pursuers made the attack. The attack was made on a hill side and I would not know where this hill is. . . ." No reference was made, up to this point in the story, of a river crossing. The Creek and Seminole men, with the other "Loyal Indian" warriors, took such protection as the place afforded—"bushes, trees, and large rocks"— and opened fire upon the attackers. "The enemy making the upgrade attack could not successfully accomplish anything. Our men gave the chase and returned with a captured flag."

Obviously, James Scott as an old man believed that the first clash with Confederate troops took place before the crossing of Red Fork (Cimarron) River. What part of his recollection came from his own observation, and how much from conversation with older men or even perusal of the J. T. Cox map, would be impossible to estimate.[9]

It cannot be determined from Scott's account at what point in the journey he was sent forward with the women and children. His story of the battle on the hill side is clear-cut, as if stamped upon his memory; and the crossing of the river immediately following is equally definite. The party in retreat was fired upon as they crossed the stream. "There was only a one way crossing and only one place to cross." The bank on the north side was "steep and slippery," dampened by wagon wheels, oxen and horses, emerging from the Red Fork. "This required a long time

[9] Indian Pioneer Papers, LXXXI, 80. Annie Heloise Abel, in 1915, included a facsimile reproduction of the Cox map in her book, *The Indian as a Slaveholder and Secessionist*, opp. p. 262.

to cross." There is no record in this story of the subsequent battles between the Confederate and Loyal forces—Chusto Talasah and Chustenalah—which suggests that James Scott was not an eye-witness of those encounters. He does give a convincing account of hardships endured by the women and children on the flight north. Particularly touching was the story of a little Indian child, abandoned as it sat under a tree unaware of any peril, waving its hands to its terrified relatives who passed in headlong flight.

A contemporary account dealing with Opothle Yahola's retreat was that of George Bruner, one of the Loyal warriors who told the story to his son. George Bruner was a full blood Creek Indian, an Uscelarnappe, "brother members of one fire" with the Opothle Yahola band. Willie Bruner, repeating his father's story in 1951, stated: "Their first battle took place on the south side of the Arkansas River, at the rounded end of the mountain ending one-fourth mile south of the Cimarron River." This agrees with the account by J. T. Cox and does not contradict the evidence of any official report.[10]

Besides Creeks under the aged Opothle Yahola and Micco Hutke, and Seminoles under Halleck Tustenuggee, John Chupco, and Billy Bowlegs, the Indians at Round Mountain included Chickasaws, Quapaws, Euchees, Keechis, Caddoes, Ionies, Delawares, Wichitas, Cherokees, and two white men who were the husbands of Euchee women. The "squaw men" were William F. Brown and George Sofley. The party also included several hundred Negroes.

In the battle of November 19, 1861, at Round Mountain south of the Cimarron, in which "Loyal Indians" drove off the Confederates, Opothle Yahola lost three men killed; the number wounded is not known. Colonel Cooper's losses were probably higher in the early stages of this clash, in which only the advance guard of the Confederate force took part. Later, at the Red Fork crossing, the attack was renewed; there were more losses on

---

[10] Orpha Russell, *Chronicles of Oklahoma*, Vol. XXIX, No. 4, 401–407; Col. Douglas Cooper's report of Jan. 20, 1862 is in *Official Records*, Series I, Vol. VIII, 5.

both sides, and the firing continued until dark when the Confederate leader withdrew his troops. During the night, Opothle Yahola moved his force across the Arkansas River and took a strong position at the horseshoe bend of Bird Creek, northeast of Tulsey Town.

On December 8, Colonel Douglas Cooper again caught up with his elusive opponent. The "Loyal Indians" had prepared to make a stand on the timbered land inside of the bend at Chusto Talasah (Little High Shoals) on Bird Creek. Apparently, however, Opothle Yahola was considering the possibility of a peace parley. His scouts had probably revealed to him that the Cherokee Regiment of Mounted Volunteers under Colonel Drew had arrived ahead of Cooper's main force; and the Creek leader shrewdly suspected that his friends among the Cherokees, including Captain J. S. Vann, would be reluctant to fight against the "Loyal Creeks." Colonel Drew sent Major Thomas Pegg to confer with Opothle Yahola whom he found in the midst of a military council. Micco Hutke and the Seminoles Halleck Tustenuggee and John Chupco were urging the old Creek chief to attack the approaching soldiers before Cooper's troops could join them. Major Pegg hastened back to Drew's camp, which was about two miles in advance of Cooper's party, then in the process of pitching camp, and reported that Opothle Yahola was likely to continue the struggle. The news passed rapidly among the Cherokee warriors, and many of them were opposed to fighting against the Loyal Indians. With the exception of minor disorders resulting from cattle theft, peaceful relations had existed along the Creek and Cherokee frontier in the West since the settlement of a boundary dispute by the Stokes Commission in 1833. The Cherokees were reluctant to make war upon the Creeks over issues that did not directly concern either tribe; and a few Cherokee warriors had already identified themselves with the followers of Opothle Yahola. During the night of December 8, about three hundred of Drew's men broke camp and left the spot. Some of them went over to Opothle Yahola at once; others slipped away to their homes, and the rest, less than two hundred, fell back to Cooper's camp.[11]

On the following morning, Colonel Cooper sent two cavalry companies to explore the approach to Opothle Yahola's position. The rest of the Confederate force followed more slowly, moving down Bird Creek toward Chusto Talasah. Captain Sam Foster, in command of the advance cavalry unit, came back with the information that Opothle Yahola was ready for battle at the horseshoe bend farther down stream.

Colonel Cooper moved forward in battle formation, with his Choctaw and Chickasaw regiment on the right wing, under the Creek war leader, Lieutenant Colonel D. N. McIntosh; Colonel William Sims and the Texans, supported by the remnant of Drew's regiment, in the center; and the Creek-Seminole column on the left, under the command of Major John Jumper, whose Seminoles had been mustered into the Confederate service on November 21. The wagons, oxen, and extra horses were left on the prairie under a strong guard, and Cooper's three columns moved up at a gallop. When they were separated from the warriors who covered their advance on foot, a party of Union Seminoles suddenly emerged from the woods along Bird Creek and opened fire upon this rear guard. Captain Young of the Choctaw-Chickasaw Mounted Rifles rode back to support the Confederate rear guard, and the Seminoles were driven back into the woods.

The steep bank of Bird Creek, about thirty feet high at the outer rim of the bend, protected Opothle Yahola against an attack from the prairie side of the stream. A house and corncrib inside the bend afforded shelter for Opothle Yahola's sharpshooters, and they were able to drive the Confederates back at that point. Douglas Cooper hesitated to order a general charge,

---

[11] Wiley Britton, in *The Civil War on the Border*, I, 168–69, incorrectly assumed that the Cherokees fled from the field through fear of a night attack by Opothle Yahola. This was one of the major changes of allegiance by Indian troops after the war began. Certainly Drew's men were not likely to be panic-stricken, with a superior Confederate force encamped within two miles of their location. Nor was Opothle Yahola so desperate as to make a night attack, instead of waiting for the enemy's advance upon a battlefield that he had carefully selected. See Foreman, *History of Oklahoma*, 107; John Bartlett Meserve, "Chief Opothle Yahola," *Chronicles of Oklahoma*, Vol. IX (1931), 446–50; M. L. Wardell, *A Political History of the Cherokee Nation*, 133.

since he was not completely confident in regard to the loyalty of Cherokee and Creek warriors after the disruption of Colonel Drew's regiment. The battle raged for four hours, with advantage first on one side, then on the other; but the Confederates were not able to drive the "Loyal Indians" from their strong position. They were giving their women and children as much time as possible for escape to the north.

Colonel Cooper, who had suffered heavy losses, ordered a retreat to the Confederate camp, and the attack was not renewed during the rest of the day. After dark, Opothle Yahola again slipped away toward Kansas, to a strong position previously chosen on Shoal Creek. Colonel Cooper reported losses of fifteen killed and thirty-seven wounded at Chusto Talasah; but if the three hundred Cherokees of Drew's Volunteers are to be included in Confederate casualties, the campaign was very costly. Cooper needed supplies and reinforcements; and he decided to fall back to Fort Gibson where he might obtain both.

The Confederate general, Ben McCulloch, had left Colonel James McIntosh in command of the division that maintained headquarters at Van Buren, Arkansas; and to McIntosh, Cooper applied for help. The commander decided to lead a force in person directly against the Union Indians; and accordingly he instructed Colonel Cooper to advance along the Arkansas far enough for an attack from the rear.

Colonel James McIntosh's force contained five companies of the South Kansas-Texas Regiment, a part of Griffith's Texas Cavalry, a company of mounted Texans under Captain H. S. Bennett, and four companies of the Arkansas Mounted Riflemen commanded by Captain William Gibson. His party numbered 1,600 well armed and mounted men. Opothle Yahola had survived the attacks of Douglas Cooper's troops and had inflicted heavier losses than those suffered by his own forces by means of his skill in selecting the battle grounds, and through the able efforts of Halleck Tustenuggee and his Seminole warriors. The new Confederate war party was far more dangerous than Cooper's Indians, however, with superior arms and equipment and better horses. Furthermore, Opothle Yahola's men were running short of ammunition, and their food supply was low. The seven days of respite, after the battle of Chusto Talasah might have been used in moving the refugee Indians closer to federal military protection; but Opothle Yahola did not know what to expect in Kansas, he had no rapid means of obtaining information on Cooper's plans from Cherokee friends of the Union cause, and he had another defensible position at Chustenalah on Shoal Creek.

Colonel James McIntosh moved fast when he started west at noon on December 22, and on December 25, after the Confederates had pitched camp, they had their first sight of Opothle Yahola's warriors. No important action took place during the night, although McIntosh sent out a regiment to follow the Union troops as a precaution against surprise. On the morning of December 26, the Confederates marched early toward the place where they expected to find Opothle Yahola; and as the advance guard crossed Shoal Creek just before noon, a sudden volley from a near-by hill revealed the Union location. Colonel McIntosh advanced upon the wooded hill and, in spite of losses, moved steadily up the slope. When the ground became too rough for mounted troops, Griffith's Regiment left their horses in the rear and charged on foot.

Opothle Yahola had posted his men near the summit of the hill, where large boulders gave excellent protection. Halleck Tustenuggee, in the front line, rallied his Seminoles again and again, but could not stop the well equipped and well trained soldiers of the McIntosh command. By four o'clock, the Union Indians were low on ammunition, and their lines were broken in many places. They scattered and retreated into the rough ground back of Shoal Creek. The ground was covered with snow, and a cold northwest wind was pelting the retreating warriors with sleet. The beaten Indian soldiers were joined by their families; and they began the final stage of their retreat to Kansas, traveling generally in small groups, and counting themselves very fortunate if they had saved back a little ammunition.

Colonel James McIntosh reported his losses as 9 killed and 40 wounded; Opothle Yahola, he thought, had lost 250 killed.

This figure was a gross exaggeration, though the rout of the Union troops was complete. The First Creek regiment under Lieutenant Colonel D. N. McIntosh and the First Cherokee Regiment under Stand Watie joined in the pursuit. Women and children, captured near Chustenalah, numbered 160. Practically all of the goods and livestock carried north by the "Loyal Indians" fell into Confederate hands, and the survivors fled across the snow with scant clothing and very little food.

The flight of Opothle Yahola and his people, after Chustenalah, was a time of indescribable horror for the fugitives. Frozen bodies lying in the snow marked the route north, and often the garments of the dead were removed to supplement the meager clothing of survivors. Of the Indians who reached Kansas, pursued by Douglas Cooper's men within ten miles of the new state's southern boundary, a large per cent had frozen hands or feet which had to be amputated after they went into camp on the Verdigris River. Some of the Seminoles and a few Cherokees who had not succeeded in joining Opothle Yahola before the march northward began, arrived in the refugee camp later. By April, 1862, there were 7,600 Indians in the camp. Medical attention could not be given to all who needed it; shelter, clothing and food were inadequate; and several hundred of the Indians, including old Opothle Yahola, died after they had reached a place of safety from Confederate bullets.

A. B. Campbell, United States Army surgeon, reporting on the condition of the refugees on February 5, 1862, stated: "It is impossible for me to depict the wretchedness of their condition. Their only protection from the snow on which they lie is prairie grass, and from the wind and weather scraps and rags stretched upon switches; some of them had some personal clothing; most had but shreds and rags, which did not conceal their nakedness, and I saw seven, ranging in age from three to fifteen years, without one thread upon their bodies. . . .

"They greatly need medical assistance; many have their toes frozen off, others have their feet wounded by sharp ice or branches of trees lying on the snow; but few have shoes or moccasins. They suffer with inflammatory diseases of the chest, throat, and eyes. Those who come in last get sick as soon as they eat. . . . Why the officers of the Indian Department are not doing something for them I cannot understand; common humanity demands that something be done, and done at once, to save them from total destruction."[12]

Before the end of cold weather, the camp was moved to a new location near Le Roy on the Neosho River, and the condition of fugitive Indians improved, though the death rate in camp was still very high. By the end of August, 1862, the camp contained over 5,000 refugees and the Indian regiments had enlisted 800 warriors from among them. Several thousand of the Indian fugitives were scattered about in smaller groups, chiefly on the Fall, Cottonwood, and Walnut rivers, at distances varying from 25 to 150 miles from the Roe's Fork camp on the Verdigris.

At the request of Commissioner William P. Dole, George W. Collamore visited the Neosho and reported upon the condition of Indians encamped there. Reverend Evan Jones, who had been driven out of the Cherokee country by the Confederates, accompanied the Agent. After pointing out that the refugee Creeks, Seminoles, and other Indians had deliberately chosen to fight for the Union, leaving comfortable homes and in some instances a large amount of property, Collamore wrote: "The battle of December last was particularly unfortunate to these people, and the disasters of the defeat left them in the helpless condition I found them. . . .

"Their march was undertaken with a scanty supply of clothing, subsistence, and cooking utensils, and entirely without tents, and during their progress they were reduced to such extremity as to be obliged to feed upon their ponies and dogs, while their scanty clothing was reduced to rags, and in some cases absolute nakedness was their condition. Let it be remembered that this retreat was in the midst of a winter of unusual severity for that country, with snow upon the prairie. Many of their ponies died of starvation. The women and children suffered severely from

[12] Meserve, "Chief Opothle Yahola," *Chronicles of Oklahoma*, Vol. IX, 446–50; Foreman, *Oklahoma*, 106–108; Commissioner of Indian Affairs, *Annual Report*, (1862), 151–52.

frozen limbs, as did also the men. Women gave birth to their offspring upon the naked snow, without shelter or covering, and in some instances the new-born infants died for want of clothing, and those who survived to reach their present location with broken constitutions and utterly dispirited."

In the second of their refugee camps, these Indians had not been able to provide themselves with shelters because they did not have tools. "Such coverings as I saw were made in the rudest manner, being composed of pieces of cloth, old quilts, handkerchiefs, aprons, &c., &c., stretched upon sticks, and so limited were many of them in size that they were scarcely sufficient to cover the emaciated and dying forms beneath them. Under such shelter I found, in the last stages of consumption, the daughter of Opothleyoholo, one of the oldest, most influential, and wealthy chiefs of the Creek Nation."

Collamore made the rounds with the physician, Dr. S. D. Coffin, visiting "nearly fifty patients in one afternoon." Many of the Indians had ailments that the doctor pronounced incurable. Amputations of frozen limbs were a daily occurence; one little Creek boy, about eight, had lost both feet. Death from frozen limbs was common—Dr. Coffin pointed out five patients suffering from frostbite who were past recovery. The Indian census as reported by Collamore on April 21, 1862, was: Creeks 5,000; Seminoles, 1,096; Chickasaws, 140; Quapaws, 315; Uchees, 544; Keechies, 83; Delawares, 197; Ironeyes, 17; Caddoes, 3; Wichitas, 5; Cherokees, 240 . . . an aggregate of 7,600 persons."

One pound of flour, a piece of spoiled bacon, and a "scanty supply of salt" was the weekly ration of each Indian—"neither coffee, sugar, vinegar, nor pepper has been allowed them, only upon the requisition of the physician for the sick. . . . They had been told by the rebel emissaries, as the chief informed me, that they would fail to obtain these articles from their Union friends, which, having turned out to be the fact, has affected them with suspicion and discontent."

Major G. C. Snow, the Seminole agent, told Collamore that the bacon issued to the Indians was "not fit for a dog to eat." He found upon inquiry, that this meat had been condemned at

Crossing Little River with oil-well equipment, 1927.

Killingsworth Collection,
University of Oklahoma Archives

Seminole, Oklahoma, during the oil boom of the 1920's.

Standard Oil Company (N.J.)

Present-day Seminole outdoor meeting place or church, at Sasakwa, Oklahoma.

The cabin, still standing, where Jennie Chisholm played with Alice Brown Davis, sister of Chief John F. Brown, south of Asher, Oklahoma.

Fort Leavenworth. "A reliable person who saw the bacon before it was sent to them, who is a judge of the article, pronounced it suitable only for soap grease." Many of the Indians who ate the bacon became ill from eating it. Collamore ended his report by an estimate of the cost for supplying immediate needs of these Indians in food and clothing: $292,000 for subsistence rations, for 365 days at 10 cents a day; $100,000 for clothing. No estimate was made for tents and other necessary articles.[13]

In the early spring of 1862, federal military officers were preparing for an invasion of the Indian country to win back the homes of the Union refugees. James G. Blunt, promoted to the rank of brigadier general and placed in charge of operations in southern Kansas and Indian Territory on April 1, selected Colonel William Weer to organize and lead the Indian Expedition; and that officer had about 6,000 soldiers ready for invasion by June, 1862. Three white infantry regiments, the Sixth Kansas Cavalry, the Second Ohio Cavalry, two artillery units—the First Kansas Battery and Rabb's Second Indiana Battery—and three Indian regiments made up Weer's troops. The third of the Indian regiments was organized under Major William A. Phillips during the actual invasion.

In its contacts with Confederate troops, the Indian expedition was a success. The battle at Locust Grove on July 23, 1862, was a smashing victory for the Union invaders. Colonel J. J. Clarkson, commanding the Confederate forces that had been sent north to meet the invaders, was the victim of a surprise attack just before daylight. Some of his troops fled leaving their guns in camp; others were shot down as they attempted to form a battle line. Colonel Clarkson surrendered with 110 men, and at the same time gave up 60 ammunition wagons, 64 mule teams, and a substantial amount of provisions.

Ordinarily, military reports made no tribal distinctions in the records of campaigns and battles in which Indian troops were engaged. The part taken by the Seminoles in the invasion of 1862 may be traced in the brief references to their activities, however. Major G. C. Snow, reporting on general conditions in the Seminole refugee camp near Neosho Falls, stated that two-

[13] Collamore to Dole, April 21, 1862, *ibid.*, 155–58.

thirds of the tribe and practically all of their Negroes had come to Kansas since the war began. "Nearly all of the able-bodied men of the tribe have joined the army," he added. "They are now with the army of the frontier, and are doing excellent service in clearing out the rebels from their homes." Major William A. Phillips, who commanded a force selected from the Indian Home Guard units after Colonel Weer's white troops were removed from the Cherokee Nation, skirmished with a Confederate raiding party at Bayou Menard on July 27, 1862.

The Confederates were commanded by Lieutenant Colonel Thomas Fox Taylor, who was killed as he tried to rally his soldiers during the surprise attack. Major Phillips reported the engagement and included an estimate of his Creek and Seminole troops. "I was very much pleased with the conduct of the whole Indian force. The only difficulty was in restraining their impetuous charge and in keeping back a reserve and guard for the wagons." The unit engaged under Lieutenant A. W. Robb was about 80 per cent Creeks and 20 per cent Seminoles.[14]

Elevated to the rank of colonel and given command of the Indian troops north of the Arkansas River, William A. Phillips faced the problem of food for his soldiers and the refugees who came back from Kansas. He was active in obtaining corn meal from northwestern Arkansas, and the greatest threat to his supply trains was from the Confederate forces under Douglas Cooper, brigadier general after October 27, 1862, who was storing supplies sent up the Texas Road at Honey Springs, and occasionally sending Stand Watie and his Cherokees across the Arkansas River on raids.

Colonel Phillips fortified an enclosed area at Fort Gibson,

[14] Maj. A. C. Ellithorpe to Wm. P. Dole, June 9, 1862; Phillips to Blunt, July 27, 1862, *Official Records, The War of the Rebellion*, Series I, Vol. XIII, 182; Snow to W. G. Coffin, supt. of Indian Affairs, Sept. 4, 1863, Commissioner of Indian Affairs, *Annual Report* (1863). There were three of the Coffin Family who were physicians in the southern superintendency of the Indian Service: A. J. Coffin, directing physician of the southern refugee Indians; A. V. Coffin, directing physician at LeRoy, Kansas; and S. D. Coffin, attending physician at the Sac and Fox agency. Col. R. W. Furnas was the leader in organization of the Indian refugee regiments, and was placed in command of the First Regiment. Britton, *Civil War on the Border*, I, 298, 309, 310.

and held it against Confederate attack even when his available troops were seriously depleted for the campaigns farther east. On May 24, 1863, a train of two hundred wagons coming down the Military Road to Fort Gibson was threatened by a regiment of Texas troops supported by Confederate Indians. Colonel Phillips sent an escort to meet the supplies, with instructions to keep moving during the night. The combined troops of the escort numbered about one thousand.

The Confederates attacked early in the morning of May 25, at a point about five miles northwest of the fort. After a sharp exchange of shots, the attacking party charged, but were driven back. The wagons kept moving, and reached Fort Gibson at sunrise. Confederate losses were thirty-five killed, mostly Indians. Colonel Phillips lost five killed and twelve wounded. The Confederate dead were brought to the fort in two wagons.

The most important military action in the entire war in the Indian country was that of June and July, 1863. General Blunt sent a supply train from eastern Kansas to Fort Gibson in June with provisions for his troops and for refugee Indians. Here was a rich prize that appealed to Stand Watie, the boldest and ablest of the Confederate Indian leaders. The train was made up of 218 mule wagons and 40 ox wagons, accompanied by an escort of 1,000 soldiers.

Major John A. Foreman was sent from Fort Gibson with a party of 600 mounted men and one howitzer, to meet the wagon train at Baxter Springs and serve as reinforcements for the escort. The train moved slowly south across the Kansas line toward the Neosho River, and news came to Colonel J. M. Williams at Baxter Springs that the Confederates were preparing an attack with a large force before the supplies could reach Fort Gibson. Colonel Williams decided to reinforce the guard with the First Kansas Colored Regiment and Captain Jack Armstrong's artillery unit. The Negro troops and Captain Armstrong, accompanied by Colonel Williams, left Baxter Springs on the morning of June 26 and caught up with the wagon train in the late afternoon of the same day.

South of the Neosho crossing, an Indian scouting party sent

out by Major Foreman killed four of Stand Watie's men and took three prisoners. From these captives it was learned that a Confederate military party under Watie and D. C. McIntosh was waiting on the south bank of Cabin Creek for the wagon train to arrive. The prisoners also stated that the strength of Stand Watie's force was approximately 1,600, and that General William C. Cabell was on the east side of Grand River with 1,500 men and three pieces of artillery, waiting for a fall in the flooded stream to join the Confederates on the west bank.

On July 1, the wagon train halted at noon, about a mile north of the Cabin Creek crossing on the Military Road. Major Foreman advanced with a mounted company from the Third Indian Regiment, supported by a second line composed of the First Kansas Colored Infantry. The federal artillery aided in exploring the north bank by dropping shells in front of Foreman's advancing Indian troops, until Colonel Williams was satisfied that Stand Watie's force had all withdrawn to the opposite side. Soundings of the stream, made under the protection of artillery fire, indicated that the ford was too deep for the wagons to cross, and Colonel Williams ordered his force to pitch camp.

It now became Stand Watie's purpose to hold the wagon train back until the Grand River subsided enough to permit a crossing by General Cabell.

While the Union forces were pitching their camp, Colonel J. M. Williams held a conference with Lieutenant Colonel Theodore H. Dodd, and Major John A. Foreman, and these officers agreed upon a plan of attack. At eight o'clock on the morning of July 2, Big Cabin Creek had fallen enough for crossing the ammunition wagons, and the plan agreed upon was put into effect without delay.

After the three artillery units had shelled the Confederate position for about forty minutes, Major Foreman and a mounted company of the Third Indian Regiment advanced across the Creek. When they had nearly reached the south bank, a line of Confederate Indians, concealed in a trench under willow boughs, rose up suddenly and fired a volley into the advancing troops. Major Foreman was wounded and had to be carried to the rear.

His men fell back to the north bank, but the second federal line, composed of the Kansas Colored Infantry, opened fire upon the Confederate concealed position, marked by the smoke from their first volley. The position of the Confederates nearest the creek became untenable and they broke for cover farther back. After another brief bombardment with shell and canister, Colonel Williams ordered his reserve units forward. Lieutenant R. C. Philbrick replaced the Indian company in advance with the Ninth Kansas Cavalry. He crossed under cover of artillery fire, formed his line on the south bank, and advanced rapidly upon the Confederates who were sheltered in the brush. Colonel Williams followed with all of the cavalry and infantry units, driving the Confederates back from their original position in the timber and brush along the creek. A few hundred yards back, on the edge of the prairie, they reformed their forces; but Lieutenant Philbrick advanced at a fast pace, and charged the front line, throwing it into confusion. Captain John E. Stewart followed the advantage with another cavalry charge, and the Confederate forces scattered in all directions, each soldier seeking his own safety in concealment or flight. Stand Watie and two companions rode hard to the south, and reported the defeat to General Douglas Cooper at Honey Springs, on the eastern border of the Creek Nation.

General Blunt's wagon train and its escort moved safely into Camp Gibson, where the commander joined them after a few days, accompanied by a party of six hundred men from the Kansas Volunteer Cavalry under Colonel William R. Judson. Two twelve-pound howitzers were added to General Blunt's artillery with the arrival of Colonel Judson's regiment.[15] Well

15 The war in Indian Territory is covered in the reports of Union and Confederate officers, in *Official Records, War of the Rebellion,* Series I, Vol. XIII, contains important material on the battle at Fort Wayne, in which Colonel Phillips' Creek and Seminole Indians played a valiant part. Series I, Vol. XXII, Part I, has material on the battle of December 7, 1862, at Prairie Grove, Arkansas, and on the battle at Cabin Creek on July 2, 1863. "General Blunt's Account of his Civil War Experiences," was published in the *Kansas Historical Quarterly,* Vol. I, No. I (1923), 211–65. For an account of the principal Union officer's career in the Civil War of the Indian country, see J. C. Hopkins, "James G. Blunt and the Civil War" (unpublished M. A. thesis, University of Oklahoma,

aware of General Cabell's intention to join Douglas Cooper at Honey Springs for a united assault on Fort Gibson, General Blunt moved rapidly. From the Arkansas River's north bank near Fort Gibson, he could see Cooper's advance guard on the opposite shore. During the night of July 15, 1863, he crossed a small party with two howitzers at Hitchiti Ford above the Confederate position, and opened fire upon them. They hastily retired, falling back to Honey Springs. General Blunt occupied his men in crossing the river on July 16, and the next morning moved against the Honey Springs supply depot. General Douglas Cooper formed his battle lines for protection of the supplies.

The Union army consisted of the Sixth Kansas Cavalry under Colonel William R. Judson, the Second Colorado Infantry under Colonel T. H. Dodd, the First Kansas Colored Infantry under Colonel J. M. Williams, and two Indian regiments. The First and Second Indian Regiments were dismounted as infantry. The whole force was divided into two brigades for the attack, with Colonel Williams commanding the First, and Colonel William A. Phillips, the Second Brigade. The Union force was supported by two howitzers and two artillery batteries of four guns each, which gave General Blunt a distinct advantage in cannon fire.

General Cooper's troops included two Cherokee regiments under Colonel Stand Watie, two Creek regiments under Colonel D. C. McIntosh, the Twenty-ninth Texas Cavalry, the Fifth Texas Partisan Rangers, and a reserve posted about two miles back of the battle line, consisting of the Choctaw-Chickasaw regiment and two squadrons of Texas cavalry. The Confederate artillery consisted of one battery of four guns, which was stationed in front of the Twentieth Texas, on the left-center of General Cooper's line north of Elk Creek.

The federal big guns proved to be the decisive factor in the battle. After a duel of one hour, the Confederate guns were disabled; and an hour later, the Colored Infantry regiment, after Colonel Williams was carried to the rear with two severe wounds,

---

1952). Wiley Britton's *The Civil War on the Border* and *The Union Indian Brigade* contain accounts of the First, Second, and Third Indian Regiments at Fort Wayne, Cabin Creek, Honey Springs, and elsewhere.

broke the center of the line on Elk Creek. The Second Indian Regiment, deployed as skirmishers, advanced against the McIntosh regiment at the same time and drove the Confederate Indians back across Elk Creek. The Texas regiment also retreated, and Stand Watie's Cherokees, along with the Fifth Texas Rangers, crossed to the south side of the creek at the lower ford.

The Confederate retreat became a rout, but General Blunt's cavalry units were challenged sharply and retarded in their pursuit by the Choctaw-Chickasaw regiment guarding the supply depot, and the Texas cavalry squadrons held in reserve. General Cabell arrived from Fort Smith with his brigade of Arkansas cavalry and four cannons, too late to help Cooper or prevent capture of the supplies.

Seminoles in this engagement fought under Lieutenant Colonel Fred W. Schaurte, Colonel Stephen H. Wattles, and Colonel William A. Phillips. The First Kansas Colored Infantry contained a sprinkling of Seminole Negroes, some of whom were veterans of the Florida campaigns. The Indian and Negro regiments were commended highly by Colonel Williams and General Blunt in their reports for steadiness under fire and in many instances for reckless courage. The Seminole Negroes, whose status as slaves or free men had often been the subject of bitter controversy, were much intrigued by the discovery of several hundred handcuffs at the Honey Springs depot which had been brought there for the purpose of securing captive runaway slaves. The Union soldiers also captured a supply of bacon and dried beef, flour, salt, and other supplies.[16]

The Union general reported definite figures on Confederates killed and captured and an estimate of the wounded. Blunt's soldiers buried 150 Confederate dead and captured 77. He estimated the enemy wounded at 400. His own losses were 17 killed and 60 wounded.[17]

After Honey Springs, war in the Indian Territory settled

[16] *Official Records, War of the Rebellion*, Series I, Vol. XXII, Part I, 378–82; 447–62; Britton, *The Civil War on the Border*, II, 115–26; *The Union Indian Brigade*, 268–71, 284, 285.

[17] *Official Records, War of the Rebellion*, Series I, Vol. XXII, Part I, 447–62.

down to a process of cleaning up details of Confederate resistance in the North, and breaking the hold of Southern military forces beyond the Canadian River. Seminole and Creek soldiers were stationed near their own homes during the last two years of the conflict, with the exception of those who accompanied Colonel William A. Phillips on his "amnesty expedition" through the Chickasaw and Choctaw country in the spring of 1864. In May and June of that year, Superintendent William G. Coffin was engaged in returning Indian and Negro refugee families from Kansas to their homes. One wagon train which arrived at Fort Gibson on June 15 was made up of three hundred baggage wagons with mule teams. On the march, this train was three miles long. Subsistence was a complicated problem, on the journey and afterward, made doubly hard by war prices that were abnormally high and by the tendency of some war contractors and government agents to defraud the Indians.[18]

Reports of military engagements during the second half of the war in the Indian country contain few references to John Jumper (Hemha Micco). The Confederate Congress conferred upon him the rank of lieutenant colonel as an honorary title, "but without imposing the duties of actual service or command, or pay, . . . as a token of good will and confidence in his friendship, good faith, and loyalty. . . ." George Cloud was advanced to major, and the following Seminole warriors held the rank of captain in the Confederate service: Thomas Cloud, Fushatchie Cochockna, James Factor, Chitto Tustenuggee, Ochee Tustenuggee, William Robinson, Sam Hill, Tulsee Yahola, and Osuchee Harjo. D. R. Patterson, Seminole adjutant and first lieutenant, was killed in the second battle of Cabin Creek, on September 19, 1864.[19]

[18] *Ibid.*, Series I, Vol. XXX, Part IV, 694–95; Vol. XXXIV, Part II, 190, 994ff.; Abel, *The American Indian Under Reconstruction*, 17–21; *The Indian as a Participant in the Civil War*, 322–23. (Unfortunately, the Confederate Indian Office, like that of the Union government, was not free from large-scale graft. "The Confederate service in Indian Territory was honeycombed with fraud and corruption. Wastrels, desperadoes, scamps of every sort luxuriated at Indian expense." *Ibid.*, 268); Debo, *The Road to Disappearance*, 163.

[19] *Statutes at Large of the Confederate States of America*, 284; Foreman Transcripts, II.

CHAPTER 19

Reconstruction and Recovery

"They took hold of the question of reconstruction and settled it at once, practically, peaceably, and firmly."

GEORGE REYNOLDS

ON SEPTEMBER 8, 1865, after the last Confederate leaders in the Southwest had surrendered, a conference was convened at Fort Smith for the purpose of beginning a resettlement of Indian Affairs.[1] On the second day of the council, Dennis N. Cooley, presiding over the meetings in his capacity as commissioner of Indian affairs, gave the Indians an item of news which had been rumored before, and which they were dreading to hear.

"The following named nations and tribes have by their own acts, by making treaties with the enemies of the United States at the dates hereafter named, forfeited all rights to annuities, lands, and protection by the United States," said the Commissioner. The list of tribes, with the dates of the Confederate alliances, was then read: Creek, Choctaw, Chickasaw, Seminole, Pawnee, Delaware, Wichita, Osage, Seneca, Shawnee, Quapaw, and Cherokee. "By these nations having entered into alliances with the so-called Confederate States, and the rebellion being now ended, they are left without any treaty whatever or treaty obligations for protection by the United States." The speaker added that the President was anxious to renew the relations which existed at the outbreak of the war.[2]

---

[1] The Choctaw chief, Peter Pitchlynn, surrendered to a federal commission on June 19, and Brigadier General Stand Watie surrendered on June 23.

[2] Commissioner of Indian Affairs, *Annual Report* (1865), 298, 252–358.

Of the seven conditions laid down by Mr. Cooley as a basis for the new understanding, the third and fifth caused the greatest consternation among tribal leaders. Permanent peace with each other and with the United States was clearly for the good of all; aid in keeping peaceful relations with the Plains Indians, all the civilized tribes were eager to give; abolition of slavery and involuntary servitude except as punishment for crime, they had expected; the formation of a single Indian government, was a project in which the tribes were interested; and exclusion from the Indian country of white persons, with certain exceptions, was a proposition generally approved.

The Commissioner's third stipulation, however, was questioned by many of the Indians. Not only unconditional emancipation of the slaves was required; the tribes would be expected to incorporate the freedmen "on an equal footing with the original members," or to make other "suitable provision" for them. This condition for the making of a new treaty gave the Seminole delegates less concern than it did the leaders of the other tribes, for the simple reason that little adjustment was required by the Seminoles for meeting it.

The Seminole delegates at Fort Smith were John Chupco, recently elected as principal chief by the Union portion of the tribe; Pascofa, Fohutshe, Fos Harjo, and Chutcote Harjo. Robert Johnson and Cesar Bruner were their interpreters; and the Seminole agent, Major George Reynolds, took an active part in the conference.

Pascofa was the Seminole spokesman, and his answer to the Commissioner was brief: "We did not know when we left home we were coming to make any new treaties," he said; and added that it was his people's desire to come to an understanding with the men who took sides with the South. On September 12, the Seminoles answered all of the seven conditions laid down by Mr. Cooley, and agreed to all of them, with the specific provision that only Seminole freedmen and free Negroes formerly resident in the Seminole Nation should be admitted to citizenship—not colored persons from elsewhere.

The fifth of the Commissioner's seven stipulations for the

new treaty was as follows: "A portion of the lands hitherto owned and occupied by you must be set apart for the friendly tribes in Kansas and elsewhere, on such terms as may be agreed upon by the tribes and approved by the government, or such as may be fixed by the government."

Micco Hutke, an influential member of the Creek delegation, answered for the Loyal Creeks, and his reply was pertinent in every respect to the status of the Loyal Seminoles. He described the march of Opothle Yahola's followers. "We were threatened with entire annihilation, and compelled to leave our homes and all we possessed in the world, and traveled north in the hope of meeting our friends from the north." He told of the suffering on the march, of the battles with superior forces, and the final clash with the cavalry of Colonel James McIntosh and Stand Watie. "We were completely routed and scattered, and a great many of our women and children were killed," he said; and those who were not captured or killed "traveled to Kansas in blood and snow."

He pointed out that the First Indian Regiment of Home Guards, "which included two companies of Seminoles," was put into service in May, 1862, and was sent to Missouri, Arkansas, and different parts of the Indian Territory, taking part in twenty-one engagements. These troops were honorably discharged on May 31, 1865. "We must now most respectfully ask if you can show us one single instance in which more suffering has been endured or greater sacrifices been made for the cause of the Union; and we most respectfully ask and beg not to be classed with the guilty."

Micco Hutke was a man of valor and his words received the attention of the officers present at Fort Smith, if they did not receive the consideration of the nation. Commissioner Cooley asked, "Can you explain why Oktarharsars Harjo's name is signed to the treaty with the rebels?"

"That was the way with many Indians," answered Micco Hutke; "their names were put to treaties when they were not there."[3] His explanation required no comment.

[3] *Ibid.*, 329–30.

After about eight days the southern Indians, who were in a council of their own at Chahta Tamaha in the southern part of the Choctaw Nation when the meetings at Fort Smith began, came up to Commissioner Cooley's council. The Confederate Seminoles had good leaders and they immediately made their presence felt, without giving the impression that they were repudiating the leadership of John Chupco. On September 18, the United Seminoles signed an agreement to permit friendly Indians from Kansas to settle on part of their land. At the head of the Loyal Indian signatures was that of John Chipco (Chupco) "his X mark;" and at the head of the Confederate delegation was John Jupen (Jumper), "his X mark."[4]

The Southern Seminoles addressed a petition to the commissioners for further consideration of the much discussed problem of adopting the Negroes; and asked also that no decision be reached on the proposal for a United Indian Territory until they had studied the matter further. John Jumper signed as chief of this group, with four other Confederate leaders: George Cloud, Fooshatche-Cochuehue, Pahsuch Yahola, and James Factor. On September 19, John Jumper wrote an appeal to Commissioner Cooley for subsistence until his people had an opportunity to make a crop.

The new treaty negotiated at Washington on March 21, 1866, was signed by D. N. Cooley, Elijah Sells, and Ely S. Parker for the United States; and by John Chupco (Long John), Cho-cote-harjo, and Fos-harjo for the Indian tribe. John F. Brown signed as special delegate for the Southern Seminoles. Officials of the government were still justifying the seizure of Indian land by claiming that the tribes had forfeited all previous rights when they entered into agreements with the Confederate States. The United States Government declared a general amnesty for all Seminoles, the Seminoles declared an amnesty for all of their own members—Confederate and Union—and it was mutually agreed that the Seminole Nation should cede all of its land to the United States for the sum of $325,362, "said purchase being at the rate of fifteen cents per acre."

[4] Ibid., 342.

The fact that a majority of the Seminoles had chosen to suffer incredible hardships on the flight from Douglas Cooper's military force rather than repudiate their treaties with the United States had no visible effect upon the treaty-makers. The statement in the preamble, to the effect that the United States required a cession of land by the Seminole Nation and was "willing to pay therefor a reasonable price," cannot be regarded as consistent with the price agreed upon. Fifteen cents an acre was not a reasonable price for the land ceded. The further provision that the Seminoles should pay fifty cents an acre for 200,000 acres to be purchased from the Creeks gave an ironical twist to the proceedings. The Creek Nation was the victim of large-scale fraud; but the Seminoles were being cheated more brazenly, because their spokesmen were less articulate.[5] Creek lands, as defined in the recent treaties by which they had given up one-half of their holdings, lay between the Canadian River on the south and the Cherokee lands on the north. The new Seminole Nation was at the southwestern corner of this reduced area, and wholly between the Canadian and its north fork.

A provision for the compensation of loyal Indians and Negroes of the Seminole tribe for their war losses was included in the treaty. A commission of three members was to be appointed by the Secretary of the Interior to investigate the claims of the loyal Seminoles, and the Agent was responsible for taking a census and making a roll of those members of the tribe who "did in no manner aid or abet the enemies of the Government, but remained loyal" through the war.

Right of way was granted to any railroad company that should be authorized by Congress to "construct a railroad from any point on the eastern to the western or southern boundary" of the Seminole Nation. The United States agreed to construct an agency building at a cost of no more than $10,000, and the Seminoles to cede one section of land for the purpose, on the site chosen. The Seminole Nation accepted in advance such legislation as Congress and the President might "deem necessary for the better administration of the rights of person and property

[5] Kappler, *Indian Affairs: Laws and Treaties*, II, 910–15.

within the Indian Territory;" provided that such legislation "shall not in any manner interfere with or annul their present tribal organization, rights, laws, privileges, and customs."[6]

The Seminole agent, George W. Reynolds, reported on August 28, 1867, that the nation was beginning to show signs of recovery from the ruin brought about by the war. The Indian citizens had been removed from the refugee camp on the Arkansas to their new reservation during October, 1866, and furnished with rations of corn and beef until crops could be raised. The Agent had obtained all that he could in the way of useful tools and farm implements—axes, saws, wedges, plows, and hoes—and the Seminoles had begun at once the erection of cabins and preparation of land for spring planting. During the winter they had made more than 100,000 fence rails, and their first corn crop was above 110,000 bushels. Many of them had also planted vegetable gardens. By a system of cash penalties for idleness, rigidly enforced by Chief John Chupco and the head men, every man and woman was compelled to work.

Reynolds advocated government purchases of livestock and farm implements for the Seminoles, with gradual abolition of all cash annuities. He gave an excellent report on the work of Reverend John R. Ramsey, who had been sent to the Seminoles by the Presbyterian Board of Home Missions. A year later, Ramsey himself reported in some detail the condition of the Seminole elementary schools: School No. 1, taught by Miss Mary M. Lilley, had an average attendance of thirty-five, for a seven-months term. "Through the untiring assiduity and tact of the teacher, very many of the pupils made astonishingly rapid progress, both in learning to read and in speaking English."

School No. 2, taught by Ramsey himself, had thirty pupils, some of whom were so eager to learn that they came to their classes through the snow without shoes. School No. 3, near the old Seminole Agency, where the people were sparsely settled, ran for three months with an average attendance of twenty-five. Mrs. H. C. Shook was the teacher. School No. 4, taught by Charles Anderson, had a six-months term with an average attendance of twenty-seven pupils.

In 1869, Commissioner Ely S. Parker reported 2,105 as the Seminole population, a slight increase over the year 1868. The freedmen had been granted "unconditional citizenship," and Parker stated that conditions in the Nation were improving in every respect, with schools well attended, teachers working diligently and effectively, and the people as a whole "in a more perfect state of peace than any of the other tribes in the Indian country." Special Commissioner Vincent Colyer wrote the Indian Office that he found Reverend Ramsey ploughing a field, with a crowd of Indians gathered around, admiring his straight furrows, and his "Virginia rail fence, run by line, straight as an arrow." Colyer added interesting details.

"I visited John Chapko (Chupco), their chief. He is a splendid specimen of his race, tall, well formed, with a cheerful and open face. In the late war he was a sergeant in the Indian regiment on the Union side. On the walls of his bedroom he has a portrait of Abraham Lincoln, which he regards with peculiar affection."[7]

W. Morris Grimes, chaplain at Fort Gibson, gave Special Commissioner Vincent Colyer a short account of the Oak Ridge Mission, southeast of Wewoka, and of the work done by Reverend John Lilley and his wife, and by John Bemo and his wife in that mission. During the war the Lilley family had been rescued by Colonel William A. Phillips and had removed to a pastorate in Nebraska.

The war had split the Seminole church. The followers of John Jumper, who spent the latter years of the war in southern refugee camps, became Baptists. "At the present he is the chief prop of the Baptist church among the Seminoles, and believed to be a true man of God," wrote the chaplain, W. Morris Grimes. Upon his return to Wewoka in 1867, Reverend J. R. Ramsey organized a Presbyterian Church of 66 members which grew to 110 by 1869. "The present principal chief, John Chapko [Chup-

[6] *Ibid.*, 912–13.
[7] Reynolds to Wortham, Aug. 28, 1867; Reynolds to Robinson, Sept. 1, 1868; Report of J. R. Ramsey, Aug. 31, 1868; E. S. Parker to Secretary J. D. Cox, Vincent Colyer to E. S. Parker, April, 1869, Commissioner of Indian Affairs, *Annual Report* (1867); (1868); (1869).

319

co], is a very orderly member of the Presbyterian Church; also several other head men of the Nation."[8]

In his report of 1869, Agent George Reynolds summarized the three years of progress since return of the Seminoles to their ruined country. Before the war, the tribe had begun to live in comfort. "Many had buildings erected with taste and elegance, surrounded with lawns, flowers, shrubbery, and parks." The largest of the cattle herds had numbered twenty thousand; and "many had herds of stock numbering from one to ten thousand." At the end of the war, they were again destitute, as they had been when they came from Florida a generation earlier.

"Again they sought the protection of the government. They found new treaties; they complied with the conditions imposed upon them; they adopted their former slaves, and made them citizens of the country, with equal rights in the soil and annuities. The Negroes hold office and sit in the councils. They took hold of the question of reconstruction and settled it at once, practically, peaceably, and firmly. They have reopened their schools and churches; they have rebuilt their homes, and are fast becoming surrounded by stock, farms, and all the comforts of life."[9]

The new agent, Captain T. A. Baldwin, estimated the value of Seminole livestock at $184,000 (2,000 horses, 4,000 cattle, and 8,000 hogs), and the value of crops at $48,000, in the fall of 1869. Baldwin reported that the bounties for Seminole soldiers, loyal to the Union, had not been paid, after the lapse of four years; that the agency building was not in repair; and that the well at the agency was not fit for use. Baldwin also stated that the new mill, promised to the Seminoles in the treaty, had not been provided, and that the old mill was being used by E. J. Brown, an adopted citizen, "for his own personal benefit. In fact, I think that it is a swindle."

Baldwin was impressed by the division of the tribe into two bands, northern and southern, each with its head chief—John Chupco for the northern band and John Jumper for the southern band. "The head chief of the Northern band attends to and

---

[8] Grimes to Colyer, Mar. 9, 1869; Mar. 10, 1869, *ibid.* (1869), 79–80.
[9] Reynolds to Robinson, July 25, 1869, *ibid.* (1869), 416.

directs all executive business, and is acknowledged the principal chief of the nation, and is so acknowledged by this department."[10]

Nine Seminole delegates attended the intertribal council at Okmulgee in 1870, and on June 4, affixed their signatures to a resolution addressed to the President and Congress of the United States. The document was a simple, dignified, and earnest appeal in favor of honest adherence to treaty obligations. The Indian leaders presented the resolution, they declared, as a "Solemn duty, . . . in view of the perils" which were closing in upon their people. They were determined to maintain peace—within the tribes, with their neighbors, and with the United States. They had been placed where they were "through the policy, and by the power of the Government, for the benefit and convenience of the Whites, with assurances and guarantees of Ownership in the Soil, and protection from interference with their privilieges [sic] of self-government, and from intrusion upon them, as strong and solemn as language could make them. If the lapse of time, the increase of the White population, and the march of events have removed us from the wilderness in which we were then plunged unwillingly, and placed us in the way of our Neighbors, the fault is not ours, nor do they invalidate . . . obligations.

"We ask nothing from the people and authorities of the United States, aside from their respect and good fellowship, but what they have promised, *an observance of their treaties.*"

The Indians were determined to make progress in the learning and the arts of civilization. They had already proved that they were not opposed to advancement, by their accumulations of property, development of schools, and regularly organized governments. "We desire only not to be overwhelmed by the influences brought to bear upon us through the ambitions of Aspiring men, the cupidity of souless [sic] Corporations, and Combinations of whatever name, or the mistaken philanthropy of the uninformed. Our forms of government are those of our own choice, modeled after your own, and such as are adapted to our condition. Under them we have prospered when allowed Quiet and rest. The tenures by which we hold our lands is [sic]

[10] *Ibid.,* (1869), 419–21.

321

such as we prefer, and such as we believe to be for the best, for the majority of our people. . . . We wish no change . . . and confidently appeal to you to arrest all attempts to enforce them upon us. . . . We do not wish any material changes in our relations to the Government, but we do wish quiet and Security."

The Cherokee, Will Ross, signed the document as president of the council, and J. M. Perryman, Creek, signed as secretary. Sam Taylor, S. H. Benge, Joseph Duval, Frog Sixkiller, and George Ross appeared among the Cherokee delegates; Pleasant Porter, Chilly McIntosh, and James M. C. Smith were among the twelve signers from the Muskogee Nation; and the Seminole delegates were headed by John Jumper and James Factor.[11]

Two major causes for discontent arose from the treaty signed by Seminole leaders at Washington in 1866. In the first place, the land purchased from the Creeks, 200,000 acres along the western border of that tribe, was not large enough to permit "elbow room" between the Seminole bands. For their combination of hunting, stock-raising, and farming, the people needed a more extensive area. Their cattle, horses, and hogs ran on common range, and the fields, usually on bottom ground, were fenced. Accustomed to sparse settlement, the people felt crowded by the restrictions of their new boundaries.

The second grievance arose from the fact that an inaccurate survey by which their east line was first marked resulted in Seminole settlement and improvement of Creek lands. The Creek tribal government claimed authority over such Seminoles as were settled in the Creek Nation, and many disputes arose over the extent of each tribe's control. Secretary Columbus Delano of the Interior Department wrote to the Commissioner of Indian Affairs, "While the Creeks are not responsible for the inaccurate survey of the western boundary of their country, the Seminoles, certainly, should not be subjected to the experience of a jurisdiction to which they are averse, and within which it was not designed to place them.

"You will therefore be pleased to notify the Creeks that their

11 O. I. A.: Southern Superintendency. D 1344. 1870 (copy in the Oklahoma Indian Archives).

claim to exercise jurisdiction over the Seminoles is not approved by this Department."[12]

In the administration of Seminole justice, the chiefs, judges, and lighthorse police took pride in the speed with which cases were brought to a conclusion. Chief John Chupco was an advocate of rigid law enforcement, and the Seminole laws, when measured by those of Indian tribes longer associated with white population, were harsh. The Creeks were disturbed by the rapidity with which their citizens were tried, judged, and not infrequently punished, when they were charged with crime in the Seminole Nation. The punishment might be whipping, with a payment of damages in cases where Seminole citizens were injured. The death penalty was quite common.

The major part of Chupco's correspondence with the Creek chiefs was concerned with jurisdiction over Seminoles who lived within Creek boundaries, and with the surrender of prisoners claimed by Seminole officers. A letter of June 6, 1877, addressed to "Honorable Ward Coachman, Chief of the Creek Nation," is one of the general pattern.

"I again ask you to have one Es-pany Harjo arrested and handed over to the Seminole authorities to be dealt with according to law," ran Chupco's message.[13] "I am informed he was arrested by your light horse and turned loose. Please advise me if such is the case. There is no question in my mind but he

[12] Delano to Commissioner, Mar. 6, 1874, Oklahoma Indian Archives, Creek-Seminole Relations, Doc. 30599.

[13] Two grades of diplomatic correspondence came from Chupco's office. One grade, generally the work of his sister, was almost illiterate. The other was obviously the work of an educated person. The strength of "Long John" was in his energetic, practical, and incorruptible administration, not in his command of English. Long John himself, a fullblood Seminole, could neither read nor write. On October 29, 1879, his interpreter wrote for him to Chief Ward Coachman: "Yours of October 14th . . . has just been read and explained to me." On September 28, 1880, his letter written by his sister to Colonel P. B. Hunt, U. S. Indian agent, ran as follows: "Dear Sir: As the two ponies got lost, as I heard it when Sodiarko was going to started it back home   So I just asked them and it was hard because there going home & Day after tomorrow I am going called all Seminol and going to have council. As our Sisters and brethren came from west, one of sister wrote this letter for me. A white man wrote one first, and I thought maybe is not right, so I wrote this one also. So I will stop writing. This all I going. I remain most truly your." (Oklahoma Indian Archives, Kiowa Foreign Relations).

is guilty of murder. But the man shall have a fair trial and every advantage extended to him admissable by law, in order that he may clear himself, and should a trial prove him innocent I guarantee he shall go as free as the day he was born. Now if it is possible I desire you to have him arrested and handed over to me about the 2d Monday in July. Believing you to be a man desirous of seeing laws executed, I urge upon you the importance of securing this man. I wish that you would push up your judges that they may stir up their light horse to make the arrest. Should Espany Harjo resist them they will be justified in complying with your law in such cases."[14]

On July 4, Chupco called attention to the fact that the accused man had not been arrested and placed in Seminole official hands. He was to be tried for murder on the Pottawatomie line. "We have an agreement with the Pottawatomie Nation in relation to crimes committed by individuals of either nation and this comes under our laws to be tried here."

Apparently Espany Harjo escaped from the custody of Seminole officers on October 2, 1877; and on July 13, 1879, John Chupco wrote to Chief Ward Coachman: "I have to inform you that on the 11th of this month one Robert Brown killed one Espany Harjo and fled the country. Both of the above are Seminoles. I respectfully request that you notify your proper officers to be on the alert for said Brown, and if possible to arrest him. On receipt of notice that he is in custody, I will send officers for him. Brown is 19 years of age, understands and speaks English, rather fair complexion, prominent nose, hair cut short, weight about 145 lbs. When last seen was with Nathan Bruner of Creek Nation."

On October 18, 1878, the subject of Chupco's letter to Coachman was two citizens of the Muskogee Nation, Cummy and Jimmy. These two young men had no permanent address, but were "coming and going constantly, in the meantime horses were missed by various persons." On the morning of October 14, L. Coker, T. Coker, and A. Harper decided to question the two itinerants, and a "fight broke out." When it was over, Cummy

14 Oklahoma Indian Archives, Doc. 30607.

and Jimmy were dead, with pistol balls lodged in vital spots. "The clothing, saddles, &c. belonging to the deceased are safe. One black pony, however, is in possession of the light horsemen. The pony is branded † on the left thigh and is supposed to have been stolen."

On July 14, 1879, a long list of Creek citizens petitioned their chief, Ward Coachman, protesting his transfer of Creeks to the Seminole jurisdiction upon demand of John Chupco. Such extradition resulted in denial to citizens of the Muskogee Nation of their constitutional right of trial by jury, the petitioners declared. The Seminole jurisdiction extended only to "their own people;" Seminole officers had "no authority whatever over the citizens of the Muskogee Nation, whether charged with a crime committed in the section of the country where they are now permitted to reside—or in any other portion of our Nation."[15] This was obviously against Seminole control in the area belonging to the Creek Nation, where they resided as a result of an error in the survey; and was also a protest against the speedy and apparently casual decisions of Seminole courts, in regard to the guilt of Creek citizens who came before them. Among the signers of the petition were James McHenry, Pleasant Porter, Micco Harjo, Robert McKillop, Motee Tiger, David Hardridge, and many others.

Ward Coachman placed the petition before the Creek Council, and wrote to Chupco concerning the attitude of the Muskogee Nation on extradition. Chupco's answer was courteous, diplomatic, and firm. "Twice the treaties were ratified by the Five Nations," Long John suggested. "Each tribe by their Delegates & all for each other—agreed to live and act as civilized people. The demand of any chief has been complied with when asking for the person of any Indian who had committed a crime in one nation and fled to another."

In answer to an enquiry concerning Nero Jones, a Creek who had been tried, sentenced, and punished in the Seminole Nation, Chupco explained that Jones had been tried on a charge of inciting another party to commit a crime. The Seminole law

15 *Ibid.*, Doc. 30626.

provided a penalty of fifty lashes for the offense. "I myself questioned Nero. He admitted to me . . . that he wrote a letter to Joka one of our citizens asking and urging him to go and steal Charley Bowlegs' best horse. . . . It makes no difference who is a prisoner be he Creek or Seminole I do . . . all in my power to give him a fair trial. . . . I have no desire to punish an innocent party. The safety of our nation depends upon the rigid enforcement of the law."

In the body of Chupco's requests for the surrender of accused men to stand trial in the Seminole Nation, are short dissertations on the law and ethics of intertribal relations. He called the attention of Chief Samuel Checote of the Creeks to Secretary Columbus Delano's decision in 1874, and added: "Your expression that we are neighbors and brothers, and should each respect the rights of the other is appropriate, and I assure you, it is my earnest desire to cultivate a friendly feeling. . . . The matter of jurisdiction is a question of law in which I conceive you to err, but I do not infer that the adjudication of the same necessitates the severing of brotherly ties, or a disregard of each other's rights. I most respectfully request that you cause the arrest and surrender of the persons herein mentioned, at an early day."[16] In answer to a proposition from the Creek Chief Samuel Checote, Chupco wrote in 1880, "I am in full accord with the suggestion of Chief Bushyhead, and shall be happy to co-operate in measures calculated to frustrate Payne in his undertaking."[17]

Chief Checote complained of the punishment inflicted upon a Creek citizen, Mechiley, who was convicted of livestock theft in the Seminole Nation. John Chupco refused to use his power as chief executive for reduction of the sentence. "The schedule of stock stolen," he wrote, "was carefully and justly compiled, being fully substantiated by evidence adduced at the trial. The punishment inflicted was in strict accordance with the law, and done without malice."

[16] *Ibid.*, Doc. 30638.
[17] *Ibid.*, Doc. 30766. The reference is to David L. Payne, leader of the Boomers, and the attitude of Cherokee, Creek, and Seminole leaders in regard to stopping Payne's project—the settlement of a white colony on Indian land—is apparent from the contents of Chupco's letter.

On February 14, 1881, a Creek committee reported to Chief Samuel Checote its progress in settling the disputed land question along the Seminole eastern border. A solution had been reached which required only the approval of Congress. By its terms, the Creek Nation would cede to the United States 175,000 acres at ($1.00) one dollar per acre, "to be located by survey so as to include the district of our country now occupied by the Seminoles." Ward Coachman, Pleasant Porter, and David M. Hodge were the signers of the report.[18]

A message from Chief Samuel Checote to John Jumper of the Seminole Nation on March 31, 1881, mentions the recent death of John Chupco. An offer by Checote to take a hand in the settlement of Seminole cases in which Creeks were involved, brought a prompt, courteous, and dignified answer from the new acting chief, John Jumper, who was far from being a novice. "For me to give official recognition establishing your right to investigate any proceedings held in this Nation would be at variance with our principles as an independent Nation. I must therefore, decline your proposition."[19]

The contest for jurisdiction over the land which the Seminoles were in the process of purchasing, along their eastern border, continued during the brief term of Hulputta-Chc as principal chief, and after the election of John Jumper in July, 1882. Tenuje and his son Peter were wanted in the Creek Nation; and on request, the Seminole Lighthorse Police were ordered to arrest them. Peter Tenuje, resisting arrest, was shot and killed by a Seminole officer.

"I shall investigate the ownership of the gun found in the possession of Peter Tenuje," wrote Hulputta-Che. "It has been taken and is now in the possession of Calhoun who claimed to have bought it from J. Chisholm & upon which representation

18 Report of Committee, Feb. 14, 1881, Oklahoma Indian Archives–Seminole Relations, Doc. 30646. Negotiations had been going on since 1876, when S. A. Galpin was appointed special agent for the purpose by President Grant. John R. Moore, for the Creeks, was offering to accept $2.50 an acre for the land at that time. S. A. Galpin thought that $.50 an acre was a fair price. See *ibid.*, Doc. 30600.

19 Checote to Jumper, Jumper to Checote, Mar. 31, 1881, *ibid.*, Docs. 30647, 30648, 30649.

the L. Horse gave it into his possession." The Seminole Chief also wanted to know whether or not Tenuje, the father of Peter, was still at large. "I would like to hear from you about this. Unless I do, our officers will discharge their duty in the premises if Tenuje is found."

A month after his election as principal chief, John Jumper wrote to Chief Samuel Checote: "Dear Brother: Recently I received a note from one of our Seminoles which is the occasion of my writing to you. I learned . . . that some of your people are pursuing your offenders against your laws into our country, disarming one man and shooting around generally among the Seminoles. This is to respectfully ask you to have such disorderly proceedings stopped; and if any offenders . . . escape into the Seminole Nation . . . I will do what I can to have them turned over to your authority. The Seminoles are not informed about your troubles and some of them might resist and make the troubles worse."[20]

John Jumper's letters to Chief Checote and Chief J. M. Perryman were filled with requests for arrests and surrender of fugitives by Creek officers. Horse stealing was perhaps the commonest charge. Cotcha Lusta (Black Tiger) was accused of stealing a saddle; Wilsey, with killing cattle—"and left them lying near his place;" Jim Grayson, Cato, Mechaley, Harker, John Tecumseh, and Charles Roberts, with theft of horses; George Doyle, for the murder of Fus Miccoche; and Bennie Walker, "to answer charges of murder."

Jumper also wrote a letter of advice to Chief J. M. Perryman. "As you know, your country joins ours and the young men living along the line fall out sometimes and accuse each other of all sorts of things to get the Deputy Marshalls to arrest them, or your, or our light horse to do so. Please instruct your Judge or Light Horse Captain to look into a thing good before acting on it."[21]

The *Atoka Vindicator*, on April 3, 1875, before John Jumper

[20] Hulputta-Che to Checote, July 16, 1881; Oct. 17, 1881; Oct. 26, 1881; Nov. 10, 1881; Jumper to Checote, Aug. 17, 1882, *ibid.*, Docs. 30653; 30658; 30660; 30677.

[21] *Ibid.*, Docs. 30679, 30680, 30684, 30685, 30686, 30687, 30688.

had come back into public office during his later years, published a letter from Dr. G. J. Johnson of St. Louis, Missouri, in which an estimate of the Seminole chief was attempted. "John Jumper is a noble specimen of an Indian man, a Christian and a Baptist Minister," the letter ran. He was further described as a fullblood Seminole, born in Florida about 1820. Physically, he was large—six feet four in height and 255 pounds. He was baptized by John Bemo and became an active member of the Seminole Presbyterian Church; but during the war he found himself associated principally with men of the Baptist denomination, and he joined their organization. After serving for ten years following the war, as leader of the Confederate Seminoles, he resigned the office of chief to devote his full time to preaching. Following the death of Long John Chupco in 1881, and a brief term of office by Hulputta-Che, Jumper became principal chief of his nation.

By 1887, John F. Brown had become chief executive of the Seminole Nation. On May 25, 1887, Chief J. M. Perryman requested Brown to arrest and turn over to Creek officers three colored citizens of the Muskogee Nation—John Sango, Tom Barnett, and Israel Charles—for crimes committed east of the Seminole border.

During 1893 the Seminole second chief, Hulputta Micco, sent most of the requests for extradition. On June 28, his interpreter wrote from Fort Smith, Arkansas, asking Judge Timiye Curnell of the Coweta District to surrender George Menacks to answer a Seminole charge of murder.[22] On January 6, 1894, Hulputta Micco addressed a letter to "Hon. Elick McIntosh," requesting the surrender of Tippie Canard and another Creek (name unknown). "They came in our Nation and violated our laws," Hulputta stated. "They came up here and stold [sic] 2 horses. . . . One of the horses is a roach Main [sic] you will have Horse and man both turned over   If they have the Horse as yet. this men was seen passing Wewoka with the Horses   the roach

[22] George Menacks was charged with the murder of Fus Miccoche. The name of the Coweta District Judge is spelled "Temiye Kernells" in the Creek Roll (*ibid.*, Doc. 30701).

main Horse has a little white in forehead not entirely white but kinder roan trusting you will accept thanks in advance, your friend, Hulputta, 2d chief."

"P. S. they lives near the High Springs."

Chief Perryman of the Creeks wrote from Tulsa to Judge Alexander McIntosh in March, 1894, that Benny Walker had been arrested but had shot one of the guards on the way to the Seminole Nation and escaped. "Now I have just received a letter from Char Che Hutke stating that this young man is disturbing the peace of the people & trouble may arise from it. This man is accused by the Seminole authorities for the crime of murder, as I have no doubt you have his name on your court records I would advise that you have him arrested and turn him over to the Seminole National authorities." It seemed that trouble arose in any community where Benny took up his residence; and neighboring Indians were very happy to surrender such persons as Benny to the Seminoles.[23]

[23] Hulputta to McIntosh, Jan. 6, 1894; Perryman to McIntosh, Mar. 19, 1894, Oklahoma Indian Archives. Doc. 30710.

CHAPTER 20

Transition
to United States Citizenship

"This country is made up of a class of cold-hearted land gobblers
who've left all thoughts of fair dealing behind."

CRAIN

LAST OF THE SEMINOLE principal chiefs before Oklahoma statehood was John F. Brown. Until the year of his death, 1881, "Long John" Chupco had been recognized by United States officers as chief of the Seminole Nation, with John Jumper, nephew of Chief Jumper of Florida, the head man of the Confederate faction. During the last four years of Chupco's administration, Jumper had been in retirement from public office, and had devoted his full time to the pastoral duties of his church at Sasakwa; but in 1882 he was signing his official letters as the principal chief of the Seminole Nation after Hulputta-Che had held the office a single year.

John F. Brown was a new-model chief for the Seminole Nation in 1885. Chupco had been illiterate, though shrewd, experienced in tribal leadership, and possessed of a keen intellect. Hulputta also was illiterate, and John Jumper needed a great deal of help in the mechanics of writing his official letters. Chief Brown, on the other hand, was accustomed to business correspondence, and had been serving in official capacities for his tribe since the Washington Conference in 1866, when he aided his father-in-law, John Jumper, in negotiations for the Confederate Seminoles.

His father, Dr. John F. Brown, was a Scottish-American whose first connection with the Seminole tribe was his employment as a surgeon on May 1, 1837, by the United States Disbursing Agent at Fort Brooke, Florida.[1] Dr. Brown accompanied a party of Seminoles to the West and married a fullblood Seminole girl of the Tiger Clan, Lucy Redbird. He settled at Fort Gibson and served as government physician for the Seminoles who were encamped in the vicinity. His sons, John F. and Andrew J., were born in the Cherokee Nation, and also his daughter, Alice, who was born at Park Hill on September 10, 1852. The children attended several of the Cherokee schools, and the records show that one of Alice Brown's teachers at Fort Gibson was Carrie Bushyhead, the sister of Chief Dennis Bushyhead of the Cherokee Nation.

After the Civil War, Dr. Brown's family moved to Greenhead Prairie near the village of Wanette, where a number of Seminole Indians had settled. The tribe was about to be removed again, this time to a restricted area with its western limit some twenty miles east of Greenhead Prairie. The Brown family lived in the old Agency building, not many miles from the ranch homes of the Chisholm brothers, Jesse and Bill. Jennie Chisholm became a close friend of Alice Brown.[2]

In the summer of 1867 a cholera epidemic in the Wanette vicinity gave the frontier doctor more cases than he could attend. He was going at all hours, and overwork was the immediate cause of his death. His son, John F. Brown, Jr., took charge of the family and moved to Wewoka, which became the capital of the new Seminole Nation. Alice attended Reverend Ross Ramsey's school north of Wewoka. As young John F. Brown was developing his business interests—principally merchandising and cotton ginning at Sasakwa and Wewoka, Alice also followed a career of her own. In 1874, she was married to George Davis, a white man. Ten children were born to the family, four boys and

---

[1] O. I. A.: Seminoles—Emigration. National Archives. Quarterly Statement of persons employed in removal and subsistence of the Seminoles at Ft. Brooke, 2d Quarter, 1837. Dr. Brown appears on the list of employees as surgeon at $150.00 per month.

[2] Jennie Chisholm (Davis) is buried in the Little Indian Church Yard near Wewoka, and Bill Chisholm is buried on the Bagwell Farm, across the Canadian River south of Asher. Jesse Chisholm's grave is farther west, beyond the Chisholm Trail.

six girls. The husband died and Alice Davis carried on her trading post at Arbeka, in the northeastern part of the Seminole Nation, near the North Canadian River.

The choice of John F. Brown as principal chief was a natural development. He had done a great deal of official work for John Jumper, John Chupco, and Hulputta-Che over a period of twenty years. The people had confidence in him, and once he had taken over the duties of chief, his fitness for the office was obvious.

In the summer of 1892, Chief John F. Brown was taking steps toward a better understanding with the Creek Nation in regard to territorial jurisdiction. In July, 1892, Indian Agent Leo E. Bennett informed Brown that the commissioner had ruled in favor of Creek jurisdiction in a disputed area along the border. The exact location of the strip was not stated in Bennett's letter—probably could not be stated, for lack of an accurate survey and clear boundary markers. On August 5, Commissioner T. J. Morgan wrote to Leo Bennett that Brown had asked for a survey to determine "whether the 375,000 acres heretofore purchased of the Creeks, if properly surveyed, does not in fact include the 25,000 acres in dispute." The Seminole Chief must have made a strong case, for Morgan added this instruction to the Agent: "Pending the consideration of this request and until further orders, the instructions of July 11, 1892 are withdrawn, and if you have communicated them you will so notify the parties of interest."[3]

The Dawes Commission, authorized by Congress on March 3, 1893, to take steps toward dissolution of the Five Civilized Tribes, required the better part of four years to determine its method for the great change. Members of the Commission—Henry L. Dawes of Massachusetts, Meredith H. Kidd of Indiana, and Archibald S. McKennon of Arkansas—organized in Washington for their work, then came to Indian Territory and met the tribal leaders to determine their attitude toward change. The Seminoles did not send representatives to the intertribal council called by the Commission, but the Seminoles were in full agreement with the other tribes whose representatives voted not to

[3] Oklahoma Indian Archives. Docs. 30697, 30698, 30699.

333

negotiate with respect to giving up their status as separate governmental units.

The attitude of the Seminoles is shown by a series of resolutions passed by the council on April 23, 1897, and approved by Chief John F. Brown. No allotments to individuals would be accepted, unless an additional quantity of land, other than that covered by their present improvements, be secured to the Nation; no territorial organization would be accepted by the Seminoles, "but ample time be given for statehood, say 25 years"; no further railroad charters without consent in advance by the council; acts of the Seminole Council not to be "subjected to change or supervision by the President of the United States"; and a United States court to be established at Wewoka.[4]

Congress, in the meantime, had moved rapidly toward establishing practical control over all the Indian nations. The Dawes Commission was reorganized in 1895, with two added members. Later, the Commission was authorized to make tribal rolls for the purpose of alloting lands in severalty. A survey of the Indian lands was ordered, and money was appropriated for the job. Tribal courts were ordered to cease functioning after January 1, 1898, and all cases, both civil and criminal, were to be tried before United States courts. No act of the Indian councils was to be valid without approval of the President of the United States.

Revolutionary changes were taking place along the western border of the Seminole country. After the great run for Oklahoma homesteads on April 22, 1889, by which the unassigned lands, formerly the property of Creeks and Seminoles, were occupied by white population, the Indian residents of Little River Valley were surrounded by new and threatening conditions. The peril was not tangible, like the invasion of a hostile army, but it was present and was recognized vaguely by many fullblood Indians who could not speak the language of the new neighbors, nor grasp the hidden sources of their laws and customs. Some of the Indian leaders were well aware of the dangers lurking in bottled beverages that could be bought in the new towns, and some of the Indian families maintained an attitude

[4] Oklahoma Indian Archives. Seminole Miscellaneous Documents. 39510–F.

Voting for principal chief of the Seminoles. Probably photographed in 1901, when the contest was between Hulputta Mico and John F. Brown. Voters for each candidate lined up on opposite sides of the street in Wewoka, Oklahoma.

Florida Seminoles at Chestnut Billy's Indian Camp, Tamiami
Trail, in the Everglades.

of distrust toward all white men, whether they sold whiskey stealthily, or hardware openly, visited sick people with their little medicine bags, or preached sermons in open-air tabernacles. Between the Seminole and Creek Indians and the homesteaders of newly settled Oklahoma Territory west of them lived bands of Sac and Fox, Iowa, Shawnee, Pottawatomie, and Kickapoo Indians. Some of these native Americans had settled on Creek lands between the Canadian and its north fork before the Civil War; but most of them had been brought from Kansas or elsewhere as a part of the government's policy of removing the Indians to land of the Five Civilized Tribes. The number of these resettled Indians who had accepted allotments of land in severalty after the passage of the Dawes Act in 1887 was about 2,700; and there were about 400 Kickapoos who refused at first to give up their tribal holdings.[5]

On September 22, 1891, the area between Oklahoma Territory and the Seminole-Creek lands east of it, with the exception of the Kickapoo holdings, was opened to white settlement. After the Indian allotments were made, more than 5,500 claims were available in this run for homes, and nearly all of them were occupied on the day of the opening. Townsites were reserved by the government at Chandler and Tecumseh, and little settlements quickly grew up around stores at various other points in the settled area. Along the Seminole border, some of these communities were peculiarly sinister in character.

People who came into Oklahoma in the races for homes were generally peaceable, law-respecting citizens, intent upon building farm homes for their families, or upon establishing retail stores, law offices, or some other legitimate enterprise in one of the rapidly growing towns. But whiskey sales to the Indians, in violation to federal law, could be made to yield big profits. It was this illicit trade that characterized the border towns—Keokuck Falls, on the North Canadian; Earlsboro, Maud, and Violet Springs, at intervals along the Seminole western boundary. Some of the lawless men who engaged in the Indian liquor trade had friends and relatives who also made their livings by means not

[5] Roy Gittinger, *The Formation of the State of Oklahoma*, 151, 197–98.

approved in the federal or the territorial statutes. Horse thieves had a tendency to congregate in this area, and the whiskey stores were sometimes used as hiding places for bandits from distant places, as well as local thugs.

With variations in minor details, the border between Oklahoma Territory and the Seminole Nation, from 1891 to 1907, was a reproduction of many another American frontier region. In Florida and Georgia, and all the region between the Atlantic coast and the Indian Territory in the West, white settlers swarming about the lands occupied by native Americans had coveted their soil; and during the period of waiting for an opportunity to take it, had found many ways to harvest a profit from the uneducated Indians.

On December 30, 1897, the murder of a white woman near the western Seminole border touched off a series of events which are reminiscent of the Florida provincial frontier, one hundred years earlier. Julius Laird left his wife and two sons, aged four and eight, and the baby a few weeks old, at their house on a Seminole lease three miles east of the Oklahoma line. He had bought a farm about five miles away, in Pottawatomie County, and was engaged in hauling furniture to the new place. He expected to be away from home during the afternoon and night, and to drive back the next day, after doing some work at his new place.[6] Apparently Julius Laird had left his wife and children alone at the house on other occasions, and felt no apprehension in leaving them, since the country was quiet, and Thomas McGeisey, the Seminole from whom he leased the land, lived only a mile away. McGeisey held office in the Seminole Nation as superintendent of schools, and had just been appointed as a delegate to visit Washington on tribal business. With him lived his grown son, Lincoln McGeisey.

The details of Mrs. Laird's murder were told later by her little boy, Frank. Two Indians came to the house, and on the pretense of trying to borrow a saddle looked about until they

[6] Geraldine Smith, "The Mont Ballard Case" (unpublished M. A. thesis, University of Oklahoma, 1957), 1–2; Commissioner of Indian Affairs, *Annual Report* (1898), 96–99; *Report* (1899), 130.

were sure that the woman and children were alone. They broke into the house, and when she attempted to protect herself with a rifle, they smashed her skull with the gun, raped her, and left her dead body lying in the yard. The children were unable to move their mother into the house, and during the night hogs came out of the timber, attracted by the smell of fresh blood, and ate part of her flesh. The next morning, little Frank Laird walked to the Post Office at Maud, carrying the baby, and told the gruesome story. Julius Laird was notified of his wife's death, and he came back to his house, accompanied by several friends.

The men from Pottawatomie County began the formation of a posse to hunt down the murderers. Their method was to ride along all the roads near the border and to take every Indian they found to the Laird house, for possible identification of the guilty persons by the boy, Frank Laird. Thomas McGeisey came, at Laird's request, and remained from noon on December 31 until late in the evening. The armed men from Oklahoma Territory who were arresting young Indians brought in twenty boys, about dark, and Lincoln McGeisey was one of the number. Frank Laird was given a good opportunity to see each of the persons in custody; and after they had been questioned for about two hours, they were released and told to go home. Young Mc-Geisey and some of the others went to Prusack Harjo's settlement, four or five miles south of Laird's.[7] Prusack Harjo was Lincoln McGeisey's grandfather.

From evidence that was brought out later at the trials of Oklahoma men in the Federal District Court on charges of criminal conspiracy and kidnapping, the mob's activities at Laird's house can be traced. The Seminole officers at Wewoka received no official notification from the men who were active in arresting and questioning Indians. When no positive identification could be obtained through Laird's children, the angry white men began a process of torturing each suspected person in the hope of obtaining a confession. On Sunday, January 2, Thomas Mc-

---

[7] *U. S. v. Mont Ballard,* 13. (Unpublished manuscript, transcript of testimony in the case of *U. S. v. Mont Ballard,* Kidnapping, No. 4786, U. S. Court, Northern District of Indian Territory, May term, 1899).

Geisey learned that his son had been arrested a second time, and recalled what Julius Laird had said to him early in the man hunt. "He said he would have to have revenge," McGeisey quoted later on the witness stand in the Federal Court at Muskogee. "If he didn't find the real murderers of his wife he would have to have revenge to kill two or three Indian boys."[8] Disturbed by the second arrest of his son, Lincoln, and faced with the necessity of beginning his official visit to Washington, McGeisey went to the United States Commissioner W. S. Fears at Wewoka, and told him that the young Indian was in danger of his life. The Commissioner at once made out a warrant for Lincoln McGeisey's arrest, and ordered Deputy Marshal Nelson Jones to bring him in. Jones assured Thomas McGeisey that his son would be in custody on the following day, and the father left for Washington. The next news that he had from the Seminole Nation, after he reached the national capital, contained the report that Lincoln McGeisey had been burned to death by the mob in Pottawatomie County.[9]

The steps that led to the burning are not matters of general agreement among the witnesses who were called in the conspiracy cases. The men at Laird's who had appointed themselves to investigate the murder, apprehend the criminals, judge as to their guilt, pass sentence upon them, and execute the sentence, gradually narrowed their suspected persons from twenty-four to seven. In spite of the fact that the eight-year-old Frank Laird did not identify any of the seven as the murderer of his mother, each of them was subjected to torture as a means of extorting from him a confession, and two of them, Lincoln McGeisey and Palmer Sampson, were burned at the stake after alleged confessions to the mob leaders.

Probably the accusers became more excited and angry as their technique for finding the murderers failed to get positive results. In short, the situation which civilized men try to prevent by the establishment of courts, guided by well accepted principles of justice, had arisen because the entire mob was acting

[8] U. S. v. Mont Ballard, 27.
[9] Geraldine Smith, "The Mont Ballard Case," 8, 9.

without legal restraints. The greatest blame rested upon the representative of the United States marshal's office, Nelson Jones, who was officially bound to prevent mob action, and who might have stopped it if he had served his warrant for Lincoln Mc-Geisey's arrest promptly.

The mob, varying in size from a dozen to several hundred, contained many men who were accepted by their neighbors as respected citizens. There was, however, a sprinkling of the criminal fringe; some of whom, apparently, were shadowy figures without legitimate occupations who spent their time mainly at one or another of the border whiskey "places," that specialized in illegal sales to the Seminole Indians. At least two ministers of the gospel, also, were identified by witnesses as being connected with the mob, and one of these men took a prominent part in the welcome of Mont Ballard to the Maud community when he returned from serving his penitentiary sentence in 1906.

Palmer Sampson was a fullblood Seminole who could not speak or understand English; perhaps the nod of his head, wrung from him by prolonged torture, was enough to constitute a confession of murder in the view of that aroused mob. For those who were motivated by strong racial hostility, the choice of Lincoln McGeisey as Sampson's accomplice in the crime was peculiarly fitting. Young McGeisey was the son of a Seminole tribal official; his execution would express with emphasis the vague hostility of the mob toward tribal government, common land-holding, annuity payments from the United States Treasury, and the effrontery of descent from stock that was not of European origin. Perhaps a nod from Palmer Sampson, barely conscious after his exposure to mob cruelty, was enough to implicate McGeisey.

It is inconceivable that little Frank Laird should have failed in an immediate identification of Lincoln McGeisey, if he had been one of the murderers. The son of the Indian from whom Laird leased his house was known to the family, and was regarded by them with confidence. Frank Laird, surrounded by friends and in the presence of his father, would not have hesitated to name the neighbor as one of the murderers, if he had been guilty.

As for the uneducated Sampson, evidence was brought to light by officers of the United States, investigating Seminole claims for damages from the mob activities, which proved conclusively that he was many miles away from the Laird home on the afternoon when Mrs. Laird was murdered. Henry L. Dawes, former United States senator, and chairman of the commission which guided the transition from tribal to individual land ownership among the Five Civilized Tribes, gave his view of the Indian burnings in these words:

"If the Seminoles had burned two white boys at the stake, the white inhabitants of Oklahoma would have exterminated the whole tribe within ten days. But when the white inhabitants of Oklahoma burn two young Indians, one of whom is known to be innocent and the guilt of the other greatly in doubt, the Indians remained quietly at home and appealed to the great father for protection and justice."[10]

W. F. Wells investigated damage claims for personal injuries of Seminole Indians at the hands of the mob. Twenty-four members of the tribe received payments that varied from $25, for those who were merely arrested and detained, to a sum over $5,000 to the heirs of the Indians who lost their lives. Each of four members of the Seminole Lighthorse Police force who were deprived of their liberty, but not mistreated in other respects, was paid $50. Sam Ela, George Kernell, George Harjo, and William Thlocco received additional damages for personal injuries. John Washington received $500 for severe personal injuries and an additional sum of $33 for property lost. His brother, Albert Washington, stated on the witness stand of the Federal District Court in Muskogee, that John died in January, 1899. The witness also stated that three members of the mob forced him to show them Palmer Sampson's house, by threats to kill him. For the burning to death of her son, Palmer Sampson, Mrs. Sukey Sampson was paid $5,000, and in addition the sum of $82.50 for property destroyed. Thomas McGeisey was paid $5,000 for the killing of his son, by burning; and property damages in the amount of

[10] Statute providing for Dawes Commission, *United States Statutes at Large,* 648; quoted by Geraldine Smith, from the *Indian Chieftain* (Vinita), Jan. 27, 1898.

$1,113.25, for the burning of the house where the Lairds had lived before the tragedies.

Sixty-nine persons were indicted for taking part in the mob activity which resulted in the burning of Lincoln McGeisey and Palmer Sampson. One of the number was Nelson M. Jones, United States deputy marshal, who was convicted in the District Court at Muskogee and sentenced to serve twenty-one years in the Missouri State Penitentiary.[11] Andrew J. Mathis was sentenced by Judge John R. Thomas to serve ten years in the penitentiary at Leavenworth, Kansas. Mont Ballard of Maud, Oklahoma served about seven years of a ten-year sentence at Leavenworth. George Bird Ivanhoe and Sam Pryor were also tried in the District Court at Muskogee, and sentenced to three-year terms of imprisonment. Sam Pryor, who was called the "Ranger" at Maud, began serving his time at Leavenworth but was transferred later to the Ohio State Penitentiary.

When Mont Ballard ended his term of imprisonment at Leavenworth, with time off for good behavior, he returned to his home at Maud and was received with honors by his fellow townsmen. One of the territorial newspapers which printed an account of the celebration gave him this glowing tribute: "No one present felt that he was assisting in extending a welcome to a criminal, but regarded him as a martyr who gave up his liberty in defense of American womanhood."[12]

Judge John R. Thomas, of Muskogee, who presided over four of the conspiracy trials in the Federal District Court, was among the men most responsible for obtaining justice in the Seminole burning cases. Chief John F. Brown of the Seminole Nation deserves great credit for his example of calm reliance upon legal remedies, and for his insistence upon the treaty rights of the Seminole people. There were other men who demonstrated that a century of contact between Europeans and American Indians had not been entirely devoid of results in creating tolerance, sympathy, and understanding between the races. Among the

[11] Geraldine Smith, "The Mont Ballard Case," 103. (From "Judgments and Sentences in Criminal Cases, U. S. Court, Northern Judicial Division," Book D, 385.)

[12] *Mangum Star*, May 17, 1906.

officials who showed some evidence of progress were the attorneys, Thomas F. McMechan, Bird S. McGuire, Roy Hoffman, Horace Speed, and Pliney L. Soper; Walter T. Fears, commissioner at Wewoka; W. F. Wells, who investigated the Seminole claims at Wewoka; W. A. Jones, commissioner of Indian affairs; and the secretary of the interior, Cornelius N. Bliss.

Perhaps the greatest progress was shown by the Indians themselves, who refused to be drawn into the desperate contest in retaliation. The fact that the real murderers of Mrs. Laird were not found, however, may indicate that no Seminole Indian was willing to give evidence in a case where members of his own tribe had already been sacrificed to satisfy the white man's demand for vengeance. It is quite possible, too, that the murderers of the white woman were not Seminoles, but members of some other tribe. As Chief John F. Brown of the Seminoles pointed out, "Our nation is a small one. . . . People are crossing it all the time. On the border where Oklahoma joins, there is a a long line of doggerel saloons patronized by the worst elements of the population."[13]

In 1895, the Choctaw, Oklahoma, and Gulf Railroad Company extended its lines through the Seminole Nation, connecting the McAlester coal mines with Oklahoma City and El Reno. Later, the Oklahoma City, Ada and Atoka road crossed the Seminole border at Maud, and was extended through Konawa in the southwestern corner of the nation, to Ada and Atoka. A branch of the St. Louis and San Francisco road, connecting Holdenville with Ada, also cut across the corner of the Seminole country, through the town of Sasakwa. In 1902, the Chicago, Rock Island and Pacific Railroad Company obtained possession of the Choctaw, Oklahoma and Gulf lines, which passed through Earlsboro near the western border of the Seminole Nation, connected it with Wewoka near the eastern border, and extended to Holdenville. Thus, before the end of tribal government and before the period of the automobile and hard surfaced roads as dominant factors in its transportation, the Seminole Nation had three railroads.

13 Quoted in *Guthrie Daily Leader*, Jan. 12, 1898.

Mekasukey Academy for boys was constructed at a cost of $65,000, near Little River at a point three miles southwest of Seminole townsite, in 1891. Emahaka was constructed two years later, and opened in 1894 as a boarding school for girls, on the border of the Seminole Nation, five miles south of Wewoka.[14] With the support of new legislation strengthening its authority, the commission headed by Senator Dawes quickly came to terms with the tribal governments of Indian Territory. The Atoka Agreement of April 23, 1897, with the Choctaw and Chickasaw tribes, was followed by the Seminole Agreement on December 16. The United State commissioners, in addition to Henry L. Dawes, were Tams Bixby, Archibald S. McKennon, Frank C. Armstrong, and Thomas B. Needles. For the Seminole Nation, Chief John F. Brown, Okchan Harjo, Wilburn Cully, K. N. Kinkehee, Thomas West, and Thomas Factor signed the document. The secretary of the Dawes Commission at this time was Allison L. Aylesworth.

All land belonging to the Seminole Nation was to be divided into three classes: First Class, to be appraised at $5 an acre; Second Class, at $2.50; and Third Class, at $1.25. Each member of the tribe was to be allowed to select his allotment so as to include his own improvements, and each was to have an equal share in value, "so far as may be, the fertility of the soil and location considered." Allotments were to be made under direction and supervision of the Dawes Commission, "in connection with a representative appointed by the tribal government." Provisions were included for mineral leases, and each allottee to receive one-half of the royalty payments, the other half to be paid to the tribal government for the purpose of equalizing the value of the allotments.[15]

---

[14] Readjustments were made for earlier mission schools, upon the completion of Mekasukey and Emahaka academies. The Sasakwa Female Academy, a Methodist school opened in 1884, was placed under the control of the Seminole Council in 1887, and consolidated with Emahaka in 1894. The teaching staff and many pupils of Reverend Ross Ramsey's mission north of Wewoka, were transferred to Nuyaka Mission, on Deep Fork in the Creek Nation during the same year.

[15] Commissioner of Indian Affairs, *Annual Report* (1898), 448–51; (1899), 197; (1900), 14, 28, 56, 85–86; (1902), 164; (1904), 231; (1905), Part I,

The provision of the agreement relative to the townsite of Wewoka, which involved the Seminoles in a controversy for more than fifty years, was as follows: "The townsite of Wewoka shall be controlled and disposed of according to the provisions of an act of the General Council of the Seminole Nation, approved April 23, 1897, relative thereto; and on extinguishment of the tribal government, deeds of conveyance shall issue to owners of lots as herein provided for allottees; and all lots remaining unsold at that time may be sold in such manner as may be prescribed by the Secretary of the Interior."

Land was reserved from the allotment—320 acres for each of the academies, Mekasukey and Emahaka; 80 acres for each of the eight district schools; one-half of an acre for each of 24 churches; and one acre in each township to be sold to the United States for non-citizen schools. For the protection of the Seminole citizens who were not competent to make business contracts in regard to their property, it was provided: "Each allottee shall designate one tract of forty acres, which shall by the terms of the deed, be made inalienable and non-taxable as a homestead in perpetuity."

The Dawes Commission reached an agreement with the Seminole representatives, that such "Loyal Seminole Claims" as were still unsettled should be submitted to the arbitration of the United States Senate. If the claims were sustained, they were to be paid within two years. The 250 claims varied from that of Toos-Harjo, $9,341, and Pascofa, $8,200, down to the claim of Sava-Chee, $280.[16]

By 1902, Seminole Indians and Negro freedmen had received allotments that totaled 346,861.75 acres. The seven appraisers had completed their work on November 1, 1899, and moved their camp into the Choctaw Nation, to aid in land classification there. The Seminole Roll had been completed on August 30, 1898, with 2,826 names listed. An additional agreement

---

516; Loren N. Brown, "The Dawes Commission," *Chronicles of Oklahoma*, Vol. IX (1931), 71–105; Charles F. Meserve, *The Dawes Commission and the Five Civilized Tribes;* Kappler, *Indian Affairs: Laws and Treaties*, I, 662–65.
16 Seminole Miscellaneous Documents, Doc. 39522-A.

between the commission and Seminole representatives, on October 7, 1899, had provided that children born to Seminole citizens up to and including the last day of December, 1899, should be added to the roll. It was also stipulated that when parents were the heirs of deceased minors, the property should first descend to the mother, or in the event she was not alive, "to brothers and sisters, and their heirs, instead of the father." The Seminole population, by 1905, was reported as 3,049—2,099 of Indian blood and 950 Negro freedmen.

The appraisement of land resulted in this classification:

First class	$5	(arbitrary value per acre)	24,055.89 acres	$120,279.45
Second class	2.50		248,837.48 acres	622,093.70
Third class	1.25		96,961.02 acres	121,201.28
		Total	369,854.39	863,574.43

In the allotments of 1898, acreage reserved for schools and churches, together with land for children born after the roll was made, amounted to 18,992.64 acres. An act of Congress on March 3, 1905, allotted 14,200 acres of this land, 40 acres to each of 355 children born after the first rolls; and 1,470 acres, 10 acres to each of 147 citizens who had received land, "not of standard value."[17]

Deeds were to be issued for the Seminole allotments after the extinguishment of tribal government on March 4, 1906. After that date, land might be alienated, excepting the forty acre homestead of each citizen. Non-citizens might lease Seminole lands for a period not longer than six years, subject to approval of the principal chief. When the legal restriction was lifted from sale of Seminole allotments, the work of exploitation began at once. A letter to the Secretary of the Interior gives the view of one observer at Earlsboro, on the border of the Seminole area.

"I write this explaining as near as possible the condition of things here in the Seminole Nation among the Freedmans and mix-bloods.

"It is a burning shame in the sight of God the way these

[17] Commissioner of Indian Affairs, *Annual Report* (1900), 28, 56; (1902), map, 164; (1905), Part I, 516.

345

people are being treated in this land-buying business. This country is made up of a class of coldhearted land gobblers who've left all thoughts of fair dealing behind and are here for no other purpose than to rob and cheat these ignorant people out of their homes, for a few baubles barely enough to cover notary fees, and the paper which the so-called deeds are written upon. Can nothing be done to stop this? . . . They are more to be petied [sic] than blamed. They are all uneducated. It is true they've had schools but the faculties were either of a class that was all for the money or they were uneducated themselves. . . . Second class lands are being sold from .26 cts. [sic] $3.00 to $10.00 per acre."[18]

In the Seminole election of 1901, John F. Brown was defeated for the office of principal chief by Hulputta Micco.[19] Grave accusations had been made against Chief Brown in regard to the handling of tribal funds—charges which could not be proved or disproved quickly, but which could become factors in the national elections. Apparently the Chief made no great effort to win the election, but simply rested his claim to the office upon his reputation for service over the years.

The charges against Chief Brown grew out of the activities of the Wewoka Townsite Commission, a body created by act of the Seminole Council, approved on April 23, 1897. This act authorized the commission to select a suitable tract, not exceeding 640 acres, for the establishment of a town to be known as Wewoka. The commissioners were made responsible for surveying and dividing the tract into lots, blocks, streets, and alleys, and were empowered to grant to any citizen who occupied a portion of the land selected, an interest in the town equivalent to "one-fourth the entire number of acres which they may occupy or claim." The Townsite Commission was further authorized to sell or lease town lots to Seminole citizens; provided that no transfer of title should be made, except upon the condition that

18 Crain to Hitchcock, May 5, 1906, Seminole Miscellaneous Documents, Doc. 39519-A.
19 Commissioner of Indian Affairs, *Annual Report* (1902), 164.

a building or other valuable improvement should be erected thereon within six months of the lease or purchase.

The Townsite Commission was required to pay over to the treasurer of the Seminole Nation once every six months the net proceeds of sales; and was authorized to appoint a city marshal, a city attorney, and police judge; and to organize a city government with elected officers when the population should reach two hundred. Authority was also granted to levy and collect taxes for improvements and the expenses of city government, but with the proviso that no taxes should be levied or collected during the existence of the Indian government. The commissioners were named in the act of the National Council by which the body was established: A. J. Brown, Thomas McGeisey, Thomas Factor, W. L. Joseph, and Dorsey Fife. The instrument was signed by Nuth Cup Harjo, president of the Seminole council, and by Thomas McGeisey, secretary. It was approved by Principal Chief John F. Brown.

Very few town lots were sold by the commissioners during the first three years, due to the restriction against purchases by non-citizens, and the provision requiring improvements within six months, by any person who might seek to gain title to property in Wewoka. On February 12, 1900, an offer was made by Chief John F. Brown, to purchase all the remaining lots for the sum of $12,000. The Townsite Commission accepted the offer, and the Seminole Council, in special session on April 18, 1900, "accepted and ratified" the contract. The Council further resolved that the sum of $12,000 obtained from the sale should be added to the next installment of annuity, payable per capita to the Seminoles.[20]

An act of July 25, 1900, provided for the employment of Captain A. S. McKennon, the Arkansas member of the Dawes Commission, as national attorney for the Seminole Nation for a term of five years, at an annual salary of $5,000. That Mr. McKennon was making, at least, some visible effort toward attempting to earn his salary is proved by various references to his activities

[20] Oklahoma Indian Archives, Seminole Laws (39350-C), 1–6, 7, 17.

in the documents of the Seminole Nation. A letter of Thomas Ryan, acting secretary of the interior, to the United States Indian Inspector in 1903, stated that the national attorney had raised the question of "wrongful transactions with the Seminole Indians by the First National Bank of Wewoka." The United States Attorney for the Western District of the Indian Territory decided that the facts did not warrant criminal proceedings against the bank "unless it can be shown that the property involved was taken and that the bank did not have a mortgage on such property, or that it was taken without the process of court." McKennon decided not to prosecute.[21]

In the spring of 1905, the United States Indian Inspector reported the death of Chief Hulputta Micco, and requested an opinion from the secretary of the interior as to determining the Chief's successor. Thomas Ryan, acting secretary, on the advice of the United States attorney general's office, stated that the safer plan would be to cause an election to be held. But the Seminoles, according to their custom when a chief died, selected his successor by action of the General Council. J. Blair Schoenfelt, U. S. Indian agent, reported this action on May 12, 1905, and sent the certificate of election, signed by Thomas Palmer, President of the Council, showing the election of John F. Brown as principal chief. The oath of office executed by the new chief was enclosed.[22]

Before the death of Hulputta Micco, an opinion of the United States attorney general's office was requested in regard to the legality of the Wewoka Townsite sale to John F. Brown. The opinion, ten typewritten pages by Frank L. Campbell, assistant attorney general, was sharply critical. "Certainly the advisability of such a sale to the Principal Chief and his brother, a member and secretary of the townsite commission, might be questioned," Mr. Campbell wrote. "The Commissioner of Indian Affairs expresses the opinion that the townsite commissioners exceeded their authority in attempting to sell as a single tract all the lots

21 Oklahoma Indian Archives. Seminole Miscellaneous Documents (39518-F).
22 *Ibid.* (39518-J).

in the townsite to the principal chief and that the execution of the deed was entirely beyond their powers, and that no title was conveyed thereby."[23]

The Commissioner stated that the Seminole officials were in sympathy with the Browns, and "there is no official complaint for the Department to take action on." The Assistant Attorney General, however, supported his opinion by a complete analysis of the sale. The act of the Seminole Council, he asserted, by which the contract for sale of the town lots was approved, "in effect read the tribal law into the agreement. That tribal law became to all intents and purposes a part of the compact between the Seminole Nation and the United States, so that the latter had and has the right to demand that the town lots shall be disposed of only as therein provided." Specifically, Mr. Campbell argued, the townsite commissioners had no authority to waive the requirement that the purchasers of lots should construct buildings or other improvements within six months after obtaining title. In the sale to John F. Brown, the requirement was waived, which in effect rendered his title invalid.

"The fact that the principal chief and his brother, member and secretary of the commission, became the purchasers, is, of itself, sufficient to raise a doubt of the *bona fides* of the transaction, even if it did not, of itself, render the sale invalid. Persons holding fiduciary relations, such as A. J. Brown did in respect to the sale of this townsite, are not as a rule permitted to become purchasers at their own sale." Mr. Campbell ended his analysis by proposing an act authorizing the secretary of the interior to adjust the rights of the purchasers, and to recover unsold lots for the Seminole Nation. Ethan Allen Hitchcock, secretary of the interior, approved the Campbell report.[24]

In 1903 the Seminole Council investigated the sale of the townsite to John F. Brown, and on December 17 passed an act ratifying the same. The act was signed by Okkoske Miller, chairman of the Council, and attested by Thomas S. McGeisey,

[23] *Ibid.* (39518-H, "Opinion of Frank L. Campbell," Mar. 19, 1904).
[24] *Ibid.* (39518-H, "Opinion of Frank L. Campbell," Mar. 19, 1904).

clerk; and by A. S. McKennon and James H. Johnson. It was approved by Hulputta Micco, principal chief, with his signature indicated by an (X) mark.

Congress, on March 3, 1905, ratified and confirmed this action of the Seminole Council. The United States Court of Claims, in *Seminole Nation* v. *United States,* held that fraud had not been proven in the sale of the Wewoka Townsite.[25] But the case was to be argued and re-argued many times before a decision was reached by the Indian Claims Commission in 1952. Many persons seemed to be pleased that a man of Indian blood had at last been able to recognize the possibilities of the unearned increment; and to consider that the choice lay between a handsome profit for the beloved chief of the Seminoles, John F. Brown and his associates, and the same or a larger profit for a noncitizen corporation.

[25] *Seminole Nation* v. *United States,* 92 C. Cls. 210.

CHAPTER 21

The Seminoles
as United States Citizens

*"Conferring citizenship upon an allottee Indian is not inconsistent
with retaining control over his disposition of lands allotted to him."*

JUSTICE CHARLES EVANS HUGHES

A N ACT PASSED by the United States Congress on March
3, 1901, made all the members of the Five Civilized Tribes
citizens of the United States. At that time the population of the
Seminole Nation was approximately 3,000, of whom slightly
over two-thirds were Indians and slightly under one-third, Negro
freedmen.[1] The Dawes Commission ended its activities on July
1, 1905, leaving in the hands of the Interior Department the
work of closing out tribal business. Under the terms of the Seminole agreement, tribal government was to be abolished by March
4, 1906; but Congress continued the functions of some tribal
officers—governor, secretary, and interpreter, beyond that time.
The secretary of the interior took over the management of tribal
funds and property, and tribal documents were turned over to
the Indian commissioner at Muskogee.[2]

The changes inaugurated by the Dawes Commission were
not put into effect without opposition from the Seminoles. A
"letter of remonstrance" was sent to the Secretary of the Interior
on January 24, 1898. The grievances stated were on the subject
of Seminole money. "There was the sum of $191,294.20 which
never entered the treasuries of the United States or the Semi-

[1] 31 *Stat.*, 1447; Department of the Interior, *Annual Report* (1905), Part I,
516. The Secretary reported Seminole population as follows: Indian, 2,099;
Freedmen, 950; total, 3,049.
[2] 34 *Stat.*, 137.

noles," the protest ran. When the citizens attempted to trace the sum, they were informed, they stated, that a lawyer had taken that amount for his services in negotiating the Seminole agreement. "The name of the lawyer was never mentioned and no receipt of the alleged deal was ever shown."

A second grievance was the matter of Wewoka town lots. "We ask that you take note of the townsite laws of Wewoka and see to whom only these laws are beneficial and whom they oppress." The absence for any provision in the Seminole laws for an auditor, these citizens thought, would justify placing Seminole finances and management of the schools under the secretary of the interior.[3]

Perhaps much of the criticism concerning Seminole finances was inspired by partisan politics within the tribe; for much of it centered upon Governor John F. Brown and his brother, the tribal treasurer. After investigating the system used for paying Seminole money to tribal citizens, an inspector for the Department of Justice reported in 1905: "It is not too much to say that, in view of the ignorance of these Indians, this system of credit is dishonest. It should be condemned because it keeps these Indians in a constant state of poverty."

Eleven years later a special investigator for the Interior Department, William L. Bowie, made similar charges and recommended abolition of the remaining functions of the Seminole tribal government. "In my opinion, Governor Brown has shown in his transactions with John Smith and Lizzie Yahola, that he has little regard for the welfare and protection of the Indians in general, and it is unfortunate that he occupies a position which enables him by reason of the confidence placed in him as such official to impose upon them."[4]

During the years immediately following completion of the Dawes Commission's work, the great contest in the counties of the former Indian Territory was over the question of restricted Indian property. Terms of the Seminole agreement of 1897 carried restrictions for the sale of surplus property only until

[3] Quoted in *Seminole Nation* v. *United States*, 316 U. S. 305.
[4] *Ibid.*, 306.

the termination of tribal government. Section 19 of the Five Tribes Act of April 26, 1906, provided: "No full-blood Indian of the Choctaw, Chickasaw, Cherokee, Creek, or Seminole tribes shall have power to alienate, sell, dispose of, or encumber in any manner any of the lands allotted to him for a period of twenty-five years from and after the passage and approval of this act, unless such restriction shall, prior to the expiration of said period, be removed by act of Congress." Seminole mixed bloods and freedmen, in 1907, were free to sell their surplus land; but the restricted lands, forty acres in extent, were "inalienable and nontaxable as a homestead in perpetuity."[5]

The early years of statehood in Oklahoma were filled with the struggle for removal of legal restrictions designed to protect new Indian citizens. The land hunger of white men, intensified by the gradual disclosure of mineral wealth, created a steady pressure against inalienable property. Congress held the key to removal of the restrictions, and Oklahoma members of both houses, representing a public that was eager to gain control of Indian holdings, took the lead in clamoring for the change. At a meeting of the Trans-Mississippi Commercial Congress held in Muskogee a short time after Governor Charles N. Haskell took office as first governor of the state of Oklahoma, leaders for restriction and against restriction of Indian lands had a chance to express their opinions. Robert L. Owen, the choice of Oklahoma voters for a seat in the United States Senate, as he was about to be officially named to the office by the legislature of the new state, attended the Commercial Congress as a speaker, and was in the audience, along with many other notable figures, as Chief Moty Tiger of the Creeks gave the conservative view of many thoughtful Indians.[6]

Referring directly to the Cherokee statesman, Robert L. Owen, Chief Tiger said: "The polished and educated man with

[5] 30 *Stat.*, 567; Kappler, I, 662 (55 Cong., 2 sess., chap. 542. "An act to ratify the agreement between the Dawes Commission and the Seminole Nation of Indians," Approved, July 1, 1898); III, 169–81 (59 Cong., 1 sess. "An act to provide for the final disposition of the affairs of the Five Civilized Tribes. . . ." Approved, Apr. 26, 1906).

[6] Angie Debo, *And Still the Waters Run*, 171.

Indian blood in his veins who advocates the removal of restrictions from the lands of my ignorant people, apart from governmental regulations, is only reaching for gold to ease his itching palms, and our posterity will only remember him for his avarice and his treachery. . . . It is a fight between greed and conscience with this great government as arbiter, and upon the decision rests for generations, the fate of these untutored children of nature." Owen answered the challenge, in an eloquent plea for freedom of the Indians to make their own contracts, as other citizens were able to do. It was the federal official putting "words into the mouths" of Indian Territory men, who was back of the design to restrict sales of Indian property, Owen declared.[7]

Chief Moty Tiger's opinion was vitally important to all Indians of the Five Tribes. It was of peculiar consequence to the Seminoles, and the wisdom of his insistence upon inalienable lands must have been apparent to many members of the tribe, during the years that followed when petroleum began to appear as a factor in Seminole economy.

The history of the Seminoles rapidly merged with that of the other citizens of the United States who lived in the same area. The process was hastened by three revolutionary changes in Seminole society: replacement of tribal law by federal and state law; the new responsibility for land held in severalty; and the discovery of vast quantities of mineral wealth in the Seminole country. These changes covered the period from the agreement with the Dawes Commission in 1897, to large-scale oil production a generation later. Like the previous transformations in Seminole life, some of the new conditions were imposed upon a reluctant people who were not ready for them, at a speed which left them in a state of confusion. Again, as on many previous occasions, the Indian's ignorance of property and business provided white men with opportunities for easy profits. But intermarriage with whites had changed the character of the population considerably, and some of the persons who obtained great wealth from Seminole oil were of mixed Indian blood. There were full-blood Seminoles, also, who received substantial royal-

[7] *Ibid.*, 172–74.

ties from oil and gas; and some of the Seminole freedmen became wealthy by the quick process of rich mineral discoveries. Perhaps more than any other appointed officer, John D. Benedict, superintendent of school in the Indian Territory, was responsible for the cynical references to "Uncle Joe Cannon's Province." Appointed to the office of superintendent in 1899, his attitude toward the schools already in operation was highly critical from the start. When it was known that his appointment under President McKinley was due to the influence of Representative Joseph G. Cannon of Illinois, which was also Benedict's home state, the term "carpetbagger" seemed to many of the Arkansas and Texas men in the Indian Territory a natural designation for the superintendent of schools. As his patron's power in Congress increased, Superintendent Benedict's influence became strongly partisan. Cannon was chosen speaker of the House in 1903, an office he was to hold for eight years, and Benedict's stature in the Republican party grew. He devoted a great deal of attention to his private business ventures, and sent scathing reports on educational and other conditions in the Indian Territory.[8]

With the passage of the Five Tribes Act in 1906, the control of tribal revenues passed to the Department of the Interior. Both Ethan Allen Hitchcock and his successor, James R. Garfield, understood this to mean that Indian education and schools for white children in the Indian Territory were automatically transferred to the secretary of the interior. Superintendent Benedict was instructed to take charge of the tribal schools.

The Superintendent was not thoroughly prepared for the task. He could see weaknesses in the educational attainment of Indian children and adults, but he lacked the imagination to grasp the full extent of the progress made by many of them in the brief period of their contact with books and the process of learning. He found teachers and superintendents in the boarding schools, with many years of service behind them, whom he regarded as incompetent by the standards of teachers in the schools

[8] Department of the Interior, *Annual Report* (1899), I, 86–92; Debo, *And Still the Waters Run*, 66.

of his own state. He wanted to change the character of the courses offered, with emphasis upon cooking, sewing, and housekeeping for girls; farming, carpentry, and the care of livestock for boys. He wanted to eliminate nepotism and tribal politics from the choice of teachers and administrators in the schools.

On September 22, 1906, Superintendent Benedict sent to the Commissioner of Indian Affairs a list of the fifteen Seminole day schools that were in operation with the length of term and the teacher's salary for each school:[9]

Brown	8 mo.	$45	$360	Seminole Union	8 mo.	$45	$360
Carr	7 mo.	40	280	Tate	8 mo.	45	360
Good Hope	8 mo.	40	320	Tidmore	8 mo.	40	320
Jarvis Ranch	7 mo.	45	315	Tidmore (colored)	8 mo.	40	320
Macedonia	8 mo.	40	320	Wewoka	8 mo.	50	400
Rocky Point	8 mo.	40	320	Wewoka (colored)	8 mo.	45	360
Red Mound	8 mo.	45	360	Wolf	8 mo.	40	320
Sasakwa	8 mo.	45	360				

On November 3, 1906, Mr. Benedict indicated some difficulty in regard to gaining control of Emahaka Academy. "I have the honor to report that on Sept. 22 I received a telegram from your office . . . stating that Amhaka [sic] Academy, Seminole Nation, could not be administered in accordance with the contract which Mrs. Davis made with the Seminole authorities, and notified me that she was removed as such superintendent."

The Commissioner of Indian Affairs ordered Benedict to make a contract with Walter Ferguson or some other suitable person, for the management of Emahaka. The Indian Inspector, however, advised Mr. Benedict to take no further action until attorneys for the Seminole Nation had filed briefs with the secretary of the interior. In the meantime, Mrs. Davis remained in charge of Emahaka. Benedict's letter to the Commissioner explains his difficulties:[10]

"When I first heard that the Seminole authorities had contracted with Mrs. Davis, I instructed Supervisor Walter Folwell to go to Wewoka and explain to Mrs. Davis and to the Seminole authorities that their schools would have to be conducted in

9 Seminole Miscellaneous Documents, Okla. State Archives. Doc. 39538-A.
10 Ibid., Doc. 39538-B.

accordance with the new rules and regulations of the Secretary of the Interior. I told him to inform them that we would employ and pay all the employees needed, and that Mrs. Davis might submit a bid for furnishing board, fuel, lights, and stationery. Supervisor Folwell carried out these instructions but instead of attempting to comply with them, Mrs. Davis went ahead and appointed all of her employees, several of whom were members of her own family, fixed their salaries herself, and went ahead with her school totally regardless of all instructions we had given her. Instead of submitting a bid in accordance with our instructions, she submitted a statement, showing the cost of provisions which she estimated would be needed, and adding thereto her own salary at $1,000 per year, making a total of $11,500 which she said would be required to maintain her school during the year, in addition to salaries of all employees.

"Upon receipt of the telegram above mentioned, I notified the attorneys of the Seminole Nation that the Honorable Secretary of the Interior had ordered Mrs. Davis removed and asked them to turn over the school to me without further trouble. They wrote me that they declined to do this, and that they were preparing a statement to be forwarded to Washington. Since that time I have heard nothing further from the matter, but I am informed that Mrs. Davis is going ahead with her school, conducting it in accordance with Seminole customs, buying whatever provisions she thinks are needed and charging the same to the Seminole Nation. I respectfully ask for further instructions in this matter."

Chief John F. Brown wrote to the Indian inspector, J. G. Wright, that he had advised Mrs. Davis to surrender the Emahaka School to Superintendent Benedict. Willmott and Wilhoit, Wewoka attorneys, also informed the United States Indian Inspector that the Seminole authorities would turn over the property of Emahaka Academy "in a peaceable manner." Mrs. Davis surrendered her office under protest, claiming all rights under her contract with the Seminole Nation, "or the Government acting for it."

Later, Superintendent Benedict submitted an itemized statement of Mrs. Davis' claim for service at Emahaka, and added his opinion that the bill was "correct and just and the various persons therein mentioned should be paid out of Seminole school funds and I recommend that this be done." He added, however, that Mrs. Davis had purchased provisions and "quite a good deal of furniture from the Wewoka Trading Company, a company owned and controlled largely by Seminole officials."[11]

Litigation concerning Seminole lands depended, in some cases, upon the tribal laws under which contracts were made. The Wewoka townsite cases depended upon such enactments, and a translation was undertaken by G. T. Grayson as a basis for determining the legality of the original townsite sale. By a resolution of the National Council, approved by Principal Chief Hulputta Micco on January 28, 1903, the principles set down in the Grayson code were held to be the laws of the Seminole Nation. In some respects, the instrument resembles the written constitution of the Creek Nation; but many of the provisions were clearly of temporary effect only, and not a part of the tribe's basic custom.

The National Council was composed of two houses. The Upper House contained three members from each of the fourteen towns. The town chief was one of the three; the other two were chosen by the town council to serve for four years. The Lower House also contained forty-two members, three from each town, elected by the voters for one-year terms. Fourteen delegates— one from each town—served as a nominating convention, to present two names to the voters for the office of principal chief. A majority of the votes gave the election to one of the candidates; and in the event of a tie, the Council was empowered to fill the office. The Chief held office for four years.

The captain, lieutenant, and eight privates of the Seminole Lighthorse Police were respected officials. The law contained specific provisions protecting the officer in the performance of his duties. "If, notwithstanding the orderly deportment of the officer, the person to be arrested shall make resistance by force of arms, then the arresting officer shall have the right to kill

[11] *Ibid.*, Doc. 39543.

him."[12] It was the strongly executive character of the Seminole law, and the trend toward prompt enforcement, that was resented by Creeks and other Indians who sometimes came in contact with the Lighthorse Police of the little nation; the effectiveness of the police was discouraging to criminals, too.

Slander was punishable by whipping—twenty-five lashes for the first offense, fifty for the second, and one hundred for the third. The penalty for theft also was whipping; but when the series of additional lashes reached 150 for repeated thefts, the culprit was entitled to a new start, with fifty lashes for his next offense.

Safeguards were provided in the law for the protection of Seminole women against hasty, ill-considered marriage. In this the ancient Indian custom of consultation with the woman's relatives was recognized, with a specific provision for filing with the Seminole Council objections to a proposed union. Sections four to seven of the article were intended for protection against interference with an established marriage relation. "After persons have married . . . and entered into the duties of housekeeping, if another person shall in any way attempt to effect their separation, the person so interfering shall be carefully advised to desist. . . . If such person shall continue to annoy the family . . . and it shall appear . . . that the annoyance . . . was wrong and unjust, he shall suffer a penalty of twenty-five lashes." A fine of $50, and additional lashes were provided for repetition of the offense.

"Dancing after the music of a violin" was prohibited from Christmas through New Year's day, with a penalty of $5 for violation of the law. An interesting attempt to adjust Indians to the white man's concept of title to personal property was set forth in the 26th article, or chapter. "Persons who swap, trade or exchange property, and thereafter become dissatisfied, may undo the trade by paying the sum of five dollars. It was provided, however, that an exchange after ten days "shall stand undisturbed by either party."

In the case of a credit transaction, the contract to pay was enforceable. If, however, the purchaser was unable to pay on

[12] Laws of the Seminole Nation, Oklahoma Archives.

the date agreed upon, it was provided that "the Chiefs shall name a further date when payment shall be made." Seizure of property, on the order of the chiefs, was the final resort for recovery on a debt.

There were provisions against grazing the cattle of noncitizens upon tribal lands, and provisions governing the use of allotted lands by noncitizens. Drovers were required to pay ten cents per day for each head of livestock held on Seminole range for one day, and to pay damages for any crops destroyed or consumed. There were restrictions against the cutting of pecan trees, and against card-playing at public meetings. Regulations for keeping forest fires under control were implemented by the provision that all citizens should help. In corn-planting time, "everybody of sound health including children" was bound to assist in fire-fighting.

The penalty for adultery was 80 lashes; for disturbing the peace at a public gathering, 25 lashes or a fine of $25; for transporting whiskey into the Seminole Nation, a fine of $10. If any person attempted to prevent a legal arrest by a member of the Lighthorse Police, and conducted himself in such manner as to endanger the life of the arresting officer, "then the officer whose life is thus threatened shall kill him." Also, a person who attempted to break away with stolen livestock in his possession, was liable to be killed, through "the rightful operation of the law of the land."[13]

In some instances the United States Supreme Court, with a measure of detachment from immediate political consequences, was able to protect the Indians of the Five Tribes from the greed of Oklahoma settlers who were eager to obtain quick returns from the lifting of all property restrictions. In 1912 the Court ruled that Congress had constitutional power to extend the restrictions upon the alienation of allotted Indian lands.[14] Justice Charles Evans Hughes, in the Court's opinion, stated principles of basic importance. "The placing of restrictions upon the right

13 *Ibid.*, Chapters L, LIII, LVII.
14 *Tiger* v. *Western Investment Co.*, 221 U. S. 286; *Heckman* v. *United States,* April 1, 1912, 224 U. S. 413.

of alienation was an essential part of the plan of individual allotment of tribal lands. . . . Conferring citizenship upon an allottee
Indian is not inconsistent with retaining control over his disposition of lands allotted to him. . . . During the continuance of . . .
guardianship, the right and duty of the Nation to enforce by all
appropriate means the restrictions designed for the security of
the Indians cannot be gainsaid."[15] In a Seminole freedman's case,
the Court answered important questions concerning the property of Negro allottees. Conveyances of homestead lands were
held to be invalid; conveyances of surplus lands made by minor
freedmen were also held invalid, as were conveyances by adult
freedmen before the act of Congress, April 21, 1904, which removed restrictions on the surplus land of white and Negro
allottees. Conveyances of freedmen adults after that date were
held valid.[16]

Only a small amount of tribal lands remained to the Seminoles after individual allotment; but per caput payments were
made from their trust funds, between 1909 and 1920. Each
member received $734, in seven separate payments. The dis-
covery of oil on tribal ground at Mekasukey after that date
resulted in the payment of $35 to each Seminole.[17]

Oil production on a large scale began in the Seminole country
during the years 1923 and 1924. By 1926 the boom was going
at full speed and several new pools were opened. By January 1,
1930, the Wewoka Pool had produced 29,500,000 barrels, the
Cromwell Pool, 38,400,000 barrels, and the Earlsboro Pool,
lying in Pottawatomie and Seminole counties, 94,000,000 barrels.
The Bowlegs Pool, three miles south of Seminole, produced over
73,000,000 barrels up to January 1, 1930, and the Seminole City
Pool, 86,400,000. Other great pools, such as the South Little
River, with 57,000,000, and the Searight with 21,800,000 barrels,
together with smaller producers—the Konawa, Mission, Sasakwa,
and others, brought the total of Seminole County above 500,-
000,000 barrels by January 1, 1930. The rate of production rose

---

[15] *Ibid.*, 436–37.
[16] *Goat* v. *United States*, 224 U. S. 458 (Apr. 29, 1912).
[17] Debo, *And Still the Waters Run*, 266.

and fell, with a general decline over the following decades—in part the result of the Oklahoma oil conservation policy. Accumulative production for the greater Seminole area in 1950 was above 1,000,000,000 barrels. Every township in the county at that time had contributed to the total oil production of Seminole County.[18]

On April 22, 1952, the Indian Claims Commission handed down a decision in the Wewoka Townsite case.[19] The Seminole Nation claimed an original loss of $500,000 on the sale of Wewoka town lots to Chief John F. Brown, and interest on that sum from March 3, 1905, to date. The total claim amounted to $1,600,000. In reviewing the origin of the case, the Claims Commission began with the Seminole Treaty of August 7, 1856, when the Oklahoma branch of the tribe became a self-governing nation, and followed with the treaty at Washington on March 21, 1866, which affirmed the right of self-government in the Seminole Nation.

The act of the Seminole Council, April 23, 1897, provided for the establishment of the Wewoka Townsite Commission, and defined its duties. The Townsite Commission selected 640 acres of Seminole land and caused it to be surveyed and platted into 4,234 lots. The tract was acquired from A. J. Brown, a member of the Townsite Commission. Under an act of the Seminole Council, A. J. Brown was entitled to one-fourth interest in the townsite. The two brothers, A. J. Brown and Governor John F. Brown, in January, 1900, held 1,102 lots.

The Dawes Agreement, December 16, 1897, in addition to providing for allotment of Seminole tribal lands in severalty, contained a clause which gave full control of the Wewoka Townsite to the National Council. Under the terms set up by the Townsite Commission for the purchase of lots, very few were sold or leased during a period of nearly three years, up to February, 1900. One condition was that no lots should be sold to non-

18 William F. Tanner, The Geology of Seminole County, 136; The Daily Oklahoman, April 18, 1932; The Times Democrat (Wewoka), March 17, 1930; R. R. Brandenthaler, and others, Engineering Study of the Seminole Area, 5.

19 Indian Claims Commission, Docket No. 53 (transcript from the office of Commissioner Edgar E. Witt, in Oklahoma State Library).

citizens until the termination of the tribal government. Another was that title should not be given to any person, "except upon condition that a building or buildings, or other valuable improvements" should be erected thereon within a period of six months from the date of lease or purchase; "Provided that said Commissioners may in their discretion, for good cause shown, extend the time for completion of such buildings or improvements."

In February, 1900, Chief John F. Brown submitted a bid of $12,000 for all the unsold lots in Wewoka, which was accepted by the Townsite Commission and approved by the Seminole Council on April 18, 1900. By the terms of the conveyance, the six-months time limit for buildings on the lots was extended indefinitely. The sum obtained for the unsold portion of the town lots was added to the next installment of the Seminole annuity, and distributed per capita to the members of the tribe, by the treasurer of the Seminole Nation, A. J. Brown.

After investigating the transaction, in every phase, the Seminole Council passed an act ratifying the same, signed by Okkoske Miller, chairman, and approved by Principal Chief Hulputta Micco, who fixed his signature to the document by use of the cross (X) mark.[20] Thomas S. McGeisey, clerk, and A. S. McKennon, Seminole national attorney, attested the signatures.

On March 3, 1905, Congress ratified and confirmed the action of the Seminole Council; hence the later claims of the Indian Nation against the United States extended back to that date. It was charged the two brothers, John F. and A. J. Brown, conveyed their town lot titles to the Wewoka Realty and Trust Company, which was principally owned or controlled by them. The two tribal officials were accused of taking advantage of their position in the Seminole Nation to "conclude an unconscionable agreement of the Nation in acquiring practically all the lots of the Wewoka Townsite."

The opinion of the Indian Claims Commission in 1952 was written by Louis J. O'Marr, associate commissioner. In effect,

[20] Hulputta Micco (Alligator King) had defeated John F. Brown for the chief executive post in 1901, which he held until his death in 1905, when John F. Brown again became principal chief.

it held as follows: The Claims Commission was not bound to pass upon the charges against the principal chief, John F. Bown, and the treasurer of the Seminole Nation, A. J. Brown. In that connection, however, Commissioner O'Marr called attention to the decision of the United States Court of Claims, that "it had not been proven that the sale of the Wewoka Townsite was fraudulent."[21]

The question before the Claims Commission was limited to the liability of the United States. The Seminole Nation was self-governing. "Its autonomy was complete and supreme in the handling of its internal affairs and property, except where surrendered to the Federal Government or . . . limited by the policies of, or action by said government."

The United States was doing what the Seminole Nation desired, at every step in the disposition of the townsite. "The United States did not appropriate the land for its own benefit, nor did it appropriate it for the benefit of another, unless the sale to Brown was fraudulent and the United States was a party to the fraud." Evidence of fraud consisted only of the inadequacy of price, the fact that the purchaser was principal chief, and that Congress was cognizant of these facts. "This falls short of sufficient proof of fraud." The opinion added that the "Dawes Agreement excepted the Wewoka townsite from the allotment provisions of that contract and assured the Seminole Nation of its independence in handling and control of its capital."

Congress and the President in all of this matter, simply "did what the Indians wished and without doubt they acted for what they conceived to be the best interests of the tribe, in fact, that could have been the only motive prompting the action. . . . We conclude, therefore, that the petition must be dismissed, and it is so ordered."[22]

It will be recalled that the Dawes Commission gave as one of its reasons for advocating the termination of tribal governments, the unequal distribution of property use between two classes, the uneducated majority and the wealthy, well-informed

[21] *Seminole Nation v. United States,* 92 C. Cls. 210.
[22] Indian Claims Commission, Docket No. 53, Transcript.

handful of tribal leaders. Probably Henry L. Dawes and his associates had regarded the promise of independence in handling the townsite a small price to pay for tribal support on their broad program. Both of the parties to the agreement, the commissioners and the Seminole officials, were driving a bargain with astute politicians.

Bibliography

I. MANUSCRIPTS AND TRANSCRIPTS

The manuscript materials examined by the author in the preparation of this study are chiefly the official correspondence and other records of the Seminoles in the National Archives; two manuscript collections in the Library of Congress; the Seminole Documents in the Archives of the Oklahoma Historical Society; two letters in the Florida State Library at Tallahassee; the Seminole Records in the Newberry Library at Chicago; the Stand Watie Letters in the Phillips Collection, University of Oklahoma Library; and the Union Agency Files, Office of the Superintendent of the Five Civilized Tribes, Muskogee, Oklahoma. The Library of the Oklahoma Historical Society at Oklahoma City contains seven large volumes of the Foreman Transcripts, copied in the Office of Indian Affairs, National Archives. The Oklahoma State Library at Oklahoma City contains a transcript of the testimony in the case *United States* v. *Mont Ballard,* No. 4786, United States Court, Northern District of the Indian Territory, May term, 1899; and a transcript from the Office of the Indian Claims Commission, Docket No. 53, determined in 1952.

A. National Archives

Office of Indian Affairs: Apalachicolas (Emigration), 1834–38.
Letter Book Twelve, Apalachicolas, 1834.
Rector's Letter Book.
Seminole (Emigration), 1832–48.
Seminole. Letters Received and Letters Sent, 1832–60.
Seminole (Miscellaneous File).
Seminole (Special File).
Special File No. 87 (Claims of the Loyal Seminoles).

Adjutant General's Office: Old Files Division.
Old Records Division, War Department Files.
B. Library of Congress, Manuscript Division
The A. J. Donelson Papers, Volume VI.
The Andrew Ellicott Papers, Volume II (Correspondence).
C. The Oklahoma Historical Society, Archives
Autobiography of Mary Ann Lilley.
Indian-Pioneer Papers. Foreman Collection. 112 volumes.
Photostatic copy of letter, Capt. John C. Casey to Jefferson Davis,
secretary of war. Tampa Bay, July 29, 1855.
Seminole Documents. 12 volumes (includes Seminole Laws).
Seminole Miscellaneous Papers—Schools Miscellaneous.
D. The Oklahoma Historical Society, Library
Foreman Transcripts, Office of Indian Affairs. 7 volumes.
Reminiscences of J. S. Murrow. Dictated by Rev. J. S. Murrow, writ-
ten by Czarina C. Conlan, in 1924. Transcript.
Rev. J. S. Murrow, Diary, 1867-69. Transcript.
Photostatic copies of *The Indian Advocate,* Louisville, Ky., March,
1849; Oct., 1852; Jan., 1854.
E. Union Agency Files, Office of the Superintendent of the Five
Civilized Tribes. Papers relating to Seminole affairs. Muskogee, Okla-
homa.
F. University of Oklahoma Library, Archives
Transcript of the testimony, *United States* v. *Mont Ballard,* 1899.
G. University of Oklahoma Library, Phillips Collection
E. C. Boudinot Letters. 3 volumes.
Indian-Pioneers Papers. 116 volumes.
Oklahoma and Indian Territory Bar Association, Proceedings of the
Third Annual Meeting.
Stand Watie Letters. 11 volumes.
H. Oklahoma State Library, Oklahoma City
Transcript from the Office of the Indian Claims Commission, Docket
No. 53.
I. Florida State Library, Tallahassee
O. T. Hammond Letter, May, 1838; O. T. Hammond Letter, Nov. 4,
1838. This Library contains an excellent collection of rare books
on early Seminole History.
J. Newberry Library, Chicago
Seminole Records (Manuscript record of subscribers to support of
war against the Seminoles, 1836).

II. FEDERAL AND STATE DOCUMENTS

American State Papers. 38 volumes. Washington, 1832-61.

Board of Indian Commissioners. Report for 1876.

Bureau of American Ethnology: Capron, Louis. "The Medicine Bundles of the Florida Seminole and the Green Corn Dance," *Bulletin No. 151,* 155–210.

Swanton, John R. "Early History of the Creek Indians and their Neighbors," *Bulletin No. 73,* Washington, 1922.

——. "Social Organization and Social Usages of Indians of the Creek Confederacy," *Forty-Second Annual Report,* Washington, 1928.

——. "Religious Beliefs and Medical Practices of the Creek Indians," *Forty-Second Annual Report,* Washington, 1928.

——. "Aboriginal Culture of the Southeast," *Forty-Second Annual Report,* Washington, 1928.

——. "The Indians of Southeastern United States," *Bulletin No. 137,* Washington, 1946.

Commissioner of the Five Civilized Tribes, Second Annual Report, 1895; *Fifth Annual Report,* 1898; *Eighth Annual Report,* 1901; *Fourteenth Annual Report,* 1907.

Compilation of all the Treaties Between the United States and the Indian Tribes. Washington, 1873.

Kappler, Charles J., ed. *Indian Affairs: Laws and Treaties.* 3 vols. Washington, 1892–1913.

Malloy, William M., ed. *Treaties, Conventions, International Acts, Protocols, and Agreements Between the United States and Other Powers, 1776–1902.* 2 vols., Washington, 1910.

Oklahoma Geological Survey, Bulletin 74. William F. Tanner, *The Geology of Seminole County.* Norman, 1956.

Opinions of the Attorneys General of the United States. IX–XII (ed. by J. Hubley Ashton); XIII–XIX (ed. by A. J. Bentley). Washington, 1852–.

Statutes at Large of the United States, 1789–1956. 70 volumes.

United States Congress. Documents and Records:

> *Annals of Congress. Debates and Proceedings in the Congress of the United States, 1789–1824.* 42 volumes. Washington, 1834–56.
>
> *Congressional Debates. Register of Debates in Congress, 1825–37.* 29 volumes. Washington, 1825–37.
>
> *Congressional Globe, Containing Debates and Proceedings, 1833–73.* 109 volumes. Washington, 1834–73.
>
> *Congressional Record, Containing Debates and Proceedings, 1873–.*

Volumes cited: *Annals,* 12 Cong., 2 sess.

> 15 Cong., 1 sess., Vol. VII, No. 173; Vol. XXXIII.
>
> *Register of Debates,* 21 Cong., 1 sess., XII.
>
> *Globe,* 24 Cong., 1 sess., *House Ex. Doc. No. 271.*

25 Cong., 2 sess., *House Ex. Doc. No. 327.*
25 Cong., 3 sess., *Ex. Doc. No. 225.*
26 Cong., 1 sess., *Senate Doc. No. 278.*
Record, 59 Cong., 2 sess., *Senate Report No. 5012,* I.
United States Bureau of the Census, *Eleventh-Seventeenth Reports.* Washington, 1890–1953.
United States War Department. *The War of the Rebellion: a Compilation of the Official Records of the Union and Confederate Armies.* 130 volumes. Washington, 1880–1901.

III. OTHER COLLECTIONS OF DOCUMENTS, LETTERS, AND PAPERS

Adams, John Quincy. *Memoirs of John Quincy Adams* (ed. by Charles Francis Adams), 12 vols. Philadelphia, 1874–77.
Bassett, John Spencer, ed. *The Correspondence of Andrew Jackson.* 7 vols. Washington, 1924–33.
Field Museum of Natural History, *Anthropological Series.* XXXIII, Chicago, 1941.
  Spoehr, Alexander, "Camp, Clan, and Kin among the Cow Creek Seminoles of Florida," Vol. XXXIII, No. 1.
  ——, "Kinship System of the Seminole," Vol. XXXIII, No. 2.
  ——, "The Florida Seminole Camp," Vol. XXXIII, No. 3.
Morse, Jedidiah. *Report to the Secretary of War on Indian Affairs.* New Haven, 1822.
Richardson, James D., ed. *A Compilation of the Messages and Papers of the Presidents. 1789–1897.* 10 vols. Washington, 1896–99.
Smithsonian Miscellaneous Collections, Vol. XCV, No. 16. Gabriel Díaz Vara Calderón, "17th Century Letter." Translated by Lucy L. Wenhold. Washington, 1937.

IV. MISCELLANEOUS SOURCES

Baum, Laura Edna. "Agriculture Among the Five Civilized Tribes." Unpublished M.A. thesis, University of Oklahoma, 1940.
Brandenthaler, R. R., and others. *Engineering Study of the Seminole Area.* Department of Commerce, United States Bureau of Mines, May 30, 1930. Washington, 1930.
Carter, Bruce. "A History of Seminole County." Unpublished M.A. thesis, University of Oklahoma, 1932.
Chaney, Margaret A. "A Tribal History of the Seminole Indians." Unpublished M.A. thesis, University of Oklahoma, 1928.
Dictionary of American Biography (ed. by Allen Johnson, Dumas Malone, and H. E. Starr). 21 volumes. New York, 1928–36.
Dictionary of American History (ed. by James Truslow Adams). 6 vols. New York, 1940.

Gallagher, Art, Jr. "A Survey of the Seminole Freedmen." Unpublished M.A. thesis, University of Oklahoma, 1951.
Hopkins, J. C. "James G. Blunt and the Civil War." Unpublished M.A. thesis, University of Oklahoma, 1952.
Moore, Audis Neumeyer. "The Social and Economic Status of the Seminole Indians." Unpublished M.A. thesis, University of Oklahoma, 1939.
Oklahoma Red Book, II. (Sequoyah Convention, 623–74).
Payne, Charles Raymond. "The Seminole War of 1817–18." Unpublished M.A. thesis, University of Oklahoma, 1938.
Sameth, Sigmund. "Creek Negroes: a Study of Race Relations." Unpublished M.A. thesis, University of Oklahoma, 1940.
Smith, Geraldine M. "The Mont Ballard Case." Unpublished M.A. thesis, University of Oklahoma, 1957.
Tanner, William F. The Geology of Seminole County. Oklahoma Geological Survey, Bulletin 74. Norman, 1956.
Wells, W. Alva. "Osceola and the Second Seminole War." Unpublished M.A. thesis, University of Oklahoma, 1936.

V. CASES CITED

Fletcher v. Peck, 6 Cranch 87.
Goat v. United States, 224 U. S. 458.
Heckman v. United States, 224 U. S. 413.
Seminole Nation v. United States 92 C. Cls. 210; 316 U. S. 305.
Tiger v. Western Investment Co., 221 U. S. 286.
United States v. Mont Ballard, Federal Court, Northern District, Ind. Ter., 1899.

VI. NEWSPAPERS

The Cherokee Advocate. The Newspaper Division of the Oklahoma Historical Society contains a limited number of issues. Mar. 20, 1845; May 1, 1845; July 30, 1846; Oct. 29, 1846; Dec. 9, 1847; June 5, 1848; Dec. 9, 1849.
The Daily Chieftain, Vinita, I. T., June 8, 1899.
The Daily Oklahoman, April 12, 1898; June 6, 1899; Feb. 18, 1912; April 18, 1932.
The Daily Oklahoma State Capital, Guthrie, Jan. 10, 11, 13, 1898.
The Guthrie Daily Leader, Jan. 12, 1898.
The Indian Advocate. The Library of the Oklahoma Historical Society contains photostatic copies of a limited number of issues.
The Indian Chieftain, Vinita, Jan. 27, 1898.
The Lexington Leader, Feb. 25, 1899.
The Mangum Star, May 17, 1906.

The Maud Democrat, May 12, 1906.
The Muskogee Phoenix, Dec. 24, 1907; Jan. 18, 21, 30, 1908; Feb. 27, 1908; Apr. 18, 1908.
The Muskogee Times-Democrat, July 25, 27, 1908; Dec. 11, 1911.
Niles' Weekly Register, Baltimore, 1811–49 (Published at Washington, 1837–39; at Philadelphia, 1848–49), 76 vols.
The Sapulpa Evening Democrat, Feb. 7, 17; April 26, 1913.
The Seminole Capital, Wewoka, May 26, 1904; July 30, 1908.
The Seminole County News, April 17, 1908.
The Times-Democrat, Wewoka, Mar. 17, 1930.
The Wewoka Daily Democrat, May 30, 1928.
The Wewoka Democrat, June 22, 1916; June 30, 1917.

VII. ARTICLES IN PERIODICALS

Abel, Annie Heloise. "Indian Consolidation West of the Mississippi," *Report of the American Historical Association* for 1906, Vol. I, 393 ff.
Boyd, Mark F. and Latorre, José Navarro. "Spanish Interest in British Florida, and in the Progress of the American Revolution," *Florida Historical Quarterly,* Vol. XXXII, No. 2 (Oct., 1953), 92–130.
Boyd, Mark F. "The Arrival of DeSoto's Expedition in Florida," *Florida Historical Quarterly,* Vol. XIV (July, 1935).
———. "Asi-Yahola or Osceola," *Florida Historical Quarterly,* Vol. XXXIII, No. 1 and No. 4 (Jan. and April, 1955).
Brevard, Carolyn Mays. "Richard Keith Call," *Florida Historical Quarterly,* Vol. I, No. 1 and No. 3 (July and October, 1908), 7–18.
Brown, Loren N. "The Dawes Commission," *Chronicles of Oklahoma,* Vol. IX (1931), 71–105.
Debo, Angie. "The Site of the Battleground of Round Mountain," *Chronicles of Oklahoma,* Vol. XXVII, No. 2 (1949), 187–206.
Dodd, Dorothy. "Horse Racing in Middle Florida," *Apalachee,* Tallahassee Historical Society, 1948–50 (double volume), 2–29.
Foreman, Grant. "Report of the Cherokee Deputation in Florida," *Chronicles of Oklahoma,* Vol. IX (1931), 423–38.
Meserve, John Bartlett. "Chief Opothle Yahola," *Chronicles of Oklahoma,* Vol. IX (1931), 446–50.
Monroe, Kirk. "A Forgotten Remnant," *Century Magazine,* March, 1890.
Morrison, William B. "Father Murrow," *My Oklahoma,* Jan., 1928.
Porter, Kenneth W. "Wild Cat's Death and Burial," *Chronicles of Oklahoma,* Vol. XXI (1943), 41–43.
———. "The Hawkins Negroes go to Mexico," *Chronicles of Oklahoma,* Vol. XXIV (1946).

——. "The Seminole in Mexico, 1850–61," *Chronicles of Oklahoma*, Vol. XIX (1951).

——. "The Early Life of Luis Pacheco, nee Fatio," *The Negro History Bulletin*, Vol. VII (1943), 52.

——. "Seminole Flight from Fort Marion," *Florida Historical Quarterly*, Vol. XXII, 113–33.

——. "The Episode of Osceola's Wife, Fact or Fiction?" *Florida Historical Quarterly*, Vol. XXVI (1947), 92.

Robertson, James A., translator. "Letter of DeSoto to the Secular Cabildo of Santiago de Cuba," *Florida Historical Quarterly*, Vol. XVII (1938).

Russell, Orpha. "Ekvn-hvlwuce, Site of Oklahoma's First Civil War Battle," *Chronicles of Oklahoma*, Vol. XXIX (1951), 401–407.

Swanton, John R. "The Landing Place of DeSoto," *Florida Historical Quarterly*, Vol. XVII (January, 1938).

VIII. BOOKS

Abel, Annie Heloise. *The American Indian as a Slaveholder and Secessionist*. Cleveland, 1915.

——. *The American Indian as a Participant in the Civil War*. Cleveland, 1919.

——. *The American Indian Under Reconstruction*. Cleveland, 1925.

Adair, James. *The History of the American Indians*. London, 1775. A later edition was published at Johnson City, Tenn., in 1930.

Adams, Henry. *History of the United States*. 3 vols. N. Y., 1903.

Babcock, Kendrick C. *The Rise of American Nationality*. N. Y., 1906.

Bartram, William. *The Travels of William Bartram*. Mark Van Doren, ed. N. Y., 1928.

Bassett, John Spencer. *The Federalist System, 1789–1801*. N. Y., 1906.

Benton, Thomas Hart. *Thirty Years' View*. 2 vols. N. Y., 1854.

Bolton, Herbert E. and Marshall, Thomas M. *The Colonization of North America*. N. Y., 1922.

Boyd, Mark F., Smith, Hale G., and Griffin, John W. *Here Once They Stood*. Gainesville, The University of Florida Press, 1951.

Boyd, Mark F. *Florida Aflame* (Reprinted from *Florida Historical Quarterly*, Vol. XXX, No. 1, 1951).

Brevard, Carolyn Mays. *A History of Florida*. 2 vols. Deland, Florida, 1924.

Brinton, D. G. *Notes on the Florida Peninsula*. Phila., 1859.

——. *The American Race*. Phila., 1901.

Britton, Wiley. *The Civil War on the Border*. 2 vols. N. Y., 1890–99.

——. *The Union Indian Brigade in the Civil War*. Kansas City, 1922.

Brownell, Albert E. *The Indian Races of North and South America*. N. Y., 1856.

Campbell, John. *Campbell's Abstract of Seminole Indian Census Cards and Index.* Muskogee, Oklahoma, 1915.

Campbell, Richard L. *Historical Sketches of Colonial Florida.* Cleveland, 1892.

Catlin, George. *The North American Indians.* 2 vols. London, 1876; Edinburgh, 1926.

Channing, Edward. *The Jeffersonian System.* N. Y., 1906.

Chatelain, Verne E. *The Defense of Spanish Florida, 1565–1763.* Washington, 1941.

Chitwood, Oliver H. *A History of Colonial America.* N. Y. and London, 1931.

Cleaves, Freeman. *The Rock of Chickamauga.* Norman, 1948.

Coe, Charles H. *Red Patriots.* Cincinnati, 1898.

Cohen, Myer M. *Notices of Florida and the Campaigns.* N. Y., 1836.

Connor, Jeannette Thurber, ed. *Colonial Records of Spanish Florida.* 2 vols. Deland, Florida, 1925.

Corse, Mrs. C. D. *Key to the Golden Islands.* Chapel Hill, 1931.

Cotterill, R. S. *The Southern Indians.* Norman, 1954.

Cox, I. J. *The West Florida Controversy, 1798–1813.* Cincinnati, 1918.

———. *The Early Exploration of Louisiana.* Cincinnati, 1906.

Crane, Verner. *The Southern Frontier, 1670–1732.* Durham, 1928.

Cubberly, Frederick. *The Dade Massacre.* Washington, 1921.

Dale, Edward Everett. *The Range Cattle Industry.* Norman, 1930.

———, ed. *Frontier Trails.* Boston, 1930.

———. *Cow Country.* Norman, 1942.

———. *The Indians of the Southwest.* Norman, 1949.

Debo, Angie. *And Still the Waters Run.* Princeton, 1940.

———. *The Rise and Fall of the Choctaw Republic.* Norman, 1934.

———. *The Road to Disappearance.* Norman, 1941.

———. *Tulsa: From Creek Town to Oil Capital.* Norman, 1943.

———. *Prairie City.* New York, 1944.

———. *Oklahoma: Footloose and Fancy-Free.* Norman, 1949.

———. *The Five Civilized Tribes.* Philadelphia, 1951.

Ellis, E. S. *The Indian Wars of the United States.* Chicago, 1902.

Ettinger, A. A. *James Edward Oglethorpe, Imperial Idealist.* Oxford, Clarendon Press, 1936.

Fairbanks, G. R. *History of Florida.* Philadelphia, 1871.

Foreman, Grant. *A Traveler in Indian Territory.* Cedar Rapids, Ia., 1930.

———. *Indians and Pioneers.* New Haven, 1930.

———. *Indian Removal.* Norman, 1932.

———. *Advancing the Frontier.* Norman, 1933.

———. *The Five Civilized Tribes.* Norman, 1934.

———. *History of Oklahoma.* Norman, 1942.

373

Frazier, Franklin. *The Negro Family in the United States.* Chicago, 1939.

Giddings, Joshua. *The Exiles of Florida.* Columbus, Ohio, 1858.

Gideon, D. C. *Indian Territory.* N. Y. and Chicago, 1901.

Gittinger, Roy. *The Formation of the State of Oklahoma, 1803–1906.* Norman, 1939.

Haines, Elijah. *The American Indian.* Chicago, 1888.

Hanna, A. J. *A Prince in their Midst.* Norman, 1946.

Herskovitz, Melville J. *The American Negro.* N. Y., 1928.

Hitchcock, Ethan Allen. *Fifty Years in Camp and Field.* N. Y. and London, 1909.

Hodge, Frank Webb, ed. *Handbook of American Indians North of Mexico.* Bureau of American Ethnology, *Bulletin No. 30,* Parts I and II (2 vols.). Washington, 1907, 1912.

Irving, Theodore. *The Conquest of Florida.* London, 1835.

Kappler, Charles J., ed. *Indian Affairs: Laws and Treaties.* 3 vols. Washington, 1892–1913.

Kenny, Michael. *The Romance of the Floridas.* N. Y., 1934.

Kimber, Edward. *Oglethorpe's Attack on St. Augustine.* Boston, 1935.

Lindquist, G. E. E. *The Red Man in the United States.* N. Y., 1923.

McAfee, George F. *Presbyterian Missionaries to the Indians of the United States.* N. Y., 1915.

McCall, Maj. Gen. George A. *Letters From the Frontier.* Phila., 1888.

MacCauley, Clay. *The Seminole Indians of Florida.* Bureau of American Ethnology, *Annual Report, 1883–84.* Washington, 1884.

Marcy, R. B. *Thirty Years of Army Life on the Border.* N. Y., 1866.

McKenney, Thomas L. *Memoirs, Official and Personal.* N. Y., 1846.

———, and Hall, James. *The Indian Tribes of North America.* 3 vols. Edinburgh, 1934.

McLaughlin, A. C. *The Confederation and the Constitution, 1783–89.* N. Y., 1905.

McMaster, John Bach. *A History of the People of the United States.* 8 vols. N. Y. and London, 1937.

Meserve, Charles F. *The Dawes Commission and the Five Civilized Tribes.* Phila., 1896.

Morse, Jedidiah. *Report to the Secretary of War on Indian Affairs.* New Haven, 1822.

Parrish, J. O. *Battling the Seminoles.* Lakeland, Florida, 1930.

Parton, James. *The Life of Andrew Jackson.* 3 vols. Boston, 1886.

Patrick, Rembert W. *Florida Fiasco.* Athens, Ga., 1954.

Pickett, Albert James. *History of Alabama and Incidentally of Georgia and Mississippi. Annals of Alabama,* Birmingham, 1900. (Author's preface dated 1851.)

Potter, Woodburne. *The War in Florida.* Baltimore, 1836.

Pratt, Julius W. *Expansionists of 1812*. N. Y., 1925.

Sherman, William Tecumseh. *Memoirs of General William T. Sherman*. 2 vols. N. Y., 1904.

———. *Sherman's Home Letters*. N. Y., 1909.

Simmons, W. H. *Notices of East Florida, with an Account of the Seminole Nation of Indians*. Charleston, 1822.

Smith, W. W. *Sketches of the Second Seminole War*. Charleston, 1836.

Sprague, John T. *The Origin, Progress, and Conclusion of the Florida War*. N. Y., 1846.

Thoburn, Joseph B. *A History of Oklahoma*. 5 vols. N. Y. and Chicago, 1916.

———, and Wright, Muriel H. *Oklahoma: a History of the State and its People*. 4 vols. N. Y., 1929.

Wardell, Morris L. *A Political History of the Cherokee Nation, 1838–1907*. Norman, 1938.

Williams, John Lee. *The Territory of Florida, or Sketches of the Topography, Civil and Natural History, etc.* N. Y., 1837.

Winsor, Justin, ed. *Narrative and Critical History of North America*. 8 vols. 1884–89.

Woodward, Thomas S. *Woodward's Reminiscences of the Creek or Muscogee Indians*. Montgomery, Ala., 1859 (New edition, Montgomery, 1939).

Wright, Muriel H. *A Guide to the Indian Tribes of Oklahoma*. Norman, 1951.

Index

376

5~

University of Oklahoma Press : Norman